Political Communications in Greater China

This book examines the role played by political communications, including media of all kinds – journalism, television and film – in defining and shaping identity in Greater China, taken to include China, Hong Kong, Taiwan and the overseas Chinese. In the context of increasing cross-border interactions of people, investment and commercial products between the component parts of Greater China, the book explores the idea that identity, rather than nation-states or political entities, may be the key factor in achieving further integration in Greater China. The book focuses on the ways in which identity within and between the component parts of Greater China plays a central role in bringing about integration.

Gary D. Rawnsley is a senior lecturer in politics and director of the Institute of Asia–Pacific Studies, University of Nottingham (UK). He has published widely on international communications and the politics of Taiwan. His many publications include *Taiwan's Informal Diplomacy and Propaganda* (2000) and *Critical Security, Democratisation and Television in Taiwan* (with Ming-Yeh T. Rawnsley, 2001).

Ming-Yeh T. Rawnsley is associate research fellow at the Institute of Asia–Pacific Studies, University of Nottingham (UK). Her research interests include media, democratisation and identity issues. Her latest publications include *The World of the Media* (2001, in Chinese) and *Critical Security, Democratisation and Television in Taiwan* (with Gary D. Rawnsley, 2001).

Political Communications in Greater China

The Construction and Reflection of Identity

**Edited by Gary D. Rawnsley and
Ming-Yeh T. Rawnsley**

RoutledgeCurzon
Taylor & Francis Group

LONDON AND NEW YORK

First published 2003 by RoutledgeCurzon
11 New Fetter Lane, London EC4P 4EE

Simultaneously published in the USA and Canada
by RoutledgeCurzon
29 West 35th Street, New York, NY 10001

RoutledgeCurzon is an imprint of the Taylor & Francis Group

Typeset in Times by Taylor & Francis Books Ltd
Printed and bound in Great Britain by Antony Rowe Ltd,
Chippenham, Wiltshire

British Library Cataloguing in Publication Data
A catalogue record for this book is available from the
British Library

Library of Congress Cataloging in Publication Data
Political communications in greater China: the construction and reflection
of identity/edited by Gary D. Rawnsley & Ming-Yeh T. Rawnsley.

Includes bibliographical references and index.
1. Communication in politics–China. 2. Communication in politics–
Taiwan. 3. Communication in politics–Hong Kong (China). 4. Group
identity. I. Rawnsley, Gary D. II. Rawnsley, Ming-Yeh T.

JF1525.C59 P65 2003
324.951'001'4-dc21

                                  2002031696

ISBN 0–7007–1734–X

Contents

List of illustrations

Plates

Tables

List of contributors

Andrew J. Brown is a former research student at the University of Nottingham (UK), where he studied politics and film. He is now working as web editor of an online marketing magazine, and he also writes on politics, film and new technology.

Qing Cao is a senior lecturer at Liverpool John Moores University (UK). His research focuses on Western representation of China and Chinese representation of the West. He has published widely in major academic journals, and his most recent publications include a book chapter entitled 'Selling culture: ancient Chinese conceptions of "the Other" in legends' (2001).

Yingchi Chu is a lecturer in Chinese Studies and Media Studies at Murdoch University, Western Australia. Her research interests include Chinese media, Chinese diasporic popular culture and cinema studies. She is the author of *Hong Kong Cinema* (2002).

John F. Copper is the Stanley J. Buckman Distinguished Professor of International Studies at Rhodes College in Memphis, Tennessee (USA). He is the author of more than twenty books on China, Taiwan and Asian affairs. His latest book is *Taiwan in Troubled Times: Essays on the Chen Shui-bian Presidency* (2002).

Hugo de Burgh is director of the Unit for Journalism and Media Ethics, Goldsmiths' College, University of London (UK). His research interests include investigative journalism and journalism as cultural practice. He will shortly be launching the first postgraduate degree in comparative journalism.

Anthony Y.H. Fung is an assistant professor in the School of Journalism and Communication at the Chinese University of Hong Kong. His research interests include the political economy of media, cultural studies, popular culture, identity issues and new media technologies.

Stephanie Hemelryk Donald is a senior lecturer in media and communications at the University of Melbourne (Australia). Her most recent book is *Media in China: Consumption, Content and Crisis* (2002) (with Michael

Keane and Yin Hong). She is currently working on a contemporary history of film culture for children in the PRC and on a collaborative project: Nations Online.

Yu Huang is an associate professor in the Department of Journalism at Hong Kong Baptist University. His main research interests include media and journalism in mainland China and Hong Kong.

Willy Wo-Lap Lam is senior China analyst at CNN's Asia-Pacific Office in Hong Kong. A former associate editor and China editor of the *South China Morning Post*, he is the author of *China after Deng Xiaoping* (1995) and *The Era of Jiang Zemin* (1999).

Chin-Chuan Lee is a professor of journalism and mass communication at the University of Minnesota (USA). Among his recent publications are *Power, Money, and Media: Communication Patterns and Bureaucratic Control in Cultural China* (editor, 2000), *Global Media Spectacle: News War over Hong Kong* (co-author, 2002) and *Chinese Media, Global Contexts* (editor, in press).

David Parker teaches sociology at the University of Birmingham (UK). His publications include *Through Different Eyes: The Cultural Identities of Young Chinese People in Britain* (1995) and *Rethinking Mixed Race* (co-editor, 2001).

Gary D. Rawnsley is a senior lecturer in politics and director of the Institute of Asia-Pacific Studies, University of Nottingham (UK). He has published widely on international communications and the politics of Taiwan. His many publications include *Taiwan's Informal Diplomacy and Propaganda* (2000) and *Critical Security, Democratisation and Television in Taiwan* (co-author, 2001).

Ming-Yeh T. Rawnsley is an associate research fellow in the Institute of Asia-Pacific Studies, University of Nottingham (UK). Her research interests include media, democratisation and identity issues. Her latest publications include *The World of the Media* (2001, in Chinese) and *Critical Security, Democratisation and Television in Taiwan* (co-author, 2001).

Neil Renwick is a reader in international and East Asian studies and co-director of the Centre for Asia-Pacific Studies, Nottingham Trent University (UK). His research includes traditional and critical security and identity politics in the Asia-Pacific region. His recent books are *America's World Identity* (2000) and *Northeastern Asian Critical Security* (2002).

Bey-Ling Sha is a visiting assistant professor at the University of Maryland, College Park, and a public affairs specialist with the US Census Bureau in Washington. Her research interests include public relations, cultural identity, communications effects and gender issues. She is founding editor of an ongoing series, *Monographs in Multicultural Public Relations*.

Julian Stringer is a lecturer in film studies at the University of Nottingham and general editor of *Scope: An Online Journal of Film Studies*. In addition to having published essays on Chinese, Japanese and Korean cinema, he is editor of *Movie Blockbusters* (2002).

Andrea Witcomb is a senior lecturer at the Research Institute for Cultural Heritage at Curtin University of Technology in Perth, Western Australia. Her research interests revolve around the relationship between museum practices and the production and representation of community identities. She is author of *Reimagining the Museum: Beyond the Mausoleum* (2002).

1 Introduction

Gary D. Rawnsley and Ming-Yeh T. Rawnsley

This volume represents the latest attempt by the editors to understand how the forces of globalisation coincide and conflict with localisation through economic, political, media and cultural processes. In our teaching and research, we have long wrestled with questions of cultural imperialism versus protectionism in Asia (typified by the survival of the Asian values movement), Americanisation versus indigenisation, globalisation versus localisation. These concerns have led to an abiding curiosity about the way identities are formed and re-formed by the constant interaction and collision of assorted external influences. We are particularly intrigued by postmodern approaches, which understand identity as a fluid and subjective concept that is not temporally or spatially settled. In short, we dismiss the idea of identity as inert, consistent and unalterable. Rather, we prefer to regard identities as flexible, permeable, coexisting and multiple, so we can now experience our local, national, regional and even international identities, depending on the situation in which we find ourselves.

This fits perfectly with the manifold understandings of Greater China that are reviewed in this book. In commissioning the chapters, we asked the contributors to define both Greater China and political communications in the way that they thought most encapsulated the growing 'glocalisation' that we see taking place in the region. Hence, this collection of essays illustrates that 'Greater China' remains a contested term for a multi-faceted phenomenon that has greater relevance in the twenty-first century than at any time previously. We have deliberately avoided assembling any conclusions about the geographic centre of Greater China, since the meaning of that term varies according to whether one is assessing the economic, political or cultural interaction of the component parts.

This is the essence of John F. Copper's chapter on the meaning and significance of Greater China. Surveying the history of the idea, Copper argues that the value of Greater China lies in its ambiguity, thus allowing for variation according to the political, cultural and economic interests of its members. Although Greater China has no definite centre or existence as a homogeneous unit, Copper agrees that it does have a reality as a cultural and economic community. It is difficult to foresee a time when this will develop into political reality, but Copper does wonder whether the further evolution of Greater China might offer a solution to the region's more intractable problems, especially the difficult China–Taiwan relationship. In introducing the multiple representations of Greater China, Copper provides the contextual and theoretical foundations for his fellow contributors.

The three chapters in Part I converge on the People's Republic of China (PRC), the first two sharing an interest in the creation of Chinese identity and China's understanding of itself. The authors are concerned with the political ramifications of communication, and they demonstrate the impor- tance of mediated identities in reinforcing political legitimacy. Thus Chin-Chuan Lee and Yu Huang aim to elucidate the social context in which the Chinese media displayed strong pro-American tendencies in the 1980s and strong anti-American tendencies in the 1990s. In the middle to late 1980s, the authors argue, Chinese intellectuals allied themselves with the reform bureaucracy, harnessing the media to advocate 'liberal' agendas (such as supervision by public opinion) and frequently invoking the United States as a point of reference. This accounted for the Chinese media's enthusiasm for the United States as a model of comparison, if not emulation.

Lee and Huang explain how the Tiananmen Square incident of 1989 became the motif of American media coverage of China, while revived economic reforms since 1992 have fostered a renewed sense of national pride, but with an emerging consumer culture beginning to overshadow interest in political reform. What we are observing, say the authors, is the realisation of the century-old Chinese dream of pursuing national wealth and power, but with a distinctly communist twist.

These themes are developed by Neil Renwick and Qing Cao. They discuss how political discourse is crucial to the legitimation of China's ruling elite and critically informs their formulation and execution of political action. The chapter explores the theme of 'victimhood' in China's contemporary political discourse, the constructed nature of which draws upon a range of supporting sources. Of central importance is the role of history, and one of its key features is the depiction of China as victim. This offers a distinct pole of identifying attachment for the construction of a modernist reading of national Chinese political identity. Renwick and Cao conduct discourse analyses of several primary texts, concluding that objectified discursive power remains an influential factor in Chinese politics.

Hugo de Burgh analyses how Chinese journalists – the mediators of these discourses – view themselves and their chosen profession. He seeks to under- stand changes that have taken place in journalists' perceptions of their political and social roles to discover the reasons for these changes: are they reflections of cosmopolitan influences, economic and technological changes in the media industries, institutional factors in the Chinese media, or changes in attitude to politics and society? The author reviews the history of journalism and journalism education in China by drawing on his extensive interviews with journalists themselves. Their words provide a unique and instructive insight into the character and functions of Chinese reporters. Many of them have been influenced by Western myths of journalism, what de Burgh describes as the 'discourse of the Tintin journalist', for example (although few would confess to emulating a foreign model). This role is represented by the remarkable growth of investigative journalism in China. Others see their value in terms of their responsibility to the state. All agree that they are providing a valuable service to the Chinese people by 'mediating' information for their audiences, but there is no escaping the honesty of de Burgh's concluding remarks: that 'most journalists live in the world as it is constructed for them by their political masters, and probably jog along as best they can'.

Gary Rawnsley's chapter moves the discussion to another area of what we loosely term Greater China, namely the recently democratised Taiwan. Rawnsley analyses trends in election campaigning in Taiwan, with particular reference to the landmark 2000 presidential election, when the Kuomintang's (KMT) fifty-year monopoly on power finally ended. Rawnsley examines the growing professionalism in election campaigning, which stands alongside, and is shaped by, the systemic and institutional features of Taiwan's electoral landscape, such as the path dependency of the parties and the electoral system used. The chapter challenges us to reconsider the notion of how identity is shaped and communicated; globalisation has given birth to a spurious catch-all notion of 'Americanisation' that is invoked by many modern election observers. It is said to describe a trend towards a global convergence of electoral practices based on the adoption of election campaign techniques developed in the United States. The discourse on Americanisation resonates with the pejorative vocabulary more associated with cultural imperialism, suggesting the displacement of the indigenous by the foreign. Rawnsley warns that we need to be careful of using this discourse too liberally. The flows of influence and information are in fact multidirectional, with the United States absorbing cultural effects as well as supplying them. Newly democratising systems have not undergone a blanket Americanisation, because, as the Taiwan example clearly demonstrates, traditional methods of voter mobilisation remain important; the foreign coexists with the indigenous.

Bey-Ling Sha builds on Rawnsley's discussion to examine 'gendered dimensions of political activism' by focusing on the role of women and gender in Taiwan's Democratic Progressive Party (DPP). The DPP is a fascinating case study to use, since it offers a multi-layered analysis: in a relatively short period, the DPP has transformed from an illegal opposition movement to a party that has not only captured the presidency (in 2000) but also won the largest number (although not a majority) of seats in the 2001 legislative election. In short, the DPP has broken the KMT's fifty-year monopoly on power in Taiwan.

The DPP has been involved in challenging official opinion on Taiwan's identity and has, in the past, been the focus for the mobilisation of Taiwanese, as opposed to the Chinese who arrived from the mainland with the KMT in 1945. But the DPP's identity itself is undergoing thorough reconstruction as it comes to terms with its new political status, agenda and understanding of Taiwan's position in the world.

The DPP has also been a powerful voice for a political agenda that in the West we might label 'liberal'. For example, the DPP has been vocal in advocating equal opportunity for women and, as Bey-Ling Sha demonstrates, in supporting issues that can be classified as 'women's issues'. However, the party's concern for women may reflect a political strategy (mobilising women voters) more than a genuine agenda for social change. Furthermore, Sha demonstrates that gendered communication within the DPP tends to reflect a traditional and patriarchal perspective on women and women's issues; women are still identified by their 'traditional' roles of wife and mother, while articulating women's issues and concerns largely falls to women within the party. Women in Taiwan have certainly been presented with a positive role model in the Vice President, (Annette) Lu Shiu-lian, and many hoped that her high profile would invite the government to address issues of gender and the problems facing women in Taiwan today. But the DPP's political agenda has still not devoted time or space to a full and frank discussion of this subject.

The final chapter to focus on Taiwan is Ming-Yeh Rawnsley's exploration of how Taiwan's national identity has been constructed and reflected by the media. These issues frame the methods and content of political and social discourse in Taiwan, and they structure the form and substance of mediated communications there. Taiwan's media, argues Rawnsley, have helped to construct and perpetuate the problems and contradictions of identity that have challenged society since the 28 February 1947 incident. While the introduction of media liberalisation in 1987 permitted a more open and less violent debate about identity, political parties are still defined largely by their Taiwanese or 'mainland' orientation, and their election campaigns tend to be structured around this polarity.

Rawnsley uses Formosa Television (FTV) to analyse these debates. Established in June 1987, FTV was the first national television station to communicate the Taiwanese identity, long suppressed under martial law. The question is whether FTV will be an exclusively Taiwanese station and thus perpetuate the primary division of identity within Taiwan, or whether it will provide equal resources and access for other minority language programming and therefore provide a credible alternative to the Mandarin-dominated Nationalist television networks.

CNN correspondent and veteran China watcher Willy Wo-Lap Lam opens the discussion about the media and communications in the Hong Kong Special Administrative Region. He analyses the communication strategies employed by Chief Executive Tung Chee-hwa's first administration following Hong Kong's reversion to Chinese rule in 1997 (Tung was 'elected' for a second term in March 2002). Lam affirms that since 1997 Hong Kong's political culture has become more 'Chinese', by which he means that values and norms associated with political institutions and processes in the PRC can now be discovered there. In a perceptive analysis of the administration's relationship with the media, Lam examines how the political system has invoked the media to participate in the continued sinicisation of Hong Kong. Most disquietingly, Lam identifies what he calls an 'erosion of press freedom and an alarming increase in self-censorship' by the territory's media. This is demonstrated by Tung's claim that the media of Hong Kong and Macau have distinct social responsibilities and his insistence that they should play a more 'positive role' in the interests of the state and Chinese nation. As a former journalist for Hong Kong's *South China Morning Post*, Lam knows from personal experience the effects of 1997 on the territory's press, an understanding shared by his colleague, Jasper Becker, dismissed in May 2002 as Beijing bureau chief for 'insubordination' (*Far Eastern Economic Review*, 9 May 2002).

Lam's conclusions are interesting in the light of Hugo de Burgh's assessment of Chinese journalism: where de Burgh sees reason for optimism, especially in the growth of 'investigative reporting' on the mainland, Lam is concerned that journalism in Hong Kong is failing to attract bright new entrants; and this is important, because Hong Kong's survival as an Asian democracy and economic powerhouse depends on the integrity and strength of its media institutions.

Anthony Fung addresses the situation facing Hong Kong's press after 1997 from a political economy approach. He has identified several characteristics that contributed to the transition of Hong Kong's press: first, he considers spatialisation, by which he means the agreement arrived at by the press in terms of allotting market niches. This gives rise to a discussion of how the relatively small market was disturbed by a new entrant, the *Apple Daily*, in 1995. Next, Fung examines how many family-owned Hong Kong media organisations weathered political uncertainties by turning a political and cultural entity into an economic good. The media then experienced a pronounced process of extension whereby they acquired non-media businesses by acquisition or through partnership. This was intended to diversify companies' investments and to cushion the possible effects of recession and political pressure on the media after 1997. Media barons were then able to consolidate and extend their control within a particular sector of media production and to maximise the economies of scale and share their resources. Finally, Fung discusses the impact of globalisation on Hong Kong's media.

In this way, Fung observes a discrete process of commodification in the way news is reported in the territory, leading him to hypothesise that this is the only strategy available to the press to maintain commercial viability and independence from political interference. Fung concludes that those newspapers that choose populism over principle are most likely to survive the transition to Chinese rule. However, the important question is whether this commodification will help to structure the media agenda and contribute to their economic and political sensitivity. Or will the increasing concentration of media ownership turn 'mass communication' into 'mass consumption' and thereby counter press freedom in Hong Kong? These possibilities deserve close scrutiny as the story of Hong Kong under Chinese leadership continues to unfold.

Andrew Brown is concerned with political communication through popular culture and provides a political reading of Hong Kong films made in the run-up to the 1997 handover of Hong Kong to Chinese rule. Brown compares the ideological position and political interpretation of two specific film texts: John Woo's *The Killer* (1989) and Wong Kar-wai's *Chungking Express* (1994). His discussion reveals that both directors express a sense of Britain's betrayal in failing to secure satisfactory democratic safeguards for Hong Kong in their films. Hence their anxiety with discovering what it means to be a citizen of Hong Kong both prior to, and especially following, the 1997 handover. Brown's chapter provides the foundation for a deeper exploration of cinema's contribution to globalisation, claiming that in the work of both directors it is possible to discern Western and Chinese influences. Like other Asian directors, especially Ang Lee, Woo and Wong have started to experience success in Hollywood, in Woo's case by adapting to the formats and genres favoured by Hollywood but retaining his personal style of film making (seen especially in his 1997 blockbuster *Face/Off*). The contrast with Ang Lee is striking: Lee has enjoyed remarkable success in what might be termed 'mainstream Hollywood' movie making, being responsible for such films as *Sense and Sensibility* (1995), *The Ice Storm* (1997) and *Ride With the Devil* (1999), which do not employ Chinese themes or actors. Arguably, it is only because Lee was considered a 'bankable' Hollywood director that his *Crouching Tiger, Hidden Dragon* (2000) received global success as a mainstream movie, even though it was essentially a 'Chinese' film.

In contrast to Woo and Lee, Wong is more critical of the union of Western and Chinese art forms, resisting the complete appropriation of American influences. Their different approaches reveal, therefore, the divergent assessments of globalisation and its impact on identity that are apparent in film, suggesting that movie making can be as much a political act as it is a commitment to entertain.

The following three chapters focus on the overseas Chinese and their experiences of coping with coexisting and competing identities. As the chapters demonstrate, the overseas Chinese have developed discourses through which they can create and articulate their identities – to themselves, to each other, and to the wider societies in which they live. David Parker considers the community of second- and third-generation British Chinese in terms of recent conceptualisations of cultural identity. Parker argues that existing understandings of concepts such as identity and diaspora are both fledgling and decidedly Eurocentric. Parker develops a deeper understanding of notions of space, time and the social, drawing on political communications within the Chinese community in Britain. He does so by analysing how 'pan-European Chinese news media', but especially the Internet, have facilitated the creation of a new Chinese public sphere for the diaspora. The new media, he argues, satisfies the postmodern acceptance of multiple identities that incorporate orientation to a distant homeland (familiar only through media representation and inter-generational narration) and attachment to Britain. The identity of the British Chinese was tested in March and April 2001, when Chinese restaurants were identified in parts of the media as the source of the foot and mouth epidemic. The Chinese communities were mobilised by their websites, while demonstrations through London attracted Chinese participation from throughout Britain. Too often, Chinese people are considered passive, untroubled, even invisible. The events of 2001 demonstrated that the Chinese could be provoked into action when required, but more importantly they forced British Chinese to confront their identity, nurturing a new consciousness and a recognition of the importance of developing new forums for expression, debate and mobilisation. Parker's conclusions are cautionary: at the moment, there are limits to the effectiveness of this public sphere, due mainly to generational and linguistic divisions among the Chinese communities in Britain. Parker also calls for 'greater participation in civil society', otherwise the public sphere will only 'amount to a few thousand people talking to themselves'. Nevertheless, the forums that Parker describes are a step in the right direction; they create new discourses that reflect the multiple, and sometimes competing, identities of the Chinese in Britain – what Parker describes as the 'beginnings of a cultural identity'.

Yingchi Chu, Stephanie Hemelryk Donald and Andrea Witcomb analyse how Chinese children in Australia consume media and information, and thus how they contribute to the shaping of identity. Migrants from the People's Republic of China have a very recent experience of migration, due to policy changes and crises in their places of origin. The migration flow has been concentrated in the last fifteen years, and many of the new migrants are Chinese with young families. These adults share strong memories of childhoods in China and are possibly living with an alternative model of childhood and media to that used in the construction of media texts for children in Australia. Given the centralised modes of production in the 1960s to early 1980s in China, remembered media products are reasonably simple to trace for analysis. The chapter looks at such texts (film and television products) and analyses them according to the related premises that dominant concepts of childhood are (1) significant markers of the character of multiculturalism in the pubic sphere and (2) political hierarchies in the media. At the heart of the discussion is a tension between parental memories of China and children's emotional distance from their parents' experience. The chapter concludes with some suggestions for how this tension might be alleviated. These include recognition that 'children from migrant families operate between two worlds .... Media practices need to acknowledge and emulate young people's flexibility and multiple competencies'. This might facilitate the future development of a genuine public sphere for Chinese communities in Australia.

Julian Stringer's chapter builds upon the discussion offered by Andrew Brown on Hong Kong cinema to explore the cultural politics of Asian American cinema. Recent productions by both Asian American film makers and critics have emphasised the importance of agency in the formation of Asian American social identities. While much of this work has documented the evolution of an Asian American independent film practice over the past thirty years, Stringer concentrates instead on the politics of crossing over into the mainstream. With some Asian American film workers now making inroads in Hollywood, it is necessary to outline the terms of this engagement with commercial film practice as well as to consider the role that Asian American film culture plays in laying the groundwork for these recent successes. To explore these themes, Stringer focuses on the public discourse about films, and especially the Chinese actor Jet Li, who has found fame in Hollywood and thus bridges China, Hong Kong and the United States while carrying 'connotations of ethnic authenticity'. He is a genuine Asian American movie star, and Stringer is interested in determining how he is viewed by his Chinese audiences in the United States and what this means for how Chinese Americans see themselves. The Internet has facilitated the growth of distinct communities who produce, circulate and reproduce these discourses across national boundaries, providing the basis for the creation of new group identities.

Finally, Neil Renwick draws the threads of the discussion together in a broad analysis of the impact of globalisation upon the construction of culture and identity in Greater China. Renwick draws upon the work of a range of writers from complementary backgrounds and disciplines: Jürgen Habermas, especially his conception of late modernity and his theory of communication; Paul Hirst and Graham Thompson in relation to the character of globalisation; and Benedict Anderson, Anthony Giddens and Stuart Hall and their work on culture and identity. Renwick advances several hypotheses: (1) that the conceptualisation of 'Greater China' is valid; (2) that collective, societal identities in the various component parts of Greater China are, as elsewhere, constructions by powerful elites; (3) that the late twentieth century saw the established bases of these cultural-identifactory constructions become unsustainable in the face of internal and external economic and technological changes; (4) that power elites have been forced to respond to these changes to seek sustained legitimacy and societal influence; (5) that the forces of economic and cultural globalisation represent a major force for change in the collective identities of Greater China; (6) that such globalisation is experienced unevenly in both spatial and temporal terms; and (7) that uneven globalisation is simultaneously contributing to both integrative and disintegrative forces within Greater China, necessitating a reformulation or reconstruction of collective identity around new forms of communicative action. It is this reformulation that will determine the future development of a cultural Greater China and will find expression through all the means of political communication explored throughout this volume.

This project would not have been possible without the continuing friendship and cooperation of the contributors. The editors wish to thank them all for their hard work and patience, and for their response to our sometimes pedantic queries and suggestions. The chapters are their own views and do not represent the views of any organisation they may work for. We also acknowledge the vision and forbearance of Peter Sowdon of Routledge–Curzon, who liked the idea of the book and encouraged the editors to start the ball rolling. This book would not have been possible without the enduring support of the School of Politics at the University of Nottingham, and especially the Institutes of Asia-Pacific Studies, Film Studies and Contemporary Chinese Studies. Our overlapping membership of these various institutions has contributed to our commitment to approaching communications and Chinese studies from a genuinely multi-disciplinary perspective. Finally, both editors thank their families for their continued support and encouragement, and we dedicate this book to Tsai Sheng-hung, Ming-Yeh's loving father, who passed away in September 2001.

2 The meaning and significance of Greater China

John F. Copper

Defining the term 'Greater China'

'Greater China' is a term that in recent years has been employed profusely in the writings of both scholars and laymen when discussing China: Beijing's relations with other countries, but especially other Chinese entities (and *vice versa*), various countries' foreign and economic policies dealing with Chinese states or Chinese political entities, and even other actors; global economic and political developments; and East Asia. Greater China has been discussed in numerous addresses, forums and academic debates. It has even been the subject of several academic conferences and some book-length studies.[1]

However, the idea of Greater China as a topic of discussion, and hence the term, came into common use only in the 1980s, and no consistent or commonly accepted definition evolved. In fact, it had various meanings. To the layman, when the term 'Greater China' was used without a special referent, intent or argument, it usually meant the People's Republic of China (PRC), Hong Kong, Macao, Taiwan or the Republic of China (ROC) and Singapore: the five political entities in the world with a majority Chinese population.[2] Recently, the number has been reduced to three, according to some writers, because the former British Crown Colony of Hong Kong was returned to the PRC in 1997, and the Portuguese colony of Macau was reunified with the PRC in 1999. Still, Greater China is frequently considered as having five members, since Hong Kong and Macau have been designated as having a kind of special autonomy within the PRC and in some important ways (economically, politically and legally) are different from the rest of the PRC.[3] Greater China is often taken to include the overseas Chinese (or *hua qiao*),[4] although sometimes this means only those living in Southeast Asia, where the majority of Chinese outside the five political entities reside (Shambaugh 1995: 274–5).[5] Occasionally, writers discriminate between overseas Chinese who retain Chinese citizenship and those who do not and include only the former (*ibid.*: 275).

Also, quite popularly, Greater China is defined or the term used to mean only the PRC, Hong Kong and Taiwan. Macau was excluded because it was small and not economically important. Singapore was not counted because the term Greater China was thought to signify an economic bloc wherein trade and investment linked up Chinese entities in a way that affected other countries calculating their trade, especially a trade imbalance. Both Taiwan and Hong Kong (but especially the former), by transferring factories to China, reduced their trade surplus with a number of their trading partners. This allegedly made them alone constitute Greater China.[6] Some writers also considered only these three as constituting a 'natural economic region' (Robinson 1994: 189).

Still others included Macau but excluded Singapore, since (before 1999) Macau was perceived as one day reverting back to China, while Singapore was not. In other words, Singapore possessed national sovereignty; Macau did not. The criterion of being a Chinese entity that was not only linguistically and culturally China but also 'adjacent' was used, thus again not including Singapore (Martin 1997: 277–325).

The idea of Greater China has been employed quite differently to refer to Hong Kong, Taiwan, and Guangdong and Fujian provinces in the PRC. The argument here is that these four entities are more integrated than the various parts of 'cultural China', or 'China' in the broad sense of using that word, but, more importantly, are more economically linked and are the portion of China that is booming economically and is rich and modern. This is also the part of China that engages extensively in trade and other commercial relations with the rest of the world, is more progressive and will set the course for China's future (Abegglen 1994: 92–3).7

The term 'Greater China' is also used, carelessly in the minds of some, to refer to much of East Asia, but notably the part that can be perceived as culturally Chinese.[8] This would include Korea and Vietnam and perhaps more. Conversely, however, one might argue that it would not include Xinjiang Autonomous Region of the PRC and Tibet. Greater China occasionally refers to the area where a Chinese or Sinitic language is spoken, thus putting all or most of mainland Southeast Asia and possibly even Malaysia and Indonesia into the fold while excluding Korea, Manchuria and Mongolia (where Ural–Altaic languages are spoken).[9]

The use of the term 'Greater China' conveys different emotional meetings as well as value judgements. In fact, Greater China is viewed by some as an avenue for peacefully solving various problems of a historical, political or economic kind relating to China, but especially territorial issues (most notably Taiwan). It has been broached as a means of keeping Hong Kong's free market and a good human rights condition intact while perhaps promoting democracy there and reaching an accommodation in the form of a confederation or federation that would allow Taiwan to unify with the PRC while still keeping its sovereignty (at least for some time) and its democracy. Others argue that it suggests hegemonism and aggressive intentions on China's part (Mosher 2000: 98–9). It has even sometimes been likened to Japan's Greater East Asia Co-Prosperity Sphere idea and been seen as connected to Beijing's policies of irredentism and/or militarism (Shambaugh 1995). In between, some speak matter-of-factly, without suggesting good or bad implications, of Greater China as a stronger China in the wake of the economic reforms launched by Deng Xiaoping in 1978, which have resulted in an economic boom and the rise of China to assume a greater role in regional and international affairs. Some have viewed Greater China as a regional actor like the European Community, and some have even called Greater China the world's next superpower (*ibid.*). Greater China has likewise been viewed as evidence of the demise of the nation-state (Ohmae 1995: 80).

Finally, Greater China has been suggested as a solution in the event that the People's Republic of China, due to centrifugal forces operating from within and/or foreign interference, breaks up or fragments. Chinese leaders often speak of this problem. They say that some in the United States want this to occur and are planning for it. They also say this about Japan. In the eventuality that a break-up does occur, some sort of political union might be used to bring the pieces back together again.[10]

In the following pages, Greater China will be examined as a geographical, historical and cultural idea; an economic construct or bloc (although with different definitions); and a political entity or actor (or wishful thinking about one). It is expected that both the meaning of Greater China and its importance will become clearer when pursuing these three angles of analysis.

Chinese history and Greater China

While the term 'Greater China' (*da zhong guo* or *da zhong hua* – the former indicating nationhood, the latter referring more to Chinese people) is new, the concept, or the idea at least, finds its origins in China's geography, history and culture. A number of other terms were used in the past to indicate that China was big and universal, such as *tian xia* (under heaven) and *tian chao* (celestial dynasty). Thus there clearly seem to be academic grounds for an argument that there was an earlier foundation for the currently expressed idea of Greater China.

China's geography, it can be facilely argued, lends itself to the notion of an 'inner' and an 'outer' China, the combination of which, even early in Chinese history, was thought of as the larger or 'greater' China. Inner China, or the 'heartland' of China, is fertile, and the supply of water from both rivers and plentiful rainfall gave rise to successful agricultural pursuits that millennia ago produced a large population and a rich culture. Outer China, which was on the periphery of inner China, was of indeterminate size; it lacked good soil and adequate rainfall and was in some places a high plateau (southwest China) or desert (north China). Its population was much smaller.[11]

Due to the physical barriers of mountains (to the southwest), long distances (to the west) and inhospitable climate (to the north) between outer China and other peoples or civilisations in the world, plus the attractions of inner China (for cultural experience, material goods to trade or plunder, the pleasures of a more advanced civilisation, and more), outer China did not link up with any other of the planet's early civilisations (Fairbank and Reischauer 1989: 2).

Because inner China's population was many times that of outer China, and also perhaps due to the absence of significant visible physical differences between the peoples of both (except in northwest China), it became the policy of the rulers of inner China to absorb the people of outer China rather than conquer them (Mosher 2000: 31–2).[12] The latter was difficult anyway due to the considerable fighting prowess of the peoples of Outer China, a similar disdain for the soldier in inner China, the difficulty of controlling land beyond the natural limits of inner China, and the general absence of places of strategic importance to hold and defend. These factors also helped to sustain the relationship between inner and outer China.

Early in Chinese history, perhaps even before the beginning of recorded history, the societies or kingdoms of inner China developed the notion that their land (not yet called 'China') was located in the centre of the world, surrounded by all sides by outer China barbarians; hence the term *zhong guo* or Middle Kingdom emerged (Fairbank and Reischauer 1989: 20).[13] This notion of centrality persisted throughout Chinese history, although the term was not used very much until later.[14] It also lent itself to the notion of a larger or expanded China, Greater China, because the Chinese were aware of people on the periphery that China had necessary and important relations with, yet were not exactly part of China.

Similarly contributing to the historical concept of Greater China, or at least to ties between inner and outer China, was the fact that 'China' was predominantly a cultural notion. Hence there was little or no notion of borders in the sense of nations being defined by physical limits or boundary lines, as was the case when nation-states developed in Europe (Mancall 1984: 30).[15] Chinese culture was therefore not limited territorially, and China went wherever Chinese culture went.

By definition, culture is largely a matter of the level of civilisation. The civilising relationship between inner and outer China linked the two together. Inner China offered science, technology and knowledge of various other sorts, the arts, and the accoutrements of a more comfortable lifestyle to outer China. Thus it had an attraction to less sedentary non-Chinese on inner China's periphery. Chinese culture was in considerable measure also linked to literacy. Since the Chinese language developed in its written form as a system using pictographs or ideographs and was not phonetic, it was transferred to others in inner China from the central core notwithstanding the different spoken languages or dialects used there. In fact, early in Chinese history, policies were set forth unifying the written language but not the spoken language (Gernet 1996: 33).

As inner China evolved from a large number of kingdoms, which spread their culture to each other but also engaged in warfare, into less independent political entities that recognised a 'centre' or predominant authority (a king in the European sense), China entered an age of feudalism. This occurred very early in China's history (well before the Christian era in the West). The concept of 'China' at this time was therefore transformed into the reality of a 'Chinese empire' or a 'Great China' something like Europe at the time of the Holy Roman Empire. The notion of Greater China, or at least a precursor, is clearly in evidence at this time.[16]

Unlike Europe, however, which evolved (or devolved, depending upon one's point of view) from empire to a family of nation-states, China developed much earlier into a large, bureaucratically ruled, centralised (in theory at least) 'state'.[17] Some say that this happened in large measure owing to the need to build public works, in particular for the purpose of water control. Outer China remained on the periphery and became more distant or separate from inner China. In fact, various leaders of inner China preferred this. The Qin Dynasty, China's first, undertook to build the Great Wall to keep the 'barbarians' of outer China away; but this did not work very well or only operated successfully in combination with military divide and conquer tactics or successful policies of conquer, subdue and maintain hegemony over the peoples on China's borders. However, the inner China–outer China relationship was not destroyed by these efforts.

In fact, a Chinese view of the world matured that saw China as the civilised world and the peoples or societies on China's borders that had considerable contact with China as partly civilised or somewhat enlightened. This became a widely accepted and semi-permanent worldview for the populations of both inner and outer China. Some writers have portrayed the Chinese perspective on the world (which, incidentally, others in East Asia generally accepted) as a series of concentric rings, with inner China or civilised China in the middle surrounded by partly civilised people, who were in turn surrounded by barbarians and then the rest of the world, the unknown world. According to this worldview, China (or inner China) had an obligation to civilise the people around it if and when it could.

From this outlook grew both the theory and the practice of Chinese diplomacy. It was not egalitarian but hierarchical, and it espoused a superiority complex. China received emissaries or diplomatic missions; it did not send them. China required outsiders to learn Chinese diplomatic practices (actually demeaning rituals such as the *kowtow*). This system, and the worldview that accompanied it, were paternalistic. China treated the people on its periphery with kindness (when not at war at least) and according to moral and ethical principles. As part of this system, and to some observers to make it work, China engineered a system of tribute (which in economic terms was generous because China as a practice gave better and more expensive gifts than it received) and a vassalage arrangement whereby the Chinese emperor gave titles bestowing political authority and rights of rule. This system was often described as involving a 'special relationship' between the centre and the proximate periphery. On this basis, Chinese emperors claimed some rights, ownership or jurisdiction over these areas and people on its periphery by virtue of this system of 'international' relations. This was clearly a kind of early Greater China (Fairbank and Reischauer 1973: 96).[18]

Another factor contributing to the idea of Greater China developing in early Chinese history was 'foreign' rule. Since for considerable periods during its long history China has been governed by people from outer China, who as a rule resided in and exercised political control from a major Chinese city, core China or inner China and a larger area of outer China came under a single jurisdiction. It was as if the governance of inner China over outer China was reversed. This seemed to add proof to the idea of Greater China, since the whole was kept together during periods of foreign rule and in many ways the ties between various parts of the 'empire' were even stronger. This was true of the Yuan Dynasty, when the Mongols ruled China. It was also true of the Qing Dynasty (1644–1911), China's last dynasty, when the Manchus ruled China.

The Qing Dynasty created a situation that now lends itself to the concept of Greater China in the sense that Beijing had effective and lasting (nearly 300 years) political jurisdiction over vast territories that were not populated by Chinese, or where Chinese were a minority, but wherein links to inner China were formal and important. During the Qing Dynasty, China's territory was almost double the size it had been during most previous dynasties. Qing China ruled all of what is now the People's Republic of China (including so-called autonomous regions such as Tibet and Xinjiang) plus Outer Mongolia, Taiwan, and some land in Russia and other border countries.[19]

The Nationalist government, which ruled China after the fall of the Qing Dynasty and a brief hiatus of weak central government and warlord rule, defined China to include all territory that was 'China' during the Qing plus some additional lands. To a considerable degree, Chiang Kai-shek successfully implemented a policy of territorial restoration in the course of his efforts to unify China, although what he accomplished was quite tenuous, and some territories were not recovered. Mongolia, which had been nominally independent before Chiang began his unification efforts (in fact, from 1921), became a Soviet satellite state, and Taiwan remained part of the Japanese Empire. Nationalist China subsequently lost Manchuria to Japan in 1931. Internal political struggles, war (which began with Japan in 1937) and various other problems encountered during the Nationalist era made it impossible for the government to even attempt to restore China's Qing Dynasty territory completely. On the other hand, Chiang did not give up the effort, and after the Second World War ended, he was able to recover Manchuria and Taiwan.[20]

The definition of Greater China was also broadened by the Nationalist government to include Chinese living outside the borders of China. This had been done only vaguely by earlier regimes so may be considered unique. There were special reasons for the Nationalist government to do this: overseas Chinese had been major contributors, financially and otherwise, to Sun Yat-sen's movement, which overthrew the Qing Dynasty. It was also said that Chinese living abroad constituted the 'backbone' of Chinese nationalism (Kim and Dittmer 1993; Wang 1991: 142). Following this, the Nationalist government defined citizenship as legally based on *jus sanguinis* (by blood) in order to make a bid for the loyalty of Chinese living outside China. At the same time, it included China's minority nationalities in the definition of 'Chinese citizen'. Provisions for giving the right of representation in the government and for establishing special ties with overseas Chinese were formalised in the Constitution and the structure of the government.

When Mao Zedong defeated the Nationalists and announced the establishment of the People's Republic of China in 1949, he also made territorial claims that were based on the maximum territory of China during the Qing Dynasty (or Manchu Empire). Accordingly, he spoke of 'lost territories' that were to be recovered. Mao clearly propounded a policy of defining China as a combination of inner and outer China. However, Mao's view of the world, in the early years at least, was one of a communist bloc led by the Soviet Union, which would win a victory over the capitalist camp. In the context of this communist–capitalist global struggle, he seemed to have little immediate concern about Chinese territory or of creating a Greater China. Likewise, Mao said little about Outer Mongolia (which the Nationalists continued to claim) being a Soviet satellite, or the colonial status of Hong Kong and Macau. No doubt part of the reason for Mao's 'neglect' was the PRC's alliance with the Soviet Union, the incessant power struggles that Mao launched, and the fact that China under Mao practised a policy of economic autarky. Finally, after the initial period of postwar reconstruction economic performance was not good.

On the other hand, Mao vowed that Hong Kong and Macau would be returned to China. And although he had earlier made a statement in which he suggested that Taiwan was not part of China, after 1950 he declared it to be a territory of China 'occupied' by American imperialism that would be 'liberated', although he also said that it was an issue that could be resolved in a hundred or even a thousand years (Snow 1938: 88–9). When Mao negotiated a *rapprochement* with the United States in the early 1970s, he broke a vow he had made earlier never to improve relations with the United States until the Taiwan issue had been resolved to China's satisfaction. Perhaps he thought that he was more likely to get Taiwan back by dealing with the United States. It is probably accurate to say that Mao calculated that both the Soviet Union and Japan had designs on Taiwan and that in the long term, the United States did not. In any event, during the negotiations with Nixon and Kissinger Mao demanded that the United States agree to a one-China policy, and he stuck adamantly to his claim that Taiwan is a part of China. Yet Mao never suggested a specific formula or plan for accomplishing this.

Mao's new government also took the position that Chinese living outside China were its people. Nevertheless, in 1955, Beijing reached an agreement with the government of Indonesia and subsequently some other countries in Southeast Asia to the effect that Chinese who had obtained local citizenship where they resided were no longer considered to be under this claim. However, due to the fact that Chinese in Southeast Asia have been persecuted regularly (often in spite of acquiring local citizenship and while abandoning Chinese education), and because they have played a vital role in providing China with investment capital (a point to be discussed in greater depth below), and also considering the scope and popularity of networking among these Chinese and Chinese in China, Beijing still views them in many respects as belonging to China (Lever-Tracy *et al.* 1996).

It is probably fair to say that the bottom line was that Mao was too preoccupied with social change and engineering, destroying capitalism as a global force, liberating the Third World, and later fighting Soviet revisionism and hegemonism to think about Greater China in ways that did not connect to his other objectives. His style of communism, which alienated other Chinese entities and Chinese living outside China, together with a policy of self-reliance (essentially isolationism), did not lend itself to pursuit of a Greater China. That was left to Deng Xiaoping.

Greater China as an economic concept

As noted above, the term 'Greater China' first appeared in its current form or usage in the early 1980s. Soon thereafter it became a widely heralded idea. This happened following, and because of, Deng Xiaoping's consolidation of political power in late 1978 and his subsequent decision to launch new and revolutionary economic plans to promote rapid growth in the PRC, which were eminently successful.[21]

Deng's new economic plans, dubbed 'Socialism with Chinese characteristics', were in essence free market capitalism. Deng began his reform efforts in rural China with agriculture. He established a free market, encouraged incentives, allowed private property (usually labelled leases, although some ran for as long as 99 years, with provisions whereby they could be bequeathed to one's children), and rationalised crop selection. China's peasants responded enthusiastically, and agricultural productivity increased markedly. Deng then moved to industry, especially light industry, where he put managers in control and removed cadres from decision making in areas related to production (Overholt 1993).[22] He also encouraged greater labour and other specialisation and making goods or products for export. All this suggested that China's economy should be opened to the outside world.

In fact, Deng made a central tenet of his economic development plans the so-called 'Open Door' policy. This meant that Deng's 'New China' sought foreign investment and trade, constituting a major break with previous, Maoist, economic ideals. Needless to say, these policies had a profound impact on China economically, especially its external economic relations. In 1978, the year in which Deng's reforms were made official policy (in

December), China was ranked 32 in the world in global trade, even though its population ranked it number one, with between one-fifth and one-quarter of the world's population people (van Kemenade 1998: 95). Similarly, before the Deng era China had been the recipient of very little foreign investment. Mao's policy of self-reliance (similar to dependency theory in the West) meant that China engaged very little in trade and had little or no debt.[23]

Deng's economic reforms impressed businesses and investors around the world, but they especially attracted the attention of business leaders in other 'Chinas', who saw Deng as replicating their approaches to economic development and in fact said so. Chinese in Hong Kong, Macau, Singapore and Taiwan soon understood that the PRC was in the process of momentous positive change. They soon supported Deng's policies and sought to participate in China's boom (Mackerras *et al.* 1984: 228).

Hong Kong, physically an appendage of China, was a beehive of commercial activity in East Asia and the site of huge amounts of capital (much of it liquid or private). An expansion of economic ties with a PRC that was on the capitalist path to economic development was natural.[24] Commerce increased by more than 31 percent per annum over the next decade. By 1991, China and Hong Kong had become each other's largest trading partners. A large portion of China's sales to Hong Kong was for re-export, but this did not matter in terms of the economic integration it fostered. Meanwhile, investment capital flowed both from and through Hong Kong to China. By 1993, Hong Kong accounted for 65 percent of foreign investment in China. There was noteworthy reciprocity: China also invested in Hong Kong, funds that accounted for nearly a quarter of the income of Hong Kong's insurance industry, nearly that percentage of the value of its trade, and a quarter of its cargo shipments. China was the destination for half of Hong Kong's tourists (Chang 1998: 159–61). Trade and investment ties between Macau and China grew almost in tandem with Hong Kong's, although it was much less in every category, Macau being much smaller and less commercial.

The economic link-up of Hong Kong and the PRC was facilitated by other factors. One of the most important was the fact that, in 1979, the United States granted the PRC most favoured nation status and concluded a textile agreement. Since the latter involved quotas, China could circumvent them to some degree, or at least *de facto* increase its quota, by exporting through Hong Kong and Macau. Second, Deng's new economic policies included the building of Special Economic Zones (SEZ) for the purpose of attracting foreign investment by eliminating regulations of various kinds that impeded commercial relations. Three of the four originally built were located near Hong Kong. They were eminently successful, as evidenced by the more than 20 percent economic growth they experienced over a number of years (Lam 1999: 236).

Taiwan's economic ties with the PRC lagged behind Hong Kong. Nevertheless, they soon became extensive and meaningful. They were especially significant because political barriers had prevented such ties before this, and Beijing and Taipei had competed for economic ties with the overseas Chinese. While economic relations between China and Taiwan changed, so did political relations, and Beijing's links with overseas Chinese business communities shifted in a decidedly positive direction. Economic ties between China and Taiwan also had the effect of dampening the Taiwan independence movement, which had grown in influence with the acceleration of democratisation in Taiwan.

In 1987, Taiwan ended the ban on its citizens travelling to the mainland, resulting in a huge number of people making the trip.[25] Many who went were in business, hence trade and investment ties followed. Trade blossomed (although legally it had to be indirect, so most of it went back and forth via Hong Kong). Still, it increased from US$77 million in 1979 to US$14.3 billion in 1993 – a 185-fold jump. Investment capital also flowed. By 1996, Taiwan accounted for US$24 billion in investment in the mainland, making Taiwan the second largest investor there (Chang 1998: 162–3). Taiwan-owned businesses employed five million people and created employment indirectly for that many more. Taiwan's commercial ties with China were encouraged by rising labour costs and pressures to cut the trade surplus with the United States. They were also facilitated by an SEZ in Fujian province, where most of Taiwan's Chinese population hails from and by a common dialect with southern Fujian and pro-business policies in the province.

The government in Taiwan, under Lee Teng-hui's leadership, initially established policies to encourage commercial links with China aimed at making Taiwan an 'Asia–Pacific regional operations centre' with the mainland as an important market. After 1993, however, Lee took measures to impede economic links, suggesting that businesses invest in Southeast Asia rather than China. This became known as the 'Go South' policy. This effort slowed Taiwan's investment in China somewhat and redirected some commercial ties to countries in Southeast Asia. In 1996, Lee announced another policy, called 'Go Slow, Be Patient', advising businesses to avoid over-dependence on commercial relations with China. Adopting this policy resulted in some businesses in Taiwan cancelling big projects in China. However, Lee's efforts did little to reverse the tide of Taiwanese business activities in China. The Asian 'meltdown' of the late 1990s hit several countries in Southeast Asia hard, and Taiwan's business there was hurt, prompting many businessmen to turn back to China (Sheng 2001: 139).

The economic slowdown in the United States that began in 1999 also dampened China–Taiwan trade somewhat, but it continued to be important to both sides and was said to be a stabilising factor in cross-strait relations. Contrary to some expectations, the election of Chen Shui-bian as president in March 2000 had a positive effect on Taiwan's investment in China. With pledges by the Chen administration (which were generally fulfilled) to abolish Lee Teng-hui's policies of impeding or limiting commerce with the mainland, Taiwan's investments increased by 108 percent in 2000, with nearly three-quarters of that coming in the second half of the year, when Chen was in office. Of Taiwan's total external investment during that time, one-third was in China and in June 2000 reached a total of US$45.7 billion (*Taiwan Weekly Business Bulletin*, 8–14 February 2001).

Taiwan's economic relations with China are likely to intensify in the future beyond the already broad and extensive ties. In fact, some say that the government in Taiwan cannot control this anymore. There are a number of reasons for believing this. Investment ties, already extensive, are probably much larger than official data suggest. In fact, Taiwanese investment in China may top US$100 billion. It has reportedly caused 500,000 Taiwan business people to become long-term residents of China (33,000 in the city of Shanghai alone). Taiwan's showcase industries, computers and semiconductors, have in large part moved to China (accounting for 70 percent of China's production in these areas).[26] These trends will probably continue due to the attraction of China's cheaper labour and its increasingly efficient trade-oriented economy.

Singapore also established significant trade and investment links with China, although not to the extent of those of Hong Kong and Taiwan. Singapore's economic links with the PRC were unique: Singapore 'sponsored' a self-contained industrial township in China near Shanghai (Rower 1995: 170). It was almost as if Singapore was running an enterprise zone in China. There were political implications in the relationship, since Beijing regarded Singapore as a nation; moreover, Singapore did not have diplomatic ties with the PRC when Deng launched his economic reforms. Some observers opined that China's quest for an economic Greater China involved throwing a big net and that political factors did not matter. Others said that Beijing viewed Singapore as a nation-state like any other and did not see any significance in most of Singapore's population being Chinese.

Since 1978, the overseas Chinese, especially those living in Southeast Asia, have established vital economic links with the PRC. They already had extensive ties with Taiwan, Hong Kong and Macau. Adding the PRC thus resulted in much expanded commercial ties and gave rise to the notion of a broader Greater China economic community that included Chinese living in other countries. Given the Chinese economic prominence in a number of Southeast Asian countries with excess capital as a result of their rapid economic growth, combined with family ties in China and China's new credibility as a place to invest, they became major participants in Deng's new economy.[27] According to one estimate, made in 1990, if the gross national product (GNP) of the overseas Chinese in four Southeast Asian countries were to be added to Greater China, 'Super Greater China' would be economically half again the size of Japan, the second largest economy in the world (*ibid.*: 228).[28]

One other factor, in fact an especial one that adds to the notion that there is a Greater China economic bloc that includes the overseas Chinese in Southeast Asia, is the phenomenon of commercial networking between Chinese there with those in the other Chinese entities. One author called the overseas Chinese a 'network of networks' and a 'new paradigm for a new formation within the framework of the world's economy' (Naisbitt 1995: 21). If the world is moving towards a collection of networks that will replace the nation-state, then this development is consequential. Chinese network for business and other reasons more than other people (especially Japanese, who are group-oriented), and there are growing links between the Chinese communities in Southeast Asia and the PRC, Taiwan, Hong Kong, Macau and Singapore.

The implications of an economic Greater China are staggering. A decade ago the World Bank predicted that in 2002 Greater China (defined as the PRC, Hong Kong, Macau and Taiwan) would be twice as big as Japan in GNP and would surpass the United States in economic output. In 1994, Greater China surpassed Japan (previously number one in the world) in foreign exchange. By that time, Greater China accounted for a quarter of the world's foreign exchange reserves (Rower 1995: 229). To many observers, it seemed natural that such a powerful economic bloc would also become a political bloc.

However, there have been some bumps along the road in the development of a Greater China economic community. There were frequent accusations that Beijing used its economic ties with Hong Kong and Macau to get around import quotas in the United States and some other countries. Taiwan reduced its trade surplus by relocating to factories in China that exported to the USA, while China claimed that this did not count in its trade surplus with America. In 1997, Beijing accused Taiwan of devaluing its currency to hurt Hong Kong and to force China to devalue and thereby undermine the 'One Country, Two Systems' formula.[29] In 2001, Taiwan blamed its investment in China for its economic slowdown. Meanwhile, China rejected Taiwan's proposal for a more formal Greater China common market and repudiated the notion that it would lead to political links. However, these problems do not appear to have slowed the momentum of economic ties by much, but they do raise the question of the need for political agreements and a political Greater China.

Greater China as a political idea

While the idea of Greater China originated with China's new economy, it soon came to acquire a political meaning, and the idea of some kind of political union followed. In many ways, the notion of a 'political' Greater China became more important than the hopes for a Chinese 'economic community'. The former, it was thought, could not fully develop, or perhaps even survive, without the latter.

A China confederation, federation, commonwealth and union were all discussed. The debate initially did not focus so much on what kind of Greater China political organisation should be sought as on why seek it at all. Many, especially in China, opposed the idea of anything other than Beijing incorporating Chinese entities that were once part of China.

Some, both in the PRC and the other Chinas, as well as individual Chinese, felt that creating a political Greater China was, or should be, connected to the problem of governance. In other words, it offered to some a solution to the 'problem' of ruling China. For some years, there had been serious discussions about the question of the system for governing a nation of more than 1.2 billion people. Many doubted that China's unitary system of government would continue to work. Although China's polity was always in theory one governed by the centre, it was a *de facto* confederacy throughout much of its history. Now with a much larger population and with the economic system having been decentralised to promote economic development and allow China to compete in the global economy, China perhaps needed a new political system to reflect that.

The question that China might disintegrate was also on the minds of many Chinese. If that happened, and China had to be put back together again (presumably there would be such an effort), how would that be done? A Greater China union might be the best approach. There has also been a proposal, although one not taken very seriously by anyone, that China should be cut into seven or so parts so that it could be governed better and so that economic growth could continue as China's economy became more complex.[30] Presumably, the new nations would not destroy 'China', and provisions for a Greater China would be retained. Another question was democracy in China; some felt that China had to be decentralised politically as well as economically to democratise, and if that proceeded then integration of the Chinese parts would be easy. Clearly, the political side of Greater China became more challenging than its economic aspects.[31]

Putting the question of a political Greater China on a more practical level, most advocates of those promoting a political Greater China assumed in the 1980s that Hong Kong and Macau were not much at issue, if at all, in constructing a Greater China union.[32] Neither possessed national sovereignty, and both were inevitably going to become part of the PRC (probably soon). Singapore had sovereignty, and it was not territory claimed by Beijing, thus most observers perceived that it would remain separate from China politically, at least in the short run and probably in the long run. Taiwan was thus Beijing's target and consequently the main issue at hand. Taiwan's reunification (or, as Taiwan put it, unification), became the paramount challenge and objective of those seeking a politically defined Greater China.

It was thought in Beijing that the incorporation of Hong Kong and Macau would set a precedent for Taiwan's incorporation. By giving them a special status after joining the PRC, the foundation could be built for enlargement by recovering other 'lost territories' – meaning Taiwan. However, Chinese leaders, including Deng Xiaoping, did not cite a political Greater China or any of its variants in this context.

On the other hand, Deng clearly espoused more positive ideas about a Chinese union than Mao did. His Taiwan policies also departed dramatically from Mao. Soon after he assumed power, Deng gave a speech entitled 'On the United Front and the Chinese People's Political Consultative Conference', which may be said to have contained the seeds of a Greater China that was not just economic.[33] Deng mentioned the role played by Taiwan, Hong Kong, Macau and Chinese nationals overseas in China's economic modernisation. In the same breath, and ostensibly in an effort to include them in a political Greater China, he mentioned patriotism and the goal of reunifying the motherland. Deng also stated his intention to promote democracy and establish a legal system in China, which many took to be the domestic prerequisites to building a political union of some kind linking the three.[34]

However, Deng realised that engineering a political Greater China would not be easy. He knew that he needed to persuade members of his own Communist Party and government; the leaders and the populace of Taiwan; and the world community (most importantly the United States). He viewed these three tasks as connected, although each would require a different strategy.

Deng's framework for making the idea of Greater China acceptable to his cohorts involved the use of already laid out formulas. One was the idea of a united front, which had fallen out of favour during the Cultural Revolution but was subsequently revitalised. It was melded with the notion of 'peaceful reunification' and the view that many patriots in Taiwan could be mobilised against 'secessionist forces and their foreign supporters'. Deng sought to give the impression that he was pursuing both a soft and hard approach and would succeed one way or the other (Hughes 1999: 131).

Deng's initial approach to Taiwan was (in Beijing's eyes at least) a soft approach, based on 'peaceful reunification'. On 1 January 1979, at his request the Standing Committee of the National People's Congress (China's 'legislature') issued a 'Message to Taiwan Compatriots'. It called for cooperation in national development and academic, cultural and trade contacts – the so-called 'three exchanges'. The message also spoke of 'present realities' in Taiwan and China's willingness to maintain the *status quo* there. Coinciding with these friendly overtures, Beijing announced that the shelling of Quemoy would cease in order to 'convince' civilians to make visits and facilitate shipping and production activities in the Taiwan Strait. The next year, Beijing announced that since Taiwan was a part of China its products could enter China duty free. Deng subsequently spoke of a two-party system in China and 'joint leadership' of China.

Deng made the approach to Taiwan cited above at the time the PRC and the United States established formal diplomatic relations. Deng underscored the importance of the Normalisation Agreement with the United States when making his pitch. He played down or ignored the Taiwan Relations Act (which treated Taiwan as sovereign), passed into law by the US Congress a few months later. He told his domestic audience that better relations with the United States would perforce move Taiwan to negotiate and bring Taiwan 'back into the fold'. Deng sought to leave the impression that Taiwan was isolated diplomatically and had to come to some agreement on unification.

Deng's soft approach prevailed for several years. In September 1981, China's president, Ye Jianying, at Deng's bequest issued a 'Nine Point Proposal', which advanced the idea of talks and various exchanges with Taiwan. Ye guaranteed Taiwan's investments in China. He said that Taiwan could retain its socio-economic system and its military after unification. One point cited autonomy for Taiwan, an offer more generous than any proposal Beijing had yet made. In the new 1982 Constitution, Article 31 provided for administrative regions that were in many ways legally separate from the rest of the PRC. Taiwan would have this status (Sheng 2001: 17).

Deng elaborated on Ye's proposal two years later, saying that Taiwan could have an independent legislature and judiciary and could handle its own foreign affairs. He declared that official acts and even laws of the Chinese government would not necessarily apply to Taiwan. Deng seemed to be suggesting a commonwealth to resolve the 'Taiwan issue'.

Taiwan did not take the bait. Its leaders pointed out that sovereignty was at issue. They also noted that China's so-called autonomous regions were badly treated and pointed to Tibet and Xinjiang. Because of Taiwan's response, Deng met resistance at home to what some labelled his 'weak' Taiwan policies. As Taiwan more openly resisted unification and invoked its democratisation as justification, concern grew among Chinese leaders that time was not on Beijing's side. Washington was also a problem. Contrary to China's expectation, the USA continued significant arms sales to Taiwan, enabling Taipei to parry China's military threats. To Beijing, Taiwan formally claiming independence seemed more likely than it deciding on unification. Deng's approach thus changed.

Beijing stepped up its pressure on Taipei with concerted effort to isolate Taiwan using various kinds of diplomatic pressure. China managed to terminate Taipei's membership in the World Bank, the International Monetary Fund and other international organisations. Deng's approach seemed to be a carrot and stick one and reflected deep differences in views among Chinese leaders concerning how to handle the Taiwan matter.

In 1984, Deng Xiaoping's strategy shifted to Hong Kong. Incorporating Hong Kong, he thought, would put pressure on Taiwan in a variety of ways. In September, Beijing and London held talks that resulted in an agreement whereby Hong Kong would be returned to China in 1997.[35] Deng sought to make Hong Kong a model for incorporating both Macau and Taiwan. He promised that Hong Kong's socio-economic system would be preserved for fifty years and that Hong Kong would be a 'special administrative region' after reversion, in many respects separate from China. Deng's approach for doing this was called the 'One Country, Two Systems' formula.

Taiwan did not respond in a positive way to the 'One Country, Two Systems' formula when it was first proposed or when it was implemented in incorporating Hong Kong. Basically, Taipei said that it could not apply to Taiwan. Leaders in Taipei pointed out that Hong Kong had been a colony and had not possessed sovereignty; Taiwan, in contrast, had sovereignty. Also, Hong Kong could not defend itself; Taiwan could. The media and various commentators in Taiwan noted that Hong Kong was to be made a 'special region' and was promised autonomy, but this had been applied to Tibet and it had been treated very badly. Officials in Taipei argued that the 'One Country, Two Systems' concept when applied to Taiwan did not take into consideration Taiwan's history, its democratisation and China's bad human rights record.

In 1988, Lee Teng-hui became president in Taiwan upon President Chiang Ching-kuo's death. Under Lee's leadership, Taiwan responded with its own formulas. One of these was 'One Country, Two Governments'. This supported the ROC's sovereignty but also the principle of one China. It was rejected by both Beijing and opposition politicians in Taiwan. Another approach, that of 'One Country, Two Entities', was broached by leaders in Taiwan with the intent of using creative ambiguity to resolve their differences. Still another, 'One Country, Two Areas', was proposed; it was also passed in the form of a resolution by Taiwan's Legislative Yuan in 1992, although it did not become the prevailing stance in relations with the PRC. The political opposition in Taiwan meanwhile adopted the policy of 'One China, One Taiwan' (Copper 2000a: 144–5). Opposition leaders argued that Taiwan had the right of self-determination and that its future should be decided by it alone, which it deserved more than ever due to its successful democratisation.

Nevertheless, in 1990 and 1991, Taiwan established three organisations, two governmental and one non-governmental, to carry on and ostensibly improve relations with the PRC: the Mainland Affairs Council, the National Unification Council and the informal Straits Exchange Foundation. The National Unification Council, in 1991, set up guidelines for Taiwan becoming part of China.[36] At the same time, Taipei ended the 'Period of National Mobilisation for the Suppression of the Communist Rebellion', thereby terminating a state of war with Beijing that had existed since the 1940s. In this act, Taipei recognised the legitimacy of the government of the PRC. This seemed a friendly gesture towards Beijing, yet it also suggested that there were two sovereign Chinese states. Taiwan's claim to rule all of China before this, although condemned by Beijing and by this time seen almost universally as chimerical, nevertheless was not opposed by Beijing, and dumping it broke a link between China and Taiwan.

In April 1993, historic talks were held between representatives of Taipei and Beijing in Singapore. The two sides agreed to legalise some documents, to establish formal channels for communication and to hold future meetings (Chiu 1993). Beijing and Taipei agreed to the concept of one China, with each entitled to its own definition. Some viewed the talks as groundbreaking and promising in terms of building a Chinese union of the PRC, Hong Kong, Macau (which were at this time already scheduled for reunification) and Taiwan.

However, optimism generated by this meeting was dampened by a 'White Paper' on unification issued in the fall by Beijing and by an ugly incident involving the murder of more than twenty tourists from Taiwan in China (Copper 1995). As a result, from 1994 onwards, Taiwan almost stopped mentioning the one-China principle (Sheng 2001: 144). Taiwan also issued a White Paper and it in talked of 'two legal entities in the international arena'. This implied that both sides had sovereignty and appeared to contradict the idea of one China. In its White Paper, Taipei also categorically rejected Deng's 'One Country, Two Systems' formula. In addition, Taipei demanded that Beijing respect its 'democratic system', saying that 'freedom and democracy in China was a precondition for unification' (*White Paper on Cross Strait Relations*, 24 July 1994).

Notwithstanding Taipei's recalcitrance, in January 1995, Jiang Zemin made a Chinese New Year speech in which he proposed unification on terms that were more generous than Deng's early ones. He cited a high degree of autonomy and judicial powers that would have final jurisdiction. He promised that Taiwan would retain its armed forces and that the PRC would not station troops in Taiwan or send administrative personnel there. With an emphasis on how unification would take place, as opposed to Taiwan's status after unification, which was the mainstay of the 'One Country, Two Systems' formula, Jiang suggested that the process would take a long time. Jiang also offered negotiations on an equal footing, suggesting, some say, political (although not sovereign) equality (Sheng 2001: 105). Jiang's offer was seen by China's leaders as 'envisioning the development of a common "greater" Chinese civilisation through efforts across the Strait' (Lam 1999: 172).[37]

Taiwan did not respond immediately. Three months later, President Lee Teng-hui issued a 'Six Point Proposal' in reply. He said that reunification should be pursued based on the reality that the two sides are governed by two governments and that the two should join international organisations on an equal footing. Lee was demanding sovereign equality, a rebuttal of Jiang's eight points, which some said Lee saw as a sign of weakness (*ibid.*: 54). In any case, he embarrassed Jiang, or worse, and soured cross-strait relations (*ibid.*: 173).

Progress towards serious talks on unification was brought to a complete halt in 1995 when President Lee Teng-hui visited the United States, deeply angering Chinese leaders in Beijing. In fact, many observers sensed that Beijing had a change of heart about Lee and from that time saw him as a proponent of independence rather than someone being influenced by others (Sheng 2001: 27–8; Zhao 2001).[38] Lee sought the visit as part of his 'pragmatic diplomacy'. He contended that Taiwan must avoid being isolated by Beijing, which in his eyes had become China's policy some time before this.

Tensions increased again the following year when President Lee was re-elected in Taiwan's first direct presidential election and Beijing conducted a second set of missile tests near Taiwan's shores. The tests in 1995 had been seen to reflect Beijing's anger over Lee's visit; in 1996, they were to disrupt the election and perhaps affect its outcome. Taiwan's response was that it was now a democracy and therefore should not be forced to become part of China against its will and that the election results indicated that the populace of Taiwan did not favour unification at the present time.

However, as a result of the 'almost war crisis', in 1996, Taipei began to seek some framework for accommodation with Beijing or at least some way to reduce tensions. The United States also wanted this. Before this, scholars in Taiwan had discussed a commonwealth, confederation and even federation, but before the mid-1990s the government had not, since it opposed the concept. Nevertheless, in 1997, Vice-President Lien Chan said that national unification was a goal 'without a timetable or set form, and so we do not rule out the possibility of any system'. Later he suggested 'one country, one good government' (meaning democracy) as a formula (Sheng 2001: 145).

In 1998, Beijing sought support from the Clinton administration to pressure Taiwan to negotiate. President Clinton obliged and while in China on a state visit publicly stated the 'three noes' policy: no independence for Taiwan; no two Chinas or one China, one Taiwan; and no participation for Taiwan in international organisations that require statehood for membership. Taiwan was intimidated, but the US Congress did not let Clinton's policy stand. It responded by passing a bill supporting the Taiwan Relations Act, which in essence had returned sovereignty to Taipei in US eyes after it had been taken away by the Normalisation Agreement negotiated between Washington and Beijing a few months earlier by the Carter administration. Congress took other actions to 'give Taipei a choice', such as announcing support for theatre missile defence (TMD) and larger weapons sales to Taiwan.

In July 1999, President Lee Teng-hui announced that relations between Beijing and Taipei would henceforth have to be special 'state-to-state' relations. This became known as his 'two-state theory'. Some said that he made this provocative declaration because Beijing was still attempting to isolate Taiwan, others that his statement was in response to Clinton's statements while in China the previous year. In any event, Lee's words were viewed with anger and hostility in Beijing. Beijing cancelled talks, which were scheduled, and China threatened Taiwan with military force. Relations across the Taiwan Strait hit another low point at this time, and any kind of agreement on reunification, Greater China or whatever appeared unlikely.[39]

In March 2000, Taiwan held a second direct presidential election, won by opposition leader Chen Shui-bian. This further strained relations between China and Taiwan, even though Chen had repudiated his call for Taiwan's independence and had adopted a moderate stance on cross-strait relations during the campaign. Beijing preferred another candidate and had said so.

During the campaign, China issued another 'White Paper' on Taiwan. This one was more demanding and more intimidating than such policy statements in the past because it put a time limit on negotiations, saying that if Taiwan did not negotiate within a reasonable period of time this would be justification for taking military action against the island. To ratchet up the level of the threat, Chinese Premier Zhu Rongji made a televised statement warning the electorate in Taiwan not to vote for Chen as there 'would not be a second chance'. This created a backlash and according to election analysts in Taiwan helped Chen (Copper 2000b).

During campaign speeches, Lien Chan, the Nationalist Party's presidential candidate cited, although without defining what it meant, a political 'union' as a means of resolving cross-strait problems. Some months later, Lien proposed a 'Chinese confederation' as a means for resolving cross-strait problems (*Taiwan Weekly Business Bulletin*, 17–24 January 2001). In January 2001, former premier Vincent Siew proposed a 'cross-strait common market'. He said that the idea came from the successful European Union, which began with a 'transitional economic integration' and moved towards political integration. He also spoke of it producing a 'sharing of sovereignty' (*ibid.*).[40] In mid-year, Siew visited China and made the proposal again but found no takers (Wang 2001).[41]

After winning the election, Chen Shui-bian made what members of his party called 'major concessions' to Beijing in the form of a 'four noes' policy: no independence, no change in the country's name, no constitutional amendment to formalise Lee Teng-hui's two-state formula, and no referendum to decide Taiwan's future. Chen then added a 'fifth no': no change in the National Unification Guidelines. Chen, meanwhile, had suggested a 'Chinese confederation' as a means of resolving political issues between Taipei and Beijing. Chen also endorsed Siew's cross-strait common market idea, saying that mutual trust can be built only when political issues are put aside. President Chen then introduced the concept of 'integration' to resolve cross-strait problems. He spoke of both economic and political integration but said that the former would precede the latter. His advisors subsequently turned this into what has been called an 'integration theory'. Chen later elaborated on the meaning of this idea when he told members of the European Parliament visiting Taipei that Taiwan should seek permanent peace through 'political integration' in the form of federation, confederation, commonwealth or something like the European Union (Hahn 2001).

However, Chinese leaders expressed no interest in these ideas. The Beijing-controlled Hong Kong newspaper *Wen Wei Po*, at the time of Vincent Siew's proposal, quoted an official as saying that a confederation would violate the one-China principle and is 'not suitable' (*Wen Wei Po*, 21 January 2001). Shortly afterwards, Chinese leaders reiterated their position that proposals that did not adhere to the one-China principle constitute efforts to divide Chinese sovereignty and to split China. They said that proposals resembling the German formula could not be accepted because, unlike Germany, China is a big and growing power and foreign countries would like to keep China divided and weak. Some leaders in Beijing also believed that the Chen government was weak in view of the fact that his party did not control the legislature. Hence they thought that Chen might eventually be more accommodating to Beijing's overtures and eventually accept the one-China principle (Sheng 2001: 210–13). Others disliked and distrusted Chen so much that a friendly policy was not feasible. In any event, Chen could not accept one China, except as a negotiating topic, and refused it as a starting principle.

Conclusions

The concept of Greater China found its inception in the 1980s as a consequence of Deng Xiaoping's successful economic reforms. However, it arguably had a historical basis or foundation. It was also a concept that as it developed was in many respects in consonance with how most Chinese view their culture and, in some ways, how Beijing and other Chinese entities view the world.

The notion of an economic community of Chinese 'participants' became widely heralded in the early 1980s after it began to garner strong support from various Chinese political actors and the overseas Chinese. By most standards, in fact, Greater China became more dynamic in some ways and just as viable as most regional economic organisations, including the most famous one, the European Union. Economic Greater China soon offered great promise, producing vast mutual advantage for all while increasing the clout and the influence of Chinese in the region and even in the international community.

Subsequently Greater China came to have very salient political implications, especially as the 'Taiwan issue' became more heated and difficult with rapid democratisation on the island. However, a political Greater China did not win such broad and enthusiastic support as an economic Greater China.

One might conclude, then, that economic Greater China succeeded, but political Greater China had not. That is too simple a generalisation. One needs to recall that there were, and remain, several different and indeed conflicting definitions of an economic Greater China. An economic bloc comprising Fujian province, Guangdong province, Hong Kong and Taiwan had and still has considerable support. Some say that Greater China includes Singapore, the overseas Chinese and possibly Korea, Outer Mongolia and all or part of Southeast Asia. How to define economic Greater China thus awaits a consensus. Beijing sees this as a splittist notion and opposes it, at least in the sense of it taking on any political meaning, which one would think it must in order to evolve further. Chinese leaders have also labelled it too narrow in scope. They view as provocative and thus bad policy the inclusion of areas not traditionally part of outer China and the overseas Chinese. Thus economic Greater China usually, and certainly in Beijing, means the PRC, Hong Kong, Macau and Taiwan.

There is a general consensus about the composition of political Greater China, but especially as far as Beijing is concerned. It will comprise the PRC, Hong Kong, Macau and Taiwan. Hong Kong and Macau have already been reunified with the People's Republic of China; Taiwan will. However, for Taiwan, whether it becomes part of Greater China is yet to be decided.

With the continuation of commercial ties and as the economic gap between the PRC and Taiwan closes, constructing a meaningful and more formal economic Greater China will presumably become more likely. A political union is a different story. The fact is that the political systems in the two remain very different. In addition and probably more importantly, Taiwan possesses sovereignty, in its view anyway, and the international community generally agrees, in some senses at least. There has been no effort by the global community or any international organisation to pressure Taiwan to join China, not even any serious suggestion of this. Thus Taiwan may be unwilling to give up its present status no matter what the PRC does or offers. Taiwan also has outside support, most importantly from the United States, for keeping its democracy, and at present its population does not want to join China. All of these 'realities' present serious problems. So does the fact that Beijing has not been willing to accept any compromise and views with great suspicion any proposal for a political union based on anything other than its one-China formula. Complicating matters, both Beijing and Taipei justifiably view the other as deceitful and untrustworthy.

Alternatively, Taiwan may change its views under intense long-term pressure. Many in Taiwan admit that China is too big to ignore, and this feeling will only increase. The realisation may also grow in Taiwan that in standing alone it will be historically insignificant and will be a pawn to the United States and/or Japan. Becoming part of China will make Taiwan relevant and important. People in Taiwan do talk this way, and so do government officials.

A commonwealth has also been suggested as a means of formalising Greater China. According to this approach, Taiwan would join a loosely structured, voluntary organisation (which presumably Beijing leads) that does not require it to sacrifice its sovereignty, something like the British Commonwealth. Presumably the relationship would evolve. Beijing–Taipei relations might then progress from the status of a commonwealth to a confederation (which is sometimes described as a 'halfway house' between a system wherein the units are sovereign to one where they give up some or all of that sovereignty). This might work for Taiwan if no time limit were to be put on the organisation 'progressively' evolving. It might happen anyway if extensive and growing commercial activities across the Taiwan Strait weaken Taiwan's resistance to political ties and Beijing were to accept some other formula than the one-China one. Some say that Greater China might thus follow the course of the European Union, which saw economic links turn into political ones and the system evolve as advantages to the organisation and the members increased.

To date, however, Beijing has rejected these ideas. China has nominally supported something similar being sought by the two Koreas but at the same time has categorically denied that there is any lesson in the two Koreas unifying by forming a confederation that would be transformed into a federation later. Beijing has rejected a cross-strait common market, yet it has endorsed, even proposed, a common market for Southeast Asia. It may be that domestic politics in China explain this seemingly contradictory attitude. The military and hard-liners, who comprise leftists in the Chinese Communist Party and the government, oppose this 'weak' solution to resolving the question of China's territorial integrity. There may be other problems as well. The People's Republic of China is a unitary political system, and while it has decentralised both economic and political authority over the last two decades to make reform work, no constitutional provisions have been made for a federal system or anything resembling one.

Yet this situation may change. The military's clout has certainly waxed and waned in the past. The PRC is democratising on many fronts, and a 'fourth generation' of leaders may perceive that continued economic growth requires more technology and that this mandates a more open, free and democratic political system; and they may act accordingly. And no matter what Chinese leaders say, some kind of political union, most commonly a federation, has been discussed frequently in private over the last several years.[42]

Beijing's continued hostility towards Taiwan may be the key. Taiwan has alternatives. In the most extreme case, it may decide, if all of these proposals fail, to eschew an economic Greater China in favour of pursuing broader commercial ties with the United States, Japan, Southeast Asia and the rest of the world. Based on history, geography, current politics and security considerations, Taiwan is inclined to move away from China more than towards it. The United States, Japan and ASEAN may encourage this if their relations with Beijing sour, which has been the situation in recent years. However, this scenario assumes that strategic objectives predominate over economic links and that Taiwan's commercial ties with China do not become more important and Taiwan's economic ties with the United States and Japan remain vital and perhaps increase or Taiwan diversifies its trade and other economic ties internationally in a very significant fashion. These are iffy assumptions. The 'secret view' (that of the intelligence community and the military) in the United States is another uncertain factor. So is Japan.

In any event, tranquillity and stability in East Asia seem to be a much better environment for reconciliation and one in which Taiwan is more likely to join China in some kind of 'union with Chinese characteristics'. Peace will also reduce the probability of interference in this process.

Greater China is currently an economic reality and is likely to be more so in the future. While its definition is not fixed, that will hardly matter in terms of its growing importance. Taiwan is a partner it seems, whether or not it wants to be in terms of government policies. In other words, economic ties are irreversible. However, whether Greater China succeeds probably depends on whether it also becomes a political reality, and that is difficult to discern at the present time.

Notes

1 For example, Greater China was the topic of a conference in the early 1990s, and the papers filled a subsequent issue of *China Quarterly* (December 1993) and were later published in book form (see Shambaugh 1995). The Hoover Institution sponsored a conference at Stanford University in late 1994, also resulting in a book (see Metzger and Myers 1996). A Nobel lecture was published on the subject (Wang 1995). An issue of *China Quarterly* was also devoted to elections and democracy in Greater China: no. 162, June 2000.

2 As of mid-2000, the population of these five Chinese 'entities' was PRC – 1,264,536,000; Taiwan – 22,256,000; Hong Kong – 7,002,000; Singapore – 4,001,000; Macau – 445,000. Source: Population Reference Bureau, *2000 Population Data Sheet*.

3 Hong Kong is called a 'Special Administrative Region' of China. Macau has a similar appellation.

4 The number of Overseas Chinese was 34,505,000 as of the end of 1999. Source: Republic of China, Overseas Chinese Affairs Commission, cited by China News Agency, 5 May 2000.

5 The author of the article, in Shambaugh (1995), Guangwu Wang, prefers the term 'Chinese overseas' since overseas Chinese, which in Chinese is *hua qiao* and implies temporary residence, is not accurate. This author agrees with that but will stick to the more common term 'overseas Chinese'.

6 This is the thesis of a long book-length study. See, for example, van Kemenade (1998). The only reference to Greater China in this set of books is to US trade with Greater China as defined this way. A number of other authors concur: see, for example, Tucker (1994: 195) and Zhao (1997: 192–4).

7 Abegglen notes that the 'Greater South China regional zone' compares very closely to the Association of Southeast Asian Nations (ASEAN) in size, economic dynamism and more. Also see Chang (1998: 158).

8 Although this point of view is usually based on historical and cultural perspectives, it has also been proposed as a means whereby China and Southeast Asia can form an economic bloc that will stop Japanese economic penetration of the area and perhaps become a fourth global economic bloc (in addition to the North American Free Trade Association, the European Union and Japan). See Abegglen (1994: 21).

9 Even serious scholars view China's history as in many ways inseparable from that of East Asia. Fairbank and Reischauer state: 'China is so large a part of East Asia and was for so long so dominant in the region that any study of China involves some consideration of the whole East Asian area' (1989: 2).

10 Chinese leaders have often spoken of hostile foreign forces that seek to divide China. This was one of the main themes in the nationalistic literature that became common in China after the Tiananmen Square massacre. More was said after the US–China confrontation in 1996 resulting from missile tests by China to intimidate Taiwan during a presidential election. Beijing referred to the United States using Lee Teng-hui and the Dalai Lama in its 'splittist' crusade. It also mentioned Japan. At the 15th Party Congress in 1997, party leaders called on the Chinese Communist Party's 3.4 million grass-roots cells to become fortresses against 'peaceful evolution', which Chinese leaders define as *Western*

efforts to penetrate and fragment China to keep it weak (see Lam 1999: 267, 351). In fact, Lee Teng-hui advocated the break-up of China into seven parts in his book *Voice of Taiwan*, published in 1999. Chinese leaders have never mentioned a union or any other such term as a means of putting China back together again as they strive to prevent its disintegration at all costs.

11 For a discussion of inner and outer China, see Blunden and Elvin (1998: 14–15).

12 Mosher contrasts China's policy of assimilation with a different policy pursued by Rome during the Roman Empire, observing that China probably had three times as many men under arms to do this. Another writer notes that the rate of China's assimilation of other people was slow and accompanied by war and slaughter (see Lattimore and Lattimore 1944: 36–7).

13 A number of authors have argued that the present government has to a large degree adopted this view (see, for example, Elegant 1968).

14 The term *tian xia* and other words suggesting China to be large and universal were used instead. The terms *da Han* (big Han Dynasty) and similar terms for other dynasties were common. The term *da Qing guo* (big Qing country) was used after the West had impacted China. The fact that *guo* was not used before this indicates that the Chinese saw China as an empire rather than as a nation, which to them was lower in status.

15 Mancall states: 'In the Chinese world view, legal boundaries could not exist between societies since all societies were part of a socially and culturally hierarchical, not a legal and egalitarian, universe'.

16 According to the *Cambridge History of China* (p. 21), 221 BC (the start of the Qin Dynasty) 'marks a shift from state to empire'.

17 Chinese would say that this was progressive change compared with what happened in Europe. What happened there was a 'fragmentation of the empire'. Western historians, for the most part, would disagree.

18 Fairbank and Reischauer (1973) say that the relationship between inner China and outer China compares to *yin* and *yang* and that foreign (meaning outer China) conquest brought new blood and a martial spirit to China and thus China became strong and expanded.

19 In so far as the Manchus did not allow the immigration of Chinese into their homeland, Manchuria, and as recent documents indicate, their intent was to create a Chinese empire by incorporating territory that was not populated by Chinese and that was traditionally defined as outer China to facilitate their control of inner China and the Chinese people. This has been reversed by the governments of both Nationalist and Communist China to mean that these territories were part of China. They are now defined as 'lost territories', and the view is that they should be returned. The best way to do that is to employ the term 'Greater China' (see Horner 2001: 86–96).

20 Some would say that the return of these lost territories was the work of the United States. Chiang's close relations with Washington, which he pursued with focus, were relevant. This was especially the case with Taiwan, since it had been acquired fifty years earlier and was not categorised as 'recently seized territory' that was to be stripped from Japan.

21 It is worthy of note that the term 'Greater China' did not originate with, nor was it connected by Chinese policy makers to, concepts such as globalisation (*quanqiuhua*), economic integration (*jingji yitihua*) or world economic interdependence (*shijie jingji de xianghu yicun*) (see Moore 2000): 105).

22 For a less complimentary version of China's reform, or one that supports Maoist communism, see Chossudovsky (1986).

23 Mao's belief was that economic ties, especially with Western countries, but later the Soviet Union as well, would lead to a dependency relationship that would hurt the country both economically and politically. In 1979, China had a debt of 3.5

billion yuan, including foreign and domestic loans, and outstanding bonds. This was 3.3 percent of total government revenue (see Donnithorne 1989: 355–89).

24 In the 1940s and 1950s, China had been Hong Kong's main trading partner. That situation changed in the 1960s due to China's isolationist economic policies.

25 Soon a million people from Taiwan were visiting China each year. By 1997, there had been eleven million visits and over 200,000 visits by people from China to Taiwan. Many went to visit relatives and for educational and cultural exchange, but many went to conduct business (see Clough 1999: 51).

26 Beijing reports that Taiwan's investments in China total US$28 billion; the Ministry of Economic Affairs in Taipei reports US$50 billion; Taiwan's central bank reports US$100 billion (see Tkacik 2001: 2).

27 Chinese are particularly dominant in the economies of Indonesia, Thailand, Malaysia and the Philippines. Chinese comprise 4 percent of the population of Indonesia, but they own or control seventeen of the twenty-five largest business groups. In Thailand, they make up 10 percent of the population and control 90 percent of commercial and manufacturing assets and half of the nation's bank capital. In the Philippines, they are 1 percent of the population and account for two-thirds of the sales of the largest commercial enterprises. In Malaysia, Chinese comprise nearly 40 percent of the population and dominate nearly every sector of the economy. For further details, see Rower (1995: 228).

28 Rower estimates that the overseas Chinese in these four countries would add US$500 billion to US$600 billion in GNP if measured by purchasing power parity.

29 Fred Bergstem said this in testimony before a congressional committee at this time (see Lampton 2000: 197).

30 This is Lee Teng-hui's famous, or some would say infamous, 'theory of seven parts' (*qi kuai lun*). Beijing was furious about the proposal and accused Lee of intending to destroy China's sovereignty.

31 Many advocates of a political Greater China looked at the European Union as their model. The argument was that economic cooperation and extensive commercial relations would create an economic union and that in turn would lead to a political union. However, others noted that the European Union was also closely linked to the North Atlantic Treaty Organisation (NATO) and that a military component was needed to ensure the viability of a political union.

32 It is necessary to point out that the government of the People's Republic of China did not openly use the term 'Greater China' to refer to either an economic bloc or a political union. Chinese officials found the term too sensitive in Southeast Asia, in particular where many overseas Chinese resided. It is not clear whether before or during the early 1980s the term was taboo for other reasons, namely that it might make it possible for foreign countries to challenge Beijing's sovereignty over Taiwan and possibly some other claimed territories. In any case, this view evolved as discussed in this chapter.

33 The CPPC, established in 1949, was designed to bring together 'persons from all strata of society' as well as patriotic organisations and various political parties (including a faction of the Nationalist Party). It heard various points of view and represented an early effort to build democracy.

34 The speech was entitled 'The United Front and the Tasks of the Chinese People's Political Consultative Conference in the New Period' and was given on 15 June 1979 (see Deng 1984: 76).

35 In the nineteenth century, two parts of the British Crown Colony of Hong Kong (Hong Kong Island and the Kowloon peninsula) had been transferred to Britain 'in perpetuity' and therefore, one could argue, did not legally have to be returned. However, since the era of colonialism was over and Hong Kong was not econom- ically and in other ways viable without the New Territories, which had been

leased by the UK for ninety-nine years (to expire in 1997), the deal provided that all of Hong Kong be returned to China.

36 According to the guidelines, unification would take place in three stages: (1) exchanges and reciprocity; (2) building trust and confidence; and (3) consultations and unification. No timetable was set. It has long been debated whether the guidelines were serious or whether Taipei was seeking to establish a means of impeding the process.

37 However, Willy Lam notes that the generals did not 'utter a word of support' for Jiang's eight points and that the vice-chairman of the Party's Central Military Commission, General Zhang Zhen, commented about 'cowardly behaviour'. Jiang and several other officials connected with making Taiwan policy later made self-criticisms.

38 However, Zhao believes that Beijing became hostile towards Lee earlier.

39 Beijing cancelled talks with Taipei at this time, and the war of words escalated.

40 James Lilly, former US ambassador to China, responded by saying that it was a 'very good concept'.

41 However, some said that the mere fact that Siew went indicates some interest on Beijing's part.

42 Mao discussed it as a means of dealing with Tibet and Xinjiang province. Jiang Zemin's think tanks studied it. After the 1990s, papers were written about it that went to the Chinese Communist Party's Central Committee (see Lam 1999: 263–4).

References

Abegglen, J.C. (1994) *Sea Change: Pacific Asia as the New World Industrial Center*. New York: Free Press.

Blunden, C. and Elvin, M. (1998) *Cultural Atlas of China*. New York: Checkmark Books.

Chang, M.H. (1998) *The Labors of Sisyphus: The Economic Development of Communist China*. New Brunswick, NJ: Transaction.

Chiu Hungdah (1993) *The Koo–Wang Talks and the Prospects for Building Constructive and Stable Relations across the Taiwan Straits*. Baltimore: University of Maryland School of Law.

Chossudovsky, M. (1986) *Toward Capitalist Restoration? Chinese Socialism after Mao*. New York: St Martin's Press.

Clough, R.N. (1999) *Co-operation or Conflict in the Taiwan Strait*. Lanham, Md: Rowman & Littlefield.

Copper, J.F. (1995) *Words Across the Taiwan Strait: A Critique of Beijing's 'White Paper' on China's Unification*. Lanham, Md: University Press of America.

—— (2000a) *Historical Dictionary of Taiwan (Republic of China)*. Lanham, Md: Scarecrow Press.

—— (2000b) *Taiwan's 2000 Presidential and Vice Presidential Election: Consolidating Democracy and Creating a New Era of Politics*. Baltimore: University of Maryland School of Law.

Deng Xiaoping (1984) *Deng Xiaoping: Speeches and Writings*. Oxford: Pergamon Press.

Donnithorne, A. (1989) 'The reform of the fiscal and banking systems in China', in J.Y.S. Cheng (ed.), *China: Modernization in the 1980s*. Hong Kong: Hong Kong University Press.

Elegant, R.S. (1968) *The Center of the World: Communism and the Mind of China.* New York: Funk & Wagnalls.

Fairbank, J.K. and Reischauer, E.O. (1973) *China: Tradition and Transformation.* Sydney: George Allen & Unwin.

—— (1989) *China: Tradition and Transformation.* Boston: Houghton Mifflin.

Gernet, J. (1996) *A History of Chinese Civilization.* New York: Cambridge University Press.

Hahn, L. (2001) 'Toward a resolution of the Taiwan Strait problem: Chen Shui-bian's "theory of integration"', Foreign Policy Research Institute, e-notes distributed on 21 May 2001.

Horner, C. (2001) 'China and the historians', *The National Interest* (spring): 86–96.

Hughes, C. (1999) 'Democratization and Beijing's Taiwan policy', in S. Tsang and H.-M. Tien (eds), *Democratization in Taiwan: Implications for China.* Hong Kong: Hong Kong University Press.

Kim, S.S. and Dittmer, L. (eds) (1993) *China's Quest for National Identity.* Ithaca, NY: Cornell University Press.

Lam, W.W.-L. (1999) *The Era of Jiang Zemin.* Singapore: Prentice Hall.

Lampton, D.M. (2000) *Same Bed Different Dreams.* Berkeley: University of California Press.

Lattimore, O. and Lattimore, E. (1944) *The Making of Modern China: A Short History.* New York: W.W. Norton.

Lever-Tracy, C., Ip, D. and Tracy, N. (1996) *The Chinese Diaspora and Mainland China: An Emerging Economic Synergy.* New York: St Martin's Press.

Mackerras, C., Taneja, P. and Young, G. (1984) *China Since 1978: Reform, Modernization and Socialism with Chinese Characteristics.* New York: Longman Cheshire.

Mancall, M. (1984) *China at the Center: 300 Years of Foreign Policy.* New York: Free Press.

Martin, H. (1997) 'Cultural China', in M. Brosseau, Kuan H.-C. and Y.Y. Yueh (eds), *China Review 1997.* Hong Kong: Chinese University of Hong Kong Press.

Metzger, T.A. and Myers, R.H. (eds) (1996) *Greater China and U.S. Foreign Policy: The Choice between Confrontation and Mutual Respect.* Stanford, Calif.: Hoover Institution Press.

Moore, T.G. (2000) 'China and globalization', in S.S. Kim (ed.), *East Asia and Globalization.* Lanham, Md: Rowman & Littlefield.

Mosher, S.W. (2000) *Hegemon: China's Plan to Dominate Asia and the World.* San Francisco: Encounter Books.

Naisbitt, J. (1995) *Megatrends Asia: The Eight Asian Megatrends that Are Changing the World.* London: Nicholas Brady.

Ohmae Kenichi (1995) *The End of the Nation-State: The Rise of Regional Economies.* New York: Free Press.

Overholt, W.H. (1993) *The Rise of China: How Economic Reform is Creating a New Superpower.* New York: W.W. Norton.

Robinson, T.W. (1994) 'Interdependence in China's foreign relations', in S.S. Kim (ed.), *China and the World: Chinese Foreign Relations in the Post-Cold War Era.* Boulder, Colo.: Westview Press.

Rower, J. (1995) *Asia Rising: Why America Will Prosper as Asia's Economies Boom.* New York: Simon & Schuster.

Shambaugh, D. (ed.) (1995) *Greater China: The Next Superpower.* New York: Oxford University Press.

Sheng Lijun (2001) *China's Dilemma: The Taiwan Issue*. Singapore: Institute for Southeast Asian Studies.

Snow, E. (1938) *Red Star over China*. New York: Random House.

Tkacik, J. (2001) 'Chen visit would promote Asia–Pacific stability', *Taiwan Outlook* (July): 2.

Tucker, N.B. (1994) *Taiwan, Hong Kong and the United States, 1945–1992*. New York: Twaye Publishers.

van Kemenade, W. (1998) *China, Hong Kong, Taiwan, Inc.: The Dynamics of a New Empire*. New York: Vintage Books.

Wang Gungwu (1991) 'Among Non-Chinese', *Daedalus* (spring): 142.

—— (1995) *The Chinese Way: China's Position in International Relations*. Stockholm: Scandinavian University Press.

Wang, D. (2001) 'Strait common market won't work', *Taipei Times*, 1 June, available at http//www.taipeitimes.com.

Zhao Suisheng (1997) *Power Competition in East Asia*. New York: St Martin's Press.

—— (2001) 'Deadlock: Beijing's national reunification strategy after Lee Teng-hui', *Problems of Post-Communism*, March–April.

Part I

The People's Republic of China

3 Peddling party ideology for a profit

Media and the rise of Chinese nationalism in the 1990s

Yu Huang and Chin-Chuan Lee

> The characterisations of the United States as being a hegemony, as a country determined to dominate the world and to contain and dominate China are simply untrue .... Yet we see constant references such as this appearing in the Chinese media, which only provokes a negative reaction on the part of many in my own country.
>
> (William Cohen, US Defense Secretary, Beijing, July 2000)

> Shortly after Cohen made the irresponsible remarks misleading world opinion, the U.S. press including the *Washington Post*, *USA Today* and *Newsweek* did not hesitate to follow suit and publish articles demonising the Chinese media. Given the embarrassed situation the United States is in, the U.S. media should really learn to recognise their own faults rather than just throwing dirt at others.
>
> (*China Daily*, 31 July 2000)

Arriving in Beijing to mend fragile US–China, ties which had been damaged fourteen months earlier by NATO bombing of the Chinese embassy in Belgrade, Secretary of Defense William Cohen was greeted by the official English-language *China Daily* with a banner headline, 'U.S. a Threat to World Peace', across its front page (13 July 2000). The article accused the United States of 'going against the will of the world and seeking military supremacy'. This public display of anti-Americanism betrayed mutual desire for conciliation and symbolised the convergence of statist and populist nationalism in China, which has been on the rise since the 1990s. The media have been quick to seize particularly emotive external events and frame them in a variety of sensational ways as an affront to China's national pride and sovereignty. Media discourses have harped on the themes of the US media's demonisation of China (Xiao and Liu 2001) to stir up public sentiment. Media production of orchestrated nationalism fits into official craving for legitimacy and recognition that is commensurate with China's increased economic prowess, while filling the void left by a dying communist ideology (He Zhou). The end of the Cold War has stripped China and the United States of the basis for strategic alliance against the Soviet Union and has exposed China to international criticism of its human rights abuses. The selling of orchestrated nationalism also satisfies the consumerist logic for a collective therapy, hence garnering a huge profit for the media in a more secular post-Tiananmen Square China (Lee 2000a).

Scholarly attention given to Chinese nationalism has ranged widely. Segal (1996) argues that Chinese nationalism has developed from an 'affirmative' to an 'assertive' position, while Zhao (2000) and Yan (2001) interpret it as a 'situational' and defensive reaction to external challenges. Friedman (1997) and Liu ,Alan P.L. characterise recent waves of nationalism as more 'aggressive' and 'chauvinistic' than ever before, a product of deliberate manipulation to bolster the regime's fragile legitimacy. Other writings on this topic include Whiting (1995), Shambaugh (1996), Unger (1996), Rosen (1997), Zheng (1999) and Chang (2001). This chapter seeks to analyse the shifting trajectory of the media in the construction of nationalism in post-Tiananmen Square China.

Pro-Western media discourses in the 1980s

Before the modern era, China was seen as a 'closed' civilisation marked by static stability rather than as a nation (Duara 1996; Pye 1996). Nationalism being a Western concept of modernity, invasion by Western powers and Japan in the nineteenth century dragged imperial China into the modern world and gave birth to nationalism in China (Levenson 1967; Townsend 1996). The motif of Chinese nationalism has been the pursuit of wealth and national strength in its struggle against foreign domination (Zhao 2000: 2–5). Schwartz (1993: 247) thinks of nationalism as 'a fundamental "turn" in modern Chinese culture'. China has had to accept the West as a mentor of modernisation and reject it as a hostile oppressor. It is important to remember this vacillating ambivalence towards the West as the larger historical backdrop of current nationalism.

In a way, the seeds of nationalism in the 1990s were sown in the 1980s, when public discourses seemed to be much more receptive to Western liberal thought as an alternative to bankrupt Maoism. Deng Xiaoping emerged from the Cultural Revolution to push his modernisation projects as a way of bringing party legitimacy back from the brink of collapse and from the depth of a prevailing crisis of confidence.[1] The loss of faith in Marxism, the Communist Party and socialism reflected what Max Weber (1958) called 'the disenchantment of the world' among the intellectual elite and the workers. The *People's Daily* was a leading enlightened voice of reform ideology that supported Deng against the Maoist remnants and from time to time fell into sharp criticisms of the propaganda police for endorsing reformist leaders Hu Yaobang and Zhao Ziyang. Many reformist intellectuals sought to give a more liberal and less dogmatic interpretation to the texts of Marx, Engels, Lenin and Mao (Lee 2000a). Others, notably Wei Jingsheng and Fang Lizhi, looked up to the liberal positions for inspiration. Liberal advocates had a contested relationship with reformist Marxists, but as the pace of political reform stalled and party reformists became more disillusioned, both sides seemed to find considerable ground for agreement towards the second half of the decade (Su 1996). Infatuation with Western thought was not limited to the intellectual circle: during the mid-1980s, nationwide surveys showed the vast majority of the population and the political elite expressing a strong interest in Western culture and political ideas (Min 1989).

In the years leading to the Tiananmen Square crackdown in 1989, many leading intellectuals who were allied with the reform bureaucracy launched the New Enlightenment Movement, which not only rejected Maoist *praxis* but also favoured Western liberalism. They harnessed the media, most notably the *World Economic Herald* in Shanghai, to advocate Western liberal norms such as press freedom, public opinion, and the rule of law as prerequisites for sustained economic development. In 1988, the paper provoked a heated debate when it argued that if China should fail in its economic and political reform, it would be expelled from the international community (Hsiao and Yang 1990; Yu 1992). The forced closure of the paper by the authorities became a focal point that escalated the Tiananmen Square protests in 1989.

The New Enlightenment Movement promoted Western-style institutions, technology and value systems to replace the existing feudalistic Chinese culture (Goldman *et al.* 1993). Others termed this movement as a 'culture fever' (*wen-hua-re*) (Barmé 1999; Wu 1988). Besides the media, this movement also involved publishing journals and book series, actively promoting a wide range of Western ideas, from philosophy, economics and political science to literature. Their major forums included *Dushu* ('Readings', started in 1979),[2] *Zouxiang Weilai* ('Striving towards the Future', 1984), *Qingnian Luntan* ('Youth Forum', 1985), *Wenhua: Zhongguo yu Shijie* ('Culture: China and the World', 1987), *Xin Qimeng* ('New Enlightenment', 1988) and *Sixiangjia* ('Thinker', 1988). At the same time, many of the influential Western books on the social sciences and humanities were translated and sold in large numbers to an eager audience.[3] The effect of this fever is difficult to gauge, but Western ideas appeared to be effectively disseminated across most sectors in urban China. Media reform was on the agenda. The media's appeal to liberal values, by way of launching popular anti-traditionalism, culminated in the production of a six-part TV documentary entitled *Heshang* ('River Elegy'), which was aired on China Central Television (CCTV) in 1988 (Su *et al.* 1998). The programme fused together nihilism and nationalism in mourning over the decline of the once great Chinese nation, and then in relating today's authoritarian leadership to the static and backward nature of traditional culture. For China to develop, the programme concluded, it must embrace Western civilisation. It engendered an enormous debate. China was searching its soul.

The decade was interspersed with intermittent spurts of anti-liberal backlash (including the short-lived Anti-Spiritual Pollution campaign in 1983, the Anti-Bourgeois Liberalisation campaigns in 1987 and the Tiananmen Square crackdown in 1989) as Maoist remnants waged a losing ideological battle and Deng tried to maintain a precarious power balance between various leadership factions. But media and intellectual discourses were persistently enthusiastic about the imperative of political reform, which they thought would constitute a structural guarantee for sustained economic modernisation, and they did so with the tacit approval of – and in some cases active collaboration with – the reform bureaucracy. The reform bureaucracy looked favourably on Western technology and management while trying to resist Western democracy with such dubious formulations as Zhao Ziyang's neo-authoritarianism (Ruan 1990). Even those who sought to revive the relevance of Marxism to China's reform programme in the face of public disillusionment with the Maoist debacle (such as Su Shaozhi and Sun Xupei) had varying degrees of appreciation for Western press freedom and democracy (Lee 2000b). On the other side of the Pacific Ocean, the US media were also romanticising China as a country that had begun to embrace capitalist democracy at the expense of communist ideology (Lee 1990). Most dramatically, the spirit of young protesters in Tiananmen Square, who were the descendants of Wei Jingsheng and Fang Lizhi, was symbolised by the Goddess of Democracy, a replica of the Statue of Liberty that looked more Caucasian than Chinese. We do not wish to suggest that liberal thought had a linear or smooth path in China, because official dogma and other forces constantly contested it. But despite this contestation, Western liberalism was obviously gaining the ascendancy in intellectual and media discourses.

Anti-Western media discourses in the 1990s

China's officialdom conveniently blamed the West for inspiring the Tiananmen Square protests in 1989. Official crackdowns strangled the life of the New Enlightenment Movement, thus rendering liberal–reformist–elitist programmes of the 1980s futile. The regime's legitimacy was again put to a severe test. As Huang (1995: 57) points out:

> The post-Tiananmen regime has eagerly embraced Chinese nationalism as a new fount of legitimacy. The Chinese Communist Party began in earnest to revive traditional values that the Maoist regime had tried for years to eliminate. The strategy has worked, as evidenced by the recent rising anti-American sentiment.

Deng's renewed effort at greater economic liberalisation in 1992 has brought about a small middle class whose energies have been diverted away from political reform towards economic pursuits. Partly because of growing afflu-ence, this privileged class – in an increasingly depoliticised nation – has also become nationalistic in its restricted and superficial encounter with the West and Western media (Zhang 1998: 10). The Western media's negative portrayal of China was so exaggerated as to trigger public xenophobia, fear and frustration.

Nationalist rhetoric did not come solely from within the party *apparatchiks*. Public apathy and distrust of straitjacketed party propaganda were prevalent. After the Tiananmen Square bloodshed, it was from He Xin (1991, 1996), a self-professed independent academic researcher turned state-endorsed media celebrity, that we first heard the high-pitched rhetoric of 'defending Chinese national interests'. He lambasted the New Enlightenment Movement as importing hostile Western thought to subvert China's socialist system, while justifying the military crackdown as necessary for maintaining China's stability and social order. He reframed core issues of the discourse from human rights to national interest and sovereignty. With He Xin playing into the desperate need of the Communist Party, the *People's Daily* published his 20,000-word interview with a Japanese economist, entitled 'The World Economy and China', on 11 December 1990. A long editorial preface praised his patriotism. Defining nationalism in terms of unifying the motherland, He Xin quickly became something of a media phenomenon when all of the official media rushed in to give him prominent coverage. His argument, although not sophisticated, appeared to gain some validity as he drew the scenario of Soviet break-up as a contrast to China. He's limelight dimmed in 1992 when the media turned their attention to Deng's effort to revive economic liberalisation during a tour of the South. He Xin nonetheless ushered in the first wave of post-Tiananmen Square nationalist discourse.

A 'patriotic education campaign' was conducted under the supervision of the newly installed party boss, Jiang Zemin, who asked the media to educate the younger generation as to why only the communist leadership could make China strong and prosperous. Patriotic education courses were included in all college and high school curricula (Barmé 1999: 256–8). In 1990, the Central Party Committee's theoretical journal, *Qiushi* ('Seeking Truth'), proclaimed editorially:

> Patriotism is history-specific, possessing different contents under different historical circumstances. Today, if we want to be patriotic, we should love the socialist New China under the leadership of the Communist Party. As Comrade Deng Xiaoping pointed out in one of his speeches in 1981, 'Some people say that not loving socialism is not the same thing as not loving our motherland. Is motherland an abstract concept? If you do not love the socialist New China led by the Communist Party, what else can you love?'
>
> (1990: 8)

Another article in *Qiushi*, by Ming Lizhi, a member of the Propaganda Department of the Central Party Committee, declared: 'Patriotism is the premise of China's socialism and socialism is the inevitable conclusion of genuine patriotism' (1990: 15). Meanwhile, by late 1991, the 'crown princes', the offspring of high-ranking party officials, implored the party to alter its political strategy in the post-Cold War environment. In a widely circulated pamphlet (written under the name of the Ideology and Theory Department of the *China Youth Daily*), they argued that nationalism and patriotism would be more effective than traditional communist ideology in combating the Western conspiracy of 'peaceful evolution' (Chen 1997; *China Spring* 1992: 35–9; He Zhou: 283). This meant that no Chinese could expect to criticise the government without being impugned as unpatriotic (Pye 1996: 108).

Furthermore, the authorities have stage-managed the issue of nationalism, hoping to drip it into the popular consciousness by drawing on dramatised external events. The transfer of the sovereignty of Hong Kong from Britain to China gave the media an opportunity to play up nationalistic pride and to glorify the Communist Party as the saviour of the Chinese nation that brought the long-lost child back into the embrace of the motherland from British imperialists (Lee *et al.* 2000; Pan *et al.* 1999). Besides, in 1993, the media heavily promoted China's failed bid to host the 2000 Olympic Games, shouting the slogan of 'giving China an opportunity' and emphasising that the twenty-first century will be the Chinese century. When Sydney won the Games, Beijing accused the United States of leading a Western conspiracy that wrestled the deserved prestige from China (Song *et al.* 1996: 156, 342–4; Yan 2001: 36). A Beijing lawyer was quoted as saying: 'That was the moment when the Chinese started believing that the U.S. wanted to contain China' (Chanda and Huus 1995: 20). Beijing has now been awarded the 2008 Olympics, something that satisfies China's longing for international legitimacy.

The 1990s saw a train of media events that touched the nerve of Chinese nationalism: (1) NBC sports anchor Bob Costas, while commentating on the parade of the opening ceremony at the 1996 Olympic Games in Atlanta, implied that Chinese athletes regularly took drugs; (2) the visit of Taiwanese President Lee Teng-hui to the United States in 1995 and subsequently, in 1996, the overwhelmingly positive Western media coverage of Taiwan's first democratic presidential election; (3) the annual debate in the US Congress over the granting of 'most favoured nation' status to China, which regularly turned out to be a forum for harsh criticism of China's human rights record; and (4) the NATO bombing of the Chinese embassy in Belgrade.

On 14 July 1995, the *China Youth Daily* reported that 87 percent of respondents to a survey considered the United States to be the 'most hostile country to China'. Adding salt to the wounds were provocative treatises by some Western scholars and journalists, such as *The Clash of Civilizations* (Huntington 1996), *Containing China* (Rachman 1996) and, most threateningly, *The Coming Conflict with China* (Bernstein and Munro 1997). These books were seen as further evidence of the West's China bashing and its scaremongering bully-boy tactics to contain China's legitimate aspirations. The media quoted Yan Xuetong, an international relations scholar, as saying: 'The Chinese government and its people believe that the United States is attempting to prevent China from growing strong so that the U.S. can continue to dominate the world' (Yan 2001: 36).

Media discourses have become more populist in tone. The market-driven media in particular have been at the forefront of exploiting nationalist sentiments as a profitable commodity. From the mid-1990s onwards, *China Can Say No* and *Behind U.S. Media Demonisation of China* became instant best sellers that were dangerously anti-liberal, anti-democratic, arrogantly nationalistic and self-righteous, definitely anti-Western, and emotionally explosive without reasoned analysis. Not all nationalistic discourses are spontaneous expressions of public feeling; some are part of intellectual debates about nationalism, liberalism, postmodernism and other Western ideas. The New Left discourses are harshly critical of China's increasing integration into the global capitalist structure, which has allegedly resulted in mindless consumerism and growing inequality. These highly nationalistic New Left discourses pledge their allegiance to radical idealism, which allegedly goes beyond liberal democracy to achieve the conditions of socialist democracy (Wang Hui 2000; also see Lee 2000b). They occupy such forums as *Strategy and Management*, *Dushu*, *Guoxue*, *Orient*, *Chinese Culture and Scholar*, *Frontiers* and *Horizons*.

Popular journalistic writing and nationalist discourses

As has already been pointed out, since peddling popular nationalism is now compatible with the profit motive of the media, commercialised media outlets and the tabloids are undoubtedly the most sensational and aggressive exploiters of nationalist sentiments. Several themes can be identified from the spectrum of published writings:

Reverse racism

Since 1996, Wang Xiaodong (sometimes using the pseudonym Shi Zhong) has published a series of conceptually confused articles accusing pro-Western discourses of the 1980s of practising 'reverse racism'. A student of mathematics from Peking University, he picked up the term 'reverse discrimination' – referring to how whites are said to be victimised by the policy of affirmative action in the United States – while studying in Japan and (mis)appropriated it for his own use. He charged that liberal intellectuals of the 1980s worshipped Western culture and despised the Chinese as an inferior race (Shi 1997: 9–14; Wang 1999: 82–7). He singled out the TV series *River Elegy* for criticism. He argued that Chinese nationalism of the 1990s was nothing but a reversal of the 'reverse racism' of the 1980s and a return to normality from abnormality (Wang 1999: 87). What makes him different from other cheering crowds for popular nationalism is his emphasis on the importance of democratisation and political reform in China, a position most others have shunned (Fang *et al.* 1999; Wang Xiaodong 2000: 99–101).

The 'China can say no' series

If 'reverse racism' was a prelude to popular nationalism, the 'China can say no' series, together with *Behind the Demonisation of China*, was its *leitmotif*. In June 1996, a group of young writers published *China Can Say No*, a collection of journalistic essays written with hatred and prejudice. None of its authors had ever visited, let alone lived in, the United States. As an unusual gesture from the top propaganda organ, the state-run Xinhua News Agency released news recommending this volume upon its publication. The *Wenhui Daily* in Shanghai praised it as displaying the 'bravery and patriotism of the younger generation' (26 June 1996, p. 4). An instant best seller, it sold 250,000 'legal' copies within a month (Li 1997: 159).

The commercial success of this volume was a media event that accrued huge profits to its authors and publishers; it has spawned several sequels: *China Can Still Say No* (Song *et al.* 1996b), *Why Does China Say No?* (Peng *et al.* 1996) and *How Can China Say No?* (Zhang 1996). All these writings were crude, chauvinistic and jingoistic. The message was simple and sensational: good and moral China versus bad and immoral America. It argued that the United States was launching a new Cold War to contain a rising China, and China must stand up and 'say no' to US hegemony, even if it meant fighting a war. The United States, as a morally corrupt and overstretched imperialist constantly bullying other countries, is a country notorious for its problems of racism, crime, sexual harassment, and so forth. The United States is 'annoying yet futile, despicable yet pitiful, and lost in its future direction' (*ibid.*: 230). 'How can such a country', it asked, 'criticise others?' It proclaimed that the twenty-first century would be the Chinese century, that China is a source of world peace and progress, and that Chinese thoughts and values would be highly influential in future human civilisations.

The 'U.S. media demonising China' series

Unlike the authors of the 'China can say no' series, the authors of *Behind the Demonisation of China* (English version: *Demonizing China: A Critical Analysis of the U.S. Press*) have substantial experience of the USA. Li Xiguang, now a professor at Qinghua University, was once a journalist intern at the *Washington Post*, while Liu Kang has a PhD and teaches literature at Pennsylvania State University. Their credentials were crucial in convincing the public of the validity of their nationalist bashing of the US media, all written in a combination of semi-academic and journalistic prose.

Published in December 1996, the book blasted the elite US media and Hollywood as a source of demonising China. The novelty and strong impact of the word 'demonisation' may have produced many resonances with readers.

Li and Liu claimed that they were entitled to rebut the US media's demonic misrepresentation of China. The trouble is that they identified the Chinese nation as indistinguishable from the Chinese state and thus took the US media's criticism of the Chinese communist party-state to be evidence of their trying to demonise the Chinese people or nation. By completely avoiding the issue of domestic suppression, they diverted public attention to the US media as external 'hostile forces'. Between 1997 and 1999, Li, with his collaborators, published several follow-up books on the same theme, including *How Bad Is China?* (Li 1998),[4] *Demonisation and (Western) Media Bombardment* (Li *et al.* 1999), and *Gratitude and Regret: The U.S. Media as I See Them* (Xiong 2000).

Their central argument revolved around blaming the US media, which allegedly demonise China for the sake of upholding white supremacy on behalf of bourgeois national interests (Li and Liu 1998–9: 19). They claim that the US media profited from demonising China. Such 'benefits' included scaring foreign investors away from China, diverting international attention away from US hegemonism and expansionism, boosting Japanese militarism and the USA–Japan alliance against China, and building an anti-China front with other Asian countries. Instead of holding the US media's performance to criticism according to the standards of a more open and higher moral ground (such as the gaps with Jeffersonian democracy), they opted to reduce their discourses to hysterical name calling. They accused the US media of adopting a host of tricks and tactics: using false information, fabricating facts, playing the language game to build up self-serving arguments, and manipulating news sources to achieve their goals.

While the 'say no' series called for assertive resistance to US-led Western hegemony, the 'demonising China' series blamed the US media for allegedly engaging in political subversion and cultural infiltration in China. Despite his academic New Left sympathies, Liu's demagogic writing on demonisation did not display any theoretical or methodological rigour, as did that of other members of the New Left circle (see below). As an academic in a US university, Liu cannot expect such crude analysis to be publishable in any serious English outlets. The 'demonisation' volume was translated into English not for its academic value but as a barometer of the depth of anti-American feeling.

New Left critique of global capitalist domination

The most sophisticated nationalist discourses so far have come from a small intellectual circle of the New Left that grounds its nationalist sympathies in the Western 'resistance discourses' against global capitalism and Western domination. Many members of the New Left spent their formative and college years in the secularising era of Deng's economic reforms and have transformed themselves from being liberalism's admirers to its harsh critics. They (for example, Gan 1998; Zhang 1998) attack liberal intellectuals and reformist Marxists of the 1980s for being elitist, aristocratic and conserva-tive – advocating liberalisation without commitment to democracy. They (for example, Cui 1994, 1996; Zhang 1998) fashion their visions in the light of Western radical-critical scholarship and, in varying degrees, the Maoist utopia to reconstruct a radical critique of China's commercialised party journalism, said to be under the domination of cultural capital in a glob-alised economy. Many of them are Western-educated, living overseas in the Chinese diaspora and attached to various Western academic institutions, where their perspectives garner more attention than among public constituencies in China. However, in closely following Western radical discourses, they seem to have built rather ill-conceived and exaggerated narratives of capital domination in China, thus committing the 'fallacy of misplaced concreteness'. As a result, they have sometimes put themselves perilously close to aligning with statist nationalism (see Lee 2000b for further discussion).

Paying special attention to media representation and cultural identity, they proclaim that one of the major problems facing Chinese intellectuals is that they lack a discursive framework of their own to resist the dominant Western discourse. Zhang Kuan (1995: 36–7), who holds a PhD from the United States and was one of the first people to introduce Edward Said's work on orientalism and postcolonialism into China, argues:

> For some time, we have fundamentally lost our courage to challenge and resist Western hegemonic and colonial discourses. As a result, we always appear to be very passive whenever we negotiate with Western countries on such issues as human rights, open markets and intellectual property. One of the reasons is that we are unable to come up with a mode of exposition that can be completely extricated from the Western frame-work .... The question of preserving and upholding our own subjectivity in cultural terms and reinforcing identification with our own culture so as to enable victory in future international conflicts rightly deserve serious consideration by all responsible Chinese intellectuals.

Ironically, the New Left constructs its critical discourse by radically trans-forming the imported Western *avant-garde* theories into, as Said (1983: 327) himself criticises, 'new uses, new position in a new time and place'. Zhang (1995) has also completely ignored Said's (1994) insistence on upholding democracy and human rights as universalistic values.

The New Left elite views US-led global capitalist expansion and market domination instead of the despotic Leninist party-state as the pre-eminent problem for China in its drive towards modernisation (see Li 2000). China collides with the West in basic interests; thus, for them, advocating Chinese nationalism is seen as tantamount to waging international resistance against global capitalism (Wang Hui 2000: 10–14). This position stands in stark contrast to that of the reform-minded intellectuals of the 1980s, who sought to break free from the shackles of Mao's doctrine and statism. With its discourses incorporated into the state-sponsored cultural market, the New Left sees the Chinese party-state as a bulwark against US hegemony and the 'universal' values of democracy and human rights.[5]

Unrestricted war

Still another version of nationalist discourse comes from a highly ruthless and militaristic book published in 1999, *Unrestricted War* (*chao xian zhan*), in which two air force colonels advocate fighting a kind of superwar that defies all the existing international rules and conventions. They argue that China should be able to defeat the United States by resorting to twenty-four different illicit tactics (among them the spread of computer viruses, computer 'hacking', financial and physical terrorism, cross-border drug trafficking, and environmental degradation). Because China cannot win a conventional war, they continue, it should try to learn global terrorist tactics from Osama bin Laden in order to win a boundaryless war in the future.

Having exploited anti-American fervour over the US bombing of the Chinese embassy in Belgrade, the book sold a total of 70,000 copies within a year – the highest figure sold in this category in recent years. Qiao Lian, one of the authors, boasted that 120 Chinese generals have approached him for the book, and a deputy commander of the Chinese Air Force has reportedly made it required reading in training. Even the USA's West Point Military Academy is reported to have included this book on its list of references for students (*Yazhou Zhoukan*, 2000). This militaristic–nationalistic call to arms goes beyond mere resistance discourses and openly invites extreme action in the name of defending the motherland.

Characteristics of nationalistic writings

This nationalistic genre of journalistic writings mushroomed from 1996 to 2000. A survey of a sample of such titles is revealing: *U.S.–China Military Confrontations: Before and After* (Hong *et al.* 1996); *The Grand Portrait of U.S.–China Confrontation* (Chen *et al.* 1996); *Confrontation with the United States* (Wu *et al.* 1997); *Listening to China: The New Cold War and the Future Strategy* (He *et al.* 1997); *Nine Times China Said No* (Li 1999); *The Invisible War that Threatens China: The U.S. Invisible Economic War and the Pitfall of Reform* (Yang 2000); and *The Future Hope of Humankind Rests on China* (Ju 2000). In addition, numerous articles and essays have appeared in newspapers and magazines, further fuelling the flames of popular and emotional nationalism. Several characteristics of these writings are noteworthy:

1   All these writings are based on a framework that is quick to point the finger at the other side, thus making constant references to the United States as a superpower that should be held responsible for the soured relations with China since 1989. They claim that the US-led Western world has tried to contain a rising China through military bullying (by intervening in China's missile tests off Taiwan in 1996), political subversion (by supporting Chinese dissidents, Tibetan independence and the Falun Gong, and by condemning China's human rights record in the United Nations), cultural infiltration, and media demonisation.

2   Save for a few academic publications by members of the New Left, all of the writings are emotionally charged, full of hatred, xenophobia and nationalistic jingoism, and sometimes bordering on hysteria. Their demagogic style of writing is at once filled with self-confidence, self-hate and nihilism, all sensationalised to the maximum, competing violently to incite pubic resentment. Some of the hyperbole approaches the level that could only be found during the Cultural Revolution. Exaggeration, distortion, factual errors and misleading information are common. Some are subtler and more skilful, others more deliberate and systematic. An illustrative example comes from a report in the *New York Times* on 14 May 1999. The lead of the story on Beijing's public reaction to the NATO bombing of the Chinese embassy in Belgrade reads: 'Ever since NATO bombs hit the Chinese Embassy in Belgrade last Friday, China's *state-run* media have dished up a ceaseless stream of banner headlines and jarring photos' (emphasis added). But Li and Liu (1999: 94) twisted the more descriptive 'state-run media' into the more connotative 'government-manipulated (*zhengfu caozong*) media' to fit their plot line of conspiracy and demonisation. This kind of subtle or not so subtle twisting, given the authors' academic titles and claimed credentials, has created a certain credibility among Chinese readers, especially those who do not read English.

3   Methodologically, none bar a few New Left publications follow any social science or humanistic approaches to collecting systematic data for substantiation. They tend to rely on selective anecdotes to draw their posited scenarios. Some even cite their own stories. Song Qiang (1999: 134), the main author of the 'say no' series, told university student audiences that because his girlfriend had high TOFEL scores, he was fearful of being dumped if she should go to the United States for further study. He then conceived of writing such a book to achieve 'shock value'. When the book became successful, he boasted, she decided to stay with him instead of going abroad.

4   Commercial interest is a major driving force behind the America-bashing enterprise. Most titles are similar, repetitive, imitative, sensational and hastily put together to make quick money. The media and their publishers became commercial winners without having to worry about offending the authorities. Many free-riders also tried to

catch the commercial train. No sooner had the original *China Can Say No* volume sold 250,000 copies within a month of publication in 1996 than many copycats appeared. That year alone, 400,000 legal copies of such books swamped the Beijing market, and within months the bookstores were inundated with piles of 'say no' books: *Still Say No, Just Want to Say No, How to Say No, Why Say No?* and *Not Just Say No*. Some authors managed to make a profit, but others failed. Readers' appetites had been ruined.

Patterns and strategies of media-produced nationalism

The rise of nationalism is one of the most important developments in Chinese politics during the 1990s, a process in which the media played a key role in shaping public attitudes. Nationalist discourses mixed with economic incentives may have altered the media's relationship with the state; the four patterns of media-produced nationalism are summarised in Table 3.1.

First, the media have conformed to the party line by adopting its patriotic slogans to frame the news. They staged the 'patriotic education campaign', constantly reminding people of China's century-long humiliation at the hands

Table 3.1 Four major media patterns of nationalism

	Affirmative	*Assertive*	*Aggressive*	*Rational / democratic*
Central position	state nationalism/ patriotism	state-cum-popular nationalism	popular nationalism	rational nationalism
Core frame	the Communist Party represents China's national interests and pride	China redeems itself from a century-long humiliation by the West	the USA, by containing a rising China, is the chief national enemy	call for political reform to build a democratic China
Agenda-setting strategy	strictly following the party line	stretching the party line to include media agendas.	mainly media-initiated, alternating between the party line and the bottom line	pushing the boundaries of the permissible
Discourse approach	mobilising, propagandistic	emotional, sensational	bellicose, demagogic	argumentative, analytical
Party's attitude	fully supportive	consenting and pro-active	tacitly endorsing	antagonistic and suppressive
Examples of media campaigns	patriotic education, Hong Kong/Macau handovers, bid for the Olympic Games	crisis coverage of the Chinese embassy bombing (1999), Chinese–US plane collision (2001)	the *China Can Say No* series, the *US Media Demonisation* series	*Southern Weekly, Open Times,* some online forums

of foreign powers, in contrast to the achievements said to have been made under the leadership of the Communist Party. This news frame of 'affirmative nationalism' (Whiting 1995) was particularly evident in the coverage of the handover of Hong Kong (Pan *et al.* 1999) and Beijing's bid to host the Olympic Games. This frame concentrates on the conflict between the positive 'us' and the negative 'them', with out-groups challenging the interests of in-groups. Moreover, the media elevated their discourses to the level of 'aggressive nationalism' (Whiting 1995: 295), naming a specific foreign country as a serious threat that requires action to be taken on behalf of China's vital interests. It should be noted that the media are not merely passive transmitters of statist and populist nationalism but actively contribute to its manufacture thanks to the lucrative commercial interests involved. The media profit from the market with the tacit approval of the Communist Party.

Second, within this larger party-defined parameter, the media can exercise their discretion in choosing preferred techniques, topics and scope to shape news frames. Media coverage of the Chinese embassy bombing appeared to be very assertive and aggressive. But despite their sensationalism, media narratives were, to quote Shambaugh (1996: 205), 'assertive in form, but reactive in essence'. They were 'reactive' to official narratives. This involved the media stretching the party-set boundaries in order to remain politically correct and commercially competitive, as the audience is increasingly hungry for more sensationalised news stories. In this regard, the party sets the tone, while the media can attach their own sub-agendas and present them in a more dramatic, eye-catching and assertive manner.

Third, capitalising on public resentment on the one hand and inspired by anti-imperialist discourses on the other, some media outlets have aggressively produced topics to stir heated debates over popular nationalism against US hegemony. They are assertive in form, style and core message. Sometimes they exploit the 'safety zone' in the party-defined boundaries to initiate various projects that have potential commercial gains. Even though the authorities were fully aware of the commercial motivation behind these media activities and were concerned about the adverse impact of public frenzy on improved relations with the United States, they found themselves ill-positioned to repudiate popular nationalism. Media tabloidisation also goes hand in hand with the audience's growing appetite for sensationalism in the commercial market. Patriotism is, for the moment, a highly saleable commodity. The media's task is hence to manage the tension between the party line and the bottom line.

Fourth, promoting 'rational nationalism' is coterminous with advocating political reform in order to build a better and prosperous Chinese nation for the twenty-first century (e.g. Liu Junning; Zhu 2000). For that to happen, the argument goes, China must devote itself to rooting out internal corruption and abandoning other outdated practices. This is a marginal voice, but it remains viable in some selected sites: *Open Times*, the *Southern Weekend*, and the forum for a strong China on the *People's Daily* website. Examples of critical opinions frequently posted in such forums are: 'if you want to build a great China you first have to replace the one party dictatorship with democracy'; and 'without political reform, there will be no future for China'. These examples point to the liberating potential of the Internet, but when and how the authorities will clamp down on the expression of such opinions is much more uncertain.

The first three patterns are commercially profitable and politically safe. The third pattern, an alliance between the media and the New Left elite, is both popular and controversial. The fourth pattern offers a more liberal alternative to party dogma, but given its subversive nature, 'rational nationalism' is susceptible to state repression and unlikely to become a major current of thought.

Conclusion

Nationalism has been one of the most potent developments in 1990s China, representing a reversal from the pro-Western discourses of the 1980s. It has become a unifying issue that fills the ideological vacuum created by the bankruptcy of statist Marxism and the crushing of a more liberal-reformist alternative in 1989. Although nationalist sentiments had been widespread in the patched-up reconstruction of post-Mao national identity, nationalism did not come to the fore to provide a new overarching ideological framework until the mid-1990s. Increasing economic prosperity has boosted the authorities' claims on legitimacy while fanning public yearning for a more prominent role for China in the post-Cold War world order. On the other hand, the legacy of the Tiananmen Square crackdown and the end of the Cold War have exposed China to more intense international criticism of China's sorry human rights record (Lee *et al.* 2001). The gap between these two agendas has been conducive to the ascendancy of statist and popular nationalism in China.

Since the Tiananmen Square crackdown, the authorities have maintained a tighter rein on political discourse. Political reform remains a media taboo. But post-1992 economic momentum has also created a climate of 'demobilised liberalisation' in which the media are allowed to make lucrative economic gains as long as they do not challenge Communist Party legitimacy (Lee 2000a, 2000b). The regime has been trading economic privileges in exchange for media loyalty. In fact, many media outlets have established themselves as formidable business enterprises and conglomerates, all intent on exploiting the market for maximum gains. Under these circumstances, what could be a better topic for the media to cash in on than popular nationalism, which is enormously appealing in the marketplace yet does not present political offence to the authorities?

Nationalism, in other words, has considerable consumption value. As the London-based International Institute for Strategic Studies notes, Chinese editors recognise that 'headline-grabbing, bellicose rhetoric sells better than diplomatically worded argument' (*South China Morning Post*, 24 June 2001, p. 11). The media sell 'packaged nationalism' and hedonism at huge profits and with official blessing. No wonder they have joined the chorus of praise for China's economic achievement while denigrating Russia's 'shock therapy'. They have drummed up a sense of national crisis as if China were encircled by hostile external enemies (especially the Americans and Japanese) intent on demonising China, with the implication that only the Communist Party can galvanise and protect national interests. Media discourses have therefore centred on the themes of China's supposed global status and unification with Taiwan. Through the collusion of interests, all parties (the media, the regime, the market and the audience) have played with the fire of nationalism. However, the regime, mindful of historical precedent, ensures that media manipulation of nationalist sentiments is tightly controlled lest popular discontent implode against domestic corruption and internal dislocation. While rhetorically critical of Japan, Beijing poured cold water on the flame of the Hong Kong media in 1996 when they launched an ideological war against Japan over several disputed islands.

So far, the media have been the winners, making money without political risks. In their eagerness to pander to the audience's ever-increasing taste for sensationalism, many media outlets have gone down the road of tabloidisation. The more market-driven, the more likely they will exploit raw national sentiments. Market logic has given impetus to some experimentation in the style of media presentation and modes of discourses. The regime will continue to use the media in the production of popular nationalism to divert public discontent away from domestic problems. The rise and ebb of statist and popular nationalism in China will be intertwined with the perception about how well China is treated by the international community, especially by the United States. A widespread sense of international injustice, justified or not, will continue to be a source of public interest in nationalist agitation. Western media coverage of China has been conditioned by brutal images of the Tiananmen Square crackdown, while the end of the Cold War has made China the only giant communist regime that presents a barrier to the US-led liberal world order. What is intriguing is that China has joined the liberal World Trade Organisation (WTO) and will host the Olympic Games in 2008; the interplay of the national and the global will shape China's media discourses in the coming decade.

Notes

1   When a writer, Pan Xiao (a pseudonym), wrote to *China Youth*, the organ of the Young Communist League, to complain about people around him being selfish. It elicited 18,603 letters from readers within twenty-five days, all questioning party propaganda (*People's Daily*, 10 June 1980: 1).
2   *Dushu* became a New Left flagship in the mid-1990s.
3   They included translations of European classics by John Locke, John Stuart Mill, Niccolò Machiavelli, Max Weber, Sigmund Freud and Karl Popper, as well as work

by American social scientists and writers such as Thorstein Veblen, Barrington Moore, Daniel Bell, Walter Lippmann, Milton Friedman and Wilbur Schramm.

4 To fit his straitjacket, Li (1998: 82–5) distorted the tone of the remarks made by Chin-Chuan Lee, one of the authors, at a Washington policy conference regarding Western media coverage of the Hong Kong handover. Li did not attend the conference, but one of his collaborators provided him with Lee's taped talk without permission. For our research on this topic, see Lee *et al.* (2000, 2001).

5 Jürgen Habermas, for example, protested during his trip to China in the spring of 2001 that some members of the Chinese New Left, in their zeal to construct an anti-imperialist discourse, had (mis)used his theory in such a way as to amount to rationalising the authoritarian Chinese regime.

References

Barmé, G. (1999) *In the Red: On Contemporary Chinese Culture*. New York: Columbia University Press.

Bernstein, R. and Munro, R. (1997) *The Coming Conflict with China*. New York: Knopf.

Chanda, K. and Huus, K. (1995) 'The new nationalism', *Far Eastern Economic Review* 158(45): 20–6.

Chang, M.S. (2001) *Return of the Dragon: China's Wounded Nationalism*. Boulder, Colo.: Westview Press.

Chen Feng (1997) 'Order and stability in social transition: the neoconservative political thought in post-1989 China', *China Quarterly* 151: 593–613.

Chen Feng *et al.* (1996) *Zhongmei Jiaoliang Da Xiezhen* (The Grand Portrait of US–China Confrontations). Beijing: Zhongguo Renshi Chubanshe.

China Spring (1992) 'Sulian jubian zhihou Zhongguo de xianshi yingdui yu Zhanlue Xuanze' (Realistic responses and strategic choices for China after the disintegration of the Soviet Union), *China Spring* (January): 35–9.

Cui Zhiyuan (1994) 'Zhidu chuangxin yu dierci sixiang jiefang' (Institutional innovation and a second liberation of thoughts), *The Twenty-First Century* 24: 5–15.

—— (1996) '*Mao Zedong "Wenge" lilun de deshi yu "Xiandaixing" de Chongjian*' (An assessment of Mao Zedong's Cultural Revolution theory and the reconstruction of Chinese modernity), *Hong Kong Journal of Social Sciences* (spring): 49–74.

Duara, P. (1996) 'De-constructing the Chinese nation', in J. Unger (ed.), *Chinese Nationalism*. Armonk, NY: M.E. Sharpe.

Fang Ning, Wang Xiaodong, Song Qiang *et al.* (1999) *Quanqiuhua Yingyinxia de Zhongguo zi Lu* (China's Road in the Shadow of Globalisation). Beijing: China Social Science Press.

Friedman, E. (1997) 'Chinese nationalism, Taiwan autonomy and the prospects of a larger war', *Journal of Contemporary China* 6(4): 5–32.

Gan Yan (1998) 'A critique of Chinese conservatism in the 1990s', *Social Text* 16: 45–66.

—— (2000) 'Chongjian Zhongguo zhuoyi tupu' (Reconstructing the landscape of the Chinese Left), *Ming Pao* (Hong Kong): October 1, E4; October 2, D4.

Goldman, M., Link, P. and Su, W. (1993) 'China's intellectual in the Deng era: loss of identity with the state', in L. Dittmer and S. Kim (eds), *China's Quest for National Identity*. Ithaca, NY: Cornell University Press.

Gu Xin (1993) *Zhongguo Fan Chuantongzhuyi de Pinkun* (The Poverty of Chinese Anti-Traditionalism). Taipei: Fengyun Shidai Chubanshe.

He Degong *et al.* (1997) *Qingtin Zhongguo Xinlengzhang yu Weilaimolue* (Listening to China: The New Cold War and the Future Strategy). Guangdong: Guangdong People's Press.

He Jiadong (2000) 'Jinri Zhongguo xinbaoshouzhuyi' (Neoconservatism in today's China), in Li Shengzi and He Jiadong (eds) *Zhongguo de Daolu* (China's Road). Guangzhou: Southern Daily Publishing House.

He Xin (1991) *Shiji Zhijiao Zhongguo yu Shijie* (China and the World at the Turn of the Century). Chengdu: Shichuan People's Press.

—— (1996) *Wei Zhongguo Shengbian* (Defending China). Jinan: Shandong Friendship Publishing House.

He Zhou (2000) 'Working with a dying ideology: dissonance and its reduction in Chinese journalism', *Journalism Studies* 1(4): 599–616.

Hong Yonghong *et al.* (1996) *Zhong Mei Junshi Chongtu Qianqian Houhou* (US–China Military Confrontations: Before and After). Beijing: Zhongguo Shehui Chubanshe.

Hsiao Ching-chang and Yang Meirong (1990) '"Don't force us to lie": the case of the *World Economic Journal*', in C.-C. Lee (ed.), *Voices of China: The Interplay of Politics and Journalism*. New York: Guilford Press.

Huang Yasheng (1995) 'Why China will not collapse', *Foreign Policy* (summer): 54–68.

Huntington, S. (1996) *The Clash of Civilizations and the Remaking of World Order*. New York: Simon & Schuster.

Ju Xiang (2000) *Renlei de Xiwang Zai Zhongguo* (The Future Hope of Humankind Rests on China). Beijing: Daizhong Wenyi Chubanshe.

Lam Tong (2000) 'Identity and diversity: the complexities and contradictions of Chinese nationalism', in T. Weston and L. Jensen (eds), *China Beyond the Headlines*. New York: Rowman & Littlefield.

Lee, C.-C. (1990) 'Mass media: of China and about China', in C.-C. Lee (ed.), *Voices of China: The Interplay of Politics and Journalism*. New York: Guilford Press.

—— (2000a) 'Chinese communication: prisms, trajectories, and modes of understanding', in C.-C. Lee (ed.), *Money, Power and Media: Communication Patterns and Bureaucratic Control in Cultural China*. Evanston, Ill.: Northwestern University Press.

—— (2000b) 'China's journalism: the emancipatory potential of social theory', *Journalism Studies* 1(4): 559–75.

Lee, C.-C., Chan, J.M., Pan Zhongdang and So, C.Y.K. (2000) 'National prisms of a global media event', in J. Curran and M. Gurevitch (eds), *Mass Media and Society* (third edition). London: Edward Arnold.

Lee, C.-C., Chan, J.M., Pan Zhongdang and So, C.Y.K. (2001) 'Through the eyes of US media: banging the democracy drum in Hong Kong', *Journal of Communication* 51(2): 345–65.

Levenson, J. (1967) *Liang Ch'i-ch'ao and the Mind of Modern China*. Berkeley: University of California Press.

Li Hongshan (1997) 'China talks back: anti-Americanism or nationalism?' *Journal of Contemporary China* 6(14): 153–60.

Li Jiang (1999) *Zhongguo Jiuchi Shuo Bu* (China Said No Nine Times). Beijing: Dangdai Chubanshe.

Li Shitao (ed.) (2000) *Zhishi Fenzi Lichang: Ziyouzhuyi zhi Zheng yu Zhongguo Sixiangjie de Fenhua* (Intellectuals' Positions: Controversies on Liberalism and the Division in China's Intellectual Circles). Changcun: Shidai Wenyi Press.

Li Xiguang (1998) *Zhongguo Youduohua?* (How Bad Is China?). Nanjing: Jiangsu People's Press.

Li Xiguang, Liu Kang *et al.* (1996) *Yaomohua Zhongguo de Beihou* (Behind the Demonisation of China). Beijing: Chinese Academy of Social Sciences.

—— (1998–9) 'Demonizing China: a critical analysis of the U.S. press', *Contemporary Chinese Thought* 30 (special issue, translated from Chinese): 3–102.

—— (1999) *Yaomohua yu Meitihongzha* (Demonisation and Media Bombardment). Nanjing: Jiangsu People's Press.

Liu, A.P.L. (2000) 'A convenient crisis: looking behind Beijing's threats against Taiwan', *Issues and Studies* (September–October): 83–121.

Liu Junning (2000) 'Minzuzhuyi simianguag' (Four aspects of nationalism), in Li Shitao (ed.), *Zhishi Fenzi Lichang: Ziyouzhuyi zhi Zheng yu Zhongguo Sixiangjie de Fenhua* (Intellectuals' Positions: Controversies on Liberalism and the Division in China's Intellectual Circles). Changcun: Shidai Wenyi Press.

Ming Lizhi (1990) 'Insist on the unification of patriotism and socialism', *Qiushi* (Seeking Truth) 9: 15.

Min Qi (1989) *Zhongguo Zhengzhi Wenhua* (Political Culture in China). Kunming: Yunnan People's Press.

Pan Zhongdang and Chan, J.M. (2000) 'Building a market-based party organ: television and national integration in China', in D. French and M. Richards (eds), *Television in Contemporary Asia*. New Delhi: Sage.

Pan Zhongdang, Lee, C.-C., Chan, J.M. and So, C.Y.K. (1999) 'One event, three stories: media narratives from cultural China of the handover of Hong Kong', *Gazette* 61(2): 99–112.

Peng Qian, Yang Mingjie and Xu Deren (1996) *Zhongguo Weishenmo Shuo Bu?* (Why Does China Say No?). Beijing: Xinshijie Chubanshe.

Pye, L. (1996) 'How China's nationalism was shanghaied', in J. Unger (ed.), *Chinese Nationalism*. Armonk, NY: M.E. Sharpe.

Qiao Lian and Wang Xiansui (1999) *Chao Xiao Zhang* (Unrestricted War). Beijing: Arts Press of People's Liberation Army.

Qiushi editorial (1990) 'Give full play to the patriotism of the youths of the May Fourth Movement', *Qiushi* (Seeking Truth) 9: 8–9.

Rachman, G. (1996) 'Containing China', *Washington Quarterly* 19(1): 129–39.

Rosen, S. (ed.) (1997) *Nationalism and Neoconservatism in China in the 1990s* (special issue of *Chinese Law and Government*, November–December, 6).

Ruan Ming (1990) 'Press freedom and neoauthoritarianism: a reflection on China's democracy movement', in C.-C. Lee (ed.), *Voices of China: The Interplay of Politics and Journalism*. New York: Guilford Press.

Said, E.W. (1983) *The World, the Text, and the Critic*. Cambridge, Mass.: Harvard University Press.

—— (1994) *Representations of the Intellectual*. New York: Vintage Books.

Schwartz, B. (1993) 'Culture, modernity, and nationalism – further reflection', in Tu Weiming (ed.), *China in Transformation*. Cambridge, Mass.: Harvard University Press.

Segal, G. (1996) 'East Asia and the "containment" of China', *International Security* 20(4): 107–35.

Shambaugh, D. (1996) 'Containment or engagement of China? Calculating Beijing's responses', *International Security* 21(2): 180–209.

Song Qiang (1999) 'Jianli 21shiji de xinguoge' (Establishing the twenty-first century state character), in Fang Ning, Wang Xiaodong, Song Qiang *et al.* (eds), *Quanqiuhua Yingyinxia de Zhongguo zi Lu* (China's Road in the Shadow of Globalisation). Beijing: China Social Science Press.

Song Qiang, Zhang Zangzang and Qiao Bian (1996a) *Zhongguo Keyi Shuo Bu* (China Can Say No). Beijing: Zhonghua Gongshang Lianhe Chubanshe.

Song Qiang *et al.* (1996b) *Zhongguo Haishineng Shuo Bu* (China Can Still Say No). Beijing: Zhongguo Wenlian Chuban Gongshi.

Shi Zhong (Wang Xiaodong) (1997) 'Chinese nationalism and the future of China', *Chinese Law and Government* 30(6) (November–December): 8–27.

Su Shaozhi (1996) *Fengyu Shinian: Wengehou de Dalu Lilunjie* (The Turbulent Ten Years: Theoretical Circles in Mainland China after the Cultural Revolution). Taipei: China Times Press.

Su Xiaokang *et al.* (1988) *Heshang* (River Elegy). Beijing: Xiandai Chubanshe.

Townsend, J. (1996) 'Chinese nationalism', in J. Unger (ed.), *Chinese Nationalism*. Armonk, NY: M.E. Sharpe.

Unger, J. (ed.) (1996) *Chinese Nationalism*. Armonk, NY: M.E. Sharpe.

Wang Hui (1998) 'Contemporary Chinese thought and the question of modernity', *Social Text* 16: 9–44.

—— (2000) *Sihuo Congwen* (Old Ashes Rekindled). Beijing: People's Press.

Wang Ruoshui (1997) *Huyaobang Xiatai de Beijing* (Behind Hu Yaobang's Downfall). Hong Kong: Mirror.

Wang Xiaodong (1999) 'Zhongguo de minzuzhuyi he Zhongguo de weilai' (Chinese nationalism and the future of China), in Fang Ning Wang Xiaodong, Song Qiang *et al.* (eds), *Quanqiuhua Yingyinxia de Zhongguo zi Lu* (China's Road in the Shadow of Globalisation). Beijing: China Social Science Press.

—— (2000) 'Minzuzhuyi he minzhuzhuyi' (Nationalism and democracy), in Li Shitao (ed.), *Zhishi Fenzi Lichang: Ziyouzhuyi zhi Zheng yu Zhongguo Sixiangjie de Fenhua* (Intellectuals' Positions: Controversies on Liberalism and the Division in China's Intellectual Circle). Changcun: Shidai Wenyi Press.

Weber, M. (1958) *The Protestant Ethic and the Spirit of Capitalism* (translated by T. Parsons). New York: Charles Scribner's Sons.

Whiting, A. (1995) 'Chinese nationalism and foreign policy after Deng', *China Quarterly* 142: 295–316.

Wu Xiuyi (1988) *Zhongguo Wenhua Re* (China's Cultural Fever). Shanghai: Shanghai People's Press.

Wu Yitian *et al.* (1997) *Yu Meiguo Duikang* (Confrontation with the USA). Xinjiang: People's Press.

Xiao Xinxin and Liu Legeng (2001) 'Shijimo de yichang duihua' (Conversation at the end of the twentieth century – summary of an informal discussion among news reporters and media experts from China and the USA), *Guoji Xiwenjie* (International News Circle) 1: 5–12.

Xiong Lei (2000) '*Zanshang yu yihan – wokan Meiguo meijie'*(Gratitude and regret: the US media as I see them), in Gu Yaoming (ed.), *Wokan Meiguo Meiti* (The US Media as I See Them). Beijing: Xinhua Press.

Xu Ben (1999) *Disenchanted Democracy: Chinese Cultural Criticism after 1989*. Ann Arbor: University of Michigan Press.

Yan Xuetong (2001) 'The rise of China in Chinese eyes', *Journal of Contemporary China* 10(26): 33–9.

Yang Bin (2000) *Wexie Zhongguo de Yingbi Zhangzheng yu Gaigexianjing* (The Invisible War that Threatens China: The US Invisible Economic War and the Pitfall of Reform). Beijing: Jinjiguangli Chubanshe.

Yazhou Zhoukan (Asian Weekly) (2000) 'An interview with Qiao Liang' (12 October, in Chinese).

Yu Xu (1992) 'The press and political continuity in China: the case of the *World Economic Herald*', *Asian Journal of Communication* 2(2): 40–63.

Zhang Kuan (1995) *'Saiyide de "dongfangzhuyi" yu Xifang de Hanxue Yanjiu'* (Said's 'Orientalism' and Western Sinology), *Liaowang* (Outlook) 27: 36–7.

Zhang Xudong (1998) 'Intellectual politics in post-Tiananmen China', *Social Text* 16: 1–8.

—— (2000) 'Minzuzhuyi yu dandai Zhongguo' (Nationalism and contemporary China), in Li Shitao (ed.), *Zhishi Fenzi Lichang: Ziyouzhuyi zhi Zheng yu Zhongguo Sixiangjie de Fenhua* (Intellectuals' Positions: Controversies on Liberalism and the Division in China's Intellectual Circles). Changcun: Shidai Wenyi Press.

Zhang Xueli (1996) *Zhonguo Heyi Shuo Bu* (How China Can Say No). Beijing: Hualing Chubanshe.

Zhao Suisheng (2000) 'Chinese nationalism and its international orientations', *Political Science Quarterly* 1: 1–33.

Zheng Yongnian (1999) *Discovering Chinese Nationalism in China*. New York: Cambridge University Press.

Zhu Xueqin (2000) 'Wusi yilai de Liange Bingzhao' (Two spiritual diseases since the May Fourth movement), in Li Shitao (ed.), *Zhishi Fenzi Lichang: Ziyouzhuyi zhi Zheng yu Zhongguo Sixiangjie de Fenhua* (Intellectuals' Positions: Controversies on Liberalism and the Division in China's Intellectual Circles). Changcun: Shidai Wenyi Press.

4   Modern political communication in China

Neil Renwick and Qing Cao

Introduction

This chapter examines the character of modern Chinese political discourse. In particular, it traces the way that China's political discourse repeatedly refers to the idea of China as subject to hostile external and internal predators. This theme lies at the centre of modern Chinese political communication and is understood in complex patterns of symbolic terms, allusions and metaphors acting as linguistic and textualised codes. However, this communicative theme plays an important role as a means of gaining historical and political legitimacy for the ruling elite. This theme of subordination, marginalisation and exclusion has offered a useful means by which an 'official' story of Chinese history and destiny, in effect the 'idea' of China's political identity, can be used to consolidate the ruling elite's political legitimacy, authority and continuing power. Consequently, political behaviour has been heavily influenced by this theme. From this, it is clear that we are arguing that political identity is not an essence but a construction.[1]

At the heart of this constructed idea is the play of 'official nationalism' (Anderson 1991: 101). This by now fairly familiar conception of nationalism is grounded in cultural formations and artefacts such as ideological narratives, music, literature, poetry, drama, cinema, and the symbolic forms of flag and anthem. The significance of this nationalist form lies in its deployment as a defensive stratagem designed to build a self-legitimating discourse that consolidates the established power elite and marginalises opposition discourses.

The writing of history is central to this cultural and discursive power formation. The representation of 'history' is contingent upon the demands of dominant elites and is written and rewritten according to prevailing political patterns of power. The construction of historical discourse is thus about the play of power in the delimitation of who or what is recognised and valorised and who benefits from such a narrative. China's official history juxtaposes the building of a modern independent state against the experiences of ancient invasion, nineteenth-century occidental 'semi-colonialism', counter-revolutionary dangers and late twentieth-century criticisms of commercial piracy, human rights abuses and the country's Taiwan policy. This provides a locus of attachment by which a sense of differentiated national Chinese selfhood has been built at the heart of Chinese political discourse.

Dominant discourses

The official discourses centre on the idea of a China constantly subjected to threat. It seems, *prima facie*, to be a relatively straightforward concept with a perpetrator of hostility, aggression or violence acting upon another party, who responds with hostility and resentment towards the aggressor. Thus China's leaders and intelligentsia have repeatedly represented China as the victim of external aggression and exploitation by colonial and capitalist powers and their apologist 'running dogs'. However, there are much more complex dynamics at play here. It is inevitable that any evaluation of this theme must offer a discursive return to the interventions of external powers in China's modern history. The actions of these states in extending a semi-colonial pattern of control over nineteenth-century China, in participating in internal Chinese conflicts, in Japan's attempts to realise its imperial ambitions in China, in the assistance given to the nationalist and communist combatants in the civil war, and in the various responses to the establishment of a communist state in China in 1949 form a principal analytical focus. The territorial dismemberment of the country, the humiliation of a proud state by an avalanche of 'unequal treaties' and the dislocating tensions added to existing internal forces of disorder represent a powerful *leitmotif* of subordination, resentment and anger in nineteenth- and twentieth-century Chinese social commentary and political discourse. Chinese sensitivity to perceived subordination and exploitation is characterised by a number of simultaneously experienced and enduring characteristics: 'anti-foreignness', 'modernism', 'nationalism', 'culturalism'. These are distinct but heavily interrelated and overlapping discursive themes.

Anti-foreignness

This has exhibited two interrelated features: first, an introspective and nostalgic return to 'traditional' culture and ways of life that eschewed occidental practices and values; and, second, calls for 'self-strengthening' based upon the adoption of occidental material methods combined with superior Chinese cultural values, which together would mean that China would one day be able to end its subordination, overthrow the victimisers and restore its high standing in the world.

Anti-foreign sentiment in China can be traced back at least to AD 800 and the xenophobic reaction against the fraternisation of the imperial court and ruling classes with foreigners and the vogue for exotic fashions. As Gernet (1994: 291–2) suggested, this backlash (which lasted until the 840s) could well have had its origins in the shaming of imperial forces in the An Lu-shan rebellion (755–763) and humiliating reliance upon foreign commanders to uphold the imperial cause. As Gernet also noted, this reaction germinated within officialdom and the writing fraternity, who came to believe that the presence of barbarians 'had slowly impaired Chinese purity, corrupted ancient moral standards, and thus brought about the decadence of China' (*ibid.*: 292). Thus writers such as Liu Zong-yuan (773–819) and Han Yu (768–824) contributed to a nostalgic yearning for a largely imagined pure 'authentic tradition'. Thus one of the fundamental themes of Chinese victimhood that endures to the present day, that of the corrupting and impure consequences of foreign influence for Chinese culture, was evident centuries ago.

In the 1860s, a conflation of fear of foreigners *per se* and the threat of foreign powers to the Chinese state was also evident in the persecution of Hakka Chinese Protestant converts in the 1860s. Jesse and Rolland Lutz's study documents the ostracism, theft, beatings, kidnapping and murder of these converts during this period and quotes convert Li Zhenggao's 1864 report that the people claimed that 'the preaching of the Gospel was only a pretext under which the foreigners could gain secret power over the hearts of the Chinese with the eventual goal of appropriating both China's land and its people' (Lutz and Lutz 1998: 210). These sentiments arose again during the Boxer movement (1899–1900) with claims that 'the gods assist us to destroy all foreigners; we invite you to join the patriotic militia'[2] (Meyer and Allen 1969: 80). Foreigners were blamed by the Boxers for 'the many scourges from which we are suffering' (*ibid.*: 82), and Boxer posters denounced Catholic converts for having 'conspired with foreigners, … caused China trouble, wasted our national income, broken up our monasteries, destroyed Buddhist images, and seized our people's graveyards. All these myriad acts of evil should be bitterly resented' (*ibid.*: 81). This turn-of-the-century expression of anti-foreignness found contemporary echoes in sublimated hostility towards Manchu dominance in Chinese society embedded in a tradition of Han chauvinism reaching back at least to the seventeenth century writings of Wang Fuzhi (1619–92) (Dillon 1998: 330–1) and helped to fuel opposition to the imperial order in the Taiping rebellion (1851–64), in early twentieth-century nationalist movements (Townsend 1996: 13) and among communist revolutionaries.

Although the first of Sun Yat-sen's *Three Principles of the People* (1924) espouses a Chinese nationalism insofar as government 'should offer resistance to foreign aggression, and simultaneously it should revise foreign treaties in order to restore our equality and independence among the nations' (Meyer and Allen 1969: 115) and Chiang Kai-shek's 1925 address to the Military Council tried to draw added legitimacy for the Kuomintang (KMT) by asserting that 'imperialism and militarism are one' and that 'the imperialists aim at making profits and China is their field of plunder' (*Ibid.*: 97), it was the Chinese Communist Party (CCP) that, after 1949, adeptly drew anti-foreignness into an effective 'anti-imperialism' and 'anti-hegemony' discourse grounded in a 'siege mentality' carefully constructed by Mao Zedong and the CCP leadership.

The discourse of victimhood under the CCP incorporated Chinese anti-foreignness into a concept of anti-imperialism. This had the obvious utility of providing a unifying focus for the Chinese people against a hostile West and confirming the CCP in a protective and leadership role. 'Mao Zedong thought' clearly played a central role in defining the discursive parameters of anti-imperialism, but the CCP's leaders over the years, including Zhou Enlai, Hu Yaobang, Deng Xiaoping and Jiang Zemin, have all contributed to this rich discursive vein. In 1940, building upon a line of thought that reached back to his youthful writings of 1919[3] (Schram 1969: 163), Mao defined 'the Chinese people' as 'chiefly the Hans', and 'the history of the Hans ... shows that the Chinese people would never submit to a rule of the dark forces and that in every case they succeeded in overthrowing or changing such a rule by revolutionary means' (*ibid.*: 166). In the same year, Mao explicitly linked democratisation to anti-imperialism and defined it as distinctively Chinese rather than Western in character:

> New-democratic culture is national. It opposes imperialist oppression and upholds the national dignity and independence of the Chinese people. It belongs to our own people and bears our national characteristics .... So-called 'wholesale Westernisation' represents a mistaken viewpoint. China has suffered a great deal in the past from the formalist absorption of foreign things.
>
> (*ibid.*: 356)

But as both Whiting and Liao (1986) have pointed out, the intensity of anti-imperialist rhetoric intensifies and dissipates according to the mass mobilisation campaigns used by the various leaders in Beijing to play out their intra-elite factional contests. This is particularly true with respect to episodes such as the Cultural Revolution and the Sino–Soviet split, wherein Mao used mass mobilisations of great hysteria to move against those in the CCP power elite such as Lui Shaoqi, Deng Xiaoping and Lin Biao, whom he believed not to be unwavering in their support for him in the mid- to late 1950s and throughout the 1960s (Dittmer 1998). The so-called 'Soviet revisionism' inaugurated by Khrushchev's February 1956 'secret speech' attacking the crimes and 'personality cult' of Stalin and promoting the idea of collective leadership found receptive responses in Lui Shaoqi's and Deng Xiaoping's approach to the Eighth Party Congress in 1956, at which the prevention of a Chinese personality cult was guaranteed and the primacy of 'Mao Zedong thought' as *the* guiding ideology of the country was removed from the new constitution. This seemingly confirmed Mao's suspicions of a threat to his power and personal standing (Li 1994: 180).[4] In 1966, Mao was able to nurture perceptions of internal and external threat to his personal advantage by using the Cultural Revolution's Red Guards to 'bombard the headquarters' and purge these counter-revolutionaries and restore his power as well as encourage intensified attacks upon the Soviet Union's 'revisionist clique'. The Sino–Soviet split is particularly instructive. Following the CCP's victory in 1949, Sino–Soviet treaty relations were established in February 1950 and the USSR returned former Chinese territory to PRC sovereignty. But Mao's suspicions of Soviet intentions were evident as far back as 1936, when he told Edgar Snow that 'we are certainly not fighting for an emancipated China in order to turn the country over to Moscow' (Schram 1969: 419). Following a secret visit to Beijing by Khrushchev in 1958, Mao reportedly remarked to his personal physician Li Zhisui (1994: 261) that 'their real purpose ... is to control us. They're trying to tie our hands and feet'. Attacks upon various diplomatic missions during the Cultural Revolution included that of the Soviet Union, whose leadership came in for some particularly spirited abuse as a 'handful of filthy Soviet revisionist swine!'[5]

Anti-foreignness was thus a particularly useful political tool in limiting debate, eliminating perceived rivals and promoting a sense of common cause against external threats. By couching the threat in terms of an ideological category, namely 'anti-imperialism', 'revisionism' or 'counter-revolution', domestic and foreign realms become one and the threat made an immediate and proximate presence. Thus Zhou Enlai's denunciation of Lin Biao in 1973 portrayed him as engaged in 'collusion and compromise between Soviet revisionism and U.S. imperialism' and, consequently, it was necessary to 'maintain high vigilance and be fully prepared against any war of aggression that imperialism may launch, and particularly against a surprise attack on our country by Soviet revisionist social imperialism'.[6] The Cold War itself was useful for the purposes of national coagulation, as Mao reportedly commented privately (Li 1994: 224–5): 'Let there be tension in the world. Tension is good for us. It keeps our country united. So long as others are sharpening their sabres, no one will find me asleep'. Similarly, with respect to the Taiwan issue and in a vein that might find echoes in the late 1990s, Mao is said to have stated privately that:

> Some of our comrades don't understand the situation. They want us to cross the sea and take over Taiwan. I don't agree. Let's leave Taiwan alone. Taiwan keeps the pressure on us. It helps maintain our internal unity. Once the pressure is off, internal disputes might break out.
>
> (*ibid.*: 262)

Most evident, however, has been the political utility of anti-Japanese feeling in China. The legacy of Japanese aggression and atrocities is deeply embedded in the Chinese national consciousness and has, despite the normalisation of inter-state relations, continued to resurface intermittently to the present day. Anti-Japanese sentiment focuses upon four issues: Japan's security relationship with the USA; the potential for a revival of Japanese militarism; Japanese educational textbook revision; and the degree of China's dependence upon Japanese economic relations. The Cold War relationship saw the CCP leadership present Japan as the lapdog of

American imperialism and as a direct threat to China and the revolution. The 1950 Sino–Soviet Friendship Treaty declared mutual assistance in the event that China or the Soviet Union suffered attack by 'Japan or any states allied with that country' (Jones and Kevill 1985: 1). The expression of anti-Japanese sentiment in the 1950s and 1960s lessened during the 1970s after Richard Nixon's visit to China in 1972, Japan's consequential recognition of the PRC rather than Taiwan and the signing of the 1978 Treaty of Peace and Friendship. The utility of positioning Beijing with the USA and Japan as 'anti-hegemonic' counterweights to the Soviet Union was evident enough. However, claims to Japanese militarism have continued to surface, usually at times of tension with Taiwan or when other historically driven factors resurface. The most obvious of such factors are, first, the reluctance of Japan's political leaders and emperor to provide an unequivocal apology for the war to China's satisfaction and, second, the issue of textbook revision. In recent times, the 1985 visit of Japanese Prime Minister Yasuhiro Nakasone to the Yasukuni Shrine to Japan's war dead (including convicted war criminals) provoked official criticism and mass popular demonstrations in China (Whiting 1989: 66–79). Despite periodic apologies by Japanese leaders during the 1990s, these have fallen short of Chinese expectations. The diplomatic fiasco over the failure of the emperor to make a full apology and a joint Sino–Japanese communiqué during President Jiang Zemin's state visit to Japan in 1998 merely served to consolidate this as a lingering source of Chinese irritation. The issue of textbook revision, which is claimed (validly or by incorrect report) to downplay, justify or otherwise obfuscate Japan's wartime actions in Manchuria, Nanjing (Nanking) and other parts of China, repeatedly spurs graphic Chinese criticism.[7] Finally, the surge of economic reform and the 'opening' of China raised some student unrest in the mid-1980s that China was in danger from a Japanese 'economic invasion' (Whiting 1989: 70, 95). Such sentiments are, evidently enough, a highly useful political tool to extract negotiating concessions. But the often complicating factor of a lasting and genuine residue of Chinese historical memory should not be underestimated with respect to Sino–Japanese relations. Jiang Zemin himself recalls how his revolutionary roots were grounded in the 'strong anti-Japanese and patriotic emotion' of his youth.[8]

Jiang's national leadership began in the immediate aftermath of the military suppression of the 1989 Tiananmen Square demonstration. Given the political context and the precariousness of his new position, it is unsurprising that he began with an uncompromising statement against the protest leaders (Gilley 1998: 150) and followed it up in his national address in September with a major attack upon foreign forces manipulating Chinese dissidents:

It should be stressed here that the international reactionary forces have never abandoned their hostility toward the socialist system or their attempts to subvert it. Beginning in the late 1950s, after the failure of military intervention, they shifted the focus of their policy to 'peaceful evolution' .... They support and buy over so-called dissidents through whom they foster blind worship of the Western world and propagate the political and economic patterns, sense of values, decadent ideas, and life-style of the Western capitalist world. When they feel there is an opportunity to be seized, they fabricate rumours, provoke incidents, plot turmoil, and engage in subversive activities against socialist countries .... The struggle between infiltration and counter-infiltration, subversion and counter-subversion, 'peaceful evolution' and counter-'peaceful evolution' will last a long time. In this connection, people of all nationalities, and all party members, especially leaders, must maintain a high degree of vigilance.[9]

Clearly, the association of internal threat with external enemies forms a long-running central feature of Chinese political discourse. Moreover, as Bruce Gilley's study illustrates, Jiang Zemin has a longstanding emphasis on 'patriotism', exhibited in his quoting of Lu Xun[10]; his manipulation of foreign businesses while at the Ministry of Electronics in the 1980s[11]; his 1991 'patriotic' educational materials initiative to 'heighten the self-respect and confidence of the Chinese people, especially the young and to help them guard against worshipping and blindly trusting all things foreign' (Gilley 1998: 272); and, in a throwback to Deng Xiaoping's 'anti-spiritual pollution' campaign of 1983–84, his attacks upon 'cultural colonialism' in the mid-1990s (*ibid.*: 271). The 1990s were periodically marked by issues that raised momentary expressions of anti-American sentiment, such as US debates over China's 'most favoured nation' (MFN) status; assertions that the USA was blocking China's entry into the World Trade Organisation (WTO) for reasons of national self-interest; the failure of China's bid for the 2000 Olympic Games; and the 1993 'Yinhe Hao incident' with the United States.[12] At the close of the first decade of Jiang Zemin's leadership, his rhetoric and practice still echoes that of his early declarations, with warnings that the 'Western mode of political systems must never be copied' and a sharp reminder that 'From beginning to end, we must be vigilant against infiltration, subversive activities and separatist activities of international and domestic hostile forces' (*The Times*, 2 February 1998: 14). In attempting to police the Internet and in arresting 'cyber-dissidents' such as Lin Hai for allegedly supplying 'foreign hostile publications' outside China (*ibid.*), the Chinese authorities have sought to counter such supposed subversive infiltration (*ibid.* and *The Times*, 5 February 1996: 9).

Modernism

A second characteristic has been the embracing of a Western conception of 'modernity'. This can be understood usefully as an identification by victim with the victimiser. However, it is also bound up with a sense of self-loathing and guilt, well characterised in Bo-Yang's well-known *Ugly Chinaman* (1991) syndrome but reaching deeply into modern Chinese intellectual tradition. An urge to adopt Western ideas of modernity and progress has also involved a concomitant rejection of Chinese 'tradition'. Tradition itself definitionally becomes synonymous with backwardness and inferiority. The semiotic markers of such iconoclastic thought are evident enough in the Eurocentric 'naming' of the discursive parameters of a modern Chinese society: 'sovereignty', 'state', 'nation', 'citizenry'. In one key respect, the emphasis in this discourse is necessarily upon historical discontinuity – a fundamental breaking with the past order and its imprisoning value system. As in Japan, arguments for Chinese modernisation have often been justified as a means by which a supposedly superior indigenous civilisation could be sustained and strengthened. But, as Fourth of May veteran Hu Shi wrote in 1961:

> We have to rid ourselves of a prejudice that although the West is superior in terms of its material civilisation, we in the East can remain proud of our superior spiritual civilisation .... There is nothing particularly spiritual about our ancient civilisation at all. What type of spiritual civilisation could tolerate for over one millennium the cruel and inhuman practice of foot binding without even one peep of opposition?
>
> (Barmé and Jaivin 1992: 127)

Again, Mao (in)famously portrayed the Chinese people as 'poor and ... blank'. The CCP's victory offered renewal and a new point at which to begin the reinscription of China's political narrative: 'A clean sheet of paper has no blotches, and so the newest and most beautiful pictures can be painted on it'.[13]

Yet, simultaneously, this modernisation discourse has also sought legitimacy in a selective interpretation of Chinese history that portrays a sense of historical inevitability inherent in modernisation: a serial pattern of antecedent events that together link past, present and future in a progressive, emancipatory grand narrative. KMT nationalists and nationalistic communists shared in the utopianism of the modernist discourse. In 1928–29, for example, the KMT initiated a 'superstition destruction movement' (Cohen 1994: 105). As Ci Jiwei comments (1994: 3–4): 'For a people accustomed to attach value to the past and not to think much beyond the present, utopianism enlarged the future in their consciousness and made it the purpose and meaning of their lives .... Utopianism gave to their lives a heightened sense of meaning and purpose'. Modernity thus necessitated a collective forward-facing pro-activism distinct from the Confucian-ordained social stasis held by reformer revolutionaries to have characterised the imperial order. Thus the Boxer 'rebellion'[14] and the Fourth of May Movement in 1919 came to be depicted in CCP iconographic mythology as part of a 'progressive' historical lineage that inevitably led to the CCP and revolutionary victory. Mao's 1938 speech on the twentieth anniversary of the Fourth of May Movement claimed that 'the whole of the Chinese revolutionary movement found its origin in the action of young students and

intellectuals'. However, he added that 'every beginning must have a fulfilment' (Schram 1969: 354–6). In appropriating the 1919 movement, Mao was
able to claim that its fulfilment would come only with the victory of the
CCP.

But this discourse is, necessarily, inherently secular and material in both
content and intent. Industrialisation and agrarian reform would be the signposts of revolutionary achievement. Modernity was about production and
growth. It embodied, albeit briefly, the *jouissance* of collective effort, of
overcoming or transcending natural and human obstacles. The various
'rectification' campaigns, the Great Leap Forward, the Cultural Revolution
and the Deng–Jiang reformist programme are defined by the material
rewards promised to the Chinese people. Thus we can recall Mao's 1957
claim that China's steel production would surpass that of Britain within
fifteen years[15] or that it was 'the East wind that prevailed over the West
wind'.[16] Deng Xiaoping's post-1978 reform programme sought to modernise
China's economy and re-establish the legitimacy of the CCP through a
tangible improvement in the quality of life experienced by the Chinese
people as a whole. The historical discourse underpinning this programme
was established with the 1981 official history of the communist era,
Resolution on Certain Questions in Party History, which provided a criticism
of Mao's mistakes, depicted Deng Xiaoping as unsuccessfully trying to
prevent these mistakes and portrayed China as finally on the correct path
under Deng Xiaoping's leadership. Jiang Zemin's technocratic managerial
style consolidates the pragmatism of Deng Xiaoping's approach with
campaigns against corruption, crime and inefficiency under the rubric of
'developmental dictatorship' (Gilley 1998: 318). The politics of societal
transformation in China incur further state calls for commitment and sacrifice, but the power of the discourse to move people to such commitment is
exhausted, and the drive for change now comes from individual effort and a
pragmatic entrepreneurship in addition to calls to common cause.

Culturalism

The argument that China is 'a civilisation pretending to be a state' (Pye
1994: 18–25) is well established and is intimately related to the continuing
debate over 'culturalism'. Borrowing from James Townsend (1996: 3),
'culturalism' is properly concerned with the loyalty of China's political elites
'to principles that defined a manner of rule, not to a particular regime or
nation'. Townsend (*ibid.*: 8–9) goes on to draw a useful distinction between
adherence to a culture held to be unquestionably superior ('culture as identity') and to a culture requiring an argued defence and action to establish its
legitimacy and worth among competing alternatives ('culture as movement'). Thus proponents emphasise the presence of enduring features of the
political culture that reflect culturalism as both 'identity' and 'movement': a
conviction in the culture's innate superiority; an inherent awareness of

participating in the inclusive and historical continuity of Chinese cultural unity; and the authority of the political centre legitimated as the guardian exemplar of the culture's moral virtue. But if culturalism's conceptual categories of unity, centrism, cultural sameness and superiority have been harnessed to the revolutionary discourse, the denigration of the 'feudal' particulars of traditional culture have undermined its salience for contemporary generations and theirs search for an answer to their angst of the 'anxiety of the nation', 'crisis consciousness' and 'historical nihilism' in the 1980s and 1990s.[17]

Nationalism

These discursive traits of anti-imperialism and modernisation both engage with questions of nationalism. In a search for a restored independence, international status and internal social equilibrium, reformers and revolutionaries alike in the closing decades of the nineteenth century and early decades of the twentieth drew upon the Western idea of 'nation' and its concomitant ideology of 'nationalism'. The decisive shift was away from a sense of China as an all-embracing set of values to which societal members could adhere irrespective of blood lines, lineage or social position towards membership defined in terms of a *created* 'idea' of the Chinese 'nation' grafted onto a centralised, unified Chinese state. 'Chineseness' in the Maoist revolutionary era was a complex mix of mythical discourse of race located in the Han people of the Yellow River–Wei River region and its assimilation of Manchus, Mongols, Hui and Zang. To this was added a class conception locating the driving force of Chinese progressive history in the poor (Han) peasantry of the Chinese hinterlands. Yet such reconceptualisation was inherently flawed by sublimated tensions produced by the historical amnesia of the marginalised minority cultures; by the 'scientific' imperative to 'denationalisation' inherent in socialist modernist culture; and in the 'iconoclastic antitraditionalism' (Cohen 1994: 102) of the socialist project itself. Moreover, bereft of the cultural parameters of the imperial era, the legitimacy of post-1949 revolutionary culture rested upon a teleological story of progress and eventual material reward. This discourse has been hollowed out at the core by the loss of legitimacy caused by the 'rectification' campaigns, the failure of the Great Leap Forward, the tumult of the Cultural Revolution and social divisions emerging from the reform era. The emptiness of the creed at the heart of the constructed 'national' identity is thrown into sharp relief and opened up to the mounting challenges of the opposition discourses considered below.

The Chinese 'language of politics'

As Hodge and Louie (1998: 8) note, unlike 'word-centred' Western languages, 'Chinese culture is strongly visual and semiotically promiscuous'.

The Chinese language of politics is thus rich in metaphor and allusion. Political meanings are understood by the author and the audience to be implicit. Metaphorical references are, for individuals and masses alike, triggers to formulaic memories and to a particular, constructed, discourse and official 'grand narrative'. The language of this narrative is charged with symbolic signposts: to sacrifice and overcoming; to martial terms and a siege mentality; and to the 'terrains of power' formed by the conjunction of landscape and memory. Such language is essentialist, patriarchal and marked by historical silences. The apprehension of meaning, therefore, is made all the more complex as meaning is detached from the words themselves and reconstituted in the 'dark corners' of political discourse. This is evident not only in the bizarre Orwellian 'doublespeak' of the Cultural Revolution (Chang 1993: 298; Schoenhals 1996) but also in the less feverish and enduring practices of political discourse into the contemporary period.

At the strategic level of study, Chinese political discourse is characterised by three features: building a consensus (*gongshi*), a drive for unity (*tuanjie*) and a need for the propagation of this 'consensus' through education (*jiaoyu*). Consensus is the highest priority and the first step in mobilising the party and the people for whatever goals the power elite strives to achieve. Building a consensus is frequently assumed to be consistent with China's supposed cultural tradition, wherein a centralised, unified discourse has been habitually favoured to legitimate action. Building a consensus in political discourse therefore constitutes the major site of, and strategy for, establishing legitimacy and authority. The exercise of power and the construction of knowledge are at full play in establishing and perpetuating a supposed national political 'truth' as seemingly self-evident and thus unchallengeable. Unity is organisationally oriented, aiming at reducing internal friction to a minimum. This chiefly takes the form of producing a public consensus at the top levels of state and party and the absolute suppression of opposition discourses inside and outside the CCP. Such exclusionary practice has been and remains a process viewed not only as necessary but also perfectly legitimate by China's power elite, given the high value placed upon social stability and order in the dominant political discourse. Education is one of the principal social channels through which the discursive mythology of consensus is constructed within the CCP membership and the Chinese people more widely. The unique forms of such educational power include not only the integration of the discursive consensus into a formal national educational curriculum up to postgraduate level, but also the establishment of a national political study system operating at all levels and in every walk of life, constituting the politicisation of social life. This study therefore focuses upon the processes by which this political mechanism of discursive consensus is constructed in the PRC.

At the level of content, political consensus is constructed in two main domains: historical and theoretical. Historical discourse centres on (re)formulating and (re)defining events of the past century and a half in a Marxist view, in particular, historical materialism. The framework consists of a series of designations and/or namings: for instance, pre-modern, modern and contemporary stages of Chinese history.[18] Each of these classificatory stages is positioned historically by a particular event: the Opium War, the Fourth of May Movement and the founding of the PRC, respectively. Similarly, China's political development is etched into the social fabric by way of a historical discourse that 'names' particular events as signposts of progressive change: 'feudal reform', 'old democratic', 'new democratic' and 'socialist revolution' (led by Qing court reformers, Sun Yatsen and Mao Zedong, respectively). In such processes of 'naming' and positioning, meanings are formulated or reformulated and established as forms of historical truth. An example is the focus upon the historically progressive role that the CCP played in overthrowing the 'three mountains' on the back of the Chinese people: imperialism, feudalism and bureaucratic capitalism.

The theoretical foundations for such claims are drawn from the Marxist–Leninist doctrine of historical and dialectical materialism as reinterpreted through 'Mao Zedong thought' or, latterly, 'Deng Xiaoping thought'. Human society is seen as a progression from an original classless communitarianism to slavery, feudalism, capitalism, socialism, and finally to its most advanced form of a classless communist condition. Each stage is claimed to be economically and ethically more advanced than the previous one, and therefore history is inherently progressive and forward-oriented in character. The agent of change is material in the form of productivity (technology) and modes of production (economic base and its related superstructure). History's prime mover is portrayed as that of the Chinese people, and the leading force in the last three stages is a working class (proletariat). The working class is made conscious of itself as a class by way of class antagonism, sharpened by shifting modes of production and through raised self-consciousness by its political vanguard, the Communist Party. Over the course of the post-1949 period of CCP rule, this Marxist–Leninist reading of history, interpreted through Chinese revolutionary experience, has been established as the universal, 'scientific' truth and has become the official discursive ideology of the CCP. The intersection of the two domains of political discourse (practice and theory), *praxis*, constitutes the principal discursive site where the legitimacy of the rule of the CCP is positioned.

Opposition discourses

Three domains of opposition

The hegemonic discourse cannot be viewed in isolation from the marginalised or subordinated opposition discourses. Rather, as will be illustrated below, China's hegemonic political discourse is more appropriately understood to be actively and constantly engaged in a critical tension with a variety of opposition discourses within the CCP and in the society beyond. Opposition discourses, 'micrologies' of power or 'local determinism', form inescapable and *necessary* discursive interlocutors with the dominant, officially sanctioned political discourse. These micrological sites of contested power are to be found in a range of locations: intra-party (Leftist–Rightist contests); extra-party (aesthetic, generation, gender, sexual orientation); and extra-national (Han and non-Han ethnic narrative affiliations, regional differences and geo-historical perspectives). A brief review of some recent examples of these micrological discursive sites is perhaps useful in supporting this point.

Within the CCP, supposedly ideological contests between Leftists and Rightists have long been played out in combination with, or as a vehicle for, power struggles between the leadership and factional rivals. The reform programme has been subjected to sporadic criticism by influential Leftists such as Deng Liqun. His 1995 *Ten Thousand Character Document*[19] portrayed the reform process as threatening communism, undermining the CCP and failing the Chinese people. He renewed his criticism in late 1998, arguing that, for the present leadership, 'in their hearts, it is no longer only socialism that can save China but only capitalism that can save China'. He criticised the sale of state enterprises and consequential unemployment, arguing that 'the rights of the overwhelming majority of people would be guaranteed if state-owned enterprises were in the hands of Marxists and Leninists .... Public ownership should be the mainstay and non-public ownership supplementary'.[20]

Beyond the borders of the CCP, opposition challenges are to be found in the 'semiotic guerrilla warfare' characteristic of the youth subculture's rock music (Jones 1994: 148–65), such as Xie Chengqiang's 1990 release 'What's the nineties gonna bring?' (Barmé and Jaivin 1992: 471); feminism and women's writing, such as Ma Zhongxing's 1988 *I Wish I Was a Wolf* (Kingsbury 1994: 17–48); commentaries such as He Bochuan's 1988 *In the Hills of China*[21]; and poetry, art and television series such as the 1988 *Heshang* ('River Elegy'). The chronological bunching of these examples is not coincidental, as they were expressions of the onset of a *zeitgeist* of national questioning and reappraisal.

Extra-national opposition discourses can be explored through non-Han challenges to the hegemonic discursive themes of unity and sameness. We can briefly note three expressions of such 'local determinism': Uighur separatism in northwest China; 'southern Chineseness'; and coastal and interior geo-historical differentiated perspectives. The 1990s have seen bombings in Xinjiang province, on the streets of Beijing and on the China–Kazakhstan border by Uighur Muslim nationalists seeking an independent state of East Turkestan. While popular protests such as a riot in Yining in February 1997 were largely attributable to a claim to improve the quality of life for the

Uighur people within the existing 'autonomous' status and anti-nucle-arism,[22] the deeply held resentment against Han transmigration into Xinjiang, the desire for recognition fired by memories of a brief independence before 1949, and the proximity of post-Soviet Muslim states is not to be underestimated (*Far Eastern Economic Review*, 25 August 1988: 28–30; Gladney 1996). In the late 1980s, former provincial governor Wang Enmao publicly acknowledged that 'There are still people who oppose the Hans and want them to return to the interior ... who say those who oppose Hans are heroes and those who unify with Hans are traitors ... who say we minority nationalists are still the slaves of others' (*Far Eastern Economic Review*, 25 August 1988: 29).

A second example is a resurgent sense of southern Chineseness. The importance of local cultures and identities in China and, in particular, the distinctiveness of southern Chineseness has been noted elsewhere (Douw and Post 1996; Friedman 1996: 169–82). Friedman makes the key point that instead of

> a Mao-era nationalism that privileged poor, hinterland, Yellow River, north China peasants as the source of nation-building, national success by the late 1980s was identified with the market-oriented activities of southerners who had joined with Chinese capital from Diaspora Hong Kong, Macao and Southeast Asia to produce world-competitive products, building a prosperous China. In the new southern narrative, northern peasants were re-categorised as backward, ignorant, superstitious, insular and static.
>
> (Friedman 1994: 67–91; 1996: 175)

Thus, southern Chinese identity is increasingly made synonymous with Chineseness *per se*, challenging the mythological essentialism at the heart of the hegemonic official discourse.

A third example is the identificatory differentiation drawn between coastal and interior cultures. Lucian Pye has noted the complex psychological dispositions between 'interior' and 'enclave' populations during the era of Western imperialism. The sense of shame at China's subordination was shared by Chinese enclave workers and the interior populations alike. But divisive pressures arose as the former experienced nationalistically driven shame at their work for the foreign powers and the latter found humiliation in comparisons with the modernising coastal ports. An unsurprising defensive resort to portraying the interior culture as 'authentic' and Westernised Chinese as suspect and contaminated was fuelled by communist propaganda, which valorised the former and demonised the latter (Pye 1996: 93–109). The attention paid to the coastal provinces during the reform era has necessarily left the hinterland in the shade. As John Gittings's (1996) explorations of 'Middle China' beautifully illustrate, the sense of differentiation from the coast is readily felt.

Case study

> As for the colonial expansionism and commercial activities of some Western European countries, there were profound economic and social causes, as well as scientific knowledge accumulated over a long time and the corresponding material guarantees; they were not brought about merely because they bordered on the sea. The birth, development and evolution of the whole capitalist system was the result of the mutual interaction of the economy, government and culture of all of mankind; it was a product of a definite stage of historical development; and in history there has never existed an eternal 'blue civilisation' determined by the geographical environment. Because the influence of the geographical environment – including climate and natural resources – on mankind is different in each stage of historical development, the degree of influence of the geographical environment is in an inverse relationship to the degree of development of the civilisation; there does not exist by any means an eternal, unchanging influence or determining role.

This extract is part of an article ('Historians in the capital criticising *Heshang*: a summary'; Su and Wang 1991: 314) critiquing, from an orthodox party standpoint, the major Chinese 1988 television series *Heshang* broadcast by China Central Television.[23] Originally conceived as a tribute to Chinese tradition, the director and authors[24] reversed this goal to present a dramatically iconoclastic work. *Heshang* is the most controversial work since 1949 and 'set off a debate comparable in nature to the Death of God controversy in the West' (Bodman 1991: 1). Its central theme is the 'need for a new civilisation … industrial civilisation'. The authors use the metaphor of the river flowing to the sea to represent a flow from traditional culture to modernity. Thus Chinese (yellow) civilisation, symbolically represented by the Yellow River, should be given up completely and give way to the blue (maritime) civilisation of the West. This perspective aroused strong criticism among Leftist scholars (Tu 1991: 301–9). Even one of the authors of the series, Su Xiaokang, believes in retrospect that *Heshang* treated Chinese history and culture simplistically. Simplistic or not, its appeal to a mass television audience cannot be denied.

However, in this extract, what we are interested in is the political thrust of the critical discourse directed towards the series. This criticism is grounded significantly in the discursive schematic of Marxist–Leninist 'scientific' historical materialism. Thus the authors of the series were guilty of heterodoxy in their failure to apply Marxist–Leninist theory in the analysis of history. In this textual critique, the author uses classical Marxist historical materialism: the role of productivity and production relations in moving history forward in a dialectic relationship between economic base and superstructure, and a progressive view of history from a low-level classless society to an advanced society of communism.

This text is marked by *experiential values* throughout; the *relational value*[25] is polarised between Marxist and non-Marxist views; and the text purports to offer a straightforward evaluation of historical reality. The cumulative result is the unreconstructed application of Marxist–Leninist defined 'truth' as the benchmark for the interpretation of Chinese history and the development of civilisation.

Discursively, this extract integrates a number of key issues in a coherent account of capitalism. First, the text assumes the inevitability of colonial expansion under capitalism. Thus the nature of capitalism, the insatiable desire for profit, made it inevitable that China would fall victim to such expansionism. Second, capitalism, as a product of a definite historical stage of production and production relations, ensures that the potential for continued attempts to exploit and subordinate China remains salient. Third, the dynamics of economic, governmental and cultural interaction will eventually result in the downfall of capitalism. Fourth, the categorisation of 'blue' and 'yellow' civilisations is, clearly, non-Marxist and therefore unscientific and invalid. As a result of such a critical interpretation, based on an intertextual reading, a discursive unity is achieved by relating the past (victimisation by colonial powers and liberation of China by the CCP), the present (the need for vigilance against capitalist countries and for the rule of the CCP) and the future (the fall of capitalism and the prevailing of communism); the capitalists (victimising force) and communists (devictimising force); the blue (Western, more advanced, stage of human development) and yellow (East Asian, less advanced, stage) civilisations; truth (Marxism) and fallacy (those against Marxism); and knowledge (Marxist account of history) and power (the CCP's legitimacy to rule).

An immediate situational context is that the extract is part of an organised criticism of *Heshang* by five editorial departments of the Chinese Academy of Social Sciences (CASS) (Su and Wang 1991: 311) in 1989 following the events of 4 June. Although no new theoretical formations are made in the critique, it signals an important attempt to reassert Marxism–Leninism as *the* guiding ideology. Institutionally, a wider context exists in the relationship between the CASS and the CCP, in which the former is subject to the latter. The extract, therefore, echoes the official line of the CCP. At the social level, such criticism of a television programme could well be understood as framing a new wave of the ideological purification campaign.

The intertextual background is extremely rich, and China as a victim has been meshed into a mass of historical narratives in a variety of forms: in particular, in the domain of history. Two distinctive features of this intertextuality can be noted here: the use of an environmental metaphor and a contemporaneous discourse of pessimism and crisis. Landscape and memory are intimately connected in national cultures and consciousness (Schama 1995). The use of the 'yellow' imagery is powerfully evocative in conjuring up the sense of common origins, ethnic continuity and contact with the land that has been so evident in the mythology of the essentialist and nativist readings of Chinese history and identity to be found in 'Mao Zedong thought' and elsewhere (Dikötter 1997). The second intertextual reading is that of the 'Chinese crisis' mentality of the late 1980s and the 1990s. This has been, in part, considered above. However, as Barmé and Jaivin have noted, the conjunction of 1988 as the year of the dragon and the experiencing of natural disaster and popular unrest resurrected bad memories of 1976 (the previous year of the dragon) to fuel a sense of impending calamity. *Heshang* contributed to a sense of alienation and crisis in its challenge to the hegemonic discourse and to traditional culture. The orthodox critiques, as in the case study text, sought to emphasise the mythology misapprehension of those enamoured of Western superiority. The past strength of the Western powers was temporally specific ('a definite stage of historical development') and was thus not to be held as 'eternal, unchanging'. The future, by implication, was socialism's as capitalism's 'blue civilisation' would inevitably come to an end.

Hegemony and resistance in Chinese

In China's official political discourse, a large number of commonly used words have acquired ideologically charged meanings in daily life. They, together with other more formal 'naming' political lexicons, form a pervasive discursive space penetrating every single cell of society, contributing to the politicisation and erasure of distinctions between public and private lives. The continual elevation of 'the political' to discursive pre-eminence serves to marshal control of this discursive space to the grand narrative of Chinese revolutionary history. Political meaning is thus characterised by displacement of the linguistically signified from the signifier, opening up meaning to the contingencies of elite-driven official systems of signification and representation. These discourses, as contingent systems, are thus systems of power and, consequently, are sites of continuing tension between consensus formation and opposition contestation, which is an unresolved tension in Chinese political discourse as China seeks a legitimate and authoritative basis for its reform process on the cusp of the twenty-first century.

Notes

1 Essentialism being defined as 'the idea that humans and human institutions … are governed by determinate natures that inhere in them in the same way that they are supposed to inhere in the entities of the natural world' (Inden 1990: 2).
2 Letter of Viceroy Jung Lu to Viceroy of Fukien (Fujian) province.
3 *Hsiang-chiang p'ing-lun* ('Commentary of Hong Kong'), July 1919.
4 Khrushchev himself drew a direct comparison between Stalin's cult of personality and that of Mao. In his memoirs (1977: 34), he wrote:

> I often see films about China on television, and it seems to me that that Mao Tse-tung is copying Stalin's personality cult. He's even echoing some of

the same slogans. If you close your eyes, listen to what the Chinese are saying about Mao, and substitute 'Comrade Stalin' for 'Comrade Mao', you'll have some idea of what it was like in our time.

5 Editorial, *People's Daily*, 27 January 1967 (Jones and Kevill 1985: 79).
6 Zhou Enlai, 24 August 1973 (*Jones and Kevill 1985*: 105).
7 An authoritative article in 1982, 'Beware of the revival of militarism', spared no Japanese blushes in its criticism of reported textbook revisions:

> Your 'samurai' forebears used innocent Chinese to test bacteriological warfare and used them as living targets. They dismembered and chopped up Chinese captives who were tied to trees. You adopted such savage means as the 'iron maiden', pulling out fingernails, branding, belly cutting, electric grinding, and flesh eating to persecute Chinese compatriots. Thus, even the German fascists labelled Japanese soldiers as a 'group of beasts'.
>
> (Whiting 1989: 49)

8 His full recollection is:

> In those days when I was a student in Yangzhou, I was shocked to see and hear about the evil acts of the Japanese aggressors .... Each time I saw the tombstone of Shi Kefa with my classmates I felt a strong anti-Japanese and patriotic emotion and became determined to engage in revolutionary struggle.
>
> (Gilley 1998: 14)

9 Jiang Zemin, National Day address, 29 September 1989 (Barmé and Jaivin 1992: 396–7).
10 According to Bruce Gilley (1998: 16), Jiang Zemin quoted Lu Xun's phrase that 'we Chinese have backbone' and then followed it up with his own comment that 'we shall never yield to unreasonable pressure exerted on us by foreigners'.
11 Gilley (1998: 70) credits Jiang Zemin with a 1984 statement that 'we cannot allow our products to be excluded abroad and then let foreigners run our factories to make money'.
12 In August 1993, the Chinese vessel *Yinhe Hao* was stopped, detained for three weeks and searched for chemical weapons by US Naval Intelligence vessels.
13 Mao Zedong, article in *Hung-ch'i* ('Red Flag'), 1 June 1958 (Schram 1969: 352).
14 For an excellent recent study of the mythologising of the Boxers, see Cohen (1997).
15 Moscow Conference, November 1957. According to his physician's memoirs (Li 1994: 224), Mao commented privately that 'our country produces too little steel .... We have to do everything we can to increase our material strength. Otherwise, people will look down on us'.
16 Mao's remarks to Chinese students in Moscow, 17 November 1957 (Schram 1969: 408).
17 The first two terms are attributable to the book *World Citizenship* (1989), criticised by Wu Jianguo, *People's Daily*, 26 November 1990 (Barmé and Jaivin, 1992: 170). The latter term is attributable to Su Xiaokang in a response to a viewer's letter on the *Heshang* television programme (*ibid.*: 161).
18 The pre-modern (*jindai*), modern (*xiandai*) and contemporary (*dangdai*) periods of Chinese history start in 1840, 1911 and 1949, respectively.
19 Formally titled *Certain Factors Affecting China's National Security*.
20 Speech reprinted in the magazine *Midstream* (*The Times*, 31 December 1998: 17).

21 The full title of the commentary is *Shanaoshangde Zhongguo* ('In the Hills of China: Problems, Dilemmas, and Painful Choices').
22 The province houses the Lop Nor nuclear testing base.
23 The term *Heshang* means in Chinese the sad song for the passing away of loved ones. The translation 'River Elegy' is preferred here to 'Deathsong of the River', as used in the title of Su and Wang's 1991 volume.
24 Xia Jun, Su Xiaokang and Wang Luxiang.
25 *Experiential* value and *relational* value are defined by Fairclough (1989) as traces in the text that reflect the experience of the world and the construction of social relations of the producers of the text.

References

Anderson, B. (1991) *Imagined Communities*. London: Verso.

Barmé, G. and Jaivin, L. (1992) *New Ghosts, Old Dreams: Chinese Rebel Voices*. New York: Times Books.

Becker, J. (1997) *Hungry Ghosts: China's Secret Famine*. London: John Murray.

Bo-Yang (1991) *The Ugly Chinaman and the Crisis of Chinese Culture*. St Leonards, Australia: Allen & Unwin.

Bodman, R.W. (1991) 'From history to allegory to art: a personal search for interpretation', in Su Xiaokang and Wang Luxiang (eds), *Deathsong of the River: A Reader's Guide to the Chinese TV Series*Heshang. New York: Cornell University East Asia Programme.

Chang Jung (1993) *Wild Swans: Three Daughters of China*. London: HarperCollins.

Ci Jiwei (ed.) (1994) *Dialectic of the Chinese Revolution: From Utopianism to Hedonism*. Stanford, Calif.: Stanford University Press.

Cohen, M.L. (1994) 'Being Chinese: the peripheralisation of traditional identity', in W.-M. Tu (ed.), *The Changing Meaning of Being Chinese Today*. Stanford, Calif.: Stanford University Press.

Cohen, P.A. (1997) *History in Three Keys: The Boxers as Event, Experience, and Myth*. New York: Columbia University Press.

Dikötter, F. (1997) *The Construction of Racial Identities in China and Japan*. London: Hurst.

Dillon, M. (ed.) (1998) *China: A Cultural and Historical Dictionary*. London: Curzon.

Dittmer, L. (1998) *Liu Shaoqi and the Cultural Revolution*. Armonk, NY: M.E. Sharpe.

Douw, L.M. and Post, P. (eds.) (1996) *South China: State, Culture and Social Change during the 20th Century*. Amsterdam: North Holland.

Fairclough, N. (1989), *Language and Power*. London and New York: Longman.

Friedman, E. (1994) 'Reconstructing China's national identity: a southern alternative to Mao era anti-imperialist nationalism', *The Journal of Asian Studies*, 53(1) (February): 67–91.

—— (1996) 'A democratic Chinese nationalism?' in J. Unger (ed.), *Chinese Nationalism*. New York: M.E. Sharpe.

Gernet, J. (1994) *A History of Chinese Civilisation*. Cambridge: Cambridge University Press.

Gilley, B. (1998) *Tiger on the Brink – Jiang Zemin and China's New Elite*. Berkeley: University of California Press.

Gittings, J. (1996) *Real China: From Cannibalism to Karaoke*. London: Simon & Schuster.

Gladney, D.C. (1996) *Muslim Chinese: Ethnic Nationalism in the People's Republic*. Harvard: Harvard University Press.

Hodge, B. and Louie, K. (1998) *The Politics of Chinese Language and Culture*. London: Routledge.

Human Rights Watch/Asia (1996) *Death by Default – A Policy of Fatal Neglect in China's State Orphanages*. New York: Human Rights Watch.

Inden, R. (1990)*Imagining India*. Oxford: Basil Blackwell.

Jones, A. (1994) 'The politics of popular music in post-Tiananmen China', in J.N. Wasserstrom and E. Perry (eds), *Popular Protest and Political Culture in Modern China*. Boulder, Colo.: Westview Press.

Jones, P. and Kevill, S. (1985) *China and the Soviet Union 1949–84*. Harlow: Longman.

Khrushchev, N. (1977) *Khrushchev Remembers* (trans. S. Talbot). London: Penguin.

Kingsbury, D.B. (1994) *I Wish I Was a Wolf: The New Voice in Chinese Women's Literature*. Beijing: New World Press.

Kitahara Michio (1989) *Children of the Sun: The Japanese and the Outside World*. Folkstone: Paul Norbury.

Li Zhisui (1994) *The Private Life of Chairman Mao*. London: Arrow Books.

Liao, K.S. (1986) *Antiforeignism and Modernisation in China 1860–1980*. Hong Kong: Chinese University Press.

Lutz, J.G. and Lutz, R.R. (1998) *Hakka Chinese Confront Protestant Christianity, 1850–1900*. Armonk, NY: M.E. Sharpe.

Mao Zedong (1940) 'The Chinese Revolution and the Communist Party', in S. Schram (ed.) (1969), *The Political Work of Mao Tse-tung*. New York: Praeger.

—— (1969) 'On new democracy', in *ibid.*

Meyer, C. and Allen, I. (1969) *Source Materials in Chinese History*. London: Frederick Warne.

Morrison, D. (1989) *Massacre in Beijing: China's Struggle for Democracy*. New York: Time Books.

Newby, L. (1996) 'Xinjiang: in search of an identity' in T.-T. Liu and D. Faure (eds), *Unity and Diversity: Local Cultures and Identities in China*. Hong Kong: Hong Kong University Press.

Pye, L.W. (1994) 'China: A Superpower?' *The Oxford International Review* VI(1): 18–25.

—— (1996) 'How China's nationalism was shanghaied', in J. Unger (ed.), *Chinese Nationalism*. New York: M.E. Sharpe.

Schama, S. (1995) *Landscape and Memory*. London: Fontana.

Schoenhals, M. (ed.) (1996) *China's Cultural Revolution, 1966–1969*. Armonk, NY: M.E. Sharpe.

Schram, S. (ed.) (1969) *The Political Work of Mao Tse-tung*. New York: Praeger.

Snow, E. (1936) 'Interview with Mao Tse-tung 23 July 1936', in *ibid.*

Su Xiaokang and Wang Luxiang (eds) (1991) *Deathsong of the River: A Reader's Guide to the Chinese TV Series*Heshang. New York: Cornell University East Asia Programme.

Townsend, J. (1996) 'Chinese nationalism', in J. Unger (ed.), *Chinese Nationalism*. New York: M.E. Sharpe.

Tu, W.-M. (1991) 'Deathsong of the river: whither Chinese culture?' in Su Xiaokang and Wang Luxiang (eds), *Deathsong of the River: A Reader's Guide to the Chinese TV Series*Heshang. New York: Cornell University East Asia Programme.

—— (1994) *The Changing Meaning of Being Chinese Today*. Stanford, Calif.: Stanford University Press.

Unger, J. (1996) *Chinese Nationalism*. New York: M.E. Sharpe.

Whiting, A. (1986) 'Foreword', in K.-S. Liao (ed.), *Antiforeignism and Modernisation in China 1860–1980*. Hong Kong: Chinese University Press.

—— (1989) *China Eyes Japan*. Berkeley: University of California Press.

Wu Hongda, H. (1992) *Laogai: The Chinese Gulag*. Boulder, Colo.: Westview Press.

5 What Chinese journalists believe about journalism

Hugo de Burgh[1]

Introduction

This chapter is based on interviews with Chinese journalists of varying seniority and background between April 1998 and December 2000.[2] The objectives were twofold: first, to find out what roles they thought journalists performed in society; and, second, what they regarded as 'good journalism'.

Factors prompting the research included:

1   Speculation that the withdrawal of state control from certain aspects of the media and the vast expansion in media would reduce the commitment of Chinese journalists to the totalitarian Maoist interpretation of their professional role.
2   That commercialisation of the media would tend to liberalise content as the media became more responsive to the market and that journalists would become more reflective of the concerns of their audience – citizenry – than of their political masters.
3   That both trends would fuse with increasing influences from Western, particularly Anglophone, media in driving journalists to see themselves in the 'watchdog' and 'critical' roles perceived as being archetypally 'Western'.[3]

The interviewees were first asked to explain their understanding of what a journalist is, and some of their replies are reproduced in the following section. Contemporary quantitative studies are then referred to so the reader may compare their findings. The next section examines the interviewees' views of what kinds of journalism they took pride in and what role models they might have.

What is a journalist? Some responses

According to Ding Junjie of the Peking (Beijing) Broadcasting Academy, there have been five great changes in the Chinese media in the last five years: quantity, economic independence, autonomy, serving the audience, and relationship to the polity. By 'autonomy', Ding means that the media have taken upon themselves the task of scrutinising society 'to decide themselves what kind of news is the most important, what is most attractive to viewers, and what can contribute most to social development'. This is echoed by Du Yan, deputy editor of a current affairs programme:

> Our task is to identify the latest news facts and social phenomena and to reflect them in our recording of them. Of course, we have our own objectives, one of which is to be close to the citizenry. If there is a topic in which the citizenry have shown no interest, yet you cover it, then you will create a social effect. There are some matters that are known to the audience but not reflected upon or thought out by them .... We go into depth on these topics and demonstrate our views, perhaps providing revelation.

All journalists talk of their relationship with the audience. According to Jiang Lan of Oriental TV:

> Chinese and Western audiences approach television in different ways, because China is a country 'in development'. The Chinese audience wants truth first, and responsiveness to their interests second. It is political reports and social reports that interest me most, because I believe our job is to serve the public and to help the public understand [public] matters and their contexts and background.

An idealistic tone was given to the same basic idea by the younger regional television journalists. For example, K'ang Wei said: 'you are a reporter because you have a sense of justice. Because you want to, first, expose evil, and second, give information'. Hsia Yi also commented: 'Journalists tell people those things they don't know and provide a deeper understanding of those things they do'.

Similar ideas can be expressed in different ways and given a different emphasis: 'the job of a journalist is to process the news for the people and to supervise the government. Yes, the government must be supervised', said Chen Muli. What Chen meant by that comment was slightly less challenging than it sounds: 'Residents in an area cannot get their gas supplies properly attended to, so they come to television reporters. It's that simple'.

The question of where they stood between people and government was a vexing one for T'ang Musan:

> Journalists are the mediators between people and government. Their tasks are the communication of news and scrutiny. The responsibilities of the journalists are to making a news programme that keeps the interest of the people – but not all stations are the same. Impartiality is very necessary but the absolute is impossible. We can only do our best. If something is controversial, we get it said by others. We don't say it.

When the idea that journalists should be 'social activists' was put to senior print journalist Wu Haimin, he was very forthright: 'certainly not. "Social activists" are very different from "journalists". A reporter should try to report impartially whereas a social activist has some aims. Journalists report opinions and facts'. Emphasising the active aspect of journalism, the older reporter said about his profession:

> When you teach in a school, you teach few. As a reporter you teach many and at all levels …. A reporter works because he has a sense of justice, because he wants to do justice and to cry out about it …. There are many qualifications on the work of a reporter. For example, if an ordinary person asks for help from a reporter, the latter has to judge 'is this just helping an individual, or is it a wider issue of significance to many?' Then he has to argue it with his colleagues.

Another senior journalist, Liu Ch'ao, supported Wu's views: 'The reporter has a special role as the throat and mouth of the Party', he said, 'but should serve the people first. Since you represent the party in their eyes you are not free to speak as you might wish'. He then added an interesting further twist:

> In the eyes of ordinary people I am powerful. I can speak for them. Thus when I am interviewing a politician I represent the audience. But I must be careful; I am not representing myself. When I speak to the general public I represent power.

So did he, in his turn, see the journalist as a 'social activist'? Liu answered: 'There is not really a contradiction between the social activist and the impartial journalist'. He thinks that a journalist is 'to work on behalf of the citizenry', and this makes a journalist a social activist, because 'your aims are activist'. However, as a journalist, Liu believes that 'in the way you deal with topics you must be impartial'.

All interviewees agreed, explicitly or implicitly, that people have high expectations of journalists. As Hsia Yi put it, 'Journalists have a high social position; at least people attribute to us a high status, although to ourselves we don't seem to have that'. To summarise, the interviewees apparently incline towards social responsibility, and even a paternal view of their role. It may help us to understand this if we look at the responses to other questions: Can you tell me about any heroes? Which journalists do you most admire? Before doing so, however, we should examine some contemporary studies.

The global journalist study

From 1995 to 1997, scholars undertook a postal survey of Chinese journalists. From questionnaires distributed to 5,800 Chinese journalists, Chen and his colleagues (Chen *et al.* 1998: 26) discovered how they viewed their work:

Our respondents chose the dissemination of news quickly and accurately ('information role') as the most important [task], with 79 percent of the sample naming it as 'very important'. The next most important role, endorsed by 72 percent of the sample, requires the media to provide analysis and interpretation of major social issues, which may be called the 'correlation role' according to Lazarsfeld and Merton (1948: 95–118). The 'mouthpiece role' came in third, with 64 percent considering the dissemination and explanation of governmental regulations and CCP policies to be very important. A slightly smaller number of respondents supported the 'watchdog role' by looking over either the government (61 percent) or the negative sectors of society (60 percent).

The least popular role among the Chinese journalists surveyed is entertainment, endorsed by 19 percent of the sample. The 'public forum role', offering a free marketplace of ideas to ordinary citizens, also lacks widespread support, as less than a quarter (24 percent) viewed it as very important. Contrary to the strong support for the mouthpiece role, only one out of three respondents supported the 'indoctrination role' in promoting communist role models. The journalists preference of mouthpiece over indoctrination role is consistent with our previous studies (e.g. Zhu 1990), in which Chinese audiences were found to be responsive to media messages about governmental polices but resistant to campaigns promoting Communist ideology.

Chen and his team concluded that 'future research needs to compare the perceived and the practised journalistic professionalism by Chinese journalists' (Chen *et al.* 1998: 29). C.-C. Lee has examined Chen's study in the light of a contemporary one carried out within China and considers that they profess high-minded but unrealistic ideals. He comments:

> A scrutiny of both national surveys discloses the emergence of a mixed and ambiguous normative conception about the role of journalism in the 1990s .... Since they rebuff Western norms of separating facts from values or presenting balanced views on controversial issues, they vow to find out right and wrong before they report. But, then, 'right and wrong' from what or whose vantage points? Their answers are vague.
>
> (Lee 2000a)

The key point made by Lee, which helps to explain the interviewees' attitudes, is that their expressed goals 'remain highly abstract'. He is referring to the watchdog or supervisory role believed in by 60 percent of Chen's respondents. In order to try to get my interviewees to be more concrete, they were asked to describe reports of which they were proud, what makes for a successful report and whether reports influence the authorities.

Reports of which journalists were proud

At the time of interview, the regional television station at which he worked did not have its own current affairs programmes, but Jiang Lan was particularly proud of the investigative reports on the news: 'Last night we did a programme about a lawyer and university professor who had been charged with accepting bribes but, after 100 days of investigation was found not guilty .... Our report also discussed the repercussions of the case in law circles'. He then gave another example: 'A while ago we did a story about a primary school in Shandong where a class had been given a nutritious drink and had been taken ill with vomiting and other symptoms of poisoning'. It turned out that the drink, he continued, 'was found to contain iodine. The authorities have been extremely concerned about this. We did an investigation of the kind of drinks promoted similarly in this area and the regulatory controls'.

Regional reporter K'ang Wei concentrates on social news. For example, reports she had done recently included fairly banal ones such as on the issue of a new banknote and the opening of a park. As you would expect, these stories tend to come from the organisations responsible for them. However, she said that 'most of our news today probably derives from viewers calling in'. She admitted:

> I like to do critical reports because they get the highest ratings as people like them most. The best story I ever did last year started from a letter that came into the newsroom. A woman was incorrectly diagnosed by a fraudulent doctor as having a sexual disease, and she committed suicide. This brought out into the open that there were many unlicensed doctors being prosecuted in various parts of the province and this became an important running story. I was able to spin this out for ten more days and to be given nearly fifteen minutes each day as the top running story.

For example, K'ang explained, 'on the first day I did the introduction. On the second day I went to the hospital to interview patients. On the third day I went to the prosecution office, and on the fourth day to the accused to get them to tell me about their organisation, etc.'

Nevertheless, not all reporters could be pinned down as to what particular report they were proud of, preferring to talk in generalities; some responded better when asked what makes a successful report, citing various criteria. Initially these were banal. For example, as Du Yan put it, a successful report will (1) attract interest, (2) command ratings and/or audience share, and (3) receive appreciation/feedback. A telephone hotline is used extensively to give feedback. As Du said, 'We analyse the use of our hotline in quite a scientific way in order to understand what our audience thinks of us'.

When journalists consider the content, and the professional added value of the content, they become more impassioned: 'It must be clear in its description of the matter in hand', said Du Yan. Moreover, as Du put it, journalists must 'deal with it in depth, provide context and express it effectively'. Shi Zhengmao of *Economics Half-Hour* takes as her role models the investigative programmes *News Probe* and *Focal Point*. Her reasons for choosing them are:

1   They are realistic and concrete.
2   The topics covered are things we all care about, such as government policy, corruption and the reform process.
3   The quality of the reporters is exceptionally high.
4   The programmes express ideas with competence and authority.
5   Even with a simple topic they help us to penetrate the background.

Shi cannot cite an example from her own programme, simply saying that it is 'a very successful programme series that is a leading element in our country's economic development'. However, Li Xiaoping of *Focal Point* clearly recalls one from *News Probe* that she thought was very successful. The story was about

> teenage children who ran away from home because of family troubles and … how the local authorities tried to deal with them. The programme opened this up as a national, rather than a personal issue. It showed that the situation was not just a Beijing or a Shanghai or a Hunan issue but something much larger which all could address together. The whole society got a shock. Discussion programmes, newspapers and people everywhere talked about that.

On the other hand, Yu Min wanted to make it clear that sensationalism is not an end in itself: 'I used to think that any report that made a sensation was a good one. But I have come to think differently. I want a good result. I want the viewer to have a thorough explanation of the topic in hand'. As for Jiang Lan, he admires 'programmes that meet a public need. A programme about house buying can do this as much as one on a weightier topic'. He emphasises: 'What matters is that the report is specialist enough to be good of its type'.

Speed matters today in a way that it appears not to have done a few years ago. Chen Muli said: 'A good report reports a problem first (there's much competition), and provides information of immediate use (e.g. road construction in a vicinity and when it will start and finish)'. T'ang Musan of Zhejiang TV provides an interesting example of what he would consider good revelation:

> Actions contrary to ethics should be dealt with and make good programmes. For example, a family in which the parents do not treat the children/old people in accordance with ethics … in accordance with the

precepts of the Confucian *Canon of Filial Piety* (*lunyu*).[4] That is an important topic.

Although interesting for its citation of Confucian norms, these norms do not reflec typical practice. In general, everyone would agree that, as T'ang Musan has pointed out, the necessary features for good programmes are 'attractive pictures, audience interest, being informative and thought-provoking, and explanatory of the essence and the processes of society'.

At Sichuan Television, Hsia Yi gives two examples of programmes she would consider most successful in appearing to fill most of the criteria. The first programme was about elephants in Yunnan that were

> killed by peasants because they had invaded crops .... The programme investigated and found that the peasants were desperately poor and therefore one could feel sympathy for them, even if they had killed an endangered species. The programme went further and found that the original feeding grounds of the elephants had been polluted. The programme examined the situation carefully, showing how difficult it was to fix responsibility and to settle the problem.

Another programme that Hsia has mentioned was about the Henan bribery case:

> Although the programme was made after the police arrests, it minutely researched the social factors surrounding it and the mistakes of the government and social institutions. It interviewed the accused after sentence. It analysed and discussed the systemic problems that had given rise to the criminality.

As to what the viewers think, people apparently like 'programmes on what concern themselves; few are concerned about wider politics' (Ch'en Muli). This was widely agreed, with some additions noted by Liu Ch'ao:

> (1) Things that touch them ... like interest rates and whether they are going up or down, and (2) the story inside the news. For example, the Qianzheng Bridge was badly constructed. I reported on this and found that people wanted to know the whole saga of the investigation and court proceedings and the sequel, what punishment was meted out. There was also the story of illegally prepared pork. People not only wanted to know the event itself, but also what the government was going to do about it.

Moreover, as T'ang Musan has realised, there is a definite appetite for stories about the underbelly of society: 'Corruption. Unhealthy social phenomena. Disasters. Catastrophes. They like to see corruption dealt with very much. They like things told in story form'.

Asked whether journalism has any influence upon government and government policies, the answers, taken overall, were ambiguous. However, there was in one or two cases a desire to deny any clear influence:[5]

> Journalism should not have a direct influence upon government. We are not a law enforcement agency, an executive. We are merely keeping a watching brief; we find the appeal in a topic. It's possible that as a result of our alighting upon that topic a good solution will result such as a new regulation or law. This may occur, but it's not our responsibility to make it so. A report that has created awareness of some improper phenomenon may attract attention from both audience and government so that the matter is dealt with .... It is not our function to solve problems but to cast an impartial eye over problems. Nor is it our function to get you to go and solve the problem. There are appropriate agencies for that.
>
> (Du Yan)

Jiang Lan was more concrete about this. He said: 'We do not have specific programmes on, say, housing policy. But if after a government policy comes into effect people have doubts or an interest in exploring aspects of it, then we do it'. He believes that journalists should 'cover every area of interest or relevance to ordinary people', because journalists 'have the responsibility of looking at all matters touching ordinary people'. He elaborated further:

> Here's an example. Military affairs are not relevant to everybody, yet very many youngsters in Shanghai have to do military service. We have done reports on how they, accustomed to a soft life, cope with the toughness of army living. That's rather controversial.

Policy implementation can be compared across the country. For example, as Li Xiaoping has admitted, 'We have done programmes comparing the approaches of different regional authorities to unemployment and training, housing and education'. This relationship to the polity is theorised with much reference to a phrase that has common currency, *yulun jiandu* (supervision by public opinion). Although usually translated as 'supervision', this loses some of the meaning. Here is a Chinese journalist's explanation of the concept:

> *Yulun jiandu* has spurred on the economic reform, the political reform, and the development of culture and science. There are three aspects to *yulun jiandu*: (1) Keep functionaries in order by exposing wrongdoing and corruption. Many cadres have been criticised by the media. (2) Proposing ideas that improve government policies. There are successful examples in law, especially law of bankruptcy and law of copyright, all of which came about as a result of media opening up of the subject

leading to discussions among parliamentary representatives. And (3) reflecting and interpreting social phenomena and social problems such as women problems, the black market, gambling, drugs, peasant travails, unemployment.

In other words, *yulun jiandu* means acting like a watchdog, keeping an eye on society and drawing attention to what the authorities may have missed. This expression, for which the best translation seems to be 'scrutiny', is the core of professional self-esteem and is bound up absolutely with dedication to the ideal of responsible journalism: journalism reactive to people's needs, to the improvement of conditions and to the exposure of wrongdoers.

There was no sense that there might be any disagreement in how to tackle problems, and it was quite clear what was good and what was bad. There was no sense of any political views being represented other than a consensus managed by the government, which, metaphysically, was good, even if some of its officials or representatives might be wicked.

From these interviews, it would appear that Chinese journalists really are watchdogs, but watchdogs whose watching is circumscribed by an attachment to – or scepticism about – the state as definer of truth.

The journalists they admire

When Chinese journalists today are asked which journalists they admire, the replies are various, perhaps according to the generation of the respondent and/or the circumstances of the conversation. Aside from mentioning some names on which no information is available, presumably 'local heroes', those journalists spoken to in more formal settings, who also chanced to be older, mentioned modern names (such as Hu Jiwei), or cast back into history (such as Shao Piaoping and Tsou Taofen), and early journalist radicals (such as Liang Qichao and the founders of *New Youth*).

Shao and Tsou had much in common: they were persecuted journalists of the nationalist period who founded influential newspapers and have been incorporated posthumously into the communist pantheon. Tsou appears to have been a proponent of civil rights who denounced abuses by the KMT and called for press freedom well before he associated with the CCP. Shao was a courageous investigative journalist who also worked hard to promote professionalism through his textbooks and lectures at Peking (Beijing) University. According to Li (1984):

[Shao] believed in a free and independent press, with a public interest as its highest consideration. He argued that reporters should act as 'a king without a crown' or a 'fair minded judge' who took no sides. 'Truthfulness is the backbone of news, while human interest serves as flesh and blood', he wrote.

Gu Xuebin also extolled Shao in the same terms and attempted to explain the expression 'king without a crown' as describing someone who has a position of power with neither glory nor responsibility.

In recent years, these names have all reappeared as models to emulate, so it is not surprising that they are called to mind. Whether these men are admired because they stood up to government or because they stood up to the KMT government is a significant distinction! While it was unclear, it appears that it was the style of journalism, together with the fact that they were among the few past journalists they knew, that made them suitable for citing. Another figure that is more controversial today and not obviously attractive to modern-minded journalists is Deng Tuo. Nevertheless, Deng is an interesting case that illustrates various points about Chinese journalism and that has also been extensively researched.

Deng Tuo was the first editor of the *People's Daily* after the CCP victory of 1949 and a founder of the All China Association of Journalists. After losing his editorship in 1966 he became Secretary for Culture and Education in the Peking (Beijing) Municipal Party Committee, which, among its other responsibilities, controlled the Peking-based universities. He was thus both journalist and administrator, although he probably considered himself first and foremost a scholar, having published original literary and historical researches as well as essays, innumerable press articles and speeches. While one commentator has characterised Deng Tuo as a fighter who dared to criticise Mao Zedong's capricious leadership (Leys 1971), his American biographer Cheek (1997) sees him as a conventional, if inspired and singularly able, intellectual. To Cheek, Deng was a servant of the state in the Chinese tradition, adapting himself to a modern medium of service, namely journalism.

Such a journalist had four related functions: he was a bearer of culture, transmitting and mediating knowledge and values; he provided a framework within which the issues of the moment could be discussed and problems solved; he worked to raise the cultural level of the citizenry; and he propagated the current orthodoxy.

Deng was an integral part of the system that in time he was to criticise. He always advocated supervision of the executive by 'the masses' and saw one of the important roles of the media as the vehicle by which this supervision should be affected. He also believed that journalists themselves must speak truth to power and did so in 'veiled criticisms' in the *People's Daily* in 1957 after the disaster of the Great Leap Forward (*ibid.*: 172). Mao took offence and insulted and humiliated him, a precursor to the kind of treatment that would be the lot of all Mao's opponents in the mid-1960s.

Nevertheless, in March 1961, Deng began to publish a series of essays in the *Peking Evening News* called 'Evening chats at Yanshan', followed in October by 'Notes from a three family village'. These grew out of an investigation into local conditions and revealed that the policy of 'people's communes' was causing the most appalling dislocation and misery in the countryside. Deng and his supporters were asserting their right to be more than cogs in the Great Helmsman's machinery (*ibid.*: 267).

Retribution was so savage during the Cultural Revolution that Deng took his own life in May 1966 rather than suffer the abuses being vented on others, and perhaps in the hope of saving his family and associates.[6] In 1979, he was rehabilitated and all his works were thereafter republished as well as many hagiographic articles. He has been held up for emulation by journals aimed at young journalists.[7] Yet whether Deng is a plausible model for today's journalists is open to question. His was probably the last generation to have a high level of traditional culture; the very relationship of the intellectual to the state has changed (Goldman 1994), and there is a growing cynicism about the Communist Party that Deng would have found shocking (Barmé 1999).

Hu Jiwei of the *People's Daily*, holder of prominent posts in the national professional bodies for journalists, emerged in the 1980s as a champion of press freedoms. He was purged in the summer of 1989 and held responsible for the involvement of many of his colleagues in the protests that led to the Tiananmen Square protests. He has since been rehabilitated and perhaps serves as an icon for those still hopeful of the success of his ideas, although he himself has, reportedly, despaired utterly.[8]

Younger journalists were, if anything, even more hesitant to name fellow professionals as admirable. Only one gave a name from a past generation and, since it was that of Zhou Zuoren, the interviewer at first assumed the reference to be ironic. Zhou, a writer not immediately associated with current conceptions of journalism, was editor of *Tatler* until 1927 (Pollard 1973: 333). But he is remembered more as a writer of erudite essays, as the scholarly brother of China's 'greatest modern writer' Lu Xun, and as someone who became more and more aloof from the concerns of the activists of his generation and, eventually, a collaborator in the loathed Japanese occupation.

What can we make of a journalist in his twenties citing this man, whose very name was anathema in the PRC until recently and whose works have only just been republished, as an admired journalist? In contrast to the urge to modernity, and the rejection of the Chinese tradition and abstractionism of the Fourth of May radicals, Zhou proposed that China should look within itself for sources of change and development. He rejected what he regarded as the core assumption of many of his contemporaries, that is, the inferiority of Chinese civilisation.

His alternative to the dominant discourse was not a different kind of nationalism, such as might today be adduced from some of the 'neo-conservative' intellectuals. Zhou rejected the totalising, nationalistic ideologies of the KMT and CCP, which he regarded as almost interchangeable. Daruvala (2000: 219–20) states that Zhou is associated with 'a criticism of the notion that there is a homogeneous definition of what it is to be Chinese and a rejection of the demand that self cultivation must benefit the state'. He opposed 'education on national humiliation', which became a staple of KMT and CCP schooling and can be argued to have had a poisonous effect upon China's relations with other peoples. His construction of Chinese civilisation was one made up of diverse localities, traditions and individuals, welcoming to outside influences, with its own resources for self-criticism and rejecting the assumption that the present is always superior to the past, the Western to the Chinese.

In this connection, it is relevant that the interviewee who cited Zhou also made the remark that journalists from his area (Zhejiang) were limited in their range of expression by being obliged to voice reports and write articles in Chinese, in effect their second language. Although he drew the line at agreeing that other Chinese languages ('dialects') be made official, he nevertheless implicitly drew attention to the injustice of the totalising tendency[9] and demonstrated that his localist views of culture coincided with those of Zhou. He might not go as far as Friedman (1995), who suggests that the homogenising thrust of the CCP has disintegrated and that many, if not most, people outside the CCP now reject the centralising cultural tendencies just as they do the 'northern narrative'. Be that as it may, the initial assumption that the interviewee was being ironic when he cited Zhou Zuoren as a 'model journalist' was almost certainly wrong. Rather, he was named because he stands for an alternative, and a very radical one too.

Two other names were also mentioned, and without irony. Citation of Dai Qing, associated particularly with criticism of the Yangzi River Project, was not qualified; however, Liu Binyan seemed to be disparaged.[10]

Liu is involved in a New York-based organisation for promoting press freedom and human rights in China and is usually referred to in the West as a heroic investigative journalist. Under the patronage of his editor Hu Yaobang,[11] Liu first published exposes of bureaucratic incompetence in 1956, as well as a now famous story about restricted circulation publications (RCPs) and how the life of a young journalist is blighted by the fact that although she investigates honestly, she always finds that her work is used only in RCPs and ends up ignored in some obscure filing cabinet. In *Inside News*, reporter Huang wants to reveal the reality of a coal mine but is pressured to depict it in a manner approved by the party, far from the reality she observes. Huang's application to join the CCP is judged according to her willingness to conform, so her urge to be truthful will prevent her obtaining membership of the CCP. Another typical tale tells of a man who fakes being deaf and dumb so that he does not have to participate in any meetings or worry about any official work. The moral of the story is that only those who close themselves off from all around them can survive in such a society.

Criticised by the Left, Liu was expelled from the CCP in 1957 and sent to labour reform in the countryside. He returned to his original employer,

China Youth Daily, only to be arrested in 1969 as an established Rightist (de Goldfein 1989). Rehabilitated in 1979 and given a post on the *People's Daily*, he wrote his most arresting work, *Between Men and Monsters*, which exposed in detail a case in which an enterprising woman had come to involve a vast network of managers, businesses and officials in corruption, right up to national level. These are scandals comparable to those unearthed by Lincoln Steffens in the USA at the turn of the century (Ekirch 1974: 92) and by Ray Fitzwalter in the UK of the 1970s (Fitzwalter *et al.* 1981), and it is interesting to compare the treatments. Whereas the Anglophone journalists are factual in the approved social science manner of their times, Liu resorts to fiction, or at least 'faction', to highlight abuses.

In 1985, Liu appears to have gone too far when he published *The Second Kind of Loyalty*, the story of a minor official who, moved by his allegiance to the party, unceasingly denounced corruption in its ranks, a contrast with the party's model of blind obedience, Lei Feng. This story infuriated the party, and Liu was forbidden to write for the *People's Daily*. Discussion polarised behind him and his appearances became controversial, with the intellectuals on the whole admiring him. Liu was only associated with dissidents in March 1989 when he signed the petition for the release of Wei Jingshen, who had been imprisoned by direct personal command of Deng Xiaoping. Out of the country at the time of the Tiananmen Square massacre, Wei was placed on a wanted list by the government, did not return and later joined those dissidents who had fled successfully after denouncing the government. His experience provokes some reflections, first on his *oeuvre* and its methods, and second on what he represents.

Liu Binyan could not write his investigations in the evidential mode allowed the Anglophone. He wrote them as fictionalised reports, or, as Liu would have them, 'social realism' or 'reportage literature' not too far from what Wolfe, Mailer and Capote aimed for in the 1960s. Liu's stories demonstrate the failure of idealism, the ease with which systems can be subverted, how the high-minded are sidelined or persecuted, and the perverting influence of ideology.

On the face of it, we might imagine that Liu would be the nearest to a hero that modern journalists exercised by freedom and rights could have. When questioned on their attitude towards him, respondents referred to him as 'old-fashioned' or 'a party member'. They assigned to him a belief in the party that they considered he has never outgrown and that they, feeling superior in doing so, have rejected. Duke has suggested that his limitation has been that he never criticised the system as a whole, or drew the conclusion that seems implicit in his work, namely that the main obstacle to progress is the CCP itself (Duke 1985: 122). Perhaps it is this that diminishes Liu in the eyes of a type of journalist who is sceptical of authority's good intentions or competence.

The journalist as the good official

No less than other countries, China has mythical figures who in some manner express certain values of the culture, and that of Qu Yuan (343–290 BC), the official who stood for service to absolute values at the risk of his own self-interest, is a particularly emotive one. Several journalists mentioned him when they were probed for examples of people to admire. Since there was no guaranteed immunity for this role, the critic's success or even survival depended upon the whim of those in power, who might, or might not, honour the code that justified criticism on the grounds of respect for and obedience to the real interests of the hierarchy, as described in the *Canon of Filial Piety* (Section XV).

When journalists say or suggest that they are standing up for principles, or for the people, this may be the cynosure they have in mind. The implication is that they do see their vocation as a mandarin rather than as the outsider professed by the Anglophone equivalent. In the Anglophone myth, exemplified by the character Gray Grantham in *The Pelican Brief* (1998), the journalist is among others a lone wolf, fighting evil with his conscience alone. The Chinese equivalent is re-establishing authority and orthodoxy. The difference is great.

Conclusion

The Chinese journalist's image of the journalist appears to be made up of a mixture of ideas and myths. There is the discourse of the 'Tintin' journalist, intrepid investigator of rights and wrongs, often regarded as 'American' or 'Anglo-Saxon'. Then there is the ideal of the good public servant who risks his all in his duty to the Chinese state and thereby joins the pantheon of the righteous, with Qu Yuan at the pinnacle. Expressions used by interviewees, regardless of gender, age or seniority, appear to reflect the power of this ideal. Between humdrum daily life and these archetypes are some human-size models, journalists who clearly tried to be faithful to their ideals and suffered for them – Deng Tuo, Liu Binyan, Dai Qing. However, most journalists live in the world as it is constructed for them by their political masters and probably jog along as best they can, accepting the perks of the job, fitting in with the spin doctors and propagandists, ducking the risky opportunities to anger the bosses but still imagining themselves belonging to the congregation of the faithful. This is the only interpretation that seems to fit for a group of people who clearly believe that they are doing what in only quite rare cases they *are* in fact doing. In their practices they may not differ from their contemporaries in the USA or Europe, but their beliefs differ greatly.

This research found that, by and large, the journalists saw themselves as representing the interests of the people, although some also still adhered to the Maoist view of the media as mouthpiece of the Communist Party, without necessarily perceiving any contradiction between the two views.

Representation of the interests of the people was achieved by providing accurate and timely information, by being in touch with people's concerns and by exposing the wrongdoing of officials or exploiters. Journalists were immensely proud of the genre of investigative journalism that has developed over the past few years; although asked to restrict their comments to news,[12] they rarely managed to do so, much preferring to draw attention to such journalism as could be interpreted as reflecting *yulunjiandu*. Insofar as it was possible to judge, concepts of the journalist as 'tribune' drew more upon traditional Chinese myths of the 'hero official' than upon imported ideas of what journalism is about. Although there was pride at the way in which journalism was now able to be more responsive to the needs of the citizenry, rather than only reflective of party orders, there was no sense that journalists saw themselves as fighting to realise a foreign model.

Notes

1 The author wishes to express his appreciation for help received at Fudan, Renmin and Zhejiang Universities, and the Broadcasting Academy, Peking. He is grateful to those who agreed to be interviewed. The field trips were undertaken under the auspices of the Centre for Research into International Communications and Culture of Nottingham Trent University, directed by Professor John Tomlinson.

2 Names cited in Wade–Giles in this chapter, as opposed to Pinyin romanisation, are pseudonyms.

3 The idea that there is such a thing as 'Western' media has been challenged by *inter alios*, Chalaby (1998) and Mancini (2000). What is often called 'Western' in fact means 'Anglophone', if not American (de Burgh 2000). Thus I prefer to use the term 'Anglophone'.

4 *The Canon of Filial Piety* (*lunyu*) is one of the Confucian classics studied by all literate persons until 1911 at least and treated with as much respect as the Holy Bible in Protestant societies. It is a dialogue upon the ethics of human relationships carried on between Confucius and his disciples. A translation is available in the series by Fu Genqing (1993).

5 In these cases, the interviewees' manner was exactly the same as the two journalists from BBC Radio 4's *File on Four*, Heggie and Ross, interviewed elsewhere (de Burgh 2000: 200–2).

6 However, they were maltreated, his house was taken and his possessions were stolen by the chief of police (Cheek 1997: 281).

7 See, for example, *Xinwen Jizhe* ('The Journalist'), August 1984–February 1985.

8 Chin-Chuan Lee, 1 November 2000, London, personal communication following his interview with Hu Jiwei. Lee considered that Hu's call to young journalists to 'make money' and 'work for yourself' was the symptom of a broken heart.

9 When I lived in Hong Kong for short periods in the 1970s and 1980s, I enjoyed reading newspapers and magazines that used Cantonese vocabulary. This was a delight not available to the 100 million-odd Cantonese in the PRC. Although programmes in the other Chinese languages are available on radio and to a lesser extent on cable TV, I understand that no mainstream media reflect spoken languages other than Mandarin.

10 Liu can be disparaged because he lives as a refugee in the USA as much as for the reasons I propose in this chapter. However, from the context of the conversation I believe my reading to be correct.

11 Hu Yaobang was a protégé of Deng Xiaoping, expected to succeed him until 1987, when he was dismissed from his post of CCP General Secretary on account of his failure to suppress the student democracy movement. It was his death in April 1989 that precipitated massive demonstrations, culminating in the Tiananmen Square massacre. He was respected for his frugality, openness and passion.

12 The main study dealt exclusively with news, yet the reporters invariably preferred to talk about other programmes they (might have) worked on.

References

Barmé, G. (1999) *In the Red: On Contemporary Chinese Culture*. New York: Columbia University Press.

Chalaby, J. (1998) *The Invention of Journalism*. Basingstoke: Macmillan.

Chan, J.M. (1994) 'Commercialisation without independence: media development in China', in J. Cheng and M. Brosseau (eds), *China Review 1993*. Hong Kong: Chinese University Press.

Cheek, T. (1997) *Propaganda and Culture in Mao's China: Deng Tuo and the Intelligentsia*. Oxford: Clarendon Press.

Chen Chongshan *et al.* (1998) 'The Chinese journalist', in D.H. Weaver (ed.), *The Global Journalist*. New Jersey: Hampton Press.

Christiansen, F. and Rai, S. (1998) *Chinese Politics and Society: An Introduction*. Singapore: Prentice Hall.

Curran, J. and Park, M.-J. (eds) (2000) *De-Westernising Media Studies*. London: Routledge.

Dai Qing (1999) 'Guiding public opinion', *Media Studies Journal* (winter): 78.

Daruvala, S. (2000) *Zhou Zuoren and an Alternative Chinese Response to Modernity*. Cambridge, Mass.: Harvard University Press.

de Burgh, H. (ed.) (2000) *Investigative Journalism, Context and Practice*. London: Routledge.

de Goldfein, J. (1989) *Personalités Chinoises*, Paris: L'Harmattan.

Duke, M.S. (1985) *Blooming and Contending: Chinese Literature in the Post-Mao Era*. Bloomington: Indiana University Press.

Ekirch, A. (1974) *Progressivism in America: A Study of the Era from Theodore Roosevelt to Woodrow Wilson*. New York: New Viewpoints.

Fitzwalter, R. *et al.* (1981) *Web of Corruption: The Story of John Poulson and T Dan Smith*. St Albans: Granada.

Friedman, E. (1995) *National Identity and Democratic Prospects in Socialist China*. New York: M.E. Sharpe.

Fu Genqing (1993) *Translations of the Confucian Classics*. Jinan: Shandong Friendship Press.

Gold, T.B. (1990) 'The resurgence of civil society in China', *Journal of Democracy* 1(1): 18–31.

Goldman, M. (1994) *Sowing the Seeds of Democracy in China: Political Reform in the Deng Xiaoping Era*. Cambridge, Mass.: Harvard University Press.

Goldman, M., Cheek, T. and Hamrin, C.L. (eds) (1987) *China's Intellectuals and the State: In Search of a New Relationship*. Cambridge, Mass.: Harvard University Press.

Gray, J. (1990) *Rebellions and Revolutions*. Oxford: Oxford University Press.

Hamrin, C.L. and Cheek, T. (1987) *China's Establishment Intellectuals*. New York: Buena Vista.

He Baogang (1997) *The Democratic Implication of Civil Society in China*. Basingstoke: Macmillan.

Huang Chengjiu (2000) 'The development of the semi-independent press in post-Mao China: the future for Chinese journalism as Exemplified in *Chengdu Business News*', *Journalism Studies* 1(4) (November): 649–64.

Judge, J. (1996) *Print and Politics: 'Shibao' and the Culture of Reform in Late Qing China*. Stanford, Calif.: Stanford University Press.

Kedourie, E. and Mango, A. (1988) 'Talking about the BBC', *Encounter* 71 (September/October): 60–4.

Kelly, D. and He Baogang (1992) 'Emergent civil society and the intellectuals in China', in R. Miller (ed.), *The Development of Civil Society in Communist Systems*. Australia: Allen & Unwin.

Lazarsfeld, P.F. and Merton, R.K. (1948) 'Mass communication, popular taste and organised social action', in L. Bryson (ed.), *In the Communication of Ideas*. New York: Cooper Square.

Lee, C.-C. (ed.) (1990) *Voices of China: The Interplay of Politics and Journalism*. New York: Guilford Press.

—— (1994) *China's Media, Media's China*. Boulder, Colo.: Westview Press.

——(2000a) 'Servants of the state or the market? Media and journalists in China', in J. Tunstall (ed.), *Media Occupations*. Oxford: Oxford University Press.

—— (ed.) (2000b) *Power, Money and Media: Communication Patterns and Bureaucratic Control in Cultural China*. Evanston, Ill.: Northwestern University Press.

Lee, C.-C. *et al.* (2000) 'National prisms of a global media event', in J. Curran and M. Gurevitch (eds), *Mass Media and Society* (third edition). London: Edward Arnold.

Levenson, J.R. (1958) *Confucian China and its Modern Fate*. London: Routledge.

Leys, S. (1971) *Les Habits neufs du President Mao*. Paris: Éditions Champ Libre.

Li Lubo (1984) 'Shao's words', *China Daily*, 13 November.

Li Zhurun (1998) 'Popular journalism with Chinese characteristics', *International Journal of Cultural Studies* 1(3) (December): 307–28.

Liu Binyan (1990) *A Higher Kind of Loyalty*. London: Methuen.

Liu Mei Ching (1983) 'Liang Chi-chao and the media', *Gazette* 31: 35–45.

MacFarquhar, R. (1997) *The Politics of China 1949–1989*. Cambridge: Cambridge University Press.

Mancini, P. (2000) 'Political complexity and alternative models of journalism', in J. Curran and M.-J. Park (eds), *De-Westernising Media Studies*. London: Routledge.

Metzger, T. (1977) *Escape from Predicament: Neo-Confucianism and China's Evolving Political Culture*. New York: Cambridge University Press.

Nathan, A.J. (1985) *Chinese Democracy*. Berkeley: University of California Press.

Page, B. (1998) 'A defence of "low" journalism', *British Journalism Review* 9(1): 45–58.

Pei Minxin (2000) 'Rights and resistance: the changing contexts of the dissident movement', in E.J. Perry and M. Selden (eds), *Chinese Society: Change, Conflict and Resistance*. London: Routledge.

Perry, E.J. and Selden, M. (eds) (2000) *Chinese Society: Change, Conflict and Resistance*. London: Routledge.

Pollard, D. (1973) *A Chinese Look at Literature: The Literary Values of Chou Tso-jen in Relation to the Tradition*. London: C. Hurst.

Schneider, L.A. (1980) *A Madman of Ch'u: The Chinese Myth of Loyalty and Dissent*. Berkeley: University of California Press.

Tomlinson, J. (1997) 'And besides, the wench is dead: media scandals and the globalisation of communication', in Lull and Hinermann (eds) *Media Scandals*. Cambridge: Polity Press.

—— (2000) *Globalisation and Culture*. London: Polity Press.

Wakeman, F. (1993) 'The civil society and the public sphere debate: Western reflections on Chinese political culture', *Modern China* 10 (April): 108–38.

Wasserstrom, J. (ed.) (1989) *Popular Protest and Political Culture in Modern China*. Boulder, Colo.: Westview Press.

Wen Diya (1999) 'The Chinese TV revolution: an inside view', paper presented at the First European Symposium on the Chinese Media, February, Nottingham Trent University.

Zhao Yuezhi (1998) *Media, Market and Democracy in China: Between the Party Line and the Bottom Line*. Urbana: University of Illinois Press.

—— (2000) 'Watchdogs on party leashes? Contexts and implications of investigative journalism in Post-Deng China', *Journalism Studies* 1(4) (November): 577–98.

Zhu Jian-hua (1990) '*Information availability, source credibility and audience sophistication: factors conditioning the effects of communist propaganda in China*, doctoral dissertation, School of Journalism, Indiana University, Bloomington.

Part II
Taiwan

6 'As edifying as a bout of mud wrestling'[1]

The 2000 presidential election campaign in Taiwan

Gary D. Rawnsley[2]

Other contributors to this volume have provided a cogent analysis of political communication among and between Chinese communities. Chapters devoted to the Republic of China (ROC) or Taiwan reflect on how the media have communicated the ideas of democracy there and contributed to the successful democratisation of Taiwan's political system since 1986. Free, competitive and all-inclusive elections to high office help to define democracies (Schumpeter 1976) and are the periods in the political calendar when the benefits of communication are most clearly realised.

This chapter analyses the way candidates in elections communicate with the voters, project their image and platforms, and attack those of their opponents. Using the landmark 2000 presidential election as a case study of campaign communication and organisation, the chapter aims to evaluate the idea of a global convergence of practices – 'Americanisation' – that has penetrated discussion of political communication in Greater China. The chapter suggests that Americanisation is a useful way of describing a global trend of professionalisation and modernisation, rather than the deliberate importation of campaign techniques that originated in the United States. Does the professionalisation of campaigns necessarily mean that elections in Taiwan must be 'as edifying as a bout of mud wrestling'?

The 2000 election

During the final days of the 2000 election, Taiwan's English-language press was in no doubt about how the campaign had animated the island's voters:

> Fanatical Taiwan voters and campaigners, stricken with election mania disorders, are packing hospital wards with mental illnesses and physical pains brought on by the uncertain outcome of Saturday's presidential election. In the past two weeks, there has been a 10 to 15 percent increase in the number of patients diagnosed as having psychiatric disorders linked to the election .... Passionate advocates of the leading ... hopefuls are suffering from mania, depression, anxiety and panic attacks .... One patient diagnosed ... talked incessantly about the poll

and spent most of his time on campaign activities, surviving on less than two hours of sleep each day. When his family brought him in, the first thing he asked me was 'who will you vote for?' before he started handing out campaign literature.

(Taipei Times, 16 March 2000)

Citing a rise in the number of psychological disorders in the run-up to tomorrow's election, physicians warned members of the public to be on the lookout for symptoms of 'election syndrome'. Psychiatrist Chen Kuo-hua ... said yesterday that over the past month, his department has treated 20 to 30 percent more patients than average for symptoms such as anxiety and insomnia. Some of the patients were wearing campaign uniforms when they came to receive treatment, and some even continued campaigning for their favourite candidates after arriving at the hospital .... Officials at Taipei Medical College Hospital have publicised a case of physical injury they said had resulted from a scuffle over voting preferences ... their scuffle continued in the emergency ward .... Physicians have also voiced their concern over how well fanatical supporters of defeated candidates will adapt after the vote count is completed.

(Taipei Times, 17 March 2000)

It is not surprising that the 2000 direct presidential election campaign, only the second in Chinese history, should so capture the imagination of voters throughout Taiwan. This had been a long and tiring campaign for candidate and voter alike; while speculation of possible participants began soon after Chen Shui-bian's defeat in the December 1998 mayoral election (Rawnsley 2000), the campaign stretched through the summer, autumn and winter of 1999 and into the spring of 2000. Why did this election generate so much excitement? The first reason is that the incumbent was not running for office; President Lee Teng-hui would step aside however the electorate decided to cast their votes. Lien Chan, the Kuomintang's (KMT) candidate, had served Lee as vice-president, but enjoyed few powers, a low approval rating and a reputation for being far from charismatic. The Democratic Progressive Party (DPP) had changed its internal rules to allow Chen Shui-bian, defeated in the 1998 Taipei mayoral election, to run for office, provoking a split within the party that culminated in veteran activist Hsu Hsin-liang deciding to run as an independent candidate. The KMT too was scarred by division, as the former governor of Taiwan province, Soong Chu-yu played a 'will he? won't he?' game with the party and the media over whether he would, after all, run for office as an independent and thus risk the wrath of his party organisation. With Li Ao, scholar, self-publicist, author and litigant extraordinaire running for the New Party (but endorsing few of its policies), the personalities were in place for an electrifying contest.

The peaceful transfer of presidential power to the DPP was a moment of historical significance for Taiwan: not only did the election bring to a close fifty years of government by the nationalist KMT, but it also demonstrated that Taiwan had finally entered the 'consolidation' phase of democratisation (Diamond *et al.* 1997; Huntington 1991; O'Donnell *et al.* 1986). Electoral competition has opened the political process to previously marginalised political actors and has fostered the development of genuine multi-party politics. Equally significantly, constitutional reforms in 1994 had decreed that the national constituency should elect the president of the ROC, Taiwan's only nationally elected official, by direct vote.[3]

Democratisation and constitutional reform[4] have coincided with two other decisive processes that have transformed the campaign culture and sharpened electoral competition: liberalisation of the media has created new public spheres that allow for greater (although still less than ideal) scrutiny and accountability of politics. Taiwan boasts over 300 daily newspapers – one for every four citizens. Meanwhile, there are five network television channels and hundreds of cable channels that broadcast programming from the neighbourhood and the other side of the world to over 80 percent of homes in Taiwan (Rawnsley and Rawnsley 1998, 2001). Moreover, the information revolution and the growing popularity of computer-based communications have allowed candidates to explore innovative campaign techniques that have brought to the surface new forms and methods of interaction between politicians and voters (Glass 1996: 140–6). All the candidates in the 2000 election had websites devoted to them and their platforms. Chen Shui-bian invited 'surfers' to 'e-mail me … and tell me who should be in my Cabinet'. His website included a comprehensive biography of the candidate, a list of his most notable political achievements, photographs and regular progress reports on the campaign, all in simplified and complex Chinese characters and in English. Supporters could even donate funds to Chen's campaign over the Internet (*Taipei Times*, 22 December 1999). In short, candidates and campaign managers in Taiwan had ascertained the importance of embracing this technology in reaching voters and thus corresponding to evidence of a global trend in the use of the Internet for political communications (Norris 2001).[5]

On their own, democratisation, media liberalisation and the information revolution have a limited impact; together, they have the power to change the electoral landscape beyond recognition. Many of these changes suggest that campaigns are moving closer towards resembling American elections. In particular, the growing importance of the image of candidates is identified as a main characteristic of modern election campaigns.

Other features of American campaigns are management by small personally appointed teams of party workers with wide experience of running media-centred and candidate-oriented election campaigns; a concern with securing positive media coverage; extensive use of merchandise to reinforce 'brand name'; the placement of (usually negative) advertisements in newspa-

Plate 1   Kuomintang poster, 1996 presidential election, Taipei
Source: photo taken by Gary Rawnsley

pers and on television; in-house tracking and commissioning of opinion polls (Ger 2001); and the introduction of mechanisms to incorporate poll findings into campaigns.

We can find all of these features – and many more – in Taiwan. For example, image was a popular theme that was explored by both candidates and the media. In the 2000 election, the media repeatedly rounded on Lien Chan's lack of charisma. Wang Chien-chuang of *The Journalist* magazine wrote the following indictment of the vice-president:

> Unfortunately, Lien … does not have the genetic makeup for popular moves. He does not sound humorous when he tells a joke. He does not sound mean when he condemns others. He sounds awkward when he tries to sell himself. He is like a poker player who can screw up a great hand [incumbency].
>
> (*Taipei Times*, 19 January 2000)

In turn, the media failed to devote equal attention to Li Ao and Hsu Hsin-liang, describing them as 'minor players' in a three-horse race (*Taipei Times*, 5 March 2000). None of the candidates had to devote resources to estab-lishing a brand name in order to manufacture familiarity – in contrast to American presidential elections, where the opponent tends to be relatively unknown outside their own state (Kennedy in 1960; Clinton in 1992; Bush in

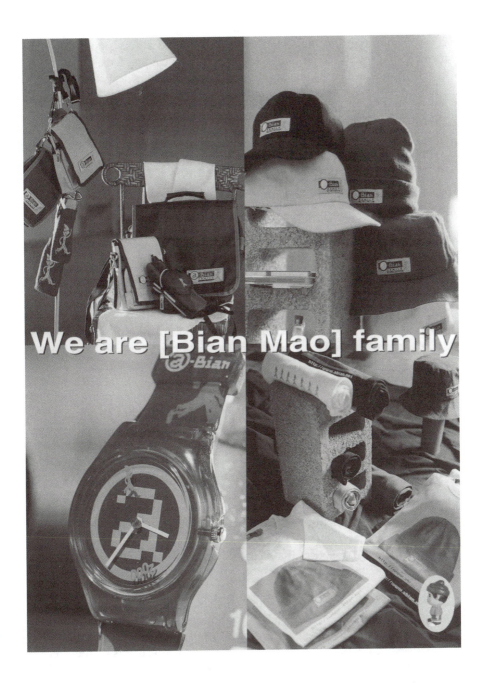

Plate 2 'Bian Mao' merchandise for sale in Taiwan during the 2000 presidential election

Source: *Bian Mao Product Autumn Catalogue*

2000) – although the 'Bian Mao' factory produced a very popular line in merchandise for the Chen Shui-bian campaign, including hats, coffee mugs and key rings, which helped to popularise the candidate, especially among younger voters, who were attracted to the image such merchandise portrayed. The Bian Mao phenomenon demonstrates that candidates in Taiwan are not above being packaged (Franklin 1994) and commodified in ways that are familiar to voters in other parts of the world.[6]

Polls too played their part. Throughout the campaign voters were pressed to reveal who they intended to vote for and who they thought would win (often the same respondent gave different answers to both questions). The opinion polls were then scrutinised by the media, ever anxious to present the campaign as a race: who's in front? Who's getting left behind? Who will fall at the first hurdle? More importantly, the polls were pored over by the candidates themselves, fully aware that they must respond to poor findings by changing the tone of their campaign or focus on different issues. The DPP has been particularly successful in this endeavour, with its own survey centre polling registered voters (and not just during election campaigns) to find out how they respond to particular issues, themes and images. Shelley Rigger (2001: 81–3) has done most to reveal the workings of the survey centre. She discovered that it conducts research in 'Party support rates and party image. Satisfaction ratings for DPP officials .... Issue preferences. Targeted surveys of social groups .... Election-related surveys' (*ibid.*: 82). The results are intended only for party workers. That they are not revealed to the press or the public suggests the importance that the DPP attaches to scrutinising public opinion when structuring the party platform and organising election campaigns.

In fact, what is happening in Taiwan – and everywhere that observers find supposed evidence of 'Americanisation' – is a global convergence of electoral practices. However, we should be careful to avoid the temptation to identify our pet variables – how do we define Americanisation? – and then make observations of the suspected indicators to suggest or prove the existence of American influence. Rather, Americanisation is a useful description of a specific set of practices that become appropriated and often indigenised by assorted political systems in response to two key factors:

1   *Political changes*: constitutional provisions that allow for the direct popular election of the head of state necessarily encourage candidate-centred campaigns. For example, the 'Élysée effect' describes the consequences of changing the institutional arrangements of the French political system, namely the introduction in 1958 of popular direct elections for the president. It implies candidate-centred politics in a national constituency, a development that critics lament for the inevitable refocus of attention towards image at the expense of policy (Charlot and Charlot 1992). But not even the most carefully designed marketing strategy can sell a defective product. As secretary-general of Taiwan's

New Party, Jaw Shaw-kong gathered his candidates together to watch video footage of American political advertisements, advising them that the party should model their election campaigns on the American experience.[7] From the perspective of comparative politics, this identifies and corresponds to a wider trend that suggests political actors are looking to alternative models of election campaigning, and that this alternative may be found in the United States. But these trends were unable to circumvent the institutional frailty of the New Party. The early electoral successes of the party seemed to confirm that 'a model of "tripartite politics" had taken root' in Taiwan, especially after its candidate in the 1994 Taipei mayoral election pushed the KMT into third place (*Free China Journal*, 9 December 1994). Where is the New Party today? Since 1997, the party's influence has declined at a dramatic rate, due primarily to the absence of a clear political programme that can mobilise both members and voters. Its support was limited to disenchanted mainlanders, its development of policy was weak, and its organisation was tarnished by infighting. Its declining credibility was suggested by its failure to nominate a plausible candidate for the 2000 election, choosing instead the vocal cultural critic Li Ao, who never failed to deliver his criticisms of the party and urged his supporters to vote for the maverick KMT heavyweight turned independent Soong Chu-yu. The rise and fall of the New Party demonstrates that campaigning cannot compensate for unpopular or unworkable platforms and an unmanageable party machinery.[8]

2 *Changes in communications technology*: David Butler and Austin Ranney acknowledged this in their 1992 study of election campaigning from a comparative perspective: 'It is the practices of politicians and the media, exploiting technical innovations and marketing approaches, that have altered the appearance of elections' (p. 4). The so-called 'information revolution' provides the most instructive test of how applicable this summation is: because candidates in America and Taiwan use the Internet as a campaign tool, does this mean that Taiwan has copied the United States, or might it suggest that candidates and campaign managers in Taiwan are able to ascertain for themselves the importance of embracing this technology?

In short, we will only understand election campaigns in Taiwan and elsewhere when we realise that we are not observing the deliberate importation of American election techniques by political societies that will then become cultural duplicates of the United States. Instead, Americanisation is a 'useful shorthand' (Scammel 1997) to describe an identifiable global trend towards the modernisation and professionalisation of politics and election campaigns.

A theory of Americanisation that proposes the deliberate importation of styles and approaches has tremendous difficulty in appreciating cross-pollination of ideas and influences, which stretches beyond the oversimplified idea of 'exporting' American ideas and influences around the world:[9] Britain's Conservative Party advising the George Bush election campaigns of 1988 and 1992; the exchange of wisdom between the British Labour Party and the US Democratic Party, which transported the 'special relationship' to a new level during the period of the Clinton–Blair administrations; the flow of ideas between Australia and New Zealand; Margaret Thatcher's advisers instructing Chile's General Pinochet on how to structure a winning campaign in that country's landmark 1988 plebiscite; French political consultant Jacques Seguela advising many states in Eastern Europe; and Saatchi and Saatchi advising anyone and everyone from Boris Yeltsin in Russia to Ernesto Pérez Balladares in Panama, stopping on the way to manage one of the campaigns in Poland's first post-communist election (Negrine 1996; Plasser 2000). The problems that are inherent in the apparent existence of a unidirectional flow of campaign influence mirror the flaws in the idea of 'cultural imperialism' that dominated media studies discourse in the late 1960s and 1970s (Rawnsley and Rawnsley 2001). Like its one-time fashionable predecessor, the suggestion of importation lacks credibility in a world where information flows are multidirectional and cultures are increasingly hybridised (Giddens 1991; Sreberny-Mohammadi, 1996). Indeed, it is no longer possible to speak of the dominant influences of either globalism or localism; instead the awkward term 'glocalism', devised as a way of describing the growing economic interdependence of the Asia–Pacific region, but also now applied to cultural flows and identity issues, seems to offer a more empirically coherent approach to election campaigns (Tu 1996). This has the greatest relevance to the area rapidly becoming known as Greater China, where the cultural similarities of people are as powerful as the political differences that separate them. The place of Greater China in the modern world demonstrates that globalisation and flows of communication, information and culture need not be a threat: identities and cultures do not replace one another, and a close study of Taiwan's election culture discredits the force of Herbert Schiller's argument that what is at stake 'is the cultural integrity of weak societies whose national, regional, local or tribal heritages are beginning to be menaced with extinction by the expansion of modern electronic communications' (Schiller 1969: 109). Rather, we can observe the rise of regional flows of ideas, information and influences, in Greater China and elsewhere, which then become indigenised so that the original source is disguised, in fact irrelevant.[10]

Taiwan's election culture has not changed beyond recognition. The defining characteristics of the pre-democratisation campaign environment have survived the transition process, and anyone who has the good fortune to observe an election campaign in Taiwan will be struck by the excitement, the noise, and the obvious enthusiasm of the participants. The quotations from the press reports that begin this chapter provide vivid testimony to such exhilaration. Boisterous rallies continue to be the preferred method of mobilising supporters; sound trucks patrol the streets of every major town urging voters to cast their ballot for their favoured candidate; every street is adorned in campaign leaflets and flags in the colours of the main parties and bearing the name of the candidate or his/her candidate number. Candidates who cannot afford to engage in such merchandising or refuse to do so on principle take a severe beating at the polls. In 2000, Hsu Hsin-liang declined to participate in a campaign that centred on gimmicks and merchandise, deciding instead to fight a clean election on the issues. For his decision, he was denied the intensive media coverage that seeks out the dramatic and the exciting campaign over the kind of dull electioneering that does not make good television. In other words, we could argue that Hsu was penalised for being a serious candidate.

However, we can also find examples where the traditional style of election campaigning is sharpened by developments in campaign structure and the use of modern communications technology. Thus rallies may still dominate the campaign calendar, but their televising projects a national image of strength and unity, allowing candidates to reach beyond the core supporters who attend such events. The Internet allows for a more personalised and intimate form of campaigning and provides opportunities for voters to e-mail the candidates with questions and comments. Again, campaigns are concerned with maximising feedback from the voters, hence 'closing the loop'.

Moreover, election campaigns use pre-existing structures of communication, socialisation and mobilisation that define the community, usually through strong personal networks and relationships. In Taiwan, politicians often attend religious and civil ceremonies, such as weddings and funerals, to strengthen their grass-roots relationship with voters. The success of former KMT heavyweight Soong Chu-yu in the 2000 presidential election was based partly on the local support he had cultivated as Taiwan's extremely popular and hard-working last provincial governor. His frequent visits to all townships and villages helped him to strengthen his personal connections with local leaders. This enabled Soong to finish the election only 3 percentage points behind Chen Shui-bian, seizing from the victor many voters who might be considered core DPP supporters (for example, Hakka minority voters). Thus we are encouraged to analyse the methods of mobilisation that occur away from the media spotlight, such as the importance of courting local factions, and *zhuangjiao*, who can deliver a specific number of votes in return for particular rewards.

However, although candidates must still canvass votes by meeting the electorate in person, this is no longer an intimate appeal for support; candidates are now shadowed by growing numbers of television crews and reporters that have been assigned to cover the activities of a particular ticket. The personal approach to campaigning is appropriate and expected, but the media magnifies its significance.

By a close comparison of the KMT's and the DPP's organisation in several key elections since 1986 it is possible to evaluate the design of the campaign as a means towards affecting voter behaviour and thus the result of the election. For example, one can assess whether the organisation is sufficiently competent and resourceful that it is able to coordinate often nebulous activities into a clearly defined strategy. The purpose of a modern campaign is to sell the client, the candidate standing for election. Behind the client stand a variety of often shadowy individuals from a number of backgrounds inside and outside the party. Each has a specific job to do, and each is a link in a different chain of accountability. Some will be party workers or volunteers, responsible only to the party hierarchy. Others may be hired from outside the party structure, such as advertising agencies and public relations consultants. In theory, success depends on unity, consistency of approach, a clear demarcation of responsibility and a discrete chain of command. However, as the Taiwan example demonstrates, the existence of such a structure can often be for the sake of appearance only. The DPP suffered in the 1996 contest because of acute and bitter differences between the party apparatus and the campaign management. In the 2000 presidential election, the lack of centralised campaign management damaged the KMT's potential.

Such deliberate organisation implies professionalism, and the greater the degree of professional competence the more chance there is of winning the election. A professional campaign seeks the same objectives as any other: to manage and monitor campaigns (their own and their rivals') and respond as quickly as possible to negative attacks and negative news coverage; to track public opinion; to commission their own polls and adjust the strategies of their campaigns accordingly; and to seek ever more sophisticated methods of guaranteeing favourable publicity, controlling the news agenda and thereby controlling the campaign. In a landmark study, Philippe Marrek has referred to these developments as evidence of 'political marketing', by which he means 'a strategy of design, rationalization and conveyance of modern political communication'. He states that this 'no longer means merely designing and printing a message on posters without consideration of to whom they are addressed. It encompasses the entire marketing process, from preliminary market study to testing and targeting' (Marrek 1995: 2–28).

As the Taiwan example demonstrates, candidates are often at the mercy of external forces, changing circumstances and the unpredictable actions of participants. Above all, they are constrained by the their very institutional frameworks and world views. Taiwan's main political parties, the KMT and the DPP, exhibit all the characteristics of 'institutions': their 'historical roots' have 'created a strong sense of path dependence in their behaviour, with connections with the past and familiar political symbols being important' for both (Peters 1999: 114). As the following analysis of its election campaign organisation demonstrates, the KMT has been concerned with promoting past victories, its record of providing stability and nurturing economic growth, and as the natural party of government. On the other hand, the campaigns of the DPP have, prior to 2000, turned on the symbolism associated with past political oppression and the struggle for democracy. In short, the narrative reveals that the electoral prospects of both parties have been damaged by their institutional path dependency. Survival is contingent on the parties maintaining their institutional structures in response to sudden systemic changes (Ponebianco 1988). Such changes in Taiwan include democratisation, the introduction of executive-level elections and the declining salience of formerly decisive issues such as identity and unification with China versus Taiwanese independence.

The KMT

Taiwan's political parties have so far resisted hiring the services of professional consultants or public relations specialists to design and manage campaigns on their behalf.[11] The parties themselves and their vote-brokers – the *zhuangjiao* (KMT) and 'third tier' (DPP)[12] – remain the focus for grassroots mobilisation and volunteer work despite the continuing importance of candidate-centred politics in a multi-party political system.[13] The campaigns themselves are managed by prominent officials within the parties. Yet the absence of hired political consultants has not prevented election campaigns from demonstrating a remarkable degree of sophistication that would not be out of place in an American presidential election. Consider for example the KMT's elaborate approach to the regional/city elections of December 1989, when the party divided Taiwan into what Chao and Myers (1998: 165–6) have called 'election combat zones'. These were 'areas where [the KMT] had lost a race for a county magistrate or city mayor and where more resources were needed to recover those seats; areas in which the KMT encountered strong DPP opposition but had a two-out-of-three chance to win; and areas where KMT surveys showed its popularity to be strong'.

This was a significant development. The KMT reorganised the party machinery around the need to fight key constituencies, and it was beginning to integrate surveys and opinion polls into its decision-making strategy. It was especially important to design particular messages for specific geographic and demographic groups, as polls indicated a rise in the proportion of voters who could not decide which candidate to support. Chao and Myers thus present an electrifying appraisal of the campaign:

> Because of its great importance, this election quickly took on the character of a small war. Party candidates mapped their campaigns like battlefield manoeuvres; they mobilised their forces, devised their tactics, and attacked their enemies to snatch the spoils of war.
>
> (*ibid.*: 164)

The problem is that the KMT had failed to modify its image, the message and its means of delivery to reflect subsequent transformations in Taiwan's political and social systems. It took the mammoth defeat in the 2000 election to shock the KMT from its complacency and finally appreciate how distant from the electorate it had grown. In the 1980 election of delegates to the National Assembly, Legislative and Control Yuans, the KMT 'claimed to represent policies of successful economic growth; material benefits; and a safe, secure and peaceful society' (Copper 1997: 193). In the December 1986 elections for the Legislative Yuan and the National Assembly, 'the KMT candidates emphasised the themes of harmony, order and stability in society, and ran on their party's performance in developing Taiwan's economy' (Domes 1999: 51). In 1991, one KMT television advertisement was described in the following way:

> Viewers see the TV screen filled with dramatic scenes of suffering, civil war and chaos in developing countries such as Haiti, Yugoslavia, Sri Lanka, the Philippines, and Vietnam. The videos play vividly upon these emotional images as a way to attest to the stability maintained in Taiwan under the KMT's rule.

Referring to this advertisement, Alan Wachman (1994: 208) concludes that the 'message was clear: a vote for the KMT was a vote for "reform, stability, [and] prosperity", but a vote for the DPP was a vote for independence'. Such themes were entirely rational during a particular time in Taiwan's political history: the Cold War, the genuine threat of military confrontation with Beijing, the often violent character of the opposition movement, and the disturbing international isolation of Taiwan, all made the KMT's record on prosperity and stability very attractive to voters (Hsu 1991: 18). In 2000, the employment of such themes and imagery was still rational, given that opinion polls suggested the popularity of the DPP's Chen Shui-bian (who had openly advocated Taiwanese independence in the past, and thus represented the possibility of military conflict with the PRC). Hence the KMT decided it was appropriate to campaign again on the platform that their candidate, Lien Chan, was 'the best choice to ensure Taiwan's safety, security and future reforms' (*Taipei Times*, 18 March 2000). Moreover, in an interview with the *Washington Post* (12 February 2000) Lien described how Taiwan risked 'domestic disturbances and foreign invasion' and 'immediate danger' if he was not elected (carried in *Taipei Times*, 2 March 2000). He appealed for the vote of Taiwan's business community, claiming that the KMT was the 'most reliable' party to guarantee stability (*Taipei Times*, 19 January 2000); and only the KMT could manage relations with Beijing (see, for example, *Taipei Times*, 10 March 2000). The KMT's campaign slogan – 'With hearts and hands joined together, Taiwan will fly' – was reinforced by the symbol of a butterfly, representing, we were told, 'the constancy of the KMT's care for the people and its resolve to establish a prosperous Taiwan into the twenty-first century' (*Taipei Times*, 24 November 1999).[14]

The problem with the KMT's strategy was that its organisation failed to realise how such themes no longer resonate with a large proportion of Taiwan's electorate, especially the strategically important voters aged between 20 and 35, who would decide this election.[15] The KMT could not even depend on the usually loyal military veterans, since they were now attracted to Soong Chu-yu (prompting a rash of KMT-sponsored newspaper advertisements urging veterans to 'dump' Soong to defeat Chen). Since 1986, the party had not made any serious attempt to respond to public opinion by changing its platform or image, a serious indictment against an incumbent institution struggling to retain its authority in a multi-party democracy. A greater familiarity with, and commitment to, democratic procedure, along with institutional and constitutional changes and a liberalised media, all meant that the political process became increasingly transparent. In this new environment, the concerns of public opinion shifted from the ubiquitous issues of relations with Beijing and national security towards a more focused domestic political agenda. Greater transparency, democratisation and serious splits inside the party exposed problems in the KMT's organisation and government and created channels whereby those problems became the focus of popular scrutiny and challenge. Hence political corruption, associated most clearly with the KMT, surfaced as a dominant issue in the 2000 election. (DPP-commissioned polls discovered that corruption was a major concern of voters; see Ger 2001: 8.) The attitudinal changes were summarised in the key television advertisement of Chen's campaign, described by one newspaper as the 'soft sell' (*Taipei Times*, 4 March 2000). Following personal endorsements of Chen by his school friends, teachers and an assortment of relations, all of whom expressed their confidence that Chen would protect Taiwan's security and maintain peace, the candidate then rounded on the negative message of his opponent: 'Some have ... tried to frighten our children by talking about declarations of war. Our responsibility is to protect them, not to join those bullies'.

Why did the KMT fail to recognise shifts in public opinion about particular issues? This is partly answered with reference to institutional weaknesses, in particular the fundamental paradox that the KMT relied on political corruption – the main issue in the 2000 election – to buy local support from *zhuangjiao*. The KMT recognised that corruption is an issue upon which they are particularly vulnerable, but abandoning its practice would mean cutting itself from its most important base of support.

Another explanation for the KMT's failure to adapt to public opinion is rooted in institutional weaknesses, in particular the internal organisation of the KMT's campaign and the limits to what the structure of the campaign could achieve. For example, the party named former foreign minister Dr Jason Hu as campaign manager, but this was merely a titular position. The manager was granted insufficient freedom in designing and running the campaign and in reality was little more than a symbol of responsibility. He was accountable to politicians higher in the party, who resisted advice from the appointed campaign manager and his team. Furthermore, a centralised campaign was impossible because the KMT depended on informal institutions – factions and vote-brokers – to mobilise supporters and deliver votes.

It was therefore important, although difficult, to reconcile and satisfy all the disparate interests. This was a serious problem for the KMT in the 2000 election, when many advertisements were produced for broadcast on television and publication in newspapers by over-eager supporters without the endorsement or even knowledge of the campaign manager. Defeat taught the KMT that it can no longer organise campaigns in executive elections in the same way that it could for local elections, where the single non-transferable vote (SNTV) system defined party structure; and it cannot depend on local mobilisation. The mobilisation of local factions and vote buying make little sense in national elections. Factional power is structured around connections to local politicians. In a national election with just five candidates, the main incentive to engage in local mobilisation is lost. The KMT also learned that it can no longer guarantee success through negative campaigning against opponents that emphasises Taiwan's security through KMT incumbency.[16]

Dangwai/DPP

Until Chen Shui-bian's victory in 2000, the opposition's success in election campaigns was also inhibited by institutional problems. The political and legal restrictions that prevented the *dangwai* (meaning 'outside the party', *dangwai* being the term used to describe the loose coalition of opposition interests that struggled against the KMT before the DPP was legalised) launching a concerted electoral challenge to the KMT during its authoritarian administration of Taiwan are well documented (Copper 1997; Rawnsley and Rawnsley 2001; Rigger 1999, 2001; Tien 1989). Less well analysed are the campaign strategies employed by the *dangwai* to overcome the natural advantages of the KMT (especially its financial resources, a strong base of organisation and mobilisation at the local level, and the advantages associated with incumbency). Because legal restrictions prevented the *dangwai* becoming a political party, it was unable to create a single organisational structure that would centralise its campaign coordination and help to disseminate a unified message throughout the island. Moreover, the *dangwai* were denied access to the mass media by control of, or influence over, newspapers and television by the KMT, the government and the military, or by private enterprises with close corporate links to the KMT (Rawnsley and Rawnsley 2001).

Once the *dangwai* movement had transformed into the DPP and had been (unofficially) allowed to campaign against the KMT in the 1986 legislative elections, it faced the challenge of how to circumvent its *dangwai* heritage (the party was viewed with suspicion by a large proportion of the electorate, who associated it with radical politics and platforms and the sometimes violent methods of *dangwai* street protest) and unite a party of factions that shared an aversion to the KMT's management of Taiwan but were divided on the issues of independence, constitutional reform and the means to further democracy. These disagreements have infused election campaign strategy throughout the DPP's brief life. The party's losses in the 1991 National Assembly election, the 1996 presidential election[17] and the 1998 mayoral election in Taipei can be explained by the insistence of prominent senior members of the party who were responsible for the DPP's campaign that it should focus on those issues that highlight social divisions, especially independence. In contrast, the DPP crafted a platform of public policy issues in the 1992 legislative election – the economy, social welfare, housing and public transport – and the party's share of the vote increased by 36.22 percent.

Ultimate authority for the 1996 and 1998 campaigns rested with veterans of the *dangwai* political movement, who controlled the campaign and were determined to run on the traditional platform. This was against the wishes of the central party organisation, especially the party chairmen, Hsu Hsin-liang and Shih Ming-teh, who wanted to avoid the divisive issue of independence at all costs. In this way, the DPP's campaigns have lacked unity and coherence and have instead been characterised by a damaging difference of opinion on policy between the party centre and the campaign managers.[18]

In 2000, the party calculated that for the first time there was a strong possibility that the DPP might wrest control of the presidency from the KMT. It therefore paid greater attention to constructing a modern campaign strategy that would compete with the organisational machinery of the KMT. The campaign was managed by the mayor of Kaohsiung, Hsieh Chang-ting, who had served as Peng Ming-min's vice-presidential candidate in 1996. Hsieh was assisted by Luo Wen-chia, who had been the director of strategy and planning in Chen Shui-bian's election campaign for mayor of Taipei in 1994. Luo represents a new generation of young media-aware activists who first gained political experience when they mobilised as students in the 1980s. This generation is not constrained by the institutional legacy of the DPP; they are not convinced that the *dangwai* platform of democracy and independence is as relevant today as it was twenty years ago. Instead, they are more concerned with transforming the party into an election-fighting and election-winning machine. This is most telling in changing attitudes towards independence, which, as we have seen, was one reason the DPP fared so badly in the 1996 election. The DPP secretary-general, Chiou I-jen, said after the election: 'Having realised the independence issue was Chen's biggest weakness, we tried to keep Chen's stance on the issue as vague as possible' (*Taipei Times*, 15 April 2000).

Working alongside a team from Fantasy Creative Company, a commercial advertising agency, they designed a strategy based on modern marketing techniques. Luo Wen-chia and Jerry Fan, the head of Fantasy, both claimed in separate interviews with the author that they found inspiration for the campaign in their own experience, by the tangible prospect that power might be transferred from the KMT, and by the redundant image of the KMT and its contrast to the youthful and dynamic image of change represented by Chen Shui-bian. Hence the campaign slogan, 'A young Taiwan, a new government with vitality' (*Taipei Times*, 26 August 1999). Most importantly, Chen Shui-bian's team had learned in 1998 the limits of what they could achieve on their own; after the complacency of their success in 1994, Chen's personally appointed team of young campaign managers had tried to run the 1998 election with little reference to the DPP machinery. The *Free China Journal* (20 November 1998) reported the techniques they were using:

> The DPP has tapped into all possible resources for promoting its candidates to Taiwan's voters, wherever they may be. The party's campaign advertisements are appearing on the Internet, on commercial television and on TV walls at train stations. They are also being shown during previews at local cinemas.

But such advertising could not prevent the KMT's Ma Ying-jeou wresting control of Taipei for his party. The loss in 1998 taught Chen's young team the importance of integrating the party organisation with the modern and innovative marketing techniques that they had applied to campaigning.[19] So the DPP was determined that the rifts of the 1996 presidential campaign would not reappear in 2000. Hence the division between party and campaign was blurred, with prominent party officials playing key roles in the campaign. For example, the DPP's secretary-general, Chiou I-jen, and its chairman, Lin Yi-hsiung, were both crucial in local mobilisation and in lending the highly factional basis of the party a sense of unity. This harmony between the party and the campaign structures was crucial to Chen's election to the presidency.

Conclusion

For the majority of citizens, regular voting provides their only opportunity to participate in the political process, and Taiwan's consistently high turnout rates suggest a strong and encouraging popular commitment to democracy.[20] Campaigns are therefore important in assessing the legitimacy of elections, first and foremost based on the liberties required to contest an election in a free and fair manner. One only needs to analyse the criticisms of the 2002 election in Zimbabwe to understand that casting a vote is not the defining feature of democracy; it is represented above all by the competition to persuade voters to cast their ballot in a particular way. This is why understanding the process of election campaigns is just as important as the result in assessing the legitimacy of the contest. Moreover, if votes are meaningful they should be based on knowledge about the candidates and their platforms. In an ideal Downsian universe, the candidates would provide full and perfect information about themselves, and voters would make their choice based on rational deliberation of that information.[21]

Unfortunately, we must settle for a less perfect society, where we rely more on the media to scrutinise the contestants and their platforms on our behalf. This implies that votes are rarely cast after judicious reflection. After all, campaigns alone do not explain voter behaviour. In Taiwan, one can identify clear structural and institutional reasons – the consequences of democratisation (leading to party competition and executive elections), the logic of the SNTV electoral system in local elections (encouraging intra-party competition and thus forcing the voters to find ways to differentiate between candidates from the same party),[22] the power of patron–client relations and factions (rational, self-interest politics of advancement, the *zhuangjiao*). Party identification is weak (Hsu 1991: 39), and split-ticket voting is common.[23] Socialisation through primary groups – family, social and professional associations – although no longer as strong as in the past, is nevertheless a compelling influence on some demographic sections of the electorate (the rural and less educated).[24] Meanwhile, the rise of the 'permanent campaign' means that voters are presented with images and issues between elections through a media determined to frame the political process in terms of the next crucial ballot. There is also a broad consensus that campaigns merely reinforce voting behaviour and that their real value lies in mobilising existing and/or potential supporters rather than converting the opposition. This has been the central purpose of campaigns in Taiwan, especially at the local level, although the 2000 presidential election with its surprising defections from one candidate to another (the loss of core DPP votes to the independent candidate Soong Chu-yu) suggests that this can no longer be guaranteed.

So an understanding of election campaigning in Taiwan requires observers to focus on the interaction of the formal and informal institutions with each other and with structural changes, such as changes to the political system brought about by democratisation and liberalisation. Taiwan's election culture has not changed beyond recognition, and the defining characteristics of the pre-democratisation campaign environment have survived the transition process. Election campaigns throughout Asia are no longer defined solely by methods of mobilisation that are culturally unique. But neither are they characterised by the simple importation of techniques from the United States or any other political system. Rather, the example of elections in Taiwan allows us to understand campaigning as a process of hybridisation that allows formal institutions and traditional methods to absorb, and coexist with, new and streamlined techniques of delivering the desired message. In this way, the excitement of election campaigns will never abate.

Notes

1 This description of the campaigns in Taiwan's presidential election (2000) is quoted in the *Taipei Times*, 4 Feb 2000.
2 I would like to thank the following for funding my research in Taiwan: the University of Nottingham, the EU–China Academic Network, and the Nuffield

Foundation. I also acknowledge the Graduate Institute of Political Science at National Sun Yat-sen University, Kaohsiung, where I was a visiting scholar, May–September 2000. I am grateful to colleagues at the University of Nottingham for their comments on earlier drafts of this paper, including graduate students Siobhan Daly and Andrew Robinson. My good friend Neil Renwick from Nottingham Trent University as ever provided valuable feedback in response to early drafts.

3 Previously, the president was elected indirectly by the National Assembly. A useful analysis of the constitutional reforms of the 1990s is provided in Wu (2000).

4 A (less that comprehensive) list of important reforms that facilitated the development of competitive politics would include the abolition of the state of emergency in 1987, the lifting of most restrictions on the media in 1988, the formal legalisation of new parties in 1989; the creation of the Central Election Commission in 1989; the 1991 decision to allow all parties that met a minimal requirement to broadcast television advertisements; the decision by the Judicial Yuan that all parliamentarians elected by mainland constituencies had to retire by 31 December 1991; the legalisation of CATV (community antenna television, also known in Taiwan as cable television) in 1993; the National Assembly's 1994 amendment to the constitution, allowing for the direct popular election of the president and vice-president (the Election and Recall Law, 1995).

5 Even in the USA, the use of the Internet is shadowed by dependence on more 'traditional' methods: in the 2000 US presidential election, the Internet was 'at the heart of both parties' organisational efforts, but the main way to reach voters on polling day remains the telephone .... The telephone appeal [is] the most effective of all last-minute campaign weapons for both parties' ('The fight for the ear of the voter', *The Guardian*, 7 November 2000, p. 3).

6 Rigger (2001: 189–91) provides a brief history and analysis of the Bian Mao phenomenon.

7 Interviews with New Party sources, Taipei, August 2000.

8 It is noteworthy that over half of the political consultants recently surveyed in the United States believed that it is difficult to sell a 'mediocre candidate' or unpopular platforms to the electorate. They believe that substance is still important (Thurber *et al.* 2000).

9 See Bowler and Farrell (2000). They structure a significant proportion of their chapter around the use of American political consultants abroad. It is interesting that the only Asian country that materialises in their table of 'Variations in election campaign "environments" in thirty-two countries' (pp. 160–1) is Japan. To their credit, however, Table 9.2, 'Survey respondents and the location of their overseas work' (p. 164), does provide basic evidence that a process of cross-pollination is taking place and that not all influences on election campaigns are American in origin.

10 Straubhaar (1997) has discussed at length the regionalisation of television flows based on distribution. See also Sreberny (2000) for a fascinating discussion of regional media flows within the Middle East. For Taiwan, Japan is the dominant source of cultural imports. As a headline in the English-language *Taipei Times* (10 February 2000) reported: 'Taipei youth say Japan hot, U.S. not'. This is reinforced by a report on the consumer boom in Asia featured in the *Far Eastern Economic Review*, 15 June 2000.

11 Sources within the KMT have revealed that party officials did meet with such consultants from the United States in preparation for the 2000 election, but they were not hired and their ideas were not accepted.

12 On DPP organisation, including full discussion of the 'third tier', see Rigger (2001: 61–7).

13 The importance of local mobilisation was evident in the 2000 election. The KMT's defeat can be partly explained by the failure to generate sufficient enthusiasm at the grass-roots level for the party's candidate, Lien Chan (interview with KMT campaign official who wishes to remain anonymous, August 2000).

14 Days later, the DPP unveiled its own butterfly symbol, the logo of the party's Youth Department for two years. 'Our butterfly actually flies, with wings spread wide, symbolising our wish to accept the world', said Chou Yi-cheng, the Youth Department's Director. 'But the KMT's butterfly's wings are closed, and it seems like it's just sitting on the flower, waiting to suck some honey from it'. See the *Taipei Times*, 25 November 1999.

15 Conversations with Professor Hung Yung-tai, National Taiwan University, Taipei, August 2000. The under-thirties made up one-third of the electorate (Sautedé 2000: 56).

16 This assessment is based on conversations with KMT sources about their election campaigns from 1996 to 2000.

17 Shelley Rigger (2001: 96) has described the 'DPP's nomination of Peng Ming-min, along with the conduct of his campaign' as 'one of the great blunders in DPP history'.

18 These insights into DPP organisation are based on conversations with key members of the party's campaign teams, 1996–2000.

19 Interviews with sources within the DPP, Taipei, August 2000.

20 In December 2001, Taiwan held elections for the Legislative Yuan with a 66 percent turnout, the lowest ever recorded. The *Taipei Review* (February 2002: 30) explained this with reference to the decline in vote buying. Ironically, the 'cleanest elections in history' were also characterised by lower rates of participation. However, Bruce Jacobs (in correspondence, 12 February 2002) is sceptical of the idea that 'people wouldn't vote if they did not have the incentive of payment'.

21 Full information is required for strategic voting, the kind of 'dump–save' electoral behaviour that many candidates in Taiwan appear to encourage (see Cox 1997). I am grateful to Nathan F. Batto, University of California (San Diego) for alerting me to this in his paper, 'From surveys to votes: strategic voting in the 2000 Taiwanese presidential election', delivered to the 42nd Annual Conference of the American Association for Chinese Studies (San Francisco, October 2000).

22 Shelley Rigger (1999) provides a full account of how the choice of electoral system has shaped elections in Taiwan.

23 If party identification was strong, we would expect to find that the votes would be spread equally in different elections. Instead, research demonstrates that the level of the election influences voter behaviour (Yang 1991: 276).

24 Professor John Copper, in correspondence, 14 February 2001. See also Chen (2001).

References

Bowler, S. and Farrell, D.M. (2000) 'The internationalisation of campaign consultancy', in J. Thurber and C. Nelson (eds), *Campaign Warriors: Political Consultants in Elections*. Washington: Brookings Institution Press.

Butler, D. and Ranney, A. (eds) (1992) *Electioneering: A Comparative Study of Continuity and Change*. Oxford: Clarendon Press.

Charlot, J. and Charlot, M. (1992) 'France', in D. Butler and A. Ranney (eds), *Electioneering: A Comparative Study of Continuity and Change*. Oxford: Clarendon Press.

Chen, W.C. (2001) 'The role of the family in political learning of elementary school students in Taiwan', *Issues and Studies* 37(4): 38–68.

Chao, L. and Myers, R.H. (1998) *The First Chinese Democracy: Political Life in the Republic of China on Taiwan*. Baltimore: Johns Hopkins University Press.

Copper, J. (1997) *The Taiwan Political Miracle: Essays on Political Development, Elections and Foreign Relations*. Lanham, Md: University Press of America.

Cox, G. (1997) *Making Votes Count: Strategic Coordination in the World's Electoral Systems*. Cambridge: Cambridge University Press.

Diamond, L., Plattner, M.F., Chu, Y.H. and Tien, H.M. (eds) (1997) *Consolidating the Third Wave Democracies: Regional Challenges*. Baltimore: Johns Hopkins University Press.

Domes, J. (1999) 'Electoral and party politics in democratisation', in Tsang and Tien (eds), *Democratisation in Taiwan: Implications for China*. Basingstoke: Macmillan.

Franklin, B. (1994) *The Packaging of Politics*. London: Edward Arnold.

Ger, Y.K. (2001) 'The politics of polling: an analysis of Taiwan's 2000 presidential election, *American Journal of Chinese Studies* 8(1): 7–12.

Giddens, A. (1991) *Modernity and Self-Identity*. Cambridge: Polity Press.

Glass, A.J. (1996) 'On-line elections: the Internet's impact on the political process,' *Harvard International Journal of Press/Politics* 1(4): 140–6.

Huntington, S. (1991) *The Third Wave: Democratisation in the Late Twentieth Century*. Norman: University of Oklahoma Press.

Hsu, H. (1991) 'Party identification and voting choice', *Journal of Humanities and Social Science* 4(1).

Marrek, P. (1995) *Political Marketing and Communication*. London: John Libbey.

Negrine, R. (1996) *The Communication of Politics*. London: Sage.

Norris, P. (2001) *Digital Divide: Civic Engagement, Information Poverty, and the Internet Worldwide*. Cambridge: Cambridge University Press.

O'Donnell, G., Schmitter, P.C. and Whitehead, L. (eds) (1986) *Transitions from Authoritarian Rule* (4 volumes). Baltimore: Johns Hopkins University Press.

Peters, B.G. (1999) *Institutional Theory in Political Science: The 'New Institutionalism'*. London: Continuum.

Plasser, F. (2000) 'American campaign techniques worldwide', *Harvard International Journal of Press/Politics* 5(4): 33–54.

Ponebianco, A. (1988) *Political Parties: Organisation and Power*. Cambridge: Cambridge University Press.

Rawnsley, G.D. (2000) 'Where's the beef? The 1998 mayoral election campaign in Taiwan', *American Journal of Chinese Studies* 7(2): 147–69.

Rawnsley, G.D. and Rawnsley, M.Y. (1998) 'Regime transition and the media in Taiwan', in V. Randall (ed.), *Democratization and the Media*. London: Frank Cass.

—— (2001) *Critical Security, Democratization and Television in Taiwan*. London: Ashgate.

Rigger, S. (1999) *Politics in Taiwan: Voting for Democracy*. London: Routledge.

—— (2001) *From Opposition to Power: Taiwan's Democratic Progressive Party*. London: Lynne Rienner.

Sautedé, E. (2000) 'Electioneering Taiwan-style', *China Perspectives* 29: 52–6.

Scammel, M. (1997) 'The wisdom of the war room: U.S. campaigning and Americanisation', Harvard University, Shorenstein Center on the Press, Politics and Public Policy research paper R–17.

Schiller, H. (1969) *Mass Communications and the American Empire*. New York: Augustus M. Kelly.

Schumpeter, J. (1976) *Capitalism, Socialism and Democracy*. London: Allen & Unwin.

Sreberny, A. (2000) 'Television, gender and democratisation in the Middle East', in Curran and Park (eds), *De-Westernising Media Studies*. London: Routledge.

Sreberny-Mohammadi, A. (1996) 'Globalisation, communication and transnational civil society', in Braman and Sreberny-Mohammadi (eds), *Globalisation, Communication and Transnational Civil Society*. Cresskill: Hampton Press.

Straubhaar, J. (1997) 'Distinguishing the global, regional and national levels of world television', in A. Sreberny-Mohammadi *et al.* (eds), *Media in Global Context*. London: Edward Arnold.

Thurber, J., Nelson, C. and Dulio, D.A. (2000) 'Portrait of campaign consultants', in J. Thurber and C. Nelson (eds), *Campaign Warriors: Political Consultants in Elections*. Washington: Brookings Institution Press.

Tien, H.M. (1989) *The Great Transition*. Taipei: SMC.

Tu, W.M. (1996) 'Cultural identity and the politics of recognition in contemporary Taiwan', *China Quarterly* 148(4): 1115–40.

Wachman, A.M. (1994) *Taiwan: National Identity and Democratisation*. Armonk, NY: M.E. Sharpe.

Wagnleitner, R. and May, E.T. (eds) (2000) *Here, There and Everywhere: The Foreign Politics of American Popular Culture*. New Hampshire: University Press of New England.

Wu, Y. (2000) 'The ROC's semi-presidentialism at work: unstable compromise, not cohabitation', *Issues and Studies* 36(5): 1–40.

Yang, T. (1991) *Elections*. Taipei: Yung-jan Cultural Publishing Ltd.

7 Gender and party politics

Case study of the Democratic Progressive Party in Taiwan

Bey-Ling Sha

This chapter derives from my research into the organisational communication and identity of the Democratic Progressive Party (DPP) in Taiwan. Part of that research examined the gendered dimensions of the DPP because, as a feminist, I believe that failure to incorporate gendered dimensions into research permits the assumption that phenomena affect organisations and individuals in gender-neutral ways. As a feminist scholar, I cannot permit the assumption that theories, research and reality are gender-neutral.

The term 'gender' is used in this chapter to designate differences between the sexes that are socially constructed, as opposed to those differences that are biologically, genetically or hormonally based. Considerations of gender include both men and women. Furthermore, I would include issues of sexual orientation, so as not to limit considerations of gendered interactions to heterosexual ones. Thus, raising the question of gender in research does not mean simply including women, women's perspectives or women's issues. Rather, the explicit inclusion of women critiques and counters gender-neutral, 'objective' research as being implicitly male-centred.

The problems of excluding gendered dimensions in research into collective action are several. First, a failure to mention gender permits the assumption that men and women invest in, participate in and gain from collective action in similar ways – an assumption that may not be true. Second, a failure to discuss gendered interactions within collective action may result in the neglect of important issues of power and negotiation internal to the collective. Finally, a failure to examine gendered differences in collective action means overlooking the possibility that the demands of activists represent only the interests of the (male) activist leaders.

Similarly, as Ware (1996) has pointed out, most political parties have, throughout history, been dominated by men, in large part because women in most countries did not have the right to vote until after male enfranchisement. However, once women could vote, they still rarely participated in party politics. Ware offered three explanations for this phenomenon:

> First, women's votes were viewed as extensions of the male votes in their families; thus, the party may establish separate women's sections to

bring women in, but these sections were segregated from the male-dominated power structure of the organisation. Second, party leaders did not want to increase the internal competition for their own positions by giving women more power. Third, women did not participate in party politics, probably because their exclusion from the power structure gave them little incentive to become involved. Consequently, women today are underrepresented in political parties and excluded from leadership positions

(*ibid.*: 81)

Thus, this chapter offers two contributions. First, the research presented here provides descriptive information on the role of women in Taiwan's DPP. Second, the explicit examination of gender in party politics problematises theories of collective action that have traditionally excluded gender as a salient variable of analysis.

Gendered dimensions of political activism

Women and gender are usually excluded from theoretical treatments of political parties (*ibid.*). Similarly, most theoretical literature on social movements and collective action fail to mention gendered dimensions of the phenomena unless the text is especially dedicated to women in politics. In most of the literature on collective action, women are usually mentioned, if at all, in terms of the women's movement. For instance, Tilly's (1978) classic study of collective action gave the women's movement one sentence. In a later work, he mentioned women occasionally, usually in connection with women's participation in various minor food riots throughout French history (Tilly 1986). Even in more modern times, Tarrow (1994) offered the women's movement only four pages and contrasted it with the French student movement of the 1960s.

In short, most social movement literature has not been gender-inclusive in that there has been little systematic treatment of gendered interactions between participants in collective action. Gender-related discussions are restricted to analyses of the women's movement or to isolated examples of women as activists. For example, in his analysis of the 1989 student demonstrations in China, Calhoun (1991) mentioned one woman activist. Otherwise, he did not discuss gender or gendered interactions within the pro-democracy movement, focusing instead on interactions between students and older intellectuals. Likewise, Tarrow (1994: 156) discussed barricades as part of Parisians' 'repertoire of contention' but did not elaborate on who mounted and defended the barricades: men, women, or both.

These kinds of omission are serious because one cannot claim to study movements based on fraternity, equality and democracy without discussing how the movement contextualised gendered fraternisation or the (lack of) equality between men and women. Tarrow (*ibid.*: 163) did provide one clue that history bore out, mentioning that 'French reformers were not so fool-hardy as to wish to extend the vote universally'. French women did not gain suffrage until after the Second World War, despite their part in democratising France through the French Revolution.

Some feminist studies of gender in political activism illustrate that women who participate in politics must fight simultaneously for both *political* and *gendered* goals. For example, L. Grunig (1993) studied the Cuban Women's Federation (*Federacion de Mujeres Cubanas*: FMC) to explore the roles that women played in that country's development. Castro's revolution in Cuba had incorporated women into production, created accessible and affordable day-care centres, eradicated prostitution, and extended educational opportunities to women. Nevertheless, these advancements were brought about primarily by the government, rather than by women themselves. Using lengthy interviews with the women leaders of the FMC, Grunig found that women had yet to achieve equality in the workplace, even though they now had the right to work outside the home. Women also were not proportionately represented in the political system, although their numbers were increasing.

Thus, although the women's movement in Cuba was successful in improving the lot of women in general, the movement 'cannot be considered an independent, feminist one. Rather, it works within the authoritarian nature of the political system' (*ibid.*: 14). Furthermore, men dominated that political system. Consequently, the federation had to battle not only for revolutionary goals but also for the gender goal of equality. An FMC statement argued that 'women must fight for their own liberation at the same time they fight for the liberation of the nation' (quoted in *ibid.*: 15).

Another example of research into women in politics is the work of Alvarez, who researched women's political participation in Brazilian regime changes. Giving historical background on her own research conducted in the 1980s, Alvarez explained how conservatives mobilised women to support the military coup of 1964, 'appealing to women's "innate" commitment to family, morality, and social order' (Alvarez 1990: 5) to convince them to support the overthrow of a democratically elected government.

In her own research, Alvarez found that the transition from authoritarian to democratic regimes contributed to fragmenting the women's movement. Some women's groups believed that the struggle for women's rights was part of the larger struggle for a democratic Brazilian society, and they affiliated themselves with political parties of the Left. On the other hand, other women's groups preferred political autonomy, seeing the struggle for women's rights as independent of the attempts to overthrow the dictatorship.

The result was that male-dominated parties vying for political power co-opted some 'women's issues' for their own electoral gain and courted women's participation in the political process. Nevertheless, the women activists interviewed by the author asserted that women's issues were still treated as secondary, that feminist activists continued to face sexist treatment within political parties, and that political parties actually remained resistant to the 'feminist political agenda' (*ibid.*: 238). Thus, despite some political gains being made by women, equity and equality were not yet among them.

In a different treatment of the same theme, Shohat (1996) discussed the movie *The Battle of Algiers* (1966) and noted the paradox in women's position as fighters for Algerian independence from France. In this documentary -style fictional film, Algerian women are critical revolutionary agents. They are effective in this capacity in large part because male French soldiers viewed veiled Algerian women as 'dominated' and 'oppressed', never suspecting that they could and did participate in revolutionary activities. The irony is threefold:

> The Algerian women fighting for 'liberation' are heroic only insofar as their actions support the struggle for *Algerian* rights, rather than for *women's* rights. These women are heroic in their submission to and obedience of male leaders of revolution. The second irony is that the Algerian women in the movie manage to accomplish their mission – planting bombs in the European quarter of Algiers – only by denying their own culture and assuming the culture of the colonisers. To pass the military checkpoints into the European quarter for their mission, the women shed their veils, cut their hair, ceased speaking in Arabic, put on European clothes, and applied make-up in the manner of French women (Shohat and Stam 1994). A third irony, external to the film itself, is that the woman who made *The Battle of Algiers* now lives in exile in Paris, a military target of the present Islamic movement in Algeria because of her 'heretical' position on gender (Shohat 1996).

In these examples from Cuba, Brazil and Algeria, the question is this: why is it that women who fight for national liberation simultaneously risk being denied their liberation as women? The related theoretical paradox is this: how can theories that explain democratisation and liberalisation at the level of the nation-state account for the simultaneous denial of democratic rights and gender liberty to women within the nation-state?

In this discussion of the gendered dimensions of collective action, the primary implication that emerges is that theoretical treatments of such phenomena do not adequately include gender as a salient variable of analysis. As this section has described, the inclusion of gender problematises any phenomenon by raising issues of justice and equity.

In this research, gendered dimensions were examined in two ways. First, I explored the roles played by women in the political party. For example, would women in the political party participate equally with men in organisational activities and administration? Second, I considered how gender dimensions and gender issues were used in the organisation's communication strategies. Would the organisation support 'women's issues'? Would any such support be truly genuine or merely strategic in its potential appeal to women voters? These research questions are summarised as follows:

RQ1   In what ways, if any, does the political party include dimensions of gender in its communication?

RQ2   What roles, if any, do women play in the political party?

Method

To answer these questions, I conducted a case study of the Democratic Progressive Party, which, at the time, was the major political opposition party in Taiwan.[1] This research involved qualitative, formal, semi-structured interviews with twenty-two party members.

In addition, I conducted participant observation in the socio-political contexts of the DPP from June 1997 to July 1998. This technique included informal interviews with nearly one hundred informants in Taiwan who were members of either the party or its communication audiences. Participant observation also involved monitoring media coverage of politics and political parties, participation in some party events and activities, and examining organisational documents. Data was collected in Mandarin.

Findings

Although some women played roles in the DPP similar to those played by men, their participation in the party could not escape the influence of traditional gender biases. In addition, the organisation's articulated support for women's issues appeared to be more pragmatic than genuine. These findings support the suggestion made above, namely that gender affects the manner in which people experience such phenomena as political activism. Before examining in depth the gendered dimensions of this case study, I first delimit this discussion by answering question RQ1.

'Gender' was included in organisational communication only in terms of 'woman' or 'female'. This research offered no indication that the party articulated any issues uniquely salient to men. Furthermore, not once did any of the DPP informants or interviewees discuss sexual orientation or issues affecting the (mostly closeted) gay community on Taiwan.

On the one hand, many people may have considered such issues inappropriate to bring up in discussions or interviews with a young woman who was a stranger. On the other hand, had issues of sexual orientation been salient, party members could have raised them in the context of political activism. This approach would have been possible because, during the period of research in Taipei, the issue of gay rights had already surfaced, with news coverage of gay literature and gay rights demonstrations.

Thus, in this section, the discussion of 'gender issues' is restricted to 'women's issues' because this reflects the DPP's emphasis, not because I am unaware of other issues related to gender. In short, women comprised important constituencies for the DPP, both externally and internally. The following sections discuss the changing nature of the relationships between the party and its women public. In addition, because interviewees suggested that women's voices in the party were not often heard, I use long quotations in this section to give fuller expression to women's voices.

Women and the activist organisation

This section discusses the relationship between the DPP and women in general, meaning primarily women external to the party. This relationship was important to this case study because of the ways in which it had evolved through the years, not only in terms of how women viewed the organisation but also with regard to how they supported it. Women in the past had shunned the DPP because of its violent image. By 1998, however, increasing numbers of women were supporting the party, believing it to be better for women than was the ruling party, the Kuomintang (KMT).

Women's identification with the party

As discussed above, the DPP in the past had the image of being a violent party, in large part because the KMT-controlled media portrayed the political opposition as violent and unstable. Furthermore, the political opposition could only obtain media coverage by taking to the streets, an action that citizens also viewed as provocative and violent. As one interviewee put it:

> In the past, why were there street demonstrations? Because of the media being controlled by the KMT. And us common people didn't know, all we saw were, like in the Legislative Assembly, people fighting. Common people didn't understand. That's why some people's impressions of the DPP were negative. Because the KMT created the image.

Interviewees, both male and female, also explained that this violent image made the party especially distasteful to women. As one participant said: 'In the past, the percentage of DPP supporters who were women was very small'. Another interviewee claimed that, until even three or four years ago, married women tended to support the KMT even in cases where their husbands supported the DPP.

By the time of this case study in 1998, however, women had increasingly become supporters of the DPP. Both male and female interviewees consistently cited evidence from public opinion polls in support of this claim. (Support for the party was especially strong among younger women, reflecting the DPP's larger support base among young people in general.) Most interviewees attributed the increase in women's support for the party to the liberalisation of the media, which corresponded to a decrease in violent portrayals of the political opposition. Furthermore, women supported the DPP because they had begun to see the party as a less corrupt alternative to the KMT.

Other interviewees, primarily women, suggested that the party's increased support among women stemmed from its support for welfare issues important to them. One participant explained that women no longer believed the KMT could successfully resolve social problems related to public safety and childcare. Another interviewee said: 'We say that the DPP wants to take care of you from cradle to grave, with childcare and old age pensions'. This quotation is illustrative of the DPP's support for issues of great concern to women in Taiwan.

Some interviewees also suggested that women supported the DPP because the DPP had supported women's rights. For example, one participant said:

> I think that, now, women, many of them, are strong supporters of the DPP .... In the past, they didn't even know they had rights. Now, many of their benefits and rights are ones that the DPP fought for. So, now [women] realise the DPP is good. In the past, [they] didn't know.

Thus, at the time of this research the DPP was more palatable to women voters for a variety of reasons. In addition, the DPP had made the effort to target women as a crucial voting segment. Interview data consistently suggested that the organisation's interest in women stemmed in large part from its realisation that women were an important constituency. For example, several interviewees explained that male voters likely to support the party already were voting for its candidates. In other words, the DPP had already maximised its support among male voters. On the other hand, the party had not yet maximised its potential base of supporters among women. As one interviewee put it: 'More and more women will identify with the DPP'.

The party's communication with women voters

One interviewee pointed out that gender was not always a salient factor in the DPP's communication. As she put it: '[We] must communicate with men as well as with women. The manner of communication is sometimes the same, sometimes different. It depends. Sometimes men and women are different only because of gender. At other times, there are other differences'. However, in its efforts to increase women's levels of identification with and electoral support for the party, the DPP's election campaign strategies consistently targeted women as a distinct public. In discussing the party's efforts to reach women, one interviewee raised an interesting point. She suggested that, although women were important to the DPP, they constituted an 'invisible' audience. As she explained:

> When speeches are made, or during public events, you see more men
> than women. It's simple. Women are [expected] to take care of their
> husbands, take care of their children, cook three meals a day, wash
> clothes and cook meals. So, like most of our speeches take place from
> 7pm to 9pm or 7pm to 10pm. During that time, husbands are done
> eating, so they can come out and listen to speeches. The wife can't.

Thus, the DPP's efforts to communicate with women were situated in a
cultural context that remained tied to traditional gender expectations.
Perhaps for this reason, the party used gender-related fear appeals in
attempting to reach women. For example, one political advertisement that
ran on television during the 1997 campaign featured a woman riding a
scooter at night, a common sight throughout Taiwan. The segment was
filmed in black and white, and a woman's sober voice-over said: 'I always
wear my helmet when riding my scooter, especially at night, so that no one
can tell I'm a woman'. The implication was that women are easier targets for
criminals and that one could increase one's safety by hiding one's female
gender.

In another example, the DPP published a comic book targeted at women.
One story segment dealt with the lack of state-supported childcare. The
comic book showed a mother who hires a Filipina maid to care for her baby
so that she could continue to work outside the home; this scenario was
commonplace among upper middle-class families in Taiwan in 1998. (The
father in the comic is playing *mah jong* with three other men and yells at the
wife for not serving tea to the guests, even though she is occupied with the
baby.) The comic book shows how the Filipina takes good care of the child,
but she speaks to him in English and Tagalog. When the mother comes
home from work and tries to hold the baby, the child screams: 'Who is your
child? She [referring to the carer] is my mother!'

In both of these examples, the DPP played on gender-related fears and
concerns. First, the common perception among Taiwan residents was that
women are more vulnerable to crime than were men. Also, the video was
aired in a climate of island-wide paranoia among women because daily news
reports pointed to a lack of progress in finding a serial rapist on the loose in
Taipei. Second, the comic book drew on the frustrations of women trying to
balance work and family commitments. The inclusion of a Filipina carer
also reflected rising tensions between Taiwanese citizens and the foreign
labour force, made up primarily of Filipinas.

Besides using gender-related concerns in communicating with women, the
party also used other means to tailor messages to this constituency. As one
interviewee said: 'We would use softer appeals, like colours that women like,
not really bold colours ... and some slogans. We would use simple ones to

ask women to feel safe, or target those television channels or programmes or newspapers and magazines that women tend to like to watch [or read]'.

The 'soft' approach to women voters was also reflected in the party's efforts to reach out to women voters without overemphasising politics. For instance, one interviewee explained that party representatives would go into the community and encourage women to be active in a variety of ways. Such activities could have included involving women in neighbourhood recycling contests or asking housewives to use their spare time to share information about the DPP with their friends and relatives.

On the one hand, the DPP's concern for women was genuine. One interviewee explained: 'For the moment, the DPP's leaders ... are really quite concerned about women's issues; or they wouldn't permit the Women's [Development] Department to become so big and powerful'. On the other hand, DPP efforts to communicate with women voters were not purely unselfish in nature, as the party's main interest lay in gaining more votes from women.

According to one interviewee, women's concerns and fears were addressed by the DPP mostly as the party sought women's votes. For instance, one participant said that party workers would try to explain to women that Taiwan's social welfare system was weak in part because the KMT spends the people's money where it should not. In this way, DPP representatives would suggest that, if voters put the DPP in power, Taiwan could change for the better.

Another interviewee was more blunt about the party's communication with women. She was asked whether she truly felt that the DPP believed in the importance of women's issues. She replied:

> I think it's passive. Passive, simply meaning, the DPP wants votes. If you want women's votes, then you have to place an importance [on women's issues] .... They know that they place an importance on women's votes, and since they place an importance on women's votes, they have to support public policies for women .... It's not self-generated. It's passive, from the outside, forcing [the party] to do this, so it is willing to do this.

Thus, keeping in mind the pragmatic aspects of the party's communication with women, we turn now to a discussion of the issues with which the DPP tried to reach women voters.

The party's emphasis on women's issues

Officially, the DPP supported equal opportunities for women, women's rights and a variety of women's issues. The party's political platform reflected these emphases, voicing support for women's legal and political rights. The party's concern for women was genuine, at least in part. As one interviewee put it: 'It is only through public policies, changing the system, that you can change the unequal situation between men and women. This is the direction we have chosen'. This interviewee meant that the DPP's appeals to women voters differed from the approach taken by the KMT.

Specifically, interviewees believed that the KMT took a more traditional approach to women, hosting such events as mothers' teas or fundraising galas for party charities. One participant suggested that the KMT approach to women was more patriarchal: 'they want to *take care* of women. Like, I love you, I care about you, and Mother is great, using those kinds of traditional angles to approach [women's issues]'. In contrast, the DPP concentrated on 'hot issues', like ensuring quotas for women in public office or hot breakfasts for children at school.

Although interviewees articulated specific differences between DPP and KMT approaches to women, these differences seem to have reflected socio-economic differences in the parties' voter bases rather than any differences in the parties' views towards women. Hence, in this author's view, both DPP and KMT approaches to women were patriarchal and traditional.

On the one hand, the KMT focused on women as traditional, revered mothers. The party's activities (e.g., fundraising dinners, charity balls) appealed to women from more comfortable economic backgrounds and a certain social class. On the other hand, the DPP concentrated on women as modern, working mothers, promising better childcare, social security and health care. This approach fitted the party's primary voter base, the middle to lower middle classes. Women from this socio-economic background were more likely to work outside the home and to be interested in concrete policies that would improve their lives.

Nevertheless, the DPP's emphasis on women's issues still reflected the party's traditional views on women's roles. Specifically, DPP policies concentrated on improving the lot of women, but only in their traditional roles as family carers. For instance, the party argued for a national social security programme, which concerned women on Taiwan because they traditionally cared for the family elderly. Likewise, national healthcare – another proposed DPP policy – concerned women because to them traditionally fell the roles of nurse and carer when family members were ill.

The DPP also supported government-funded childcare, which appealed to women as increasing numbers of them worked outside the home and as nuclear families moved away from extended family members who might have assisted with childcare. Yet, by using childcare issues to appeal to women, rather than to voters in general, the DPP seemed to suggest that the burden of finding appropriate childcare belonged to women alone, rather than also to their husbands. As one interviewee said: 'The DPP has raised women's policies. [The party] is willing to push, to take care of these [issues]. They have raised the policy that, if the DPP becomes the ruling party, the party will take care of women … including women, including children, including the elderly'. Although these policies are admirable, they also illustrated the party's traditional view that women's concerns were linked to those regarding children and the elderly.

In spite of its support for these kinds of traditional 'women's issues', the DPP leadership was less vocal about whether it supported other issues, such as equal pay for women or anti-sexual harassment laws for the workplace. Thus, it can be suggested that the party's approach to women remained concentrated on traditional aspects of women's lives, such as those related to children and family, to the neglect of other, less traditional issues that might also have concerned women in Taiwan.

In considering the DPP's articulation of public policies for women, one must also remember that, at the time of this case study, these articulations were merely rhetorical. That is, because the DPP had yet to become the ruling party at the national level, the organisation also had yet to implement any of its proposed policies for women. Thus the research questioned whether the party actually would implement such policies once it gained the power to do so. In response, one interviewee said:

> People have the perspective that, if they elect you, a woman representa-
> tive, they can have greater hope/expectation that women will be taken
> care of in the future .... We women in the DPP are also very strong ....
> So, if we women pool together our strength, I believe, if we are here to
> push them ... [we] can manage to prevent them from [dropping women's
> issues]. I feel that, still, women are more concerned about women's
> issues [than are men]. When I was running for office, I would raise this
> point. That men, mostly, they use women's issues as an election tool ....
> But, women are more easily, more likely to really carry out those issues.

In this way, this participant suggested that it was up to women within the party to make sure the DPP's emphasis on women's issues remained strong after elections were over.

Women in the activist organisation

Women in the DPP played roles similar to those played by male party members; however, women also took on the responsibility of communi-cating with the organisation's women voters. Furthermore, although the roles of women in political activism had evolved and improved since the *dangwai* ('outside the party') era, both the DPP and its women members remained tied to traditional attitudes towards gender.

Historical information shared by interviewees regarding the roles of women (specifically, of wives) in the *dangwai* during the martial law era illustrates the tensions between the party and its women members. This background is offered to highlight the progress that women have made in political participa-tion. The current roles played by women in the DPP are then discussed.

Historical roles in the dangwai

Prior to its founding in 1986, the DPP was a loosely organised coalition of opposition politicians, called the *dangwai*, literally, 'outside the party'. Historically, Taiwan had often witnessed the phenomenon of women running for office in the place of their husbands, who in most cases could not campaign because they were in jail. Both the DPP and the KMT have nominated wives to run in the stead of imprisoned husbands. Nevertheless, interviewees pointed out that DPP or *dangwai* wives and KMT wives in such instances were not in comparable situations.

First, in the martial law era, the role of women in the *dangwai* was to substitute for their husbands who had been jailed by the KMT. As one interviewee explained: 'They ran for office in the place of their husbands .... Women of that era came out [into political activities] only because their husbands were jailed'. Another participant emphasised that the *dangwai* wives had campaigned on the basis of democratic ideals, in the place of husbands who had been jailed for those ideals. Since the lifting of martial law, the DPP had not run wives in the place of jailed husbands.

On the other hand, even in 1997, the KMT was still running wives in the place of jailed husbands. Unlike *dangwai* men, who had been jailed for political reasons, most KMT candidates had been jailed for their gangland connections. As one interviewee explained, the KMT had relied on local gangs during the martial law era to extend party power into local levels. Consequently, even among KMT candidates and public officials in 1997, at least one-third were rumoured or known to have gangland connections. In recent years, the KMT had not dared to nominate gangsters for public office, but gangsters campaigned anyway as independents. Even jailing the gangsters did not help, because they would run their wives for office instead. As one interviewee said:

> The wife runs for office, but the [jailed] husband is still the force behind [her]. The [central headquarters of the] KMT has no control over the situation. These wives do not run on behalf of citizens, but for their own interests. They are just continuing the husband's monopoly over power in the gangland. It's still the jailed husband in control.

Another interviewee explained that KMT gangsters ran their wives for political office as a show of power: 'the wife has no meaning; the wife is just a symbol, representing [the gangster] and [his] power .... The wives have little interest in democracy; they just run to help [their] husbands maintain local faction power'.

Thus, *dangwai* wives ran for office to promote democratic ideals, whereas KMT wives ran to promote private interests. Nevertheless, from the perspective of Western feminism, both *dangwai* and KMT wives were serving as substitutes, rather than running on their own. For this reason, we can consider *dangwai* and KMT women to be similar in their oppressed condition.

This analysis was supported by some of the women interviewees, despite the attempts of others to portray DPP women as more independent. For example, one participant said:

> After [the *dangwai* husbands'] release [from prison], they felt, well, you wives, you can go home and cook dinner. I can run for office myself .... So, in fact, women in the DPP, especially those in publicly elected offices, were very much oppressed .... In the beginning ... it was ... 'entering the contest in the place of the husband' [*dai fu chu zheng*]. [You] were a man's substitute.

That participant later expressed her belief that the DPP had improved in this area, in that most DPP women who ran for public office no longer were doing so simply to substitute for their husbands. However, some DPP women did run for office out of familial pressures. In this blurring of the personal with the political, women in the party remained tied to traditions that deemed women to be surrogates for men. Nevertheless, their roles as members of the political opposition had improved since the *dangwai* era.

Present roles in the DPP

In this case study, the roles played by women in the organisation were as varied as those played by men, although the latter still occupied the highest-ranking party positions. In addition, women members served as communicators to women audiences and as fighters for women's issues within the DPP itself.

In terms of official roles, both women and men served as elected DPP officials, as intra-party delegates and as departmental directors at DPP central headquarters. Furthermore, a few high-profile women leaders, or 'strong women' (*nu qiang ren*), helped to give a 'female face' to the political party, articulating the organisation's position on women's issues and publicly espousing the party's concern for women.

For example, during the period of research in Taiwan, the most notable among such women leaders was Sisy Chen, who was then serving as director of the Culture and Information Department at DPP central headquarters until she resigned in the spring of 1998 to run for legislative office (party members were not allowed to run for an office while serving in another). Other high-profile DPP women included Chang Wen-ying (the mayor of Taichung, the island's third-largest city), Fan Shun-lu (a well-respected senior legislator) and Chiu I-ying (a media-worshipped National Assembly representative who was only 29 years old in 1998).

Women in the DPP appeared equal to their male counterparts, at least in terms of some of the organisational roles they played. However, men occupied the most important party roles, including those of the party chairman and secretary-general, the heads of party factions, and heads of local party branches. In contrast, women dominated low-level staff positions within the party, for example, those of secretaries or receptionists. In addition, women of all ranks were often expected to work on women's issues or communicate with other women.

For instance, in March 1998, the Women's Development Department sponsored a tour of public facilities around Taipei. The goal of the tour was to show how the design of many public facilities endangered the security of women, for example, underground crossing tunnels with no security cameras or dimly lit public parks. Despite repeated invitations to participate in the event, none of the male leaders went on the tour, viewing it as a 'women's event'.

Several women interviewees also noted that DPP women were expected to maintain communication between themselves. For instance, one female interviewee noted that she worked closely with the Women's Development Department in DPP central headquarters because she was a female elected official. Another participant, when asked how the different party factions treated women, replied: 'The factions all have women; these women keep in touch with [the Women's Development] Department'.

In short, just as factional alliances helped to improve the party's internal communication, so did gendered ones. When asked about the DPP's internal communication, one woman replied:

> Especially, we communicate most directly with the Women's [Development] Department ... because we are women elected representatives .... Like if there are activities, if the Women's [Development] Department is doing something ... they always hope that we can take part in them, to communicate with the people from central headquarters or with elected representatives from other areas.

In these ways, women within the party helped to strengthen the DPP's internal communication across party levels and localities.

In addition to working on women's issues and communicating with other women, the party's female members worked with male leaders to promote the importance of women's issues within the party itself. When asked whether the DPP genuinely cared about women, one participant said that not everyone in the party recognised the importance of women's issues. She added: 'I think it's something that needs to be fought for internal to the party'. Another participant explained that the DPP sometimes had trouble articulating its support for women's issues: 'Because now the DPP's leaders are mostly men, they can't appreciate what social welfare policies women want'. For this reason, DPP women also communicated with women voters to learn their perspectives on women's issues.

Fortunately, DPP women were willing to work on women's issues and to communicate with other women, both internal and external to the party. The women members interviewed viewed themselves as being radical and independent. They also articulated their personalities in terms of differences between themselves and their counterparts in the KMT. For example, one interviewee said that she had joined the DPP after participating in a 'radical' women's group. She suggested that her radical nature would not have fitted well with KMT women's groups, which were centred on more genteel activities such as fundraising and charity work.

DPP women also viewed themselves as more independent and willing to speak out. One interviewee said:

> Many women feel, after marriage, that they belong to their family, to their husband. If the husband says no, it's no. If the husband says yes, it's yes. I learned [with participation in the DPP] that I have my own choices. Of course, [I should] respect the family and discuss [things] with them. But [I should] decide on my own, not lose my own voice.

Like the male members, female members had joined the DPP because they believed the organisation was good for Taiwan. Furthermore, most women also believed that the DPP was good for women. Although the male interviewees in this study mentioned equal rights for women only in the context of election tactics, women participants wanted both to have those rights and to believe that the DPP could facilitate this goal. As one interviewee explained: 'In this democracy, [we] want democracy for both sexes. Women must struggle. Of course, throughout the world, men's status is higher [than women's]. But women must fight for their rights. Rights don't fall from the sky'. Although DPP women sometimes had to fight for gender democracy within the party, they were supported in this endeavour, as a general rule, by the male leaders of the DPP.

The party's role in supporting women

In this case study, interviewees cited two examples of the DPP's support for women most often. As discussed above, the party's support for women in general came in the form of proposed public policies that dealt with issues of concern to women. In terms of supporting women members, the DPP implemented the 'one-in-four' rule, which was essentially a 25 percent quota for ensuring the representation of women in positions both external and internal to the party.

The rule was originally proposed by a well-known women's rights activist, Peng Wan-ru, who also served at one point as director of the DPP's Women's Development Department. After years of lobbying by Peng and other women activists, the DPP passed the one-in-four rule for public officials in 1995, thus attempting to ensure that one out of every four elected DPP candidates would be female. As one interviewee said: 'Only from then on, after the one-in-four policy was passed, were there greater numbers of female elected officials [from the DPP]'.

However, the party continued to resist applying the quota to positions within the DPP. In December 1996, Peng disappeared after attending a party conference in the southern city of Kaohsiung. Her corpse was found two days later; she had been raped and stabbed more than thirty times. At the DPP National Convention the next summer, the delegates passed a motion to extend the one-in-four rule to apply to positions within the party.

One interviewee brought up the one-in-four rule as evidence of the party's genuine support for women. She said:

> [The rule] was passed democratically. Regardless of whether you had to scold, plead, or act coy [to get support for the rule's passage], the end result was that it was passed. This passage was not done just to show off for others .... This is for real. It's not a disguise.

This participant also pointed out that neither the KMT nor the New Party[2] had managed to pass similar proposals in support of their women members.

Although the DPP's one-in-four rule was both commendable and groundbreaking, some interview participants believed the party could still do more for women, who comprised 30 percent of DPP members in 1998. As one interviewee said: 'In fact, one of every two [humans] is a woman, so why shouldn't we ask for one of two? But I can accept one of four'. One participant was also asked whether the one-in-four rule would make some women feel like tokens. She replied: 'This is why we must nurture women's talent. No one is a born politician; [he or she] must be nurtured. There are few women politicians because women have been oppressed. If we nurture women, women can also be good political leaders'.

By implementing the one-in-four rule for party members, the DPP showed that it might actually implement its other proposed policies for women, should the organisation become the ruling party in Taiwan. Thus, the one-in-four rule also served as a means of attracting women's votes. Nevertheless, the party's motives were not purely self-interested ones. One interviewee articulated this view:

> Besides political considerations, [the one-in-four rule] is also to encourage women to get involved with politics. In the past, many women supported the KMT, not because the KMT was worthy of their support but because women just didn't care about national policies, public policies .... So, now we use this method [the one-in-four rule], first, to encourage women to get involved with politics. And second, to encourage women, as they participate in politics, to participate more in the DPP.

In short, the party supported women and women's issues to encourage women to become politically active, not only in casting their votes for the DPP but also in participating in the party's activities.

The DPP's efforts on behalf of women also were reflected in its organisational structure, with a separate department emphasising women's development. As one interviewee explained: 'Why is [the department] not called the Women's Work Department or the Women's Committee? That's because [the DPP] hoped women could be developed/nurtured .... So [the party] established the Women's Development Department'. The DPP was the first political party to have a department devoted to women's issues, and Peng had pushed for its establishment.

Another interviewee said that the DPP's male leadership both supported the Women's Development Department and recognised its importance to the organisation's goals. She said: 'They want the DPP to succeed; [they] believe that a successful political party needs both men and women'. Thus, the efforts of the department benefited from the party leaders' genuine concern for women and from their realisation that the support of women, both internally and externally, was crucial for the DPP to reach its goal of becoming the ruling party.

The Women's Development Department at central headquarters had three main objectives, which reflected the roles played by women in the party. First, the department was responsible for encouraging women to join or to like the DPP. Second, the department was expected to work on the articulation of policies that were good for women and children. Finally, the department also worked on helping male party members to treat women with respect. This latter responsibility was important because, as mentioned above, some men in the party sometimes failed to appreciate women and their significance to the party, despite the importance attached to women's issues by the party's central leadership.

Cultural influences on the party and its members

This chapter has discussed how the DPP expressed traditional views of gender roles in communicating with women voters. We now elaborate on how the influence of traditional attitudes on gender remained strong within the DPP itself, despite the party's efforts to support women within the organisation. Traditional ways of thinking affected the attitudes and behaviour of both male and female party members. These findings reflected the reality that, in 1998, traditional gender expectations remained strong in Taiwan.

As one interviewee put it: 'You have to understand that we in Taiwan have a patriarchal society .... The big male man attitude [*da nan ren chu yi*] is very strong'. Another participant agreed and added: 'The DPP, in my view ... can't completely detach itself from the big male man way of thinking .... They still say, as a man, I can do things better than a woman could'.

Although younger men were more willing to accept women as equals, men from older generations clung to traditional perspectives on gender roles. As one participant said:

My father-in-law's generation ... they still have a very strong big male man attitude. They, no matter what, they don't want their wives to be more capable than themselves, right? So, in the past, when I worked in the service centre, there were some things that I felt I was capable of doing, but my father-in-law's insistence was that those things should be done by a man.

Attitudes remained in the DPP that feminists would label male members sexist and patriarchal, despite the efforts of party leaders in supporting equal opportunities for women. In my interactions with party members, I both heard about and witnessed such traditional attitudes towards gender. For instance, one of the party events I attended during my stay in Taiwan was a campaign training seminar for candidates for low-level elected offices. The event took place on 1 March 1998.

Perhaps because of the party's one-in-four rule, the official DPP candidates who were presented at the beginning of the seminar included many women. In six rounds of presentations, there were thirty-eight men and nine women (23.7 percent of the total). True to its promise, the DPP supported women candidates for office. However, women were still excluded from male networks of communication within the party.

For instance, at the training seminar, the formal presentations seemed less important than the informal gatherings in the hall. Those gatherings were made up almost exclusively of men. Perhaps they were congregations of smokers, as no smoking was permitted inside the auditorium where the seminar took place. Perhaps the men were engaging in some personal lobbying on behalf of their favourite candidates. Perhaps the men were just old friends, reuniting and chatting. But, regardless of what those men were doing in the hallway, what was most noticeable was the absence of women in the gatherings.

Also at this seminar, I met a male party member who said that he had come just to hang out and, hopefully, to see Sisy Chen, who wanted to run for public office that spring (and thus should have come to the event to garner support for herself in the DPP primaries). I asked about Chen's run for the legislature, and this informant said that many older men in the party believed that women had no business running for public office. Apparently, despite Chen's high profile and popularity among voters, many men within the party not only refused to support her candidacy but also disliked her. (Chen later withdrew her candidacy before the elections, after a primary vote by party members ranked her second to last among all legislative candidates.)

The tension between some men in the DPP and some high-profile women members, such as Chen, was well known even outside party circles. The *China News*, one of the island's English-language dailies, published an editorial cartoon on 1 June 1998 that portrayed Chen and four men making faces at each other. The DPP party flag is in the background. The men are shown thinking: 'I really resent a woman who thinks she can tell men of power and ambition what to do'. Chen's thought bubble reads: 'I really resent men who think of nothing but power and ambition'.

The patriarchal attitudes of some men were also reflected in their disdain for the one-in-four rule. As discussed above, the rule had encountered opposition for several years and was adopted only after the rape and murder of its strongest proponent, Peng Wan-ru. Even two years later, in 1998, the circumstances surrounding her disappearance were unclear. Her murder remained a mystery. As a result, some rank-and-file party members questioned whether Peng's murder was an inside job, perhaps executed on behalf of male party members disgruntled at the possibility of losing their positions as a result of the DPP's quota for women.

This suggestion would seem outrageous, but it also represents the extreme end of the patriarchal spectrum. More commonplace was the simple lack of sensitivity to women's concerns among some male party members. For instance, during the tour of unsafe public facilities sponsored by the Women's Development Department, one of the event organisers pointed to an unlit road near the party's central headquarters. She explained that party workers had to walk along that road from central headquarters to their parking lot, and women members had complained several times about the road's lack of lighting. However, male party leaders were interested neither in providing a security escort service for party members to reach their cars safely nor in the women's petitions to the city government to rectify the lighting situation.

As another example of some DPP men's lack of sensitivity towards women, a male party member said to a female deputy director: 'Your breasts are not big, so why are you becoming a hunchback?' The woman was furious over the incident, while the man considered his comment a harmless joke. Because the woman was a deputy director, she was able to bring up the incident in a directors' meeting with the DPP secretary-general, an opportunity that would not have been available to lower-level women (Rickards 1998: 3).

In response to the incident, the DPP established a formal anti-sexual harassment committee. Through this committee, the party could accept and investigate formal complaints of harassment by rank-and-file party members and by staffers, who would not have access to the party's leadership. The director of the Women's Development Department, which was to handle the creation of the new committee, said that the DPP was not more sexist than any other organisation in Taiwan. Nevertheless, the new committee was important because 'we are the progressive party, so we must pursue this; otherwise, we will lose our progressiveness' (*ibid.*: 3).

As this last remark indicates, the DPP remained tied to traditional views on gender that some people would consider sexist or patriarchal. The research also questioned whether traditional gender expectations affected women's participation in political activities. One interviewee argued:

'Male–female differences are more expressed in daily living. [They] have less to do with political activities'. This woman's remark came in the context of how some parents did not want their children of either sex to get involved with politics, an attitude developed during the White Terror period of the 1950s and 1960s and prevalent today.

However, in cases where families put pressure on children to participate in politics, some women's reluctant acceptance of these pressures echoed the historical phenomenon of women running for office in place of their husbands. For example, two of the female interviewees in this study had run for political office primarily in response to familial pressures to carry on political work begun by a male relative. When one of these women was asked why she had run for office, she replied:

> Because I married into this … political family …. Frankly, I didn't really have any desire to take on this kind of work …. But because later, some people who supported my father [actually father-in-law] … my father's friends and his supporters wondered, why should we waste these resources on someone else? … [in Southern Min, i.e. Taiwanese] 'Those putting on the show are tired of putting it on, but those watching the show still want to watch more' (a local saying) …. [In Mandarin] We didn't want to perform [anymore], but they wouldn't let us go …. I am just continuing the [public] service for my father's old friends … my father's supporters.

The pressures of traditional culture on women in the DPP were manifest not only in their political choices but also in their personal ones. As indicated above, one interviewee consistently referred to her father-in-law as 'my father', reflecting the cultural belief that a woman 'belongs' to the family of her husband. This belonging can be either a positive one of attachment to one's in-laws or a negative one of possession by one's in-laws.

As another reflection of the persistence of tradition, one woman who held an elected public office said: 'I still cook dinner every night'. Such traditional pressures were tiring for these DPP women, who had to balance work inside and outside the home. As one interviewee explained:

> We have family responsibilities. Male councillors don't have this. When they go home, they don't have to cook or anything. This kind of work, we [women] still have to do it. We're city councillors on the outside, but when we go home, we are homemakers.

Women in the party maintained traditional roles at home in part because of family expectations. Nevertheless, they were also genuinely concerned about their family's welfare, especially that of their husbands. One woman said, very solemnly, that maintaining traditional gender roles at home was one way in which women public officials could help their husbands to adjust to being the spouse with lower political status. She said:

> When [the husband] goes out and people introduce him as such-and-such city councillor's husband, it's just not the same as when you say a person is such-and-such city councillor's wife. Upon hearing [that kind of introduction, the husband] feels uncomfortable in his heart.

For this reason, women public officials tried to soothe their husbands by maintaining traditional, subservient gender roles at home.

Although traditional gender expectations placed great pressures on DPP women to balance political work and family expectations, some female inter-viewees believed that the prevalence of traditional attitudes actually helped women to be more effective in public office. One woman gave an insightful analysis of the benefits of traditional views on gender for public officials:

Frankly, it's better to be a girl. There are fewer social engagements in the evenings, and you don't have to drink [alcohol] .... When you're a woman [elected representative], it's just less convenient for men [to socialise with you]. And we're married .... So, they consider the fact that we have families. So, they are less likely to invite us to social occasions. So, frankly, we just do our work, finish what others ask of us.

On the other hand, male politicians felt burdened by traditional gender expectations in a different way. Whereas women politicians were still expected to fulfil their traditional roles in the home, their male counterparts were pressured to assert their masculinity by meeting certain social obliga-tions:

> [Men's] social obligations are like ... one event after another .... If you don't go, people would say that you're afraid of your wife .... Women [elected representatives] are more likely to be able to serve well because they don't have social obligations in the evenings. They get enough sleep .... For men ... with their social obligations, they're out until one or two o'clock, drinking. They can't even get up in the mornings.

Thus the persistence of traditional gender expectations affected not only women in politics, but also men. Consequently, it was not surprising that some men in the DPP could not move beyond traditional views of women.

Conclusions

In short, the DPP offered support for women and women's issues. However, the party's articulation of women's issues focused on women in the tradi-tional roles of mother and primary carer. Also, the organisation's support for women's issues stemmed in part from the realisation that supporting public policies for women translated into getting more women's votes. The DPP's political communications of women's issues, or the investigation of women's concerns, were responsibilities that fell primarily to the women within the party. In the rare cases where male interviewees brought up the subject of women, they discussed the topic only in the context of gaining votes from women. Furthermore, the party had yet to concretise this support for women in society at large, because the DPP could not implement its policies as an opposition party.

Internally, however, the DPP showed its support for women primarily with the one-in-four rule, which promoted women's participation in party politics. But despite the support for women among party leaders, some men in the DPP still harboured traditional and sexist attitudes towards women. Thus official support for women's issues did not make the party less patriarchal or its members less sexist than in Taiwanese society at large. One interviewee's remark summarised the gendered dimensions of this case study: 'Women's voices are heard in the DPP, but there aren't enough voices. And they're not loud enough'. These descriptive findings illustrate not only the situation of women in the DPP but also the need to recognise the importance of gendered dimensions of political activism.

Notes

1 Since the research for this chapter was conducted, Chen Shui-bian of the DPP won the presidency in 2000, and the DPP won the largest number of seats (though not a majority) in the December 2001 Legislative Yuan elections.
2 The KMT suffered a serious internal conflict in the early 1990s. A group of young KMT legislators formed the New KMT Alliance in 1992, which clashed with the mainstream faction and finally led to the break-up of the KMT. The leaders of the New KMT Alliance established the New Party in August 1993.

References

Alvarez, S.E. (1990) *Engendering Democracy in Brazil: Women's Movements in Transition Politics*. Princeton, NJ: Princeton University Press.

Calhoun, C. (1991) 'The ideology of intellectuals and the Chinese student protest movement of 1989', in C.C. Lemert (ed.), *Intellectuals and Politics: Social Theory in a Changing World*. Newbury Park, Calif.: Sage.

Grunig, L.A. (1993) 'The Cuban Women's Federation: organization of a feminist revolution', working paper no. 238, Michigan State University Board of Trustees.

Rickards, J. (1998) 'DPP to establish sex harassment committee', *China News*, 14 May: 3.

Shohat, E. (1996) 'Globalization and the nation: towards a multicultural feminist critique', lecture presented as part of the polyseminar 'Women and Gender in an Era of Global Change: Internationalizing and "Engendering" the Curriculum', sponsored by the Department of Women's Studies and the Curriculum Transformation Project, University of Maryland, College Park, 27 February.

Shohat, E. and Stam, R. (1994) *Unthinking Eurocentrism: Multiculturalism and the Media*. London: Routledge.

Tarrow, S. (1994) *Power in Movement: Social Movements, Collective Action and Politics*. New York: Cambridge University Press.

Tilly, C. (1978) *From Mobilization to Revolution*. Reading, Mass.: Addison-Wesley.

—— (1986) *The Contentious French*. Cambridge, Mass.: Harvard University Press.

Ware, A. (1996) *Political Parties and Party Systems*. New York: Oxford University Press.

Yin, R.K. (1989) *Case Study Research: Design and Methods* (revised edition). Newbury Park, Calif.: Sage.

8 Communication of identities in Taiwan

From the 2–28 incident to FTV

Ming-Yeh T. Rawnsley

> I grew up as a Japanese during the colonial period, became a Chinese under
> the KMT dictatorship, and may die as a naturalised American, but in heart
> and soul I have always been a Taiwanese.
> (Taiwanese in the USA, in conversation with Huang Huang-hsiung; Tu 1996: 1124)

Introduction

This chapter explores the construction and reflection of Taiwan's identities
in the media over the five decades since the February 28th Incident (generally referred to as '2–28') in 1947. These issues frame the methods and
content of political and social discourse in Taiwan and structure the form
and substance of mediated communication.

Why identity? What identity?

To understand politics in Taiwan, it is very important to understand how
identities are constructed, as this construction 'affects people's views of a
wide range of choices that must be made about Taiwan's ongoing political
and social development' (Wachman 1994: 79). However, identities are
dynamic and rarely exclusive. As the quotation reproduced at the beginning
of this chapter demonstrates, individuals may have multiple, overlapping
and sometimes competing identities. Moreover, there are many types of
identity that may form the bases for a person's disparate sentiments of identification – political identity, ethnic identity, cultural identity, national
identity, and even institutional identity (such as liberalism versus communism: see Jiang 1997: 83). In the case of Taiwan, it can be extremely difficult
to distinguish the differences between political, ethnic, cultural and national
identities; further complications are added to the communication of identity
when the discourse on Taiwan's national identity is intertwined with the
emotional debate of unification versus independence.

National identity is a multidimensional concept: it is ethnic in terms of
origin and generation, cultural in terms of memory and belonging, and
institutional in terms of legitimacy and recognition (*ibid.*: 84). Therefore,

national identity 'is a philosophical problem distinct from the political issue of 'unification/independence' of Taiwan' (Jiang 1998: 165–6). Individuals may identify themselves as Taiwanese while supporting eventual reunification with the Chinese mainland, while others may identify themselves as Chinese but are in favour of Taiwan's independence. In other words, 'one's notion of national identity cannot always be determined on the basis of where one comes from' (Wachman 1994: 118); while the debate over the issue of unification/independence demands an answer framed in terms of 'either/or', identities can and do coexist. Yet national identity continues to be one of the most powerful platforms adopted by political activists to champion their particular cause and mobilise sympathisers. This has made it increasingly difficult for the people of Taiwan to separate the quest for an identity from the search for a solution to future relations with the People's Republic of China (PRC) and has subsequently become an enormous and constant pressure on the island's public psyche.

This chapter focuses on how Taiwan's national identity has been shaped and reflected in the media, especially national television, but it avoids passing judgement on the issues of independence and unification. But why are the media, and television in particular, important to the formation and expression of identities?

The importance of national television

Although the media are not solely responsible for the construction of identities, they can be significant actors in the process, regardless of whether that identity is cultural, national or political. Because of the development of modern mass media, identity is no longer confined to specific local contexts, where 'local knowledge' and local interaction determine the formation of the self. Access to the media supplements and in time displaces these local constructs, thus broadening the horizons of individuals' understanding (Thompson 1995: 211). Narrow local identities can become national identities. In turn, this understanding, and thus the construction of the 'self', will be conditioned by the primary experiences, interactions and cultural values of the audience, together with any transmission of ideology, all of which is selectively absorbed, interpreted and retained or discarded according to the framework of their existence – in other words, how the message is internalised. Together, all these influences assemble an individual's sense of his/her identity.

The media are a channel of communication between state and society, and within society itself. They give form and expression to identities and communicate the symbolism associated with them. Because identity provides a symbolic identification of the self, it is emotionally powerful. In this way, the media's communications of identities provide the framework for audience interpretation. They define, and provide the focus for, an understanding of 'us' in relation to 'them'.

Among all the media, television is the most popular in Taiwan. The criteria that can be used to measure how influential national television is are limited, but figures do exist to illustrate the reach of television in Taiwan. For example, official statistics reveal that almost every household in Taiwan owned a television set by the early 1990s (GIO 1993: 27). Market research also indicated that 78.8 percent of the Taiwanese population 10 years old or older tended to watch television evening news on a regular basis (Gallup Organisation 1994: 84). This result coincided with two academic reports published by National Chengchi University in 1994 and 1995.[1] Although these figures only indicated the percentage of the population who watched the television evening news, they at least suggest how popular national television could be.

Prior to the lifting of martial law, only the Chinese identities endorsed by the ruling Kuomintang (KMT, i.e. the Nationalist Party) could be expressed in the media, but following liberalisation in 1987, more open media have permitted a more transparent and less violent debate on identity issues. CATV (community antenna television, also known in Taiwan as cable television) proliferated in Taiwan between 1988 and 1992, when it was still illegal, and it provided the opposition with an abundance of channels to express various identities – Chinese, Taiwanese, Hakka, aborigine – together with cross-ethnicity identities such as religion, gender and green issues. However, it must be recognised that cable television is synonymous with narrowcasting, and narrowcasting creates its own problems in terms of communicating identities. In particular, it serves to divide the audience even further, since the audience will seek out those programmes that correspond to their own political orientation and thus insulate them further from alternatives. Hence, narrowcasting could never be a substitute for the national broadcasting system. Moreover, while cable television had penetrated 70 percent of Taiwanese homes by early 1996 (*Free China Review*, February 1996: 22), national television networks continued to command the biggest market share (Chiang 1994: 41–66). This suggests that the three national television companies – Taiwan Television Enterprise (TTV), China Television Company (CTV) and Chinese Television System (CTS) – remained influential and financially dominant even when the cable era arrived in Taiwan. In other words, TTV, CTV and CTS had been the most popular and powerful channels of information, entertainment and political communication in society for over three decades. Their importance in constructing and reflecting Taiwan's identities should never be overlooked.

Structuring the chapter

From the *dangwai* ('outside the party') period to the era of the Democratic Progressive Party (DPP),[2] the opposition had developed their own form of media to advocate their views and identities effectively – first journals, then videos, cable television and call-in radio. However, they were always operated underground and regarded as 'alternative' media (Rawnsley 2000: 576). Therefore, the establishment of the fourth national commercial television network, Formosa Television (FTV),[3] marked a particularly significant moment of success for the opposition movement. FTV has granted Taiwanese identities a strong presence on national television and has thus legitimised the expression of alternative identities to the 'Chinese-ness' that previously dominated mainstream television. Besides, the formation of FTV has reflected the flourishing of a multidimensional and open discussion of Taiwan's identities, even though differentiation between Chinese and Taiwanese identities, emphasised by national television, may have perpetuated the problems and their contradictions.

To understand how the communication of identities has changed alongside the political and social development in Taiwan since the island was returned to China from Japan in 1945, this chapter will proceed in three stages:

1   What are the differences between the Chinese and Taiwanese identities? Before liberalisation in 1987, how did a Chinese nationalist ideology dominate the indigenous Taiwanese consciousness in the media, and the three national television channels in particular?
2   Following the lifting of martial law in 1987, how did the opposition movement capture the popular imagination to support the liberalisation of the media and encourage the establishment of FTV in 1997? How did the opposition movement and FTV reflect, and contribute to, a growth of Taiwanese identity?
3   In its competition with the three other national commercial television networks, has FTV become an exclusively Taiwanese station and thus intensified the primary division of identities within Taiwan? The DPP's candidate, Chen Shui-bian, won the 2000 presidential election. Does this give FTV an opportunity to continue to operate as 'an opposition television station' (*The Journalist*, 21–7 June 1998: 71)?

Pre-1987

It may be true that because the ocean isolates an island, island culture will naturally be different from continental culture due to environmental and geographical factors, even though the former might have originated from, and be influenced by, the latter (Chen 1993). But the development of Taiwanese consciousness was not a consequence of simply being geographically separate from the Chinese mainland. If Taiwan does have a distinct identity, it has been influenced by its history of exposure to foreign ideas, images and cultural constructs, especially Japanese and American, together with the identities transposed to Taiwan from the mainland in 1945 by the KMT.

Indeed, the very use of the word 'Taiwan' is laden with political and cultural significance, possessing a different meaning to the frequently used 'Republic of China' (ROC). Culturally speaking, there is an indescribable 'something' that unites the Chinese on both sides of the Taiwan Strait, and wherever Chinese communities are found in the world. As cultural anthropologist Li I-yuan has pointed out, 'at a basic level, the Taiwanese are like Chinese from elsewhere in that they abide by the same notions of the temporal, supernatural, spatial, and cosmological dimensions' (Wachman, 1994: 101–2). They also share the same mentality towards 'interpersonal relations – in the family, the community, and the state', as well as the same 'attitudes toward food and health'. Hence, according to Li, 'these similarities affirm that the culture of Taiwan is Chinese' (*ibid*).

Yet, politically, the differences between Taiwan and China are fundamental and, some would say, irreconcilable. As Alan Wachman has observed:

> The identity Taiwanese feel and the reason why some have tried to promote the idea that Taiwan has a separate culture has to do with Taiwanese reactions to *political repression*. The frustration Taiwanese have endured has caused them to challenge the legitimacy of the KMT and all it represents. That has created an atmosphere in which regional distinctions that might otherwise have been ignored have become potent symbols of a group consciousness, or identity, that empowers Taiwanese to see themselves as different.
>
> (*ibid.*: 102, emphasis added)

In other words, the motivation behind the reconstruction of an independent Taiwanese culture is political. This is why Chang Chun-hung, former secretary-general of the DPP, 'accounted for the emergence of Taiwanese identity, not in cultural differences, but in persecution and repression' (*ibid.*: 101).

Chinese identities versus Taiwanese consciousness

During the 1950s, the ROC projected an image that it alone was the rightful government of China, confronting a challenge by communist rebels, and it received US support on the basis that it represented a real alternative to the politics practised in Beijing. Here we can begin to discover the origins of Taiwan's unrelenting confusion, demonstrating how its authoritarian structure was consistent with its non-communist (and therefore, in American eyes, 'democratic') credentials. This paradox meant that the political identity of the nationalist government could never be reconciled with, and therefore fully represent, the will of all the people in Taiwan.

But the turning point in the clash between mainlanders and the Taiwanese[4] pre-dates the onset of the cold war with Beijing. The February 28th incident of 1947 ('2–28') provides a dramatic demonstration of how such issues as national identity, cultural reconstruction and the search for political autonomy have had a significant impact on the development of the media.[5] Governor Chen I held the free media responsible for 2–28, believing that their excessive criticism of the provincial government helped to reinforce the division between mainlanders and Taiwanese (Lai *et al.* 1991: 76). Following the incident, identities were often invoked as justification for harsh reprisals against those involved. For forty years, the trauma of 2–28 haunted Taiwan's political and social life and poisoned the relationship between Taiwanese and mainlanders. The KMT had tried to erase the episode from the collective conscience of the nation, and only in 1992 was the ruling party able to acknowledge its role in the massacre. The government formally apologised, erected a memorial to the dead and offered compensation to the victims' families. The opposition, on the other hand, never forgot 2–28 and until the 1980s used the incident as a powerful election platform, calling on the government to narrow the gap between mainlanders and Taiwanese (Rawnsley and Rawnsley 2001: 35).

Moreover, the incident provided the grounds for the development of a harsh relationship between the government and the media. Governor Chen I closed down all those newspapers that were found to represent 'different elements outside the Kuomintang Party' (*ibid.*: 76). Clearly, the KMT now intended to control the media, and this involved the projection of its own interpretation of identities.

Television and the Chinese nationalist ideology

So by 1987, the KMT enjoyed a near monopoly on information through the legal media. The party owned four national daily newspapers, the government owned two and the military five (Tien 1989: 197). The overlapping character of government/party/military translated into an overwhelming authority over the activities of the print media. Even the remaining twenty newspapers that were privately owned tended to have close corporate ties with the KMT. Indeed, the owners of the two newspapers with the highest circulations, *Chungkuo Shih Pao* (*China Times*) and *Lien-ho Pao* (*United Daily News*) were members of the KMT Central Standing Committee. Control over the organisation and output of the media could be severe. It is true that copy was never scrutinised by a censor before publication, but Articles 22 and 23 of the National Mobilisation Law bestowed powers of confiscation after publication upon the government if a newspaper printed anything considered to be threatening to political or military interests. The vague and arbitrary wording, which left such laws open to interpretation, gave the government enormous latitude in exercising its jurisdiction over the media (Jacobs 1976).

Similarly, the television industry became part of the state apparatus. TTV, the first commercial television company in Taiwan, was established in 1962, followed by CTV in 1969 and CTS in 1971. While the Taiwan provincial government was the biggest shareholder in TTV, the KMT owned CTV, and the Ministry of National Defence dominated CTS (Cheng 1993: 88–109).[6] According to the Broadcasting and Television Law, television, like the print media, was closely supervised by the Government Information Office (GIO), a branch of the Executive Yuan. Because party, government and military were an integral unit, TTV, CTV and CTS became purely government instruments, despite being funded by advertising revenue. The three television companies would always take actions to serve the KMT's interest, even though the latter might not necessarily issue a formal order for them to do so. The KMT used national television, like other vehicles for the transmission of political values (for example, education), to project its specific world view and to spread its own version of identities. For the ruling party, all forms of mass communication, but especially television, were obliged to fulfil specific 'social responsibilities' (Rawnsley and Rawnsley 1998: 110). These all served, and were therefore subordinate to, an overriding priority – the eventual recovery of the mainland. In this way, society was forced to adopt those interpretations of identities that were consistent with the KMT's ideology. Language was an obvious battleground.

The KMT government preferred to use the term 'dialect' instead of 'language' when referring to Hakka and *Min-nan-yu* (language of southern Fujian province, which is the mother tongue of most people in Taiwan and is thus usually referred to as 'Taiwanese', the language of Taiwan). This was a deliberate attempt to foster unity among all people in Taiwan and to generate a sense of a shared 'Chinese' identity. Mandarin became the official language, while Hakka and *Min-nan-yu* were merely 'dialects' of Mandarin. Television celebrated Chinese heroes, while Taiwanese culture was denied a voice within the mainstream media and confined to the private sphere (thus prompting the opposition to seek alternative channels of expression).

At the beginning of the 1970s, the three television channels used *Min-nan-yu* programmes to compete for advertising revenue; after all, 70 percent of the population spoke the language (Cheng 1993: 223). However, the government accused these programmes of obstructing national unity and the construction of a consistent national identity. In response, the stations reduced their dialect programming in 1972 from 50 percent to less than 20 percent (Lee 1979: 155–7), and then in 1985 to less than 10 percent of the total (Lee 1989: 193).

As a result of such a language policy in programming, the prominence of 'dialects' (in particular Hakka and aborigine), and traditional folk culture and art forms was eroded. For example, in 1989 it was discovered that (1) those using the aboriginal language in everyday life had fallen by 31 percent over three generations; (2) most of the population of Taiwanese origin could not speak Hakka; and (3) only 70 percent of Hakkas could speak their own language (Cheng 1993: 224).

It is not surprising, therefore, that by the end of 1988 language had become a political issue that yet again pitted Taiwanese against mainlanders. The

Hakka Rights Promotion Union initiated the first Hakka collective social movement since 1949 and launched a campaign under the slogan 'Returning My Mother Tongue'. Its tactics included street protests demanding that television and radio programmes be broadcast in the Hakka language. It called for the 'complete liberalisation of Hakka radio programming and the revision of Article 20 of the broadcasting regulations, which limits the use of 'dialects' in broadcasting, to support the preservation of these 'dialects' and to create a pluralistic and liberalised language policy' (Rawnsley and Rawnsley 2001: 41). Feeling pressured, the GIO consequently persuaded TTV to broadcast a special programme in Hakka on Sundays in 1989; and, from September 1991 onwards, the three national television networks were required to schedule a daily 20-minute news programme in Hakka (Cheng 1993: 266–7).

From the evidence presented above, it can be concluded that national television in Taiwan reflected the domination of Chinese nationalist culture in every layer of the society. It also demonstrates how the KMT dealt with the issues of identity and communicated its ideology. Thomas Gold (1993: 171–2) has summarised the situation prior to 1987 in Taiwan:

> Although the regime acknowledged that Taiwan had regional particularities, like any other locality in China, the KMT assiduously promoted the idea that the island was the repository and guarantor of Chinese tradition as well as the mainland's rich diversity .... Popular culture stressed mainland roots, addressing history and life on the mainland, not the island. Politically and to some extent culturally, then, Taiwan became a microcosm of pre-1949 Mainland China as interpreted by the KMT.

1987–1997

It is worth noting that despite the harsh experiences of 2–28, dissident politicians continued to organise anti-KMT activities and organisations after the incident. These opposition elites, as C.L. Chiou (1995: 75) has observed:

> were not great in number in the 1950s and 1960s, and under the 'white terror' of the martial law government of the Nationalists, they could not get much popular support among the severely intimidated Taiwanese people .... Their achievements were not very impressive but they were important in terms of sustaining the opposition campaigns and establishing operational models for the following generations.

In other words, prior to liberalisation in 1987, the opposition movement and the various issues surrounding the question of Taiwan's identities had always been a strong undercurrent running through society. But the political consequences of such activities and issues were far too risky for ordinary

citizens to participate in or discuss openly. It is not that identities contra-
dicting the KMT's ideology did not exist in Taiwan before 1987, rather that
people were simply too afraid to address them.

However, the lifting of martial law in 1987 enabled the public to express
their grievances and identities openly. Activities against the mainstream electronic media – particularly the three national television stations – had also
been used as an effective method of mobilising opposition against the KMT
government, and the DPP had been especially active in this regard (Fang
1995: 102–4). As a result, media issues were highly politicised during the
process of liberalisation and democratisation. Popular demand to open up
television channels became an important part of the opposition movement,
leading to the eventual establishment of FTV in 1997.

The rise of alternative identities

The media used by the opposition to promote their platforms certainly
contributed to the pressure on the KMT to reform. In fact, the 'alternative
media' had been a thorn in the side of the KMT since the mid-1970s.
Publications such as *Formosa*, *The Intellectual*, *The Eighties* and *The China
Tide* were short-lived and under-financed, had small circulations, and were
subject to swift and often brutal suppression by the Taiwan Garrison
Command. *The Taiwan Political Review* was banned in mid-1975 after being
accused of inciting insurrection, an explanation that echoed Chen I's
suppression of the media following 2–28. These publications nevertheless
acted as an extra source of pressure on the government and 'forced the
KMT regime into reformist concessions' (Chiou 1995: 129).

Yet the media cannot be held solely responsible for the momentum
towards political reform. Liberalisation of the media opened within society
a legitimate space where issues such as identities could be discussed. The
agenda for change was publicised, and the opposition was granted a
powerful and diverse means of expression. Therefore, we can argue that the
most important development in this period concerned how the combination
of a more liberal media environment and powerful new communications
technologies contributed to the creation of new identities that crossed
ethnic, political and cultural boundaries. These were not based wholly on
the simple dichotomy of Taiwanese or mainlander (although this remains
the strongest focal point); they also express the growth of a civil society to
which both the ruling party and the opposition must appeal for electoral
success. Cable television, for example, allows for narrowcasting, enabling
broadcasters (including politicians) to target their messages at specific
demographic and geographic audiences. It has been noted that Democracy
Television, the group of clandestine cable stations launched by the DPP in
1989, not only promoted the party's political and cultural platforms
(reporting on local affairs in *Min-nan-yu*) but also campaigned on behalf of
anti-nuclear and anti-pollution movements. In this way, 'Democracy

Television ... served as a platform for the grassroots movements whose voices have been absent from the KMT-dominated state television' (Chen 1998: 27).

The alternative media, then, were important in asserting a post-martial law identity – an identity that is increasingly fragmented because the centre can no longer represent the fringe. Not only did the KMT and what it represented begin to lose the central ground, but there was also not merely one centre within the opposition movement voicing only a single identity. For example, the agenda pursued by the DPP was very different from that of the New Party.[7] Neither were the identities championed by the Formosa faction within the DPP necessarily coherent with its other faction, New Tide.[8] Liberalisation of the political system in 1987, and especially the legalisation of the DPP, created the demand for a forum free from political restraint and accessible by all. Yet the three national television companies could not keep pace with the radical social changes sweeping the island during the late 1980s and early 1990s. Nor could the speed of liberalisation in the media environment as a whole parallel the remarkable progress being made in the political landscape. Hence the Campaign to Liberalise the Electronic Media initiated by the DPP was able to catch the public imagination (see below).

Alternative media played a crucial role in satisfying opposition demands for a means of expressing their growing identities, among which an indigenous consciousness was overwhelming. It became significant that, especially during elections, DPP candidates tended to speak in *Min-nan-yu* in order to appeal to their traditional voters. This can be proved by the fact that apart from the KMT, the other three sets of 1996 presidential candidates (including those competing in the DPP's primary election) all used *Min-nan-yu* in addition to Mandarin as their main campaign languages. Moreover, the underground radio stations and cable television channels that were supportive of independence also mainly adopted *Min-nan-yu* as their principal language, while the media that supported unification usually adopted Mandarin. Consequently, cultural, political and national identities have become entangled with the issues of reunification/independence. The government's countermeasures, including confiscation of equipment, helped to unite the opposition movements and politicise the media, thus reinforcing the new fragmentation of society.

Eventually, when the KMT government recognised the growth of alternative identities, the GIO responded by including new programming within national television services that catered to the indigenous consciousness. For example, in November 1987, the three network television stations were required to include a 20-minute news and weather bulletin in *Min-nan-yu* in their schedules, while in 1988, two *Min-nan-yu* soap operas scooped the National Golden Bell Television Awards (Cheng 1993: 265–70). But these measures did not go far enough. Research has shown that while *Min-nan-yu* programming still accounted for less than 9 percent of each station's output in 1990 and 1991, other dialects remained unsatisfied and thus prompted the 'Returning My Mother Tongue' street protest by the Hakka Rights Promotion Union, as previously discussed. While English-language television programmes made up 7.99 percent of the total in 1991, only 0.85 percent of each station's programmes were devoted to the Hakka dialect, and aboriginal-language programming was virtually nonexistent (Cheng 1993: 224). Such discrimination has strengthened the idea that political and social divisions can coalesce around cultural identities. In this way, the campaign to liberalise the electronic media has become a broad church that appeals to minority groups and alternative identities. These are gradually assimilated into a greater 'Taiwan' identity during the process and contribute to an expanding Taiwanese ideology.

Liberalising television and the establishment of FTV

In its 1991 proposal to liberalise television, the DPP identified the establishment of a terrestrial national television station as one of its goals (Cheng 1993: 484). The DPP justified its ambition of creating another party-owned national television company by arguing that this was to break the monopoly of the nationalists' hold on mainstream television. In other words, the launch of the fourth national television channel had a very strong political motive from the very beginning.

In January 1992, a number of DPP National Assembly members and legislators, including Chen Shui-bian (elected president in 2000), formed a Justice Alliance, adopting media issues as their major action point (Tao 1994: 282). Their platform was able to appeal to social elites, academics and intellectuals in particular, and subsequently to combine with environmental groups to maximise their influence. Under constant pressure from within the National Assembly and especially the Legislative Yuan, together with popular support generated through the opposition movement, the KMT government could no longer resist demands to release frequencies. In March 1992, the Ministry of Transport and Communications first agreed to release fifteen broadcasting channels and eleven regional television channels, and then in October the same year, the GIO agreed to open up FM airwaves in March 1993 and AM airwaves in February 1994 (Chen 2001).

By the time the Legislative Yuan passed the Cable Television Law in August 1993, the television industry in Taiwan was changing rapidly. As James Robinson (1996: 30–1) has pointed out, 'since the 1990s, many small, limited-audience cable television stations have been set up, several of them by political figures from the … DPP …. Although the … KMT and New Party … eventually realised the value of cable television for their own campaign purposes, the DPP founders got there "firstest with the mostest"'. Clearly, the opposition movement stimulated and changed the landscape of Taiwan's television. The public was so dissatisfied with the KMT monopoly of the electronic media that the DPP was able to benefit politically and economically from the campaign to liberalise television. The irony is that if the DPP has become as dominant in the television industry as the KMT, will the party be seen as corrupt like the KMT and thus lose its credibility in the campaign?

The DPP soon recognised the possible danger. In a meeting in July 1993, the DPP Central Standing Committee vetoed its previous plan to establish a party-owned national television station in order to provide a contrast to the KMT. The party also published a White Paper, stating its communication policy to 'abolish control and to break monopolies in order to establish a new communication order with a diverse and democratic system' (DPP 1993: 337). But this policy statement does not prevent politicians being involved as individuals in the television industry. So, in reality, DPP politicians are still able to pursue profits and political influence by operating television companies.

On 28 January 1994, the GIO announced the release of a new island-wide commercial television channel, which was designed to be based in Kaohsiung, the largest city in the south of Taiwan, in order to provide geographical balance to the existing television landscape. Three groups competed for control: the first was Asian Pacific Television (APTV), organised by the Chen Tien-mao family and several Kaohsiung-based politicians, most of whom had ties with the KMT. They invested £300,000 solely in preparing the proposal and collected £125 million in capital to support the establishment of the station (Lei 1994). The second group was Formosa Television (FTV), organised by various DPP politicians including Chang Chun-hung (of the Formosa faction), Tsai Tung-jung (a strong advocate of independence), and others with roots in southern Taiwan. Its proposal cost £250,000, and its capital was £75 million, although it had raised only one-third of the total when it applied for the licence (Chen 2001). The final competitor was Harvest Television (HTV), organised by Chiou Fu-sheng, a self-made media giant in Taiwan with an estimated capital of £37.5 million.

The GIO set up a special committee consisting of eleven independent members. During the period of examination by the committee, the press predicted that APTV, with the most careful plan and a strong financial background, would be the favourite, while others predicted that the HTV had a strong chance of winning since it was the only experienced professional group in television. But the FTV organisers took political action, combining threats with persuasion. They organised press conferences and public hearings to publicise the reasons why DPP politicians deserved to be awarded a national television channel. At the same time, they warned of direct action if their application was not successful. They also appealed to the US government through the Formosan Association for Public Affairs (FAPA), an effective Taiwan lobby group based in Washington, to help the campaign to liberalise television in Taiwan (*FTV Communication*, 15 November 1996: 1). Finally, in June 1995, the GIO announced that FTV had been successful; the licence was granted on the basis of winning six votes in the committee (Fang 1998: 72–85). The fourth national commercial television channel began transmitting in June 1997.

Post-1997

> FTV's highest principle is to ensure that Taiwan will never be swallowed by China. How to protect Taiwan? It is our responsibility to cultivate ... Taiwanese nationalism. We shall not allow any colleague to use FTV to champion Chinese nationalism. All the programmes and news provided by FTV must be produced under the principle of Taiwanese nationalism.
>
> (Tsai Tung-jung, chairman of the board of governors, FTV; FTV Communication, 15 August 1997: 1)

> If a programme does not have (interesting) content, it will not appeal to any viewers even if it was shot on the Moon. I see programmes as products. As long as products have defined features, they will be able to grab the mass market.
>
> (Chen Kang-hsin, managing director, FTV; quoted in Chen 2001)

The above statements illustrate two major characteristics of FTV – 'Taiwanese nationalism' and 'commercialism'. Since its launch, FTV has competed relentlessly with TTV, CTV and CTS, not only politically but also commercially. So these are two important perspectives when we assess FTV's contribution to the communication of identities and consolidation of democracy in Taiwan.

Taiwanese nationalism

It is important to recognise that the 'Taiwanese nationalism' that FTV fosters has a stronger international dimension than the previously discussed 'indigenous consciousness'. Prior to liberalisation, the Chinese ideology that the opposition movement rebelled against was a nationalist ideology represented by the KMT. But the KMT likewise seemed confused. For over four decades, while the KMT and the government 'relentlessly drummed into the minds of the people their obligation to reunify with the rest of China', they 'earnestly tried to reinforce the idea that the communist system and the leaders of the PRC are evil'. So the people on Taiwan attested to 'feeling as though they were deceived by the KMT about political and cultural realities', which caused intense anxiety. People resented being 'caught between an abstract notion of a remote China', about which they knew too many ancient facts, 'and a concrete reality on Taiwan', about which they knew too little to make sense of their experiences (Wachman 1994: 76–84).

Democratisation has boosted Taiwan's own self-confidence, brought it to the attention of the international community and subjected it to escalating threats from the PRC. The explosive combination of the first direct presidential election, missile tests and the American Seventh Fleet steaming into the Taiwan Strait in 1996 forced Taiwan's increasingly complex identities back onto the agenda. They were political and social issues that the media naturally seized upon and reported. Media coverage accentuated identities, and the differences between the PRC and the ROC were highlighted. So the challenges of 'Chinese nationalism' that face Taiwan do not equal the nationalist ideology of the KMT but are forceful proposals for reunification accompanied by military threats and diplomatic manoeuvres from Beijing. Hence, under Tsai Tung-jung, a strong believer in Taiwan's independence, the identities reflected in FTV are not simply 'Taiwanese' against 'mainlanders' any longer but 'Taiwan' versus 'China', 'Taiwanese' (people of Taiwan) versus 'Chinese' (people of China – a cultural and historical China that is also inseparable from the political China, that is the PRC).

Therefore, since it joined the GIO's project in April 1998 to provide a daily 20-minute news programme overseas (in rotation with the three other stations), FTV has become mired in the political divisions that revolve around identities in the international arena. It has been criticised, mainly by supporters of reunification among the overseas Chinese communities in North America who receive programmes via a satellite feed. Complaints centre on its use of *Min-nan-yu* greetings; its use of the terms 'China and Taiwan' instead of 'cross-strait', 'PRC' instead of 'Chinese mainland', and 'Taiwan' instead of 'Republic of China'; and their coverage of the opposition activities of Cheng Nan-jung, who burned himself to death in protest against the KMT. However, it has also received fulsome praise from overseas Chinese communities that are supportive of Taiwan's independence (Kang 1998: 57).

Domestically, FTV has been proud of the fact that 'Taiwanese nationalism' distinguishes the station from its national rivals. It guarantees a large number of news and other programmes in *Min-nan-yu* and Hakka (although the aboriginal languages are still absent). In addition, since September 1999, FTV has provided simultaneous subtitles for the major evening news slot, the first station to do so in order to serve viewers with hearing difficulties (Chen 2001). Indeed, to compare with TTV, CTV and CTS, FTV has offered more resources and access for other dialect programming and minority groups and has thus provided a valuable alternative to the Mandarin-dominated television networks.

Similarly, FTV has been more radical and provocative in politics than its counterparts. It produced a series of documentaries, news programmes and dramas on various aspects of Taiwan, such as history, the environment, the 2–28 incident, and political and social scandals that were considered taboo under martial law. It has hosted talk shows and call-in programmes on debates such as 'Should Taiwan enter the United Nations?' and 'Should the Taiwan Independence Party Constitution be amended?' (*FTV Communication*, 10 December 2000: 1). However, it is difficult to distinguish whether this was due to 'Taiwanese nationalism' or 'commercialism'. The programmes were sensational in order to attract the highest possible ratings, but the discussions generally lacked depth and objectivity.

When it comes to news coverage during elections, FTV was heavily criticised because it favoured DPP candidates, especially in the 1998 mayoral elections (Ma 1998). It was also noticed that, in the second half of the 2000 presidential election, FTV was biased towards the DPP candidate, Chen Shui-bian. Yet FTV justified its position because it was designed to provide 'opposition views' to counter coverage found on TTV, CTV and CTS (Chen 2001). By doing so, FTV's original ambition to act as 'an opposition television station' (*The Journalist*, 21–27 June 1998: 71) was quickly reduced to merely 'an opposition party's station', despite the declaration in its 1993 White Paper that the DPP was against the idea that political parties should own national television stations. Hence, as soon as the DPP had won the 2000 presidential election, the press began to designate FTV as 'government television' (*Jin Post*, 21 March 2000).

In other words, perhaps the 'distinct' television culture that FTV has so proudly claimed to represent is not essentially all that different from that of TTV, CTV and CTS after all. From the perspective of 'Taiwanese nationalism', the fourth national television station clearly suffers from a similar level of political involvement to its three national rivals under the KMT's 'Chinese ideology'. The establishment of FTV has broken the nationalist monopoly over mainstream television, but the public is offered merely a system of duopoly as an alternative, emphasising 'Taiwanese' against 'Chinese' and thus perpetuating the primary division of identity.

However, as Table 8.1 demonstrates, identity is a fluid concept, neither spatially nor temporally bound. Although it is difficult to differentiate which part of the Taiwanese and Chinese identities respondents identify with, results suggest that many people do not wish to choose one identity over another.

Perhaps the most telling of all is that in 1996, when the missile crisis was escalating tension between the ROC and the PRC, the number of people who viewed themselves as exclusively 'Taiwanese' did not increase but actually decreased by almost 4 percent compared with the figure in 1994. On the other hand, the number of people who viewed themselves as exclusively

Table 8.1 How do the people of the Republic of China (Taiwan) view themselves?

	Exclusively Taiwanese (%)	Both Taiwanese and Chinese (%)	Exclusively Chinese (%)	Other/uncertain (%)
1992	16.7	36.5	44.0	2.8
1994	28.4	49.9	21.7	0
1996	24.9	49.5	20.5	5.1
1998	38.0	44.9	12.3	4.8
2000	45.0	39.4	13.9	1.7

Source: Chang (2000: 6).

'Chinese' also decreased, while the group who identified themselves as both 'Taiwanese and Chinese' remained as high as 49.5 percent. This may suggest that although Beijing's military exercise succeeded in preventing people in Taiwan registering themselves as exclusively 'Taiwanese', at the same time it failed to push more people into viewing themselves as 'Chinese'. In fact, many spectators believe that China's military exercise was designed to frighten Taiwan's electorate into voting against Lee Teng-hui, but that the plan backfired and only served to strengthen Taiwan's resolve to give Lee a clear mandate (Rawnsley 1997: 54). Nevertheless, while 54 percent of the population was willing to demonstrate their political commitment against Beijing's threat by voting for Lee, evidence presented in Table 8.1 shows that almost 50 percent of the population were determined not to give up their Chinese heritage despite the political hostility.

In other words, the Taiwanese nationalism that FTV endorses may have reflected, and contributed to, the trend of a growing Taiwanese identity. But this does not mean that the needs of the group that maintains or wishes to maintain both Taiwanese and Chinese identities should be sacrificed. When such needs are neglected by the Taiwanese nationalism promoted by the DPP through FTV, it is not surprising that, as a political and social consequence, the new ruling party has found it increasingly difficult to secure a strong mandate from an increasingly fragmented society.

Commercialism

As a privately owned national television company that depends on advertising revenue, FTV is subject to the same pressures as any other commercial television station in the world. In order to survive, FTV has been forced to enter a fierce ratings war with TTV, CTV and CTS since its launch.

For example, FTV has guaranteed provision of a large number of news and other programmes in *Min-nan-yu* and Hakka. As over 70 percent of the population speak the language, the popularity of *Min-nan-yu* programming has not been a problem, but programmes in Hakka have always suffered in terms of ratings. Hakka news programmes were consequently rescheduled to unpopular slots, and journalists who were originally appointed to make special features in Hakka were transferred to other divisions. Without sufficient resources and talent, news programmes in Hakka suffered from a lack of professionalism and finally became simply Mandarin news dubbed into Hakka. Hence the quality of dialect programming provided by FTV is questionable.

In addition, it is worth noting that FTV was designed by the GIO to be based in Kaohsiung to provide a geographical counterbalance to Taipei, the centre of Taiwan's media industry. Therefore, in comparison with TTV, CTV and CTS, FTV has promoted views associated with regional aspects, especially southern Taiwan. However, due to financial considerations, FTV finally transferred its headquarters from Kaohsiung to Taipei, where most resources are readily available. Although FTV cannot abandon its southern centre because of its licensing requirements, the Kaohsiung base has been reduced to a mere subsidiary.

Finally, FTV has broadcast more soap operas than its rivals in order to attract the largest possible market share and advertising revenue. If a programme proves popular, the number of episodes is increased and the series is extended indefinitely, enjoying numerous repeat showings. If ratings are low, a programme will be axed at short notice even though it may have established a small but loyal following of viewers. Public service programmes, such as educational, informational and highbrow cultural programmes, will always be scheduled in unpopular slots.

These practices should not be overly criticised; after all, profit is the goal of all commercial enterprises. But it is doubtful just how much diversity the establishment of FTV can really provide in an era of democratic consolidation when identities are increasingly fragmented. How much can the existing structure of mass culture reflected in Taiwan's national television be improved by offering a national television channel to the DPP as a contrast to the KMT-dominated TTV, CTV and CTS? Has the opposition movement really liberalised the electronic media in Taiwan by launching FTV? In fact, the evidence presented has demonstrated three points: (1) The opening up of more commercial television channels is not equivalent to more choice; (2) the establishment of another national television station biased towards one party cannot resolve the long-term identity problem; and (3) privatisation of information and cultural resources will not provide pluralism and democracy in 'television liberalisation' (Scannell 1990: 26).

A free and diverse media environment that can provide greater competition is essential if identities are to coexist, interact, assimilate and search for common ground (Tsai 2001). The prominence of the underground media in Taiwan's recent history was a reaction to the failure of the ROC to respond to such pressure, while the establishment of FTV in 1997 symbolised some progress towards the liberalisation of national television. But further liberalisation and the breaking of a duopoly are necessary for the establishment of a national broadcasting system that is free from political interference and is able to contribute more to the consolidation of democracy.

Notes

1   The research showed that 76.5 percent of the Taiwanese population watched the television evening news during the 1992 legislative election campaign; 78.7 percent of the population watched the same programme during the 1993 mayoral election (Weng and Sun 1994: 6–8); and 80.1 percent of population watched the evening news during the 1994 Taiwan gubernatorial election (Sun 1995: 102–4).

2   Under martial law, politicians who opposed the KMT were unable to establish political parties, so they formed an informal alliance that was loosely referred to as *dangwai*, meaning 'outside the ruling party'. During the mid-1980s, President Chiang Ching-Kuo began a process of widespread reform, which involved

repealing martial law, in place for thirty-eight years, and allowing the organisa-tion of viable and legitimate opposition parties. The main opposition party, the DPP, became legal in early 1989 after the law governing new political parties had been passed, and it brought together most of the politicians from the *dangwai* era.

3   The full name of this station in Chinese is *Min Jian Quan Min Dian Shi* (short-ened to *Min Shi*), literally meaning 'People's Television'.

4   To be precise, there are four major ethnic groups in Taiwan according to linguistic sociologist Huang Hsuan-fan (1995: 218): *Min-nan* people, i.e. Chinese immigrants from southern Fujian province before 1945 (73.3 percent of the entire population); Hakka, i.e. Chinese immigrants from parts of Guangdong province before 1945 (12 percent); aborigines (1.7 percent); and 'mainlanders' (13 percent), who arrived in Taiwan in large numbers only after their defeat by the communists. The term 'Taiwanese' in some literature refers only to the *Min-nan* people; however, 'Taiwanese' in this chapter refers to Chinese who have lived in Taiwan since the sixteenth century, so it includes *Min-nan* people, Hakka and aborigines.

5   After the KMT took over Taiwan from Japanese colonial rule in 1945, the islanders became increasingly frustrated under the new administration. In February 1947, a seemingly insignificant incident finally triggered a near revolu-tion. The KMT sent troops from the mainland to suppress the revolt, which wiped out almost an entire generation of the Taiwanese socio-political intellec-tual elite. For further information about the 2–28 incident, see, for example, Lai *et al*(1991), Executive Yuan 2–28 Research Committee (1994), Chiou (1995) and Zhang *et al.* (1998).

6   Since democratisation, the financial structure of the three national television stations has been reformed. According to a GIO report in 2000, their major shareholders are as follows:

- TTV: indirect investment from the Ministry of Finance (25.88 percent), foreign investors (20.51 percent), indirect investment by the KMT (10.55 percent), domestic enterprises (34.86 percent), indi vidual domestic investors (8.2 percent).

- CTV: indirect investment by the KMT (41.1 percent), domestic enterprises (23.35 percent), individual domestic investors (35.55 percent).

- CTS: Ministry of Defence (26.41 percent), Ministry of Education (9.84 percent), private and public corporations and foundations (38.69 percent), domestic enterprises and individual investors (25.06   percent).

7   Since Lee Teng-hui took over leadership of the KMT on the death of Chiang Ching-Kuo in January 1988, the ruling party has suffered a series of internal conflicts. As a consequence, the New Party was established at the end of 1992 and consisted mainly of members of the anti-Lee Teng-hui camp and second-generation Taiwan-born mainlander politicians (the children of mainlanders are still known as mainlanders, even though they were born in Taiwan).

8   The DPP has been racked by division and factionalism since its birth, because the only consensus shared by the *dangwai* politicians was an opposition to the KMT. The two major factions within the DPP are Formosa and the New Tide. Generally speaking, the former takes a more moderate and orderly approach towards political reform, while the latter is more radical and appeals for Taiwan's independence.

References

Chang Hui-ying (2000) *Lee Teng-hui: 1988–2000 Twelve Years in Power*. Taipei: Yuan-liu (in Chinese).

Chen Wai (1993) *Island Culture*. Taipei: Yang-Chih (in Chinese).

Chen Sheue Yun (1998) 'State, media and democracy in Taiwan', *Media Culture and Society* 20(1): 9–29.

Chen Yen-lung (2001) 'Television and democratisation in Taiwan: case study of FTV', master dissertation, Graduate Institute of Political Science, National Sun Yat-sen University, Taiwan (in Chinese).

Cheng Jui-cheng *et al.* (eds) (1993) *Deconstructing Broadcasting Media: Establishing the New Order of Broadcasting Media*. Taipei: Cheng Society (in Chinese).

Chiang Wen-yu (ed.) (1994) *Media Reform and Democracy*. Taipei: Chien-Wei Publication (in Chinese).

Chiou, C.L. (1995) *Democratizing Oriental Despotism: China from 4 May 1919 to 4 June 1989 and Taiwan from 28 February 1947 to 28 June 1990*. Basingstoke: Macmillan.

DPP (1993) Policy White Paper. Taipei: DPP Central Standing Committee (in Chinese).

Executive Yuan 2–28 Research Committee (1994) *2–28 Research Report*. Taipei: China Times (in Chinese).

Fang Jien-san (1995) *The Political Economy of the Broadcasting Media's Capital Movement: The Analysis of the Changes in Taiwan's Broadcasting Media during the 1990s*. Taipei: Taiwan Radical Quarterly in Social Studies (in Chinese).

—— (1998) *Big Media II: Media Social Movement*. Taipei: Meta Media International (in Chinese).

Gallup Organisation (1994) *The Direction of Public Television's News Programmes and General Programmes*. Taipei: Public Television Organizing Committee (in Chinese).

GIO (1993) *The Republic of China Yearbook*. Taipei: GIO.

—— (2000) *Television Policy and Structure Reform Special Committee Report*. Taipei: GIO (in Chinese).

Gold, T.B. (1986) *State and Society in the Taiwan Miracle*. New York: M.E. Sharpe.

—— (1993) 'Taiwan's quest for identity in the shadow of China', in S. Tsang (ed.), *In the Shadow of China: Political Developments in Taiwan*. London: Hurst.

Huang Hsuan-fan (1995) *Language, Society and Ethnic Consciousness: Research on Taiwan Linguistic Sociology*. Taipei: Wen-he Publishing (in Chinese).

Jacobs, B.J. (1976) 'Taiwan's press: political communications link and research resource', *China Quarterly* 68(4): 778–88.

Jiang Yi-huah (1997) 'National identity in liberal democracy', *Taiwan: A Radical Quarter in Social Studies* 25: 83–121 (in Chinese).

—— (1998) 'Reflections on the discourses of national identity in Taiwan', *Taiwan: A Radical Quarter in Social Studies* 29: 163–229 (in Chinese).

Kang I-lun (1998) 'FTV speaks in *Min-nan-yu*. Overseas New Party Members Criticise it for Advocating Taiwan Independence', *The Journalist*, 3–9 May: 57 (in Chinese).

Lai Tse-han, Myers, R.H. and Wei Wou (1991) *A Tragic Beginning: The Taiwan Uprising of February 28, 1947*. Stanford, Calif.: Stanford University Press.

Lee, C.-C. (1979) *Media Imperialism Reconsidered: The Homogenizing of Television Culture*. London: Sage.

—— (1989) *Media Imperialism*. Taipei: China Times (in Chinese).

—— (1992) 'Emancipated from authoritarian rule: the political economy of the press in Taiwan', in Chu and Chan (eds), *Mass Communication and Social Change*. Hong Kong: Chinese University Press (in Chinese).

Lei I-hsien (1994) 'Chiou Fu-sheng, Chen Tien-mao, and Chang Chun-hung compete fiercely', *Wealth*, May: 244–6 (in Chinese).

Ma Chih-chun (1998) 'FTV's special interview with Chen Shui-bian was protested by Ma Ying-jiu camp', *The Journalist*, 4–10 October: 86 (in Chinese).

Rawnsley, G. (1997) 'The 1996 presidential campaign in Taiwan: packaging politics in a democratizing state', *Harvard International Journal of Press/Politics* 2(2): 47–61.

—— (2000) 'The media and popular protest in pre-democratic Taiwan', *Historical Journal of Film, Radio and Television* 20(4): 565–80.

Rawnsley, G.D. and Rawnsley, M.-Y.T. (1998) 'Regime transition and the media in Taiwan', in V. Randall (ed.), *Democratization and the Media*. London: Frank Cass.

—— (2001) *Critical Security, Democratisation and Television in Taiwan*. London: Ashgate.

Robinson, J.A. (1996) 'Cable campaigning', *Free China Review* 46(2): 30–1.

Scannell, P. (1990) 'Public service broadcasting: the history of a concept', in A. Goodwin and G. Whannel (eds), *Understanding Television*. London: Routledge.

Sun Hsiu-hui (1995) 'Exploring the influence of new media on voters' political behaviours during 1994 election in Taiwan', *Journal of Electoral Studies* 2(1): 93–118 (in Chinese).

Tao Wu-liu (1994) *Chen Shui-bian Shock*. Taipei: Ta-tsun Culture (in Chinese).

Tien Hung-mao (1989) *The Great Transition: Political and Social Change in the Republic of China*. Taipei: SMC Publishing.

Thompson, J.B. (1995) *The Media and Modernity: A Social Theory of the Media*. London: Polity Press.

Tsai Ming-Yeh (2001) *The World of the Media*. Taipei: Youth Culture (in Chinese).

Tu Weiming (1996) 'Cultural identity and the politics of recognition in contemporary Taiwan', *China Quarterly* 148(4): 1115–40.

Wachman, A.M. (1994) *Taiwan: National Identity and Democratization*. New York: M.E. Sharpe.

Weng Shieu-chi and Sun Hsiu-hui (1994) 'How media use influences voters' political knowledge, party preferences and their voting behaviour in Taiwan's 1993 general voting', *Journal of Electoral Studies* 1(2): 1–25 (in Chinese).

Zhang Yen-Xian *et al.* (eds) (1998) *Collection of the 2–28 Incident Research Papers*. Taipei: Wu San-lian Taiwan Historical Material Foundation (in Chinese).

Part III

Hong Kong

Plate 3　Memorial commemorating Hong Hong's return to
the motherland.
Source: photo taken by Gary Rawnsley

9 The media in Hong Kong

On the horns of a dilemma

Willy Wo-Lap Lam

Introduction

The visit to Washington by Tung Chee-hwa, Chief Executive of the Hong Kong Special Administrative Region (SAR), in July 2001 was special in more ways than one. What was most remarkable was the high-level reception: the Hong Kong supremo not only met Secretary of State Colin Powell but also had a full thirty minutes with President George W. Bush at the White House. By contrast, Jack Straw, the British Foreign Secretary, who was in the American capital on the same day, had to content himself with a session with National Security Adviser Condoleezza Rice (*South China Morning Post* (*SCMP*), 11 July 2001).

By according Hong Kong a status even higher than that of a big province in the People's Republic of China (PRC), Washington was trying to underscore its hope that the SAR would in some ways retain a separate identity. However, in February 2001 the US State Department expressed worries about the lack of a clear-cut commitment to democratisation in Hong Kong. For example, it cited 'limitations on residents' ability to change their government and limitations on the power of the legislature to affect government policies; reports of police use of excessive force; some degree of media self-censorship ... '.[1]

Tung sees the picture differently. In his assessment of four years under Chinese sovereignty in 2001, Tung claimed that the 'one country, two systems model' had had an 'outstanding achievement' in the SAR. He cited, among other things, 'open and fair' elections in the territory, while most objective analysts would point to the singular slowness in the development of democratic institutions (*Wen Wei Po*, 1 July 2001).[2]

While most Western governments, academics and observers had been hoping that the SAR experience would stress the 'two systems', Tung has given top billing to 'one country'. More importantly, the socio-political culture of the SAR has taken on heavier and heavier doses of 'Chinese-ness' as its economy becomes more dependent on the mainland's. Particularly after the slowdown in the US economy in 2001, hopes of a recovery in Hong Kong are predicated upon the China market. This means that Hong Kong residents, from college graduates and businessmen to senior officials, see their interests in good relations with Beijing if not in the mainland itself.[3]

This chapter will examine political developments in Hong Kong between 1999 and 2001. It will look at the distinctive political culture and communication tactics of the Tung administration in the last phase of the unpopular chief executive's first five-year term. Particular attention will be paid to the development of the media, especially the erosion of press freedom and the alarming increase in self-censorship.

The Sinicisation of Hong Kong politics

The rise of 'Chinese-ness' in the socio-political milieu

In an article in the influential American journal *The Weekly Standard* in 2001, veteran Hong Kong observer Ellen Bork wrote that the situation in Hong Kong was fast becoming 'one country, one system'. Casting serious doubt on the validity of 'one country, two systems', she claimed that Beijing had boosted its influence in SAR affairs and that a number of senior civil servants had become Beijing's puppets or 'proxies' (Bork 2001).

While Bork's views may be somewhat exaggerated, there is no doubt that the SAR's political culture has become more 'Chinese', and this goes behind relatively superficial phenomena such as declining standards of English and more people taking up Mandarin Chinese. What is most disturbing seems to be that members of Hong Kong's elite – top civil servants and businessmen – are observing mainland Chinese values and political norms. Foremost among such values is a phenomenon known in Cantonese slang as *sik jo* (meaning *savoir faire*) or knowing how to anticipate the wishes of the powers that be. Often *sik jo* is couched in the Confucian terms of 'harmony', knowing one's station in life, curbing confrontation and divisiveness and maximising the collective good or the goals of patriotism.[4]

Diplomats and other observers have cited examples galore to back up their pessimistic reading of the SAR's political development. This became a certainty after Beijing had indicated in mid-2000 that it wanted Chief Executive Tung to get a second term in 2002. It was always unlikely that any heavyweight Hong Kong politician or businessman would run against Tung in 'elections' scheduled for 24 March 2001.[5] In turn, Beijing and Tung have been accused of showing favouritism and giving 'sweetheart deals' to businessmen willing to toe the Beijing line or to contribute to 'political stability' in Hong Kong.

Then there are apparently trivial but actually significant events such as the passage of a 'Chief Executive's Bill' in July 2001 giving Beijing authority to remove the top official whenever it deems necessary. The Basic Law, Hong Kong's mini-constitution, has nothing specific on the removal of the Chief Executive. Government critics such as Martin Lee, head of the Democratic Party, have accused SAR officials of self-emasculation at the prompting of

Beijing. Lee and others observed that the legislation was to ensure that if, one day, the Chief Executive were to be popularly elected, Beijing would have the legal foundation to remove the top official should he refuse to toe the line (*Asian Wall Street Journal*, 24 July 2001).

Other instances that run counter to the full autonomy ideal include efforts by the SAR administration to put pressure on groups or individuals anathema to Beijing. Since 1 July 1997, the Hong Kong immigration department has barred dissidents, including former student activists involved in the 1989 student movement in Beijing, from entering the territory. The local government has also turned a blind eye to the operations of the estimated several thousand state security agents from Beijing. The latter keep close tabs on the activities of 'anti-Beijing elements' in the SAR.[6]

In particular, the harsh treatment of the Falun Gong spiritual movement has raised doubts about the pledge of 'no change for fifty years' for Hong Kong. Beijing has apparently put pressure on the SAR to restrict the activities of the quasi-Buddhist sect if not ban it altogether. In public statements, Tung and senior Hong Kong officials blasted the Falun Gong as an 'evil cult'. However, while the sect has staged noisy demonstrations against Beijing leaders, it has largely abided by local laws.[7]

There was strong speculation that the Falun Gong was behind the earlier than expected departure of Chief Secretary Anson Chan, Hong Kong's most popular public figure, in May 2001. Chan had opposed Tung's harsh treatment of the sect.[8]

Adulterating the neutrality of the civil service

The departure of Anson Chan raised eyebrows because she represented 'Hong Kong's conscience', one aspect of which was the neutrality of the civil service. Immediately after becoming Chief Secretary on 3 May 2001, Donald Tsang reaffirmed her precept of political neutrality by saying that senior officials should not be hampered by the principles of political parties or personal political aspirations (*SCMP*, 16 February 2001; *Wen Wei Po*, 3 May 2001). After all, the efficiency and political neutrality of civil servants has all along been cited as a key legacy of the British era – and a vital component of Hong Kong's success formula.

However, fears have been raised that the civil service – and gradually, even the judiciary and the legal profession – may lose its neutrality and impartiality. Analysts in Hong Kong have criticised leading officials, including Secretary of Security Regina Ip and Secretary of Justice Elsie Leung, for bending over backwards to please Beijing and for failing to uphold Hong Kong's tradition of civil liberties. Ip has been relentless in her condemnation of the Falun Gong, and Leung is seen as too prone to ask the Standing Committee of the National People's Congress (NPA) to provide interpretations of the Basic Law in such a way as to undermine the authority of Hong Kong's highest judicial organ, the Court of Final Appeal.[9]

Doubts have also been cast on Tung's efforts to set up a quasi-ministerial system, which will be a departure from the existing model. In future, policy secretaries will be akin to ministers in parliamentary systems: while not being MPs, the top SAR officials will have to bear political responsibility. An important corollary is that they will have to defend Tung's line or that of a future Chief Executive, thus effectively losing their political neutrality. While the ministerial system will not be introduced until late 2002 at the earliest, Tung took a first step by appointing veteran banker Antony Leung as Financial Secretary in May 2001. Almost immediately, Leung raised suspicions by openly supporting Tung's 're-election'. He later apologised for this action, saying that it reflected only his private views. However, the damage was done (*Ming Pao*, 9 June 2001; *SCMP*, 9 June 2001).

Then there is the so-called 'Apei Awangjinmei syndrome', a gloss on how quite a few senior civil servants have switched their loyalty from the SAR to Beijing with the apparent goal of self-advancement. According to sources close to Beijing's Hong Kong policy establishment, even some mainland cadres were amazed at this about-face. Some officials called over-achievers among Hong Kong officials 'new Apeis', a reference to the fact that although Apei was originally a close lieutenant of the Dalai Lama, he soon switched sides and was co-opted by Mao Zedong in the early 1950s. To this day, Apei, now Vice-Chairman of the Chinese People's Political Consultative Conference, has been vociferous in condemning the 'separatist apostasy' of the Dalai Lama.[10]

With only relatively minor exceptions, Beijing has honoured its side of the commitment not to send officials to Hong Kong. The Hong Kong garrison of the People's Liberation Army (PLA) has remained largely out of sight to the public.[11] However, should the mentality of top civil servants – traditionally seen as elitist trend setters – change, it will be difficult for the SAR to convince the world that autonomy will remain undiminished.

Hong Kong's growing economic dependence on the motherland

Economics underpins politics. As Hong Kong's economy encounters problems, its dependency on the mainland becomes more obvious, and the formula of a high degree of autonomy may be dealt a big blow. After all, when Deng conceived his 'one country, two systems' model, mainland–Hong Kong relations were the other way around; that is, the mainland was dependent on Hong Kong to spearhead modernisation and to introduce foreign capital.

Hong Kong enjoyed an exceptional growth rate of 10 percent in 2000. Yet projections of gross domestic product increase for 2001 were a mere 1–2 percent. Business and consumer confidence that year was not much higher than immediately after the Asian financial crisis. One thing is clear: the SAR's much-vaunted efforts at economic restructuring in the wake of the Asian financial crisis have not been successful.

Early initiatives to restructure the economy have not been working well. One year after the handover, Chief Executive Tung unveiled an ambitious game plan to go high-tech. Major projects announced in 1998 and 1999, including the cyberport (on the western side of Hong Kong Island) and an industrial park in the New Territories near Shenzhen had not taken off by late 2001.[12] In terms of the technological content of its exports, Hong Kong lags behind developed Chinese cities such as Shanghai and Shenzhen by big margins.

Investments in high technology by companies such as those owned by tycoons Li Ka-shing, Li Shau-ki and Walter Kwok have been minuscule. Before the bursting of the dotcom bubble in late 2000, there was a spate of initial public offerings involving so-called high-tech or Internet stocks. Yet most of these companies were not really technology firms. Indeed, the great majority of local concerns spend less than 5 percent of their fiscal outlays on research and development. Hong Kong also lacks trained personnel. The shortage of information technology professionals stood at 4,000 in 2000, and this is expected to grow to 50,000 within ten years (*Ming Pao*, 24 February 2000).

In 2000, the Hong Kong securities markets raised more than US$50 billion for PRC companies. However, partly because Chinese stocks listed on mainland bourses enjoy much higher price-to-earnings ratios, many PRC firms may prefer listings back home if foreign fund management companies and other investors are allowed access to the mainland after China's entry to the World Trade Organisation (WTO). Shenzhen was due to open a NASDAQ-like second board in 2002, and the new facility is expected to pose ample competition to Hong Kong's Growth Enterprise Market second board.[13]

A way out for Hong Kong is not to compete but to work even more closely with industrialised cities in the mainland. This involves setting up direct and tailor-made cooperative relationships and ventures with coastal regions, particularly cities in Guangdong province such as Shenzhen. Hong Kong would thus derive substantial benefits as a dedicated, purpose-specific service centre for individual provinces and cities. This would go beyond Hong Kong's pre-1997 role of being a mere 'window' for the mainland.[14]

As Guangdong Governor Lu Ruihua put it in April 2001: 'Guangdong and Hong Kong are like lips and teeth. Their economies are complementary to each other. Guangdong needs Hong Kong and Hong Kong needs Guangdong'. Lu said that until now, cooperation between the two areas had been spearheaded by non-governmental sectors. He urged the provincial and SAR governments to play bigger roles to facilitate synergy between the two areas (*Wen Wei Po*, 1 May 2001).

A month later, prominent Hong Kong businessman Victor Fung unveiled a blueprint for economic integration between Hong Kong and the Pearl River delta area by 2022. The potential for symbiosis between Shenzhen and

Hong Kong is seen as immense. As officials in the Shenzhen Special Economic Zone put it, Hong Kong would provide financial and marketing support for Shenzhen's hi-tech industries (*Wen Wei Po*, 12 May 2001).

Until now, however, Hong Kong officials and businessmen have shown a considerable degree of resistance to virtual integration with Shenzhen or closer ties with Guangdong. Cooperation between Hong Kong on the one hand, and Guangzhou and Shenzhen on the other, has been restricted to areas such as water supplies to Hong Kong and repatriation of criminals. Investments by Hong Kong tycoons in Guangdong are mostly in the areas of hotels, real estate, infrastructure and relatively low-tech factories (*Wen Wei Po*, 26 July 2001).

However, since late 2000 Tung has given instructions to his aides to pay much more attention to working with mainland provinces and cities. Thus, in mid-2001, formal committees and mechanisms were set up between Hong Kong and Guangdong officials to proceed with much more specific economic and technological joint ventures, thus making synergy, and integration in some areas, a real reality.[15]

Indeed, Hong Kong is reaching out to areas much further than Shenzhen. The SAR may play a substantial role in Beijing's super-ambitious 'develop the west' programme, which will be a main driver of the mainland's economic growth for at least twenty years. Hong Kong's role in the go-west programme will be to raise capital and provide services in areas such as law, banking, accounting, marketing and public relations. In mid-2001, two Hong Kong tycoons, Li Ka-shing and Li Shau-ki, had sizeable investments in the oil and gas business in the western provinces (Yang 2001).

A prime force behind the economic integration of the mainland and the SAR is Beijing. Since the Asian financial crisis, central leaders have become worried about Hong Kong losing its advantages, and top cadres, including Premier Zhu Rongji, have expressed their desire to come to Hong Kong's aid if needed. One proposed method is to ask more major state firms and listed PRC companies to set up regional or even main headquarters in Hong Kong: 'The central government wants the more successful state-owned enterprises to become multinationals and it makes sense for PRC multinationals to establish marketing and financial offices in Hong Kong', said a party source in Beijing.

By October 2001, Beijing officials, including Premier Zhu Rongji, had pledged to give the SAR a series of dispensations. For example, cities such as Beijing and Shanghai were advised not to build Disneylands so as not to take business away from Hong Kong's Jiant Theme Park, due to open by 2005. Shenzhen was told to delay opening its NASDAQ-like second board so as not to compete with Hong Kong's growth enterprise market. The city of Beijing also indicated that Hong Kong enterprises setting up joint ventures in the capital would qualify for special treatment, such as lower taxes and land costs. Zhu later claimed that this would not violate WTO regulations, because Hong Kong was part of China.[16] Other 'special deals' for Hong Kong included permitting more businessmen and tourists, particularly from Guangdong province, to visit the SAR to help with the latter's tourism and retail trade.

The psychological and political implications of this growing economic dependence on the mainland are clear: If the lifeline of the SAR economy is the mainland, more Hong Kong residents may be resigned to the fact that in return for their jobs and high incomes, they will have to give up some of the freedoms they had become used to under the last years of British rule. After all, such residents could at least console themselves that the option of departure or emigration remains open should the situation deteriorate. Alternatively, they could at least send their riches and children overseas.

Blighted democracy prospects

If confirmed, the Sinicisation of Hong Kong life may have the impact of retarding democratisation. Reforms such as expanding the proportion of Legislative Council (Legco) members who are directly elected (currently only twenty-four of the sixty legislators are returned via universal suffrage) – one of the aspirations of Anson Chan – may be slowed down. Moreover, the prospects of direct popular election of the Chief Executive (at present, 'election' is done by an electoral college of 800 mostly pro-Beijing politicians and businessmen) seem to be receding further into the distance. Some conspiracy theorists believe that Beijing would only allow the bulk of Legco members to be elected directly if it thinks that pro-PRC parties such as the Democratic Alliance for the Betterment of Hong Kong (DAB) can win a majority.[17]

Other markers of a free society may also be adversely affected. The freedom of the press may be truncated. Sinicisation may also mean that the SAR economy will lose its reputation as a level playing field as 'pro-Beijing' business concerns and entrenched interests are seen as having unfair advantages over, say, Western or Japanese companies. There are also misgivings about an increase in corruption if the integrity of the legal and judicial systems is compromised (*Ming Pao*, 5 February 1999; *SCMP*, 5 February 1999).

Moreover, a vicious circle may be setting in. When Deng set up his 'one country, two systems' model, he did not anticipate that so many members of Hong Kong's elite – business leaders and top civil servants – would choose to chip away at their own community's autonomy by anticipating Beijing's wishes. It is already a truism in Hong Kong that often it is not a case of Beijing asking the SAR administration to do this or that. It is more likely that SAR officials are trying to score points for themselves, or simply to be politically correct, by anticipating what Beijing may like to see and hear.

This state of affairs easily plays into the hands of conservatives in both Beijing and Hong Kong who, for ideological or opportunistic reasons, are averse to a faster pace of democratisation. It is also of benefit to Tung, who was appointed to a second term in 2002, although he realised that he would not have been able to stay on if ordinary people had been given a choice in the selection of their top leader.[18]

Communication tactics of the Tung administration

Portraying Tung as a Confucian patriarch

Since he became Chief Executive, Tung Chee-hwa has tried to portray himself as a quintessentially Confucian patriarch. This self-professed fan of Singapore's Lee Kuan-yew apparently hopes that if he can successfully sell his image as 'Uncle Tung', the venerable head of the extended SAR family, his level of acceptance among the populace will rise. In sessions with college students, he likes to dwell on traditional values such as patriotism and respect for elders. It is not for nothing that Tung has always been a keen advocate of the revival of 'Chinese values' or Confucian edicts among the young in Hong Kong.[19]

Tung's status as Hong Kong's patriarch is reinforced by the fact that he seems to enjoy the ironclad support of Beijing's patriarchs: President Jiang Zemin, Premier Zhu Rongji and Vice-Premier Qian Qichen. From mid-2000, the top cadres have begun to sing the praises of Tung. Zhu indicated that Tung's performance was worth a mark of 110 percent, or, as Qian put it in early 2001, 'I hope various sectors of Hong Kong will unify themselves and support the work of the Chief Executive' (*China News Service*, 7 March 2001).

Normally neutral civil servants are expected to join the chorus. After a session with Tung in Beijing in October 2000, Qian said, 'SAR officials should of course support the head of the government. There is nothing more natural than this' (*Hong Kong Economic Journal (HKEJ)*, 27 October 2000) A month earlier, Qian had upbraided Anson Chan for not supporting Tung enough. In fact, since July 1997, Beijing had suspected that Chan, whose only boss since leaving college had been the British colonial government, had tried to form an anti-Tung faction within the SAR civil service.

Chinese-style bureaucratic harmony – in the form of officials proffering undying support for their patriarch – was neatly captured by a photograph distributed by the Information Services Department of the SAR government in mid-June 2001. Hong Kong had just been buffeted by a spate of tropical rainstorms and Tung, together with senior officials such as Tsang and Leung, were out inspecting salvage operations. However, the poses struck by the various protagonists – Tung seemed to be unlocking the keys of the future while his subordinates looked up to him with the utmost admiration – reminded observers of Cultural Revolution-era pictures of larger-than-life Helmsman Mao and his awestruck entourage. Editorialising on this notable photo, the *HKEJ* (14 June 2001) said that Tung was leading the SAR down the path of Chinese-style politics.

United front tactics

Chairman Mao used to say that there were two main weapons that led to the success of the communist revolution in 1949: naked military power and the 'united front'. Loosely defined, a united front means 'uniting and co-opting whosoever can be united and co-opted, and isolating your enemies'. Thus Mao was able to isolate Chiang Kai-shek and the Kuomintang by reaching out to a broad array of sectors, from intellectuals to underground gangs.

From the beginning, Tung knew that it would be very difficult for him to win over pro-democracy politicians, as well as intellectuals and professionals sympathetic to Western values of democracy and civil rights. He also concluded that the democrats would be his harshest critics, if not also 'troublemakers' who might exacerbate tension between Beijing and the SAR. Instead of trying to build bridges to them, the supremo decided to take a leaf out of Mao's book and use united front tactics to isolate and marginalise partisans for a faster pace of democracy.[20]

The task of isolating the democrats, including the Democratic Party led by Martin Lee, the Frontiers led by Emily Lau, and other fringe groups, is simple. As Lau pointed out, 'Tung and company just pretend we do not exist'.[21] Tung has also been helped by Beijing in this operation. The PRC government has refused to let most of the prominent democrats visit the mainland, let alone talk to them. The economic recession has also exacerbated the democrats' plight. Hong Kong's growing economic dependence on the mainland, and Beijing's refusal to acknowledge the existence of the 'rabble rousers', has convinced quite a number of Hong Kong residents and even voters that the democrats are tilting at windmills.

The sectors and groups that Tung has united or co-opted with reasonable success have included the following: the business community, including small and medium-sized enterprises; the traditional left-wing or pro-China establishment; and ordinary citizens resigned to the fact that they have to acknowledge Beijing's suzerainty in return for jobs and economic security.

Much has been written about the 'unholy alliance' between big business in the SAR and Beijing to ensure 'stability and prosperity' for fifty years. Tung's relationship with the leftist establishment merits closer study, because the Chief Executive was not, at least initially, regarded as 'one of us' by traditional pro-PRC elements. This left-wing establishment includes the increasingly popular DAB, whose bulwark of support includes a mammoth network of trade unions, as well as powerful PRC businesses in the SAR.[22]

Despite Beijing's support for Tung, there was initial resistance in 1997 and 1998 among 'old-line patriots' that a 'late-coming patriot' with a capitalist background had stolen the crown of the Chief Executive. However, Tung has done his best to give left-wing old-timers rewards such as appointments to government committees and government medals.

On 1 July 2001, however, Tung's united front work backfired when he awarded the SAR's highest honour, the Great Bauhinia Medal, to Yeung Kwong, who is a veteran and generally well-respected left-wing trade unionist.

But he was also a mastermind of the 1967 anti-British riots, which cost the lives of a few dozen innocent Hong Kong residents. Tung's controversial action reopened old wounds as newspapers and magazines went over events that residents younger than 40 would have no personal experience of (*Taipei Times*, 16 July 2001). Almost invariably, the Great Bauhinia Medal was seen as a cynical vote-getting strategy on Tung's part to secure the support of left-ists who sit in the 800-member electoral college.

'Cry wolf' tactics

The 'cry wolf' tactic was first used to good advantage by former Financial Secretary Donald Tsang to win acceptance for his annual budgets. The mode of operation was like this: a couple of months before releasing his budget, Tsang or his aides would float trial balloons about a large number of tax increases or new taxes. On budget day, however, only a small number of new levies were announced. The public, of course, would end up paying more than before, but thanks to 'it's not so bad after all' psychology, residents heaved a collective sigh of relief. In mid-2001, Tung and company again resorted to this technique by saying that the government was considering a sales tax. Tung would gain points upon announcing that the idea would be killed to spare the populace.[23]

This tactic was also used to good effect in the SAR's crusade against the Falun Gong. Immediately after Tung had condemned the group as an 'evil cult', officials claimed that the administration was considering an anti-cult law. Tung's spin doctors also obtained much mileage from the fact that France had enacted an anti-cult law in May 2001. There were also reports that SAR officials had studied similar statutes in African countries. By June, however, officials including Tsang and Ip began saying that the administration had no intention of enacting such legislation 'at this stage'.[24] Some members of the community began to say 'Tung is not that bad after all!'

Then there is Article 23 of the Basic Law, which states that the SAR administration should introduce laws to combat sedition, secession, rebel-lion and other anti-Beijing activities, including the leaking of state secrets. This draconian article would also forbid the maintenance of ties with their counterparts overseas by SAR political organisations. Since July 1997, Article 23 has hung over Hong Kong like a sword of Damocles. So far, Tung and company has been most coy about whether and when the dreaded clause would be enacted into law. One theory is that this deliberately engi-neered suspense amounts to a cynical form of intimidation against pro-democracy elements and the media (*Ming Pao*, 20 August 2001; *SCMP*, 20 August 2001).

But what if the wolf really shows up at the door, or even the bedroom, of the Hong Kong resident? By refusing to say definitely that his administra-tion will protect Hong Kong residents against the excesses of the mainland,

Tung has kept Hong Kong residents on tenterhooks. While this may be shrewd psychological warfare, the unpopular Chief Executive can hardly expect to endear himself to world opinion.

Bogeymen and red herrings

At least in the eyes of critics, the Tung administration has used the strategy of raising bogeymen to persuade, if not bully, the Hong Kong populace into supporting an otherwise starkly unpopular policy, or one that clearly undermines the SAR's autonomy. A case in point is the practice of asking the Standing Committee of the National People's Congress to interpret Hong Kong's Basic Law. Ordinarily, the policy of deferring to the NPC would be seen as undermining the autonomy of Hong Kong and the authority of its Court of Final Appeal (CFA). Yet the SAR administration chose an opportune moment to set a precedent in mid-1999 in the wake of a CFA ruling that interpreted the Basic Law in such a way as to give the right of abode to PRC children whose parents are Hong Kong citizens.[25]

To buttress its argument that it needed an NPC intervention, the SAR government marshalled statistics and made projections showing that tens of thousands of PRC residents would flood into Hong Kong should the CFA ruling stand. Numerous independent legislators and journalists have raised doubts about the authenticity of government figures. The SAR authorities have been accused of fear-mongering. Yet this method worked in terms of overall popular support for the government's asking the NPC to overrule the CFA (Ching 1999).

The same goes for the Falun Gong. Tung's condemnation of the movement as an 'evil cult', as well as measures that boosted surveillance over its 500-odd adherents in Hong Kong, has been widely criticised by pro-democracy bodies and by the Catholic Church. However, given the overall unpopularity of the Falun Gong, which is seen by a sizeable portion of the populace as having dubious if not dangerous principles, it is relatively easy for the government's spin doctors to exaggerate its threat to the community. The point is that once it is accepted that the government can use draconian measures against what is perceived as a fishy spiritual movement, it could get away with similar tactics against other political or religious groups that are not to the liking of either the SAR or Beijing authorities.[26]

Consider also how the SAR government justified its decision to let PRC courts try Hong Kong residents held on suspicion of committing crimes in Hong Kong. Again the SAR government picked a shrewd case to establish a precedent: Cheung Tse-keung made international news by kidnapping the son of Li Ka-shing in mid-1996. Cheung was seized by Guangdong police in late 1998 reportedly after Li had made a personal appeal to President Jiang in July the same year.

Since Cheung was a Hong Kong resident and his major crimes took place in Hong Kong territory, the government should have asked the Chinese authorities to hand him back to the SAR police and judicial departments. Yet it did not, apparently because Hong Kong has no death penalty and many of the most powerful figures in both Beijing and Hong Kong wanted Cheung executed. Because Cheung was such a notorious hoodlum, most Hong Kong residents were glad to be rid of him permanently. Few save legal experts saw the longer-term consequence, and few protested against the SAR government's decision to let politics get in the way of justice.[27]

Media hard sell

Tung has a well-deserved reputation for being media-shy if not downright antagonistic towards journalists. He once told an interviewer from the government's own RTHK that he was 'too busy' to spend much time on the media. However, since early 2000, when his popularity ratings began to plummet, he and his aides have adopted an aggressive carrot-and-stick approach to try to influence media coverage and public perceptions.

First, Tung began an orchestrated bid to be chummy with senior media administrators and editors, many of whom were invited to regular banquets at Government House. SAR senior policy secretaries also began to spend longer hours with the hacks. One of the first moves of Antony Leung after he became Financial Secretary was to hire a full-time press aide. Prior to this, a senior civil servant had served as press secretary to both the Chief Secretary and Financial Secretary.[28]

The new deal for the media was evident in the much-ballyhooed trip to western China in May 2001 by a large group of business tycoons and top officials, led by Chief Secretary Tsang. A team of senior bureaucrats from the Information Services Department (ISD) was on hand to cater to the needs of reporters covering the two-week journey. At the last stop, Urumqi in Xinjiang, Tsang sent special souvenirs to media personnel. Female journalists even got a peck on the cheek. As political commentator Kitty Poon pointed out, the success of the SAR government's PR exercises had made top officials such as Tsang and Leung big stars even as editors were being 'seduced' into not delving into matters that might prove embarrassing for the administration (*HKEJ*, 14 June 2001).

The government's PR tacticians have also not overlooked overseas journalists and opinion formers. Each year, the ISD sponsors all-expenses-paid trips for influential media personalities, as well as academics, politicians and legislative assistants. These VIPs are put up in five-star hotels and given access to senior officials, including the Chief Secretary and the Financial Secretary. However, whether the money and resources spent have resulted in a good overseas image for the SAR is still open to question.[29]

The media hard sell can often backfire. For example, the SAR government went to great lengths to ensure that the Paris-based World Association of Newspapers (WAN) held its prestigious annual convention in Hong Kong in June 2001. Tung and a host of top officials also agreed to be guests of honour. However, Tung went overboard when he came to the defence of China in the wake of unflattering remarks made by WAN organisers on the sad state of press freedom in mainland China. Tung countered by asking the international newsmen to visit China more regularly. 'The fact is that enormous progress is being made everywhere in China today', said Tung, adding that the current leadership under Jiang had already done much for media freedom. The response to Tung's patriotic outburst was predictably negative.[30]

Tung's often ham-fisted attempts to control public perceptions of himself and his administration are perhaps best illustrated by the so-called Robert Chung affair of 2000. A Hong Kong University academic and pollster, Chung incurred the wrath of Tung by publishing numerous polls in 2000 that reflected the lack of popularity of Tung and his policies. One of Tung's key aides, Andrew Lo, then held meetings with the head of Hong Kong University, Professor Cheng Yiu-chung, with the purpose of gagging Chung. The conspiracy was exposed in the media. Cheng resigned after failing to uphold academic freedom, and Lo insisted that, on his own initiative, he had talked to Cheng and a couple of heads of colleges whose academics had also written unflattering articles about Tung. Tung refused to fire Lo (*Asiaweek*, 8 September 2000; *SCMP*, 13 October 2000).

The erosion of media freedom

Direct or quasi-direct interference from Beijing

In October 2000, the world was given a graphic picture of Beijing's attitude towards the Hong Kong media when President Jiang lashed out at SAR reporters for being 'simple and naive'. 'I am angry', said Jiang in English in response to a question from Cable TV reporter Sharon Cheung that implied that Beijing had given a second term to Tung via 'imperial decree'. While touring Macau in late 2000 for the first anniversary for the assumption of sovereignty over the former Portuguese enclave, Tung reminded Hong Kong and Macau media of their 'social responsibility', saying that they must play a 'positive role' in matters such as the interests of the state and nation.[31]

While Jiang's outburst represented the true feelings of the powers that be towards Hong Kong media, it is also important to note that at least theoretically, there is no direct or well-established mechanism whereby Beijing, or its Hong Kong representative office, the Central Liaison Office of the Central Government (CLOCG), would pass along instructions to the Hong Kong media. The exceptions are the three left-wing papers that have since the 1940s been run by Beijing and have long been considered official mouthpieces.[32]

However, Beijing has made it clear that in several 'taboo' areas, it will not tolerate the traditional *laissez-faire* operation of the media. In these fields, what are tantamount to edicts have been passed to editors and journalists.

Before 1 July 1997, officials including Vice-Premier Qian Qichen and Lu Ping, former head of the cabinet-level Hong Kong and Macau Affairs Office, had reiterated that the media must not 'make propaganda' for the pro-independence movements in Taiwan and Tibet.

Wang Fengchao, Vice Director of the CLOCG, castigated a Hong Kong television station for broadcasting an interview with Taiwan Vice-President Annette Lu in early 2002. In the interview Lu, an outspoken pro-independence advocate, said that the mainland was a mere 'remote relative' of Taiwan's. 'The media should not treat speeches and views which advocate Taiwan's independence as normal news items, nor should they report them like normal cases of reporting the voices of different parties', Wang thundered (*Time*, Asia edition, 24 April 2000).

In May 2001, the television audience was surprised when Hong Kong's two main stations, TVB and ATV, began to use a new standard designation for Taiwan President Chen Shui-bian: 'Taiwan leader'. The two stations would not say whether an instruction had come from the CLOCG. However, Cheung Chi-kong, assistant controller of news at TVB, explained that his station 'advocates the "one China" principle and the way we address [Chen] is just to embody this principle'. ATV also responded by saying that it was company policy to abide by the one-China policy (*Wen Wei Po*, 2 June 2001).

It is easy to understand Beijing's sensitivities about Taiwan and Tibet. However, it is equally clear that if the Hong Kong media and public accept that PRC authorities can call the shots on how news about these two places is reported, this practice could easily extend to other areas deemed equally vital to Beijing's perceived national interests.

In fact, 2000 witnessed more disturbing cases of mainland cadres directly exerting pressure on Hong Kong editors and reporters. One example is what transpires when SAR journalists accompany state leaders on overseas visits. On the surface, Beijing is doing the Hong Kong media a big favour by allowing them close access to the likes of Jiang and Zhu. Arrangements for covering the activities of senior officials in countries ranging from the United States to Russia are done by press officials of the Chinese Foreign Ministry or local Chinese embassies. However, in special briefings for Hong Kong reporters, Beijing officials also try to coax the latter into presenting Jiang and Zhu in the best light. News organisations that are most amenable to doing this are often rewarded with favourable treatment such as the granting of exclusive interviews.[33]

The cancerous growth of self-censorship

More often than not, cadres in Beijing and Hong Kong try to influence the SAR media through subtle, even underhand, means. The *spinmeisters* like to work through the owners of media organisations and their senior news executives and editors. What happens is that over dinner tables or at cocktail parties, a cadre will impart the line to take in a roundabout manner, or the official may express disapproval of a certain television programme or newspaper column. Usually, the idea of following a particular orientation in presenting the news, or reining in a journalist that Beijing finds obnoxious, is presented as a suggestion, not an order. However, given the realities of Hong Kong, most media owners and editors are willing to meet Beijing at least halfway.[34]

The result of these machinations is self-censorship, which is becoming more serious in most SAR newsrooms. A discussion with senior journalists carried out by this author in mid-2001 showed that reporting about events and trends considered embarrassing to the leadership had declined. They included factional infighting in Beijing; juicy stories about the personal life of senior cadres and sons and daughters of party elders; corruption in high places; and Beijing's policies towards Tibet and Hong Kong. Self-censorship has also been cited by the respected Hong Kong Journalists' Association (HKJA) as one of the most serious problems plaguing the local media (HKJA 2001: 23–6).

However, on any given day most of the media still run a plethora of negative stories about the mainland or the SAR administration, but the phenomenon of *bizhong jiuqing* ('skirting the major issues while beating about the bush') has become common. One often-used tactic to shirk editorial responsibility concerning a major news event that might embarrass Beijing is to run Western wire agency stories. Even for such a major occurrence as the Yuan Hua smuggling and corruption scandal in Xiamen, Fujian province, very few local media dispatched special teams to do on-the-spot reporting.[35]

Self-censorship is rife even in the *South China Morning Post*, Hong Kong's main English-language broadsheet and also its oldest newspaper. According to graphic accounts by several departed senior staff, since the mid-1990s management has tried to tone down coverage to please China. Well-known British journalist Jonathan Fenby, who edited the *SCMP* from 1995 to 1999, said that the paper's owners and management tried numerous times to force him to fire or drop journalists and columnists deemed to be anti-Beijing. Efforts were also made to excise certain words or phrases (for example, 'massacre' as in 'Tiananmen Square massacre') from the paper. Fenby (2000: 178) had this to say about the interference from owner Robert Kuok: 'Kuok insisted that he did not want the *Post* to become a party-line organ, like the *Straits Times* in Singapore .... But the instructions I received would have led it to go that way and would have undermined its spirit'.

More details of efforts by the management to water down stories, change interpretations or get rid of 'unpatriotic' journalists were detailed in *North Wind* (2001) by former *SCMP* associate editor Nury Vittachi. Vittachi was forced to leave the paper after a column he wrote had been stopped because the paper's owners thought it had offended powerful figures in Beijing and

Hong Kong such as Li Peng and Chief Executive Tung. At one point, the popular columnist was even scolded for writing something satirical about the state-run *China Daily*.[36]

The obverse of self-censorship is what Chinese media critics call *gede*, or uncritical praise of the leadership. Beginning in 2001, ATV began broadcasting nightly editorials, some of whose main themes were widely perceived to be encouraging patriotism and generating support for the Tung government. These editorials were often reprinted the next day on the opinion page of *Wen Wei Po*, one of the SAR's three Beijing-run papers. Another case in point was the 'go west' programme, a multi-billion yuan (*renminbi*) effort announced by Beijing in 2000 to develop eleven provinces and regions in western China. ATV, TVB and a host of other media (electronic and print) devoted large amounts of money and manpower to producing documentaries and other reports that highlighted the investment opportunities of the hinterland.

According to HKJA chairwoman Mak Yin-ting, most Hong Kong media reports about the 'go west' programme could hardly qualify as news. 'Many media, particularly the electronic media, have adopted the mainland style of singing the praises [of western China]', she said. 'They have not reported on the problems and difficulties of the western areas' (*HKEJ*, 2 July 2001). In the summer of 2001, most Hong Kong media accepted invitations from the foreign affairs bureaus of provinces and autonomous regions in western China, including Tibet and Xinjiang, for visits to coincide with the 'go west' programme. Almost without exception, most of the reporting that resulted from these all-expenses-paid trips was positive. The television programmes and articles did not give adequate treatment of negative phenomena such as ethnic tension and the resentment of minorities such as the Uighurs to Han Chinese-dominated development initiatives.[37]

The influence of monopolistic conglomerates on the media

Was this merely a storm in a teacup? In mid-2001, HSBC, one of Asia's largest financial institutions, suddenly withdrew all its advertising from the Next Media group of newspapers and magazines owned by maverick media baron Jimmy Lai. The ostensible reason was that in an early 2001 edition, *Next* magazine ran a highly unflattering cover story on Vincent Cheng, the CEO of a key HSBC subsidiary, Hang Seng Bank. When asked why Cheng did not take the usual step of suing the magazine, a Hang Seng Bank spokesman said that libel suits usually took years and the withdrawal of advertising would be more effective.[38]

However, this incident was widely covered by the Hong Kong and overseas media. Outspoken legislator Emily Lau deplored efforts by a major publicly listed company to use advertising as a weapon to hit out at unfriendly media. But the HSBC action was not new. The companies

controlled by Hong Kong magnate Li Ka-shing had in the late 1990s with-
drawn all advertising from Lai's publications after *Next* had written stories
about his private life.

However, these instances of apparent corporate bullying also have a
China angle, given the fact that Lai has always been Beijing's *bête noire*
among Hong Kong media owners. As the *Asian Wall Street Journal* (9 July
2001) pointed out in an editorial, a legitimate question could be asked as to
whether Hong Kong companies had a different motive in targeting Lai, who
had since the mid-1990s been blacklisted by Beijing. The *Journal* said that
the HSBC action had raised the 'worrying question of whether China is
trying to interfere with Hong Kong's traditionally free and lively media
through its proxies in the business sector'.

Indeed, media watchers have concluded that apart from Beijing, major
Hong Kong companies have been a potent force in inhibiting free media and
encouraging self-censorship. In a much noted report in late 2000, the
European Parliament expressed concerns that companies controlled by Li
Ka-shing and his sons accounted for between one-fourth and one-third of
the market capitalisation of the Hong Kong stock market. The report said
that this monopolistic situation also meant that big business had undue
influence in Hong Kong's politics and the media (*Associated Press*, 26
October 2000).[39]

There is an adage among Hong Kong journalists that while few reporters
would have second thoughts about writing a piece critical of Jiang or Zhu,
most would think thrice about doing a similar thing to Li or another of
Hong Kong's seven or eight major magnates. It is not surprising that apart
from the Next group, only foreign media have dared to write unflattering
stories about the tycoons.[40]

Then there is the even more disturbing question of the so-called unholy
alliance between Beijing and big business. As former mainland officials or
operatives in Hong Kong such as Xu Jiatun and Kam Yiu-yu have noted,
well before 1997 Beijing had sought to control the local media through two
similar methods: having PRC-controlled firms take over media companies;
and ensuring that media companies are owned by tycoons friendly to
Beijing.[41]

By 2001, a substantial number of influential media were held by individuals or companies considered to have close PRC ties. Even more
importantly, most television stations and newspapers are now owned by
large corporations that have ambitious expansion plans in the mainland for
media-related and other businesses. Particularly given Hong Kong's growing
economic dependence on China, the owners of media companies all see
their future in China, and they have even more reason to ensure that a television programme produced by their own station or a column in their own
paper does not fall foul of the leadership. This is exacerbated by the fact that
there is no established 'church and state' relationship between owners and
the newsroom in Hong Kong media companies.[42]

It is not surprising that the two papers generally deemed to be most independent – the *Hong Kong Economic Journal* and Jimmy Lai's *Apple Daily* – have special corporate backgrounds. The *HKEJ* is solely owned by a former journalist, while Lai's company has no plans to go into the China market (*Taipei Times*, 26 February 2001). The *HKEJ* is the only paper in Hong Kong that regularly showcases the writings of democracy activists both in China and the United States. It also carries thorough reporting on behind-the-scenes manoeuvres on the Beijing–Hong Kong front.

Conclusion: a lose–lose situation?

At least from the points of view of partisans of democracy, Hong Kong is on the horns of a dilemma. Its survival as a regional financial and commercial hub hinges on ever closer links with China, particularly the Pearl River delta area. As former Chief Secretary and now business consultant Sir David Akers-Jones pointed out, Hong Kong cannot afford to be left out of the developments of southern Guangdong province.[43] His views are shared by many ordinary people, including new college graduates.

However, the political fall-out of economic integration is severe. As the socio-political culture of the SAR becomes more Chinese, Hong Kong risks losing many of the characteristics that are integral not only to its success formula but also to its uniqueness as a cosmopolitan city on the Chinese coast. These traits include freedom of expression and the media; Western-style democracy; a non-politicised civil service; and the rule of law.

Even in the short term, retardation of the democratic process has already engendered something that most SAR residents would regard as negative: the extension of Tung's tenure for five more years. Widely seen as lacking in political skills and vision, Tung would never have been in a position to secure another term if there really were an element of choice for the people of Hong Kong. Particularly at a time when both the economy and society are undergoing drastic changes, Hong Kong needs a dynamic, future-oriented leader, not one whose strong suits include anticipating Beijing's wishes and reviving a vulgarised form of Confucianism.

The detrimental effect is most clearly shown in the media, which is trapped in a vicious circle. Given the well-known phenomenon of political influence and self-censorship, experienced professionals are leaving the field even as bright young graduates – even those from journalism schools – are forsaking the profession.[44] Inadequate and biased reporting has in turn contributed to the deterioration of the integrity of the political process.

What will Hong Kong be in ten, or even five years? By mid-2001, officials from the SAR and from various cities in Guangdong, including Guangzhou, Tongguan, Panyu, Shunde and Shenzhen, had set up commissions and mechanisms for different aspects of joint development. New bridges, highways and railways are connecting the dozen-odd major cities in the Pearl River delta, which will become one giant business hub for south China. The most important question for the SAR is that by the time all these boom towns are intimately linked up, Hong Kong will remain not only the biggest star in the constellation but also a qualitatively different one. It is as important that the SAR media still be free to report the facts as they are, and to give their opinions without fear or favour.

Notes

1 See US Department of State Country Reports on Human Rights, February 2001.
2 Information can also be obtained from the website http://www.cnn.com/Asia, 1 July 2001.
3 See, for example, a discussion of the new psychology among Hong Kong residents in 'Will Hong Kong be better if China's economic strength increases?' *HKEJ*, 10 September 2001.
4 No clause in the Basic Law makes it obligatory for Hong Kong officials, businessmen or politicians to consult Beijing on a daily basis or to curry favour with Beijing cadres. However, most civil servants, politicians and businessmen feel that their career and business prospects will be greatly enhanced if they can anticipate Beijing's wishes and score points for themselves.
5 During the first 'election' of the HKSAR chief executive in 1997, two well-known figures, businessman Peter Woo and former Chief Justice Sir T.L. Yang, ran against Tung. In 2002, not a single community leader expressed an interest in running despite efforts by Beijing's representative office in Hong Kong, the Central Liaison Office, to persuade well-known community figures to take part in the 'election'.
6 Xu Jiatun, China's top representative in Hong Kong in the late 1980s, revealed in his memoirs that different party, government and army units maintained intelligence agents in Hong Kong. Western diplomats interviewed by the author say that the total number of such agents has increased since 1997 (Xu 1993).
7 Author's interviews with Kan Hung-cheung, spokesman for the Falun Gong in Hong Kong, and with officials at the government's security branch, September 2001, Hong Kong.
8 There were widespread reports in the Hong Kong media that Anson Chan had given approval for an international Falun Gong convention to be held in a government facility in early 2001, thus incurring the ire of Tung and Beijing.
9 On 1 July 1997, Tung retained pretty much all the senior officials who had served under former governor Chris Patten, but Elsie Leung was a newcomer brought in by Tung to oversee the sensitive justice portfolio. Leung, who had specialised in family law, is regarded as having close links with Beijing – a number of her relatives were mainland cadres.
10 The Apei designation for Hong Kong officials was circulated in Beijing in mid-2001. Author's interviews with Chinese sources in Beijing and Hong Kong, September to November 2001.
11 Diplomatic sources in Hong Kong have said that the Hong Kong garrison of the PLA consisted of only about 5,000 men, down from around 8,000 at the time of the handover on 1 July 1997.
12 The cyberport project has been delayed by the recession in the local economy. Much of the project consists of residential buildings, not technological facilities (*Ming Pao*, 11 September 2001).
13 See, for example, 'The mainland stock market is having a facelift; Hong Kong must have a sense of crisis', *HKEJ*, 21 February 2001.

14 For a discussion of Hong Kong's economic relations with Guangdong, see, for example, 'Coming Together', *Asiaweek*, 21 April 2000.

15 A series of meetings were held between Guangdong and Hong Kong officials in July and August 2001. Preliminary agreements included joint efforts to develop the Pearl River delta city of Nansha and to make better use of Zhuhai Airport near Macau (Xinhua News Agency, 25 July 2001; *SCMP*, 14 August 2001).

16 The day after China gained entry to the WTO, Premier Zhu said that it would not contravene the trade body's regulations for Beijing to grant Hong Kong special privileges, even though Hong Kong is also a WTO member (cited in news broadcasts on ATV and Cable TV in Hong Kong, 11 November 2001). However, Western trade specialists in Beijing said that after WTO accession, whatever privileges Beijing has granted Hong Kong will also have to be given to other WTO members.

17 During elections in 1999, the Beijing-nurtured DAB came close to becoming the biggest political party in Hong Kong. The Hong Kong Democratic Party lost more than 100,000 votes compared with the election in 1995.

18 In opinion polls, Tung consistently scored lower than his deputies Anson Chan and Donald Tsang did. Tung's approval rating dropped to around 30 percent in times of recession such as 1999 and 2001. See, for example, David Liebhold, 'Wrong Touch', *Time* (Asia edition), 10 July 2000, http://www.time.com /time/asia/magazine/2000/0710/hk.chtung.html.

19 In an apparent bid to popularise Chinese culture, Tung changed the medium of instruction in most of Hong Kong's secondary schools from English to Cantonese soon after 1997.

20 The Basic Law of Hong Kong spells out that the HKSAR should have an 'executive-led government', and Tung has not even tried to hide his view that the legislature is only an ancillary body. He seldom consults members of the democratic alliance despite their strong showing in the polls.

21 Author's interview with Emily Lau, October 2001, Hong Kong.

22 It has been widely reported in the local and Western press that a number of DAB stalwarts are long-time Communist Party members. During elections, large PRC corporations in Hong Kong try to mobilise their staff to vote for DAB candidates.

23 No new taxes were announced in 2001 in view of anticipated zero growth in the economy.

24 See Donald Tsang's speech to the Foreign Correspondents' Club of Hong Kong, in *The Correspondent*, August/September 2001 issue, p. 19.

25 For a discussion of the Court of Final Appeal controversy, see, for example, Ching (1999).

26 The Catholic Church was vocal in its opposition to the government's handling of the Falun Gong. See, for example, Chan (2001).

27 Only a few legislators, including barristers Margaret Ng and Martin Lee, raised the question of the impropriety of trying Cheung in a Chinese court.

28 Since May 2001, most senior civil servants, including Antony Leung and Donald Tsang, have been more accessible to the media.

29 Author's interviews with foreign VIPs who have visited Hong Kong on lavish trips arranged by the Hong Kong authorities, August to October 2001, Hong Kong.

30 For further details, see the website of the Hong Kong government: http://www.info.gov.hk, 4 June 2001.

31 See Hong Kong Journalists' Association (2001); author's interview with Sharon Cheung, August 2001.

32 The heads of the three left-wing papers in Hong Kong report to a vice-director of the Central Liaison Office; they also report to the Communist Party cell in Hong Kong, which is known as the Hong Kong and Macau Work Committee.

33 Author's interviews with editors of electronic and print media in Hong Kong, August to October 2001, Hong Kong.
34 Author's interviews with office bearers in the Hong Kong Journalists' Association and editors of Hong Kong papers, October to November 2001, Hong Kong.
35 Normally, Hong Kong media editors would rather dispatch reporters to China on trips organised by the mainland authorities.
36 Author's interview with Vittachi, March 2001.
37 Author's interviews with Hong Kong journalists who took part in trips to western China that were organised by local authorities, August to September 2001, Hong Kong.
38 Author's interviews with spokesmen for the Hang Seng Bank and *Apple Daily*, October 2001, Hong Kong.
39 Author's interview with the author of the report, John Cushnahan, December 2000, Brussels.
40 It is not an accident that it was a foreign paper, the *International Herald Tribune*, that broke the story in early 2001 that Li Ka-shing's son, Richard, had enrolled in but not graduated from Stanford University.
41 Author's interviews with Xu Jiatun and Kam Yiu-yu, 1999, Los Angeles.
42 There is no 'church and state' tradition in Hong Kong to prevent media owners intruding into the operations of newsrooms. Most media moguls have no difficulty exercising control over their chief editors. 'Disobedient' chief editors are simply sacked or laid off. Such events would hardly cause a stir outside journalistic circles.
43 Author's interview with Sir David Akers-Jones, October 2001, Hong Kong.
44 Author's interviews (September 2001) with professors at the School of Communications, Hong Kong Baptist University.

References

Bork, E. (2001) 'Hong Kong in a chokehold', *The Weekly Standard*, 12 February: 23–7.
Chan, Y.K. (2001) 'It's a matter for "One Country, Two Systems"', *Hong Kong Economic Journal*, 17 March.
Ching, F. (1999) 'The Court of Final Appeal row', in Centre for Strategic and International Studies (ed.), *Hong Kong Update*, February–March issue.
Fenby, J. (2000) *Dealing with the Dragon*. London: Little, Brown.
Hong Kong Journalists' Association (2001) *Following the Flag: China's Sensitivities Threaten Freedom of Expression in Hong Kong*. Hong Kong: Hong Kong Journalists' Association.
Liebhold, D. (2000) 'Wrong touch', *Time Magazine* (Asia edition), 10 July.
Vittachi, N. (2001) *North Wind*. Hong Kong: Chameleon Press.
Xu Jiatun (1993) *Xu Jiatun's Memoirs*. Taipei: Linking Publishing.
Yang Fan (2001) 'Hong Kong will invest in the western provinces on a big scale', *Wen Wei Po*, 1 May.

10 Media economics of the Hong Kong press in political transition

Towards a new viable political economy

Anthony Fung

New politics, new political economy

An old economy survives in an old regime. In new regimes, the media have to operate with new strategies and tactics to survive. In the mature capitalism of Hong Kong, media organisations are able to create a new market logic to overcome financial difficulties, surmount operational obstacles, meet the obligations of journalistic professionalism and, above all, dilute political pressure.

Discussion of political communication in the capitalist city of Hong Kong would not be complete without recapitulating its macro-economics. Media are not only cultural products laden with politics but also exchangeable commodities. Whereas political pressures due to the looming presence of China are subtle and intangible, economic pressures on media enterprises are real and concrete (Fung and Lee 1994, 2002). However, the discipline of media economics, emphasising competition, the invisible hand, demand and supply, and profits in a democratic and capitalist society, is non-contextual, ahistorical and an ideal predicated on an Anglo-Saxon assumption that direct political intervention is played down (Mosco 1996). In many of the developing countries and transitional states, a free market does not exists and political forces are diluted to a degree that mere media economics manifest and dictate press content. The interplay of political and economic factors for media operations is highly convoluted with *realpolitik* and is also dependent on market reactions. This is particularly true in Hong Kong, where late in the political transition, newspaper enterprises emphasised the political nature of mass media and turned themselves into sites of political struggle between Britain and the PRC, between local autonomy and national control, and between reformist/democrat and conservative. An adequate study necessitates an empirical description of how the press reacted to these politico-economic contingencies and dilemmas.

China's resumption of sovereignty over Hong Kong cast doubt on press freedom there. Under capitalism, economic rather than overt political control is most effective, putting local media corporations on the defensive. This chapter first aims to map out how the newspaper industry in Hong Kong in the 1980s and 1990s used a Western-style self-protective strategy to weather the political transition. It will explain the processes of segmentation, incorporation, extension, integration/conglomeration and globalis- ation, all of which are traditional means by which capitalists survive political and economic changes.

These are commonplace strategies for corporations in capitalist cities. However, given that these means could be easily countered by economic methods, freedom of the press in Hong Kong was at stake. While coordinated economic sanctions by China-affiliated corporations – and possibly coercion on the propaganda front – were effective in curtailing the profit margins of newspapers, hence indirectly stifling press criticism of the authorities, capitalists and politicians could also seize control by buying the shares of newspapers listed on the stock market. Could the capitalist media transform themselves to pre-empt these advanced economic controls? This would necessitate a new capitalist strategy contextualised in the specific historical moment of Hong Kong.

This chapter describes a new phenomenon that materialised prior to the political transition, when some capitalist barons had their papers cruise along with a kind of *USA Today* populism – being sensationalised and vulgarised – which attracted a considerable readership. Whenever they politicise, they are effective in sensitising the public's anger towards the authorities. This strategy, perhaps the only conceivable one – the commodification of news – was a new capitalist strategy to survive in the political economy of Hong Kong while it underwent political transition. This chapter argues that, whereas many people see press performance as psychotic and deranged, this in fact reflects another sociological/capitalistic logic or new political economy that not only enables the free press to survive commercially in the market but also in effect safeguards press freedom and maintains a diversity of opinion.

Hong Kong's press in transition

Hong Kong's press was briefly classified into five types according to political ideology and financial sponsorship: the mass-appeal popular press; the serious independent professional press; the financial press, which reports and analyses economic news; the elite English-language press, and the party press of the People's Republic of China (PRC) (Chan and Lee 1991). They passively fortified their market positions in the wake of political change to actively seek out business opportunities brought about by Hong Kong's political reunion with China. On the one hand, media organisations had long prepared for the transition. They stabilised their market share, accumulated and safeguarded their resources, and extended their empires to include other politically inert industries. On the other hand, they attempted to set up joint media ventures with China in order to expand their influence further. Capitalists toned down their critical stance of China when, in the 1980s, China's gesture to open the door for business investment tempted the local media.

However, the autonomy of the local media was at stake when the presence of China in Hong Kong began to distort the local political economy. The Hong Kong media were susceptible to ever-increasing political pressure by officials of the PRC in Hong Kong and from the Xinhua News Agency. Despite the fact that press freedom was always reported and featured as a burning issue, media self-censorship continued (Chan and Lee 1991). Economically, China had become one of the largest investors in Hong Kong. In 1990 alone, its local investment soared to an estimated HK$78 billion (Shen 1993: 426; Sung 1991; Tsang 1994: 137). China accounted for 16 percent (HK$792 million of all local print advertising, making it influential enough to tame local politics and media. The capitalist-owned popular, professional, financial and English-language press could not afford to ignore business affiliations with China, advertising sanctions and the potential of the China market (Fung and Lee 1994). At this juncture, the political and economic interests of capitalists align, so that a more pro-China stance could be conceived as viable and promising. However, thanks to journalistic professionalism, the media still provided room for intellectuals to exercise their minimal autonomy under various self-protective and pre-emptive strategies. Editors working in organisations realised how the media help to legitimise the state, but they did not necessarily conform to the editorial and political stance (Blumler and Gurevitch 1975). On the other hand, China's party press also had to consider the canons of the market and appeal to readers to survive under capitalism (He 2000).

In terms of direct control, media barons with close ties to China actively sought to buy out the Hong Kong media (Fung and Lee 1994), and the public worried about their intention to ingratiate themselves with China by changing the press's political stance or to do so by simply depoliticising the papers. The advantage of such acquisition is self-evident, since capitalists acquired more bargaining power by owning shares in the media. New media owners might reorient their ideological stance as a conciliatory gesture to China, but this risked disappointing the readers who conferred legitimacy and credibility on the press. In the 1990s, with the local capitalists' interests 'dyed red', media accountability and the interests of the market seemed to polarise economic and political interests.

This polarisation was exacerbated by a new entrant triggering a price war that not only destroyed the weak but also considerably diminished the stable, regulated profit distribution of the press giants. Important factors included (1) the price war, (2) an ailing media economy in the late 1990s, and (3) the tightening political atmosphere, which together challenged local–China media joint ventures and fuelled competition. The result was a severe local press war. In the past, the marginal profit on newspapers was linked to a stable share of advertising and circulation with no papers experimenting with content reform. Now the media had to return to the fundamentals of securing a readership base and to locating sufficient advertising revenue.

This chapter presents a macro-picture of this change in terms of how the various political and economic factors limited and circumscribed the general dynamics of media industries and capitalist economies. It also discusses how the media optimised their positioning and strategies by reallocating their capital and resources to surmount the political both before and after the transition.

Segmentation

Hong Kong has been characterised as a financial city in which the media operate in a free, 'positive non-interventionist' market (Endacott 1973; Lane 1990). This is only partially true of the media business. Although running newspapers had always been a profitable business, this was not built on a free market but on a pre-mature market – isolated from market competition – pre-stipulated and structured by major newspapers themselves. These papers defined the rules of the game – regulating their retail price, sharing their advertising profits, and dividing and targeting different niche markets – not according to the economic rules of supply and demand but instead under the protection of a *de facto* newspaper cartel. It was a segmentation of market and capital to ensure that newspapers 'competed' in concert with each other. Within the shelter of the cartel, and enjoying guaranteed revenue from sales, newspapers shared the ever-increasing annual advertising revenues of around HK$4,000 million, so that by the 1980s the press in Hong Kong had evolved into a stable market system (*Hong Kong Adex*, various years).[1]

The operation of the cartel was based on a segmentation scheme, namely an implicit agreement on the allotment of market niches in terms of circulation and audience, with only a small number of papers dominating the market (Levins 1962). However, other papers with relatively low circulations were sustained by their smaller market share. In other words, an unequal competition existed among the press, with a few papers controlling the cartel and thus able to set the news agenda and create a seemingly unanimous tone in terms of price decisions and advertising charges. Obviously, these controllers were large local papers with greater influence in the market and the ability to compel others to conform to the rules of the 'competitive' game. As a result, the widely circulated papers always enjoyed lower operating costs and higher profit margins, while those in the lower range of the circulation list, if not on the verge of collapse, barely survived.

The cartel in Hong Kong consisted of three newspapers, *Oriental Daily News*, *Sing Pao Daily News* and *Tin Tin Daily News*, which together had two-thirds of the market and half of total advertising revenue. The independent professional press, which included elite papers for professionals and the educated, lodged themselves in a secure position in the middle. *Ming Pao Daily News* enjoyed around 24 percent of the professional and executive market, a higher percentage than the top three popular newspapers, despite its relatively limited circulation of around 100,000 (*Hong Kong Adex* 1990). The prestigious English-language newspaper, the *South China Morning Post*, attracted 53 percent of high-income readers and 39 percent of professional and managerial executive readers. Also included in the top ten were *Hong Kong Daily News* (with a circulation that exceeded 100,000 in the early 1990s); *Express Daily News*, a 30-year-old newspaper with a circulation of 70,000; and *Sing Tao Daily News* (with a circulation of 65,000). The two financial papers, *Hong Kong Economic Journal* and *Hong Kong Economic Times*, were just outside the top ten. The circulation figures of these newspa-

Table 10.1   The circulation of Chinese newspapers in Hong Kong, 1993-95

	1993 circulation (000s) (market %)	*1994 circulation (000s) (market %)*	*Percentage change in circulation*	*1995 circulation (000s) (market %)*
Apple Daily News	–	–	–	300[a] (20.1)
Oriental Daily News	600 (40.4)	450 (34.3)	25	320[a] (21.5)
Sing Pao	223 (15.0)	198 (15.1)	11.2	198 (13.3)
Tin Tin Daily News	205 (13.8)	177 (13.5)	13.7	177 (11.9)
Ming Pao Daily News	120 (8.1)	109 (8.3)	9.2	109 (7.3)
Hong Kong Daily News	82 (5.5)	109 (8.3)	34.1	110 (7.4)
Sing Tao Daily News	65 (4.4)	65 (5.0)	0	65 (4.4)
Express	70 (4.7)	80 (6.1)	14.3	90[a] (6.0)
Hong Kong Economic Journal	68 (4.6)	62 (4.7)	8.8	62 (4.2)
Hong Kong Economic Times	52 (3.5)	59 (4.5)	13.5	59 (4.0)
TOTAL	1,485[b]	1,310[b]	11.8	1,490

Source: To (1995: 426). The 1993 and 1994 figures are from Social Research Hong Kong Media Index (Adex); the 1995 circulation figures were audited by ABC for the first six months of 1995.

Notes:

[a] Estimates in *Apple Daily News*, 17 December 1995.

[b] These totals also include circulation of other newspapers not listed above.

The figures do not add up to 100%; newspapers with low circulation are not included

pers reflected the stability of shared capital during the maturity of the cartel in the early 1990s (see Table 10.1). From the mid-1980s to the early 1990s, such segmentation was relatively robust until a new entrant disturbed the equilibrium in 1995.

Unequal competition was not achieved via simple informal, voluntary and natural negotiations between the powerful and the less circulated papers. Although the segmentation was to some degree subtle and implicit, and the decisions of the cartel were not legally binding, certain media organisations preserved resources, protocols and procedures by means of bureaucratisation and rationalisation (Adrich and Pfeffer 1979: 3–27). Local publishers established the Joint Newspaper Society of Hong Kong, which, together with the distribution agents, constituted a cartel that regulated and prescribed the retail price of newspapers.[2] The presence of this society distorted competition by adjusting the sales price of newspapers according to the profit requirements of the controlling newspapers in the organisation and the distributors.

Newspapers were not always happy with the retail price decisions of the society, but conflicts rarely surfaced. Financially successful papers often welcomed the cartel-instructed price increase, but others whose circulation had been in decline were well aware of their vulnerability and were often determined to resist. The society and the distributors monitored the industry vigilantly to punish any deviants. Newspapers that defied the price consensus of the cartel soon found themselves banished by newspaper vendors and local agents, who were entitled to 30 percent and 6.5 percent, respectively, of a daily's selling price (see Table 10.2).[3]

Table 10.2 The cartel-dictated pricing of newspapers since the 1980s

Date	Original price (HK$)	New price	Increase (absolute)	Increase (percentage)
1 November 1981	0.50	0.80	0.30	60
1 November 1983	0.80	1.00	0.20	25
1 November 1986	1.00	1.50	0.50	50
1 November 1988	1.50	2.00	0.50	33
1 October 1990	2.00	2.50	0.50	25
1 October 1991	2.50	3.00	0.50	20
1 October 1992	3.00	3.50	0.50	17
1 October 1993	3.50	4.00	0.50	14
1 October 1994	4.00	5.00	1.00	25

Source: *Overseas Chinese Daily*, 2 October 1994; *Ming Pao Daily News*, 9 January 1995.

To be fair, observance of the spatial allocation or compliance with the cartel did bring competitive and monetary advantages to every individual capitalist who played the game, regardless of their paper's market position. Individual capitalists did advance their particular economic interests; but on a broader level, communication industries as a whole also worked to bolster the general and collective interests of the capitalist class by means of some joint actions (Murdock 1982: 123). Given the 'collective rationality' of capitalists to defend both their personal and collective interests (Hannan and Freeman 1977: 932), the cartel acted as a power centre to counteract organisations that challenged its operations. New competitors or intruders who attempted to seize a share of the tantalising pie found the market niches filled by organisations with considerable social, economic and political resources (Stinchcombe 1965). These intruders were often ousted from the system and eventually folded, such as *Hong Kong Financial Daily*, launched in November 1987.[4] With a pre-segmented market without severe competition, the press industry reaped huge profits and accumulated capital. Since the capitalist press was not limited by keen competition and economic pressure, it could afford to equip itself financially and politically for the transition to come.

Incorporation

Political economy stresses the continuing centrality of ownership as a source of control over the policies and activities of large communications corporations (see Table 10.3). In the past, Hong Kong's newspapers were family businesses, and the editorial board was under the control of the family. The territory's most popular paper, *Oriental Daily News* (and later the *Sun*, founded after the transition) was founded by the Ma family in 1969. *Sing Tao Daily News* (established in 1939) and the *Hong Kong Standard* (founded in 1949) were owned by the Aw family; the *Hong Kong Daily News* was founded by the Law family in 1959. The longest-surviving paper in Hong Kong, the *Overseas Daily News* (*Wah Kiu Yat Po*) was owned by Shum Choi-sang, who succeeded his father Shum Wai-yau. The major owner and founder of *Ming Pao*, Louis Cha, had directly commanded the editorial pages and overseen its commentaries since 1959 (Chan 1991).

Between 1984, when China and Britain decided the fate of Hong Kong and the Basic Law was drafted, and the handover of 1997, many family-owned media organisations weathered political uncertainties through incorporation. This is a strategy defined as registering the cultural industry as a limited corporation, which means in effect turning a political and cultural entity into an economic good. This implies that the press's decision making was thereafter based upon economic concerns rather than political intentions. Accountability of the press to its investors serves to reduce any possible sanction when the press reports sensitive events and offends the authorities. It also expands capital resources, flattens the burden and spreads

Table 10.3   Ownership of Hong Kong newspapers

Newspaper	Year of establishment	Change of ownership	Readership in 1996 (000s)
Oriental Daily News	1969	Ma family	1,601
Apple Daily News	1995	Jimmy Lai	1,238[a]
Sing Pao Daily News	1939	Ho Man-fat (sold to Lee Kwok-keung in 2001)	630
Tin Tin Daily News	1960	From Ho Sai-chu to Yuk Long Int. and then to Aw of Sing Tao Group (now closed)	465
Ming Pao Daily News	1959	From Louis Cha to Yu Pun-hoi, then to Tiong Hiew Hing	345
Hong Kong Daily News	1959	Law family to Emperor Holdings	323
South China Morning Post	1903	From HKSB and Hutchison Whampoa (Li Ka-shing) to Rupert Murdoch, then to Robert Kuok	253
Sing Tao Daily News	1939	Sally Aw of Sing Tao Group (sold to Global China Technology Group in 2001)	221
Express	1963	From Sally Aw to South China Development (now closed)	209[a]
Hong Kong Economic Journal	1973	Lin Shan-muk and his wife	61
Hong Kong Economic Times	1988	Fung Siu-po	95
Wen Wei Po	1948	Shanghai Wen Wei Po	[b]
Ta Kung Pao	1948	Fei Yimin to Wang Guohua	[b]
Hong Kong Commercial Daily	1952	Economic Tribune to Joint Publishing Company (sold to Global China Technology Group in 2001)	[b]
Hong Kong Standard (now renamed imail)	1949	Sing Tao Group (sold to Global China Technology Group in 2001)	[b]
New Evening Post	1950	Ta Kung Pao (now closed)	[b]

Readership source: Social Research Group Media Report (Adex).

Notes:

[a] *Figures in 1995.*

[b] Readership below 60,000.

the political risks among a larger number of legal owners. Registration for incorporation was conducted in Bermuda to evade political interference.

Oriental Daily News was listed on the stock exchange in August 1987. While the Ma family still retained a majority shareholding, the Oriental Press Group benefited from a cash inflow of HK$254 million. *Hong Kong Daily News* was incorporated in May 1985 and was later purchased by the Emperor Group, which bought 30 percent of its shares in 1992. The Sing Tao Group and Ming Pao Enterprises were incorporated in February 1986 and March 1991, respectively. In the process, Sing Tao and Ming Pao accumulated HK$625 million and HK$217.5 million, respectively. Yu Pun-hoi's corporation, CIM, acquired Ming Pao Enterprises, which had been listed on the stock exchange in March 1991. Before the political transition, the Sing Tao Group remained in the hands of Sally Aw, who had also acquired Culture Communications (Culturecom, originally named Yuk-Long International, the parent company of *Tin Tin Daily News*). Culturecom accumulated additional capital of HK$306.8 million after incorporation. The *South China Morning Post* was incorporated in 1990 with an additional inflow of HK$149 million. *Express Daily News*, the property of the Aw family, was acquired by a listed company, South China Holdings in 1991 (see Table 10.4). Existing owners benefited in cash-flow terms from incorporation during the transition in Hong Kong, but it also sent out an important signal to other would-be investors that the media industry could operate as independently as any other business in Hong Kong. Incorporation also ensured that even if the press faced political interference after 1997, the authorities would have to respect the market, which is protected under the aegis of 'two systems'.

Incorporation did not signify the withdrawal of the original owners from the industry. Instead, families still presided over the newspapers, while other investors entrusted the business to the corporation. Poulantzas' distinction (1975: 18–19) between legal ownership and economic ownership is useful in describing the situation in Hong Kong. Technically, those who buy shares in the corporations are the legal owners of the newspaper, but not all shareholders are equal; owning shares does not necessarily confer real influence or control over the company's activities and policies. For legal ownership to become economic ownership, the shares must be voting shares, entitling the holder to vote in elections for the board of directors, or holders must be able to translate their voting power into effective representation on the board responsible for key decisions. However, this is not always possible. Economic ownership in large media corporations is typically structured like a pyramid, with the largest and best-organised voting shareholders determining the composition of the executive board, which formulates policy on behalf of the small investors who make up the company's capital base (Murdock 1982). Since the largest holdings of voting shares in Hong Kong's newspapers were still in the hands of the families, they essentially retained both financial and operating control of the organisations (Pahl and Winkler 1974: 114–15).

Table 10.4   Incorporation of media enterprises

	Date of incorporation	Price (billion K$)	Capital inflow (million HK$)
Ming Pao Enterprise Corporation	March 1991	$2.90	$217.5
South China Morning Post Holdings	June 1990	$3.08	$149.0[a]
Hong Kong Daily News Holdings	May 1988	$0.80	–
Oriental Press Group	July 1987	$1.00	$254.0
Yuk-Long International (acquired *Tin Tin Daily News* in 1987)	July 1987	$1.18	$306.8[b]
Sing Tao Group	February 1986	$1.80	$625.0

Notes:
[a] Capital inflow due to reorganisation.
[b] Difference between consolidated shareholders' funds, the nominal value of shares of Culturecom and the face value of shares.

As part of large corporations, newspapers were then tied to the complex business interests of the owning and affiliated enterprises. While administrators and barons had to observe commercial interests, middle-level personnel and editors did not have to be told of these affiliations, so journalists could boldly respond to the economic and political issues during transition. Shareholders' interests and economic benefits might arise as a pretext when the papers commented on certain political issues. The new structures also divested the interests of the investors to administrative personnel, who decided the paper's orientation, as opposed to the editor-in-chief, who was burdened with day-to-day corporate and political pressures.

Extension

Incorporation allows the listed parent company of the media business to formally acquire other non-media businesses, either by acquisition or through partnership. In this way, extension of the media empire was a means of diversifying the company's investment, enabling media enterprises to cushion the effects of recession by enjoying support from other sectors. In other words, the profitable profile of non-media businesses could subsidise losses and minimise the risks of investing in cultural interests (Murdock and Golding 1977: 28). Approaching the transition, Hong Kong's media barons must have been prepared for the possibility that their papers might have been forced to renounce some of their market interests when the authorities increased political pressure after 1997. Extension was one strategy to deal with this. It is not difficult to observe how the speed of extension can increase when there is a political crisis, for example during the 1989 Tiananmen Square demonstrations (see Table 10.5).

Extension is common in large capital-resourced media corporations, where the effect of economies of scale is more prominent. Culturecom, the parent company of *Tin Tin Daily News*, had diversified into comic books and publishing – apolitical sectors with mass appeal – which then became the major source of revenue for the entire enterprise. *Tin Tin Daily News* eventually folded in 1999, but Culturecom flourished. As long as the non-media business made a profit, the owner could choose to sacrifice his paper when the situation required, or simply shut it down all together. For example, the Sing Tao Group (Canada) invested in residential and commercial real estate in Canada, and Sing Tao's other activities include pharmaceuticals, medical and laboratory servicing, photo printing, sound recording, video filming and travel/tourism. In 1997, it also acquired the South China Printing Company. Political considerations that concern the media sector are absent from such activities.

The Emperor Group, which owned *Hong Kong Daily News*, is another example of diversification. The Emperor Group extended its business beyond publishing and hence diluted the possibility of political interference. In 1989, the group's investments included a printing service, investment and

Table 10.5 The market extension of press groups in 1989

Press group	Diversification	Market location	Investment in product (%)	Profit from newspapers (%)
Oriental Press Group	mono	Hong Kong	press (100)	39.8
Hong Kong Daily News	multi	Hong Kong Taiwan Singapore North America Australia	press (40) magazine furniture (37) equipment (23)	1.5
Sing Tao Group	multi	Hong Kong Southeast Asia North America UK	press (50) commercial printing (11) property (21) other (18)	7.7
Yuk Long International (later incorporated as culturecom)	multi	Hong Kong Southeast Asia North America Spain	press and publishing (61) printing (12) advertising (23) other (4)	loss

Source: Contemporary (18 August 1990: 45).

property holdings, the wholesale and retailing of furniture (through the local branch of Ulferts of Sweden), infoline and money-lending services, securities and futures brokerage services (through Emperor Securities and Emperor Futures), entertainment (through Fitto Entertainment Holdings and Fitto Mobile Laser Distribution), laser disc and video rental, and the supply of equipment for the pager business in Taiwan and China.

Ming Pao invested in the textile industry and property, a seemingly profit-generating business before 1997, when the government maintained a high-price land policy. The owner of Hyacynthe Ltd, Yu Pun-hoi, who briefly owned the enterprise, indicated that Ming Pao's participation in non-media investment and its plans for the future acquisition of other newspapers was a means of securing the financial situation of *Ming Pao Daily News*. He added, without reservation, that such a move was designed to reduce the impact of political change on the paper (*Ming Pao Daily News*, 13 December 1991; *Hong Kong Economic Journal*, 8 January 1992).

The Oriental Press Group, besides publishing a Chinese daily, also published *Oriental Sunday*, *Jade Magazine* and the *Sun Racing Journal*. In the 1990s, it also diversified into property investment, communications services, building management services and plant leasing. The more the media diversified, the less chance they would be subjected to political constraints.

Integration

In addition to extending into non-media businesses, newspapers in Hong Kong also conglomerated. Since the mid-1980s, there had been an underlying shift in the economic structure of Hong Kong when media ownership was increasingly concentrated in a few large corporations. Concentration is a measure of the degree to which the largest media corporation has control over production of the media message as calculated in terms of circulation (Picard 1989: 33). By buying out similar cultural products, media enterprises can increase their efficiency and diversify their market to benefit from economies of scale (Hage 1988; Picard 1989: 62). This is a process of integration through which merger and acquisition have produced media corporations or conglomerates with significant stakes in several sectors of the communications industry. Media conglomeration gives the capitalists an unprecedented degree of potential control over the range and direction of cultural production.

In Hong Kong, conglomeration and concentration were further accelerated by the government's non-interventionist policy and the absence of anti-trust laws on newspaper ownership, furthered by the enactment of the Bill of Rights, which opposed any interference in the industry. The Bill of Rights was passed in 1991, when Hong Kong people were perplexed by China's repeated and ambiguous narrative about freedom of speech in Hong Kong.

Horizontal integration has been a common local strategy for media giants and was designed to allow survival during the transition. It occurs when firms acquire additional units at the same level of production, and it results in mergers and takeovers (Hamelink 1994). This enables companies to consolidate and extend their control within a particular sector of media production, maximise their economies of scale and share resources.

The Ma family of the Oriental Daily Press Group owns *Oriental Daily News* and *Oriental Sunday*, which have mass appeal, and *East Touch* and *Eastweek*, which are directed at the young and the middle class. It also owns the highly profitable *Sun Racing Journal*, and it owned the English-language *Eastern Express* until it was closed with huge losses in 1995). Ma aimed to build an influential publication empire for all social classes. A media empire that is dominated by a single family provides bargaining power with the authorities.

Sally Aw of the Sing Tao Group used to own the *Sing Tao Daily News*, the *Sing Tao Evening Post* and the English-language *Hong Kong Standard*. Sally Aw also owned Culturecom, *Tin Tin Daily News* and the *South China Economic Daily* (*Huanan Jingji Ribao*), which closed in 1995.

The Ming Pao Group owns *Ming Pao Daily News*, *Ming Pao Weekly* and *Ming Pao Monthly*. It also acquired the Chinese *Yazhou Zhoukan* (*Asiaweek*) from Time-Warner in 1994. Ming Pao also launched the tabloid *Hong Kong Today* in November 1993 but closed it in December 1994 in the midst of keen competition. Ming Pao's subsidiaries include Ming Pao Publications, which publishes leisure and reference books, and Crystal Window Publications, which publishes *City Children Weekly*. For both the Ming Pao Group and the Sing Tao Group, the resources of their own publications (*Ming Pao Daily News* and *Ming Pao Monthly*, and *Sing Tao Daily News* and *Standard*, respectively) were shared to reduce costs and increase efficiency.

Media moguls integrate horizontally with non-political media to avoid over-concentration on news, which might increase political risk. Hong Kong Daily News Holdings owns *Hong Kong Daily News*, the *Economic Digest* and the entertaining *Fresh Weekly* and *Esquire*. Its subsidiary also owns a series of 'high-class' magazines for executives and professionals, including *Marie Claire*, *City Entertainment*, *Arch Domina*, Walt Disney's *Mickey*, *Golf*, *First Class Traveller*, *Penthouse* and *Cosmopolitan*. In 1985, Rupert Murdoch's News Corporation purchased the *South China Morning Post* for HK$241 million, and it also owned *South China Weekly Magazine*, *Hong Kong Visitor* and *Asia Magazine*. In January 1992, South China Morning Post Holdings also acquired the 70-year-old *Overseas Chinese Daily* for HK$46 million but with annual losses of HK$40 million, the newspaper was closed in January 1995 (see Table 10.6). In February and March 1996, shareholders in the *South China Morning Post* could exchange one share for two shares in Television Broadcasting Enterprise (including property investment, magazine and book publishing, music production, convenience stores, club management, the promotion and operation of foreign tours, commercial and movie production,

Table 10.6   Conglomeration of media in China and Hong Kong in the 1990s

Company	Major owner	Daily	Other media
Oriental Press Group	Ma family	*Oriental Daily News* *Eastern Express* (English) *Oriental Sunday* *Sun Racing Journal*	*Eastweek East Touch*
Sing Tao Group	Sally Aw	*Sing Tao Daily News* *Sing Tao Evening Post* (closed) *Hong Kong Standard*	*Starlight Monthly* *Liberation Daily/* Economic Section (China)
Culturecom	Sally Aw	*Tin Tin Daily News* *Huanan Jingji Ribao* (closed)	other comic books
Hong Kong Daily News Holdings	Albert Yeung	*Hong Kong Daily News*	*Economic Digest* *Fresh Weekly* *Esquire* *Marie Claire* *City Entertainment* *Arch Domina* *Mickey* *First Class Traveller* *Penthouse* *Cosmopolitan* karaoke productions
Ming Pao Enterprise	Tiong Hiew Hing	*Ming Pao Daily*	*Ming Pao Weekly* *Ming Pao Monthly* *Yazhou Zhoukan* *City Children* *Weekly* other leisure books
	Oei Hung Leong	Hong Kong Today (closed)	*Wide Angle* (sold) *Modern Mankind* (China, closed)
South China Morning Post Holdings	Robert Kuok	*South China Morning Post* *Wah Kiu Yat Po* (closed)	*South China Weekly* *Magazine* *Hong Kong Visitor* *Asia Magazine* TVB

and the operation of a chain of kindergartens). The move towards integration has accelerated the shift from differentiation (attained by the strategy of extension) to concentration (Garnham 1981: 140). Such conglomeration, coupled with growing shareholding links with other leading corporations, has become a characteristic of the capital accumulation market.

Globalisation

The increasing concentration of media control and influence is the outcome of three interlinked but analytically distinct processes: extension, integration and globalisation (Boyd-Barrett 1995; Hamelink 1994). The huge sums required for acquisition and capital accumulation might prompt businesses to enter into partnership with international corporations that are interested in expanding their business overseas. The local media diversified to invest overseas at the same time that foreign businesses began to invest in Hong Kong's media. The injection of foreign funds into a specific media organisation secured it from political risk. The Chinese authorities would be less likely to interfere and risk undermining their international reputation. Local owners might also dare to defy political pressure and report what they believed deserved to be reported.

For some, investment in Hong Kong was considered a stepping stone or a testing ground for their business's potential. Overseas Chinese jumped the queue to enter into closer business relationships with China. The *South China Morning Post*, formerly owned by Rupert Murdoch's News Corporation, was acquired by Robert Kuok, a Malaysian Chinese who had enormous investments in Burma, Malaysia and China. Ming Pao, established by Louis Cha, was sold to CIM, which involved Japanese funds. Tiong Hiew Hing, a Malaysian Chinese, finally acquired a majority stake in Ming Pao in 1995 after Yu had failed to pay an instalment to Louis Cha. Tiong also has significant investments in Singapore and Malaysia.

Some papers, like Sing Tao Daily News, the South China Morning Post, Ming Pao Daily News and the leftist press, also expanded their markets in America and some other Asian countries. The expansion of the news media overseas was crucial as a source of revenue when local prospects were gloomy. The Ming Pao and Sing Tao Groups competed in the Canadian market for a readership of 280,000 Chinese. The Sing Tao Group has published editions in New York, San Francisco, Vancouver, Toronto, London, Paris, Sydney and Melbourne, while the Ming Pao Group also launched overseas editions in Toronto and Vancouver in May and October 1993, respectively. Positioned as a Chinese journal for intellectuals, Ming Pao Monthly entered the Taiwan market in April 1995. The Hong Kong Standard also joined the Vancouver Sun to publish the Asia Pacific Quarterly Report in Hong Kong. In the early 1990s, Hong Kong Daily News Holdings planned to expand in Taiwan and obtained a license to operate and distribute a Chinese-language newspaper there. The Oriental Press Group held industrial and residential properties in the United States. In 1993, the South China Morning Post acquired 15 percent of shares in Post Publishing Company Ltd in Thailand, a long-term investment that anticipated the Post publishing in Bangkok. All these globalisation strategies – either overseas expansion or investment by foreign owners – might bring more profit to the parent mother companies but, most importantly, these were 'safe' strategies that eased worries that coverage of local issues might upset the authorities.

The end of capital accumulation

However, the various media strategies for capital accumulation seemed to be the performance of a swansong before Hong Kong's return to China. This does not mean that these strategies were inappropriate; nor does it mean that local media corporations failed to accommodate China's presence. Simply, the local economy adapted to potential integration with the China market. In part, the economic viability of the commercial sectors and media enterprises was eroded by the turbulence of the political transition in Hong Kong, as well as by China's new media policy after the Tiananmen Square demonstrations, which shattered the hope of media moguls to penetrate the China market. In part, the worsening financial situation was due to the general weakening of the Hong Kong economy. It also represented the dismantling of the cartel's protection functions, which was a prologue to restructuring the political economy of the media. This not only rendered those relatively conventional strategies impotent but also curbed the media's capital accumulation.

The vanishing hope of the China market

The local free capitalist-run economy had been flooded by Chinese capital since the 1990s. Moreover, China's financial interference in the local economy meant that media and non-media economic interests began to intertwine with and transform their political positions. To make profits, media corporations had to manoeuvre their news content and their economic resources politically. The vast market in China was tempting, as in Shanghai and Guangdong alone advertising revenue for newspapers was over HK$1 billion annually in 1990 (*Journalism Yearbook of China*, various years). Such dependency finally eroded the profits of the local media and crippled their political and economic planning.

Owners of various newspapers joined the queue to pay homage to China in the early 1990s. Paving the way for coming joint ventures, Sally Aw returned to Fujian in 1992 to lay the foundation stone of a hall to commemorate her family and also to establish a foundation for a local infrastructure project.[5] Other publishers, including Ho Man-fat of *Sing Pao* and Ma Ching-kuan of *Oriental Daily News*, followed suit by making visits to China. As a result, business tycoons and media owners donated considerable amounts of money to their ancestral homes, satisfying their duty of filial piety while winning the trust of the ruling Chinese powers.

In 1993, the Ming Pao Group set up printing facilities and a distribution network in Guangzhou for its northern expansion. In total, CIM acquired six publications on the mainland. One prominent paper was *Guangzhou Today News*, a joint company with a mainland publishing house. Although CIM owned over 70 percent of the paper, it delegated editorial to the Chinese side to desensitise the paper. In late 1993, the paper was ordered to stop publishing because of the withdrawal of the mainland company. Another example was *Qiao*, a mainland magazine, which CIM had acquired in 1993. *Qiao* was later banned because it contained articles that contravened the propaganda front (AuYang 1993). In November 1993, the Hong

Kong Social Communication Company, in which the Ming Pao Group held a majority stake, invested HK$20 million in *Modern Mankind*, a paper covering cultural affairs in Guangzhou.[6] Nevertheless, in mid-1994, the Guangdong branch of the China Council for the Promotion of International Trade withdrew sponsorship from *Modern Mankind*. Suspicious of the paper's intentions and of its possible popularity in the future, Beijing ordered *Modern Mankind* to be closed down on 1 January 1995 (*Yazhou Zhoukan* 1995). Whenever a newspaper revealed its political nature, the authorities stepped up their interference.

Buoyed by its initial success with joint ventures, the Sing Tao Group eventually encountered a similar setback. On 1 June 1993, Sing Tao established *Starlight Monthly* (*Xingguang Yuekan*) with People's Daily International Cultural Publications, a subsidiary of the official *People's Daily* (*Hong Kong Economic Journal*, 4 April 1992; *Hong Kong Standard*, 24 November 1992). This monthly publication was important because it was the first Sino–Hong Kong joint venture periodical started in China with the approval of the PRC. Freely distributed on the mainland, the magazine diluted political ideology, reported economic news and glorified the Chinese leaders. The editorship rested with the Chinese authorities, and both agreed that the monthly would avoid reporting sensitive ideological problems (Ha 1993).

In May 1993, China had drafted 'Preliminary Suggestions Regarding the Direction of Newspaper and Magazine Reform', which allowed businessmen from Hong Kong, Macau and Taiwan to invest in cooperative ventures in China. However, the suggestion was subsequently turned down when Beijing tightened its ideological control. The *Starlight Monthly* eventually ceased publication in May 1995, purportedly for 'reorganisation of the editorial department' but also following huge financial losses and an underlying realisation that northern expansion was not feasible. In the same year, the Sing Tao Group also invested HK$200 million to publish the Chinese-language business daily *Shunxing Times* for the southern city of Shenzhen. The paper's editorial independence yielded many insights for newspapers expecting publishing opportunities on the mainland. *Shunxing Times* had a circulation of less than fifty in Hong Kong. Prior to December 1996, Sing Tao had already dismissed fifty staff from the paper, including twenty in the editorial department. So far, Sing Tao's investment in the *Shenzhen Special Zone News* has been the greatest success, but the scale of operations has been significantly reduced. Aw's joint ventures, together with those of other media barons, were doomed to failure.

No matter how they repositioned themselves in relation to Beijing, these foreign capitalists were still viewed with suspicion. Beijing believed that their influence might extend beyond the political realm; the press could become empowered economically to 'negotiate' with the authorities the meaning (or ideology) of press content. The cutback in mainland investment undermined the financial structure of local media (*Ming Pao Daily News*, 6 June 1993).

Recession in the local market

When the media accumulate capital and expand, the scale of the business eventually reaches a size in which circulation can no longer be relied on to balance the budget. Profits must then be linked to the amount of advertising sold rather than simply to the circulation. However, the advertising pot shared among Hong Kong's newspapers was relatively fixed. Although total advertising revenue of the media and communications industry grew by 13 percent in 1991, this was the lowest growth rate since 1985. Taking an inflation rate of 8 to 10 percent in the early 1990s into account, it reflected sluggish growth.[7] This effective reduction in advertising revenue was potentially lethal to the press, for various papers had been accumulating resources to prepare for the handover. They were reluctant to use their reserves until the expected political and economic downturn after 1997.

In addition, production costs rose so quickly that advertising revenue could not offset the global rise in the cost of newsprint.[8] The cost of paper shot up from US$500 to $600 per tonne in 1994, while in 1995 the price even hit $1,045 per tonne. The annual cost of publishing a single broadsheet (four pages) was HK$9 million (*Price*, 7 February 1995). According to Dharmala Securities,[9] newsprint accounts for 43 percent of the total cost of *Oriental Daily News*; the corresponding figures are 20 percent for the *South China Morning Post*, 30 percent for *Ming Pao Daily News* and 16 percent for *Sing Tao Daily News*. The cost of running a newspaper, including the cost of newsprint, printing ink and wages, was so exorbitant that only large media enterprises could afford it. Dragged down by the increase in paper costs, *Oriental Daily News* earned only HK$138.2 million in 1995, representing a 36.2 percent decrease in profits; the profits of *Ming Pao Daily News* suffered a drop of 40.4 percent. Newspapers were under pressure to cut pages, but they could not reduce them to the extent of allowing advertising to exceed content.

The mounting cost of newsprint intensified tensions between the business departments and the editorial departments of newspapers (*Rising*, 31 March 1995). However, the cartel hindered the press from changing content to cut into the market of competitors in an effort to acquire more advertising and other sources of revenue. These tactics pushed small newspapers to the wall.

New entrants and price wars

In June 1995, Jimmy Lai launched the *Apple Daily News*, which eventually emerged as a successful model of how to attract readers by providing gossip, sex and crime-related stories ('sensationalism', 'yellow journalism' and 'vulgar entertainment' were all terms used to describe its content). *Apple* was also infamous for its team of thirty to forty photographers and reporters with ten vehicles and seven motorcycles to cover timely stories.

When the cartel raised its prices to an unreasonable level, the *Apple Daily* was able to enter the market easily by having a relatively low retail price.

With an investment of HK$700 million, *Apple*'s promotional strategies initially triggered criticism from the cartel.[10] Vendors refused to adjust the price, but as *Apple*'s circulation was so attractive the vendors could not resist change. The paper had soon built up a circulation of 300,000 and cut into the commanding position of the *Oriental Daily News* and other popular papers (see Table 10.7). *Apple* was able to take a share of advertising revenue from a saturated market. On its debut, advertising revenue was an estimated HK$1 million per day, and by July 1996 the figure had increased to HK$1.5 million with a net profit of over HK$1 million per day.[11]

When a competitor outside the system was able to gain a firm foothold in the industry, the other papers had no compunction in defying the cartel by using aggressive marketing tactics at a time when they were being drained of advertising revenue and circulation. These papers were soon launching promotional campaigns and mimicking *Apple*'s format, content and techniques of mass appeal, all of which required huge capital expenditure. The resulting competition forced others out of what had become a shrinking market. At the end of 1995, the press became engaged in a cut-throat price war designed to knock out competitors. The war could be regarded as an interim tactic for individual members of the press to manipulate their resources to safeguard their own futures.

The death of the cartel was finally announced when the cash-rich market leader, *Oriental Daily News*, decided to cut the cartel-imposed price of HK$5 to $2 per copy. The paper was then relaunched with a major facelift in content and layout. *Sing Pao Daily News*, *Tin Tin Daily News* and *Hong Kong Daily News* then matched *Oriental*'s price cut. The selling price of the Oriental Press Group's *Eastweek* was reduced from HK$18 to $8 and that of Lai's *Next Magazine* from HK$18 to $12.

On the surface, the price war increased circulation. The *Oriental*'s circulation rose by 20 percent and eventually shot up to 580,000. The *Daily News* doubled its circulation to 240,000, and its advertising revenue also doubled. *Sing Tao Daily News* boosted its circulation to 300,000. *Tin Tin Daily News* hit 320,000 with an average circulation of 200,000. In reality, the price war

Table 10.7   The circulation of newspapers before and after the launch of *Apple Daily*

	Before	After
Oriental Daily News	320,000	300,000
Apple Daily	–	300,000
Sing Tao Daily News	187,477[a]	140,000
Tin Tin Daily News	173,777[a]	110,000
Hong Kong Daily News	127,712[a]	110,000
Ming Pao Daily News	107,484[a]	80,000

[a] Figures based on the ABC report for January–June 1995. Other figures are from distributors (*Hong Kong Economic Journal*, 13 December 1995; *Next Magazine*, 15 December 1995).

was disastrous for profits. Because newspapers gave discount prices to distributors and special advertising rates of 30 percent (on average) for advertisers, the newspapers reaped no extra profit. What mattered was that some papers had more capital at their disposal than their competitors.

All newspapers were sold at a price below production cost. Such predatory pricing not only resulted in great losses for the price-cutting newspapers but also eroded profit margins (Bluestone *et al.* 1981). By tradition, Chinese newspapers received HK$3 for each copy sold, with the remaining $2 split between distributors (30 cents) and news vendors ($1.70). In forgoing their circulation incomes, *Oriental* and *Sing Pao* were set to lose at least HK$1 million and HK$370,000, respectively, every day even if their sales recovered to previous levels. An editor estimated that by launching the price war, *Apple* lost HK$930,000 per month.[13] The price war took less than a week to ruin those less fit to survive. While a few media corporations boosted circulations at a financial loss, newspapers that remained at the same price had sluggish circulations (*Overseas Chinese Daily*, 2 and 10 October 1994). Those less competitive papers were further damaged by vendors and distributors, who reduced their stock for sale.[14]

In 1994, the price war forced South China Holdings to extricate the 32-year-old *Express* (with an annual loss of HK$26 million) from bankruptcy by suspending it for a year. In December 1995, Culturecom closed *South China Economic Daily* (*Huanan Jingji Ribao*), a paper targeting an audience in the Pearl River area and Southeast Asia (with a HK$30 million loss). The war also triggered the closure of Taiwan's *United Daily News* in Hong Kong, which had a limited circulation of between 20,000 and 30,000. The *Television Daily* was also closed down in the same year. The *Hong Kong Economic Times*'s supplement, *Leisure Pie*, which was scheduled for launch as a separate magazine in 1996, was shelved as a result of the unfavourable situation (*Hong Kong Economic Journal*, 29 December 1995). The Oriental Group also closed its English-language daily, *Eastern Express*, since it continued to make a loss of HK$71 million. Within only a year Hong Kong also saw the closure of *Hong Kong Today News* in November 1994 and the *Overseas Chinese Daily* in January 1995.

It was no surprise that the share prices of the Oriental Press Group, Hong Kong Daily News, Sing Tao Holdings, Ming Pao Enterprises and Culturecom Holdings nosedived to record lows. Papers, including *Apple*, had reduced profits during the price war and consumed significant amounts of accumulated capital. The price war reduced *Oriental*'s turnover by HK$2.35 billion. *Oriental*'s profit was reduced by 93.8 percent, from HK$4.05 billion in fiscal year 1994/95 to HK$250 million in fiscal year 1995/96. The greatest loss was felt by relatively small papers like *Sing Tao*. It lost HK$2.88 billion between 1994 and 1995. The Sing Tao Group, which owned 43 percent of Culturecom, suffered a HK$28.2 million loss. *Hong Kong Daily News* and *Ming Pao Daily News* had record losses of HK$1 billion and HK$9.4 million, respectively. The top seven newspapers lost a total of HK$6 billion.

The two new giants, *Apple* and *Oriental*, temporarily buried their differences, and Lai proposed to lever the prices of both publications. The
cut-throat price war ended, but the implications were permanent.

Commodification

The consequences of the price war go far beyond profit and loss. The price
war not only directed the whole press market back towards the free market
and forced newspapers to reposition themselves in such a market, but it also
sent a message to the media: that to survive the transfer of sovereignty,
Hong Kong's newspapers had to consider not only pressure from the
authorities but also the market and public interest.

When the capitalist interests of Hong Kong coincided with their political
interests, the non-political formula did not always work. Media owners
modified their orientation towards China to accommodate the transition.
With the pretext of a seemingly popular strategy to report attractive sensational social and non-political news, reporters and editors could practice
self-censorship at the expense of public interest.

Whereas sensational reporting might target the largest readership, the
non-political or non-critical attitude of the press did not seem to attract
interest from the politicised masses. Media owners might have conceived of
the adjustment needed, but local voices often contradicted those of the
authorities. Had there been a stable press system protected under the cartel,
the audience's access to political news might have been completely sacrificed
to local interests.

The scenario was altered by the success of *Apple Daily*, which claimed
itself to be a 'Hong Kong newspaper' with an indigenous edge and pandered
to the needs of local readers. It sent out two signals, one to its competitors
and one to the authorities. First, in the face of keen competition from *Apple*,
other papers could not be insensitive to the market. The press had to
respond quickly to readers' needs, be sensitive to their tastes, improve print
quality, differentiate themselves from the competition and create a market
niche to survive. Financial benefits will flow only to those who can differentiate from their competitors, either territorially or in terms of content
(Hannan and Freeman 1977). Second, the authorities realised that they
could not eliminate dissident voices during the handover, especially if this
opinion was strong enough to support a new paper.

Demand and public taste could both be political. Local readers annoyed
by interference by the Chinese authorities in local autonomy were desper-
ately in need of a channel to represent their voice, and they themselves
might have formed a strong readership base for any paper that articulated
their needs. Public opinion forms a market – and hence promotes commodification – which can be in opposition to the authorities. When the new daily
felt no obligation to comply with the cartel economically and politically, it
seized the opportunity to criticise the authorities and did so at a time when

public fury had no suitable outlet. It is only under such conditions that the aforementioned analysis as well as the struggle for press freedom is meaningful. Otherwise, the press would simply have shifted towards the party line and there would have been no free press. Such a contradiction opens up the possibility of resistance.

Conclusion: the continual struggle for press freedom

The press in Hong Kong entered the transition period in the midst of dismay and consternation. The stability of the cartel-formed segmentation necessary for the press to accumulate capital and resources had been shaken by a new entrant. The price war, which required newspapers to field and risk huge amounts of capital, triggered a gradual transformation of the media, eliminating the weak and leaving only the most resourceful. The surviving papers were much better prepared to attend to readers' needs. To do otherwise in the face of strong competition would have meant failure. In the years to come, they must not only accumulate resources and capital but also manoeuvre themselves to strengthen their competitive ability. The press has to adjust its market position in relation to political forces, and it must be continually aware of political intentions, contingencies and limitations. At any given moment, political forces may either complement or contradict economic ones. Thus the press has to optimise its survival by constantly resolving this complicated politico-economic dialectic. The press can choose to minimise the sanctions of political constraints (to be politically controlled), and/or choose to satisfy the market to resist political forces.

Commodification of news has a significant implication for press freedom. The popular press has the upper hand in determining the media agenda, making economic decisions and, more importantly, in political sensibility. What has not been discussed publicly is how this populist movement might be conceived as a way of challenging authority, namely the PRC and the PRC-appointed government in Hong Kong. This explains why the government has, on more than one occasion, accused the local media of being banal and secular, and of abusing press freedom, after 1997.

Notes

1   *Hong Kong Adex* is an annual publication about readership of all Hong Kong media by ACNelson Hong Kong, formerly called the Social Research Group Hong Kong.
2   While, most of the time, the Newspaper Society, the vendors and the distributors converged to defend their interests, they were occasionally inimical to each other. First, the papers might unanimously take joint protest action to foster their bargaining power against news distributors and vendors. In October 1990, the Hong Kong Newspaper Society raised the selling price of newspapers by 50 cents, instead of the $1 that the distributors had demanded. In fact, price

increases were often pushed by distributors, who claimed that the cover price had to go up to offset increasing operating costs. This eroded the legitimacy of the Newspaper Society.

3 For example, in the 1970s the defunct *Kung Sheung Daily* (*Commerce Daily*) attempted to keep its price at 20 cents when every other paper raised its price to 30 cents. But many news vendors disregarded *Kung Sheung*'s decision and sold it at the same price as the other major papers because they shared 40 percent of the cover price. Vendors also colluded with distributors and threatened to stop selling *Kung Sheung*, forcing the paper to go along with the price increase within six months (*South China Morning Post*, 17 January 1995).

4 To keep itself intact, the cartel also served to eliminate external threats. In October 1988, nine newspapers of the cartel issued a joint statement complaining that the figures released by Survey Research Hong Kong (SRH) failed to reflect their readership and that SRH implicitly compelled the press to accept its calculations for auditing circulation (*Hong Kong Economic Journal*, 25 October 1988). The cartel planned to set up a working committee to compile its own reports, and the Newspaper Society also improvised a preparatory committee to look into the possibility of establishing a media council under the chairmanship of Sally Aw of *Sing Tao* in 1985 instead of surrendering to surveillance from without. These actions to 'clamp down' on the disclosure of their circulation figures reduced the transparency of the market and thus isolated the whole press system from market forces (*Overseas Chinese Daily*, 22 March 1988).

5 Many high-ranking government officials, including Zhang Jinsheng of Xinhua and Lu Ping of the Hong Kong and Macau Office came to the ceremony. She also visited leaders in Beijing in 1992 and was warmly received by President Jiang Zemin and Premier Li Peng.

6 The paper was started after receiving permission from the Guangzhou Propaganda Department, State Council and Guangzhou News Office.

7 According to a *Hong Kong Adex* report, the newspaper industry received 29 percent of advertising revenue (HK$4,375 million) in 1994, a reduction of 6 percent on the overall share from the previous year. Property ads, the pillar of newspaper advertising since the 1990s, were also contracting.

8 For example, one of the longest-running papers in Hong Kong, the *Overseas Chinese Daily*, lost HK$2 million per month due to insufficient advertising, even though it managed to achieve a 60 percent increase in circulation in 1994.

9 There are many (non-media-related) investment companies in Hong Kong giving figures and predicting trends for various businesses in Hong Kong. Such information helps investors in the stock and securities markets with regard to (public) listed media companies. Dharmala Securities is one of these companies.

10 While Jimmy Lai accused five Chinese newspapers of intimidating the *Apple Daily*, a spokesperson for the Joint Association of Newsstand Operators' Societies and the cartel lashed out at *Apple*'s attempt to introduce a discount voucher sales scheme.

11 Author's interview with source in the *Apple Daily News*, late 1997. The interviewee wishes to remain anonymous.

12 Audit Bureau of Circulation, an independent company providing advertisers with the circulations and profiles of newspapers so as to determine and estimate the advertising charges. However, Hong Kong newspapers are not compelled to join this organisation.

13 Author's interview with source in the *Apple Daily News*, late 1997. The interviewee wishes to remain anonymous.

14 The press had at this time been suffering from a slack economy and decreasing advertising revenues, made worse by the doubling of newsprint price in one year due to a global shortage. To compensate for the inflated cost in October 1994,

major papers put aside whatever differences might have divided them and agreed to comply with a price set by the newspaper cartel on behalf of the Newspaper Society. The compliance of the cartel bullied the small papers because rising prices reduced the readership of small papers.

References

Adrich, H.E. and Pfeffer, J. (1979) 'Environment of organizations', in M. Zey-Ferrel (ed.), *Readings on Dimensions of Organizations*. Santa Monica, Calif.: Goodyear Publishing.

AuYang Fung (1993) 'Hong Kong media rushing for the mainland market', *Frontline Magazine*, 14 May (in Chinese): 13–14.

Bluestone, B., Hanna, P., Kuhn, S. and Moore, L. (1981) *The Retail Revolution: Market Transformation, Investment, and Labor in the Modern Department Store*. Boston: Auburn House.

Blumler, J.A. and Gurevitch, M. (1975) 'Towards a comparative framework for political communication research', in Chaffee (ed.), *Political Communication: Issues and Strategies for Research*. Beverly Hills, Calif.: Sage.

Boyd-Barrett, O. (1995) 'The political economy approach', in Boyd-Barrett and Newbold (eds), *Approaches to Media: A Reader*. London: Edward Arnold.

Chan, J.M. and Lee, C.-C. (1991) *Mass Media and Political Transition: The Hong Kong Press in China's Orbit*. New York: Guilford Press.

Chan Yat-kwan (1991) 'Newspaper ownership and press freedom', *Hong Kong Economic Journal*, 22 December (in Chinese).

Endacott, G.B. (1973) *A History of Hong Kong* (2nd edition). Hong Kong: Oxford University Press.

Fung, A. and Lee, C.-C. (1994) 'Hong Kong's changing media ownership: uncertainty and dilemma', *Gazette* 53(1/2): 127–33.

—— (2002) 'Market and politics: Hong Kong press during sovereignty transfer', in Jia, Heisey and Lu (eds), *Chinese Communication Studies: Contexts and Comparisons*. Norwood, NJ: Ablex.

Garnham, N. (1981) 'Contribution to a political economy of mass communication', in Wilhoit de Boch (ed.), *Mass Communication Review Yearbook*, Volume 2. Beverly Hills, Calif.: Sage.

Ha Man-sze (1993) 'Setback of Hong Kong media's northern expedition', *The Open Magazine*, 21 July (in Chinese): 20–1.

Hage, J. (1988) *Future of Organizations: Innovating to Adapt Strategy and Human Resources for Rapid Technological Change*. Lexington, Ky: D.H. Health, Lexington Books.

Hamelink, C.J. (1994) *Trends in World Communication: On Disempowerment and Self-empowerment*. Penang, Malaysia: Southbound and Third World Network.

Hannan, M.T. and Freeman, J. (1977) 'The population ecology of organization', *American Journal of Sociology* 82(5): 929–64.

He Zhou (2000) 'Chinese Communist Party press in a tug-of-war: a political economy analysis of Shenzhen Special Zone daily', in C.-C. Lee (ed.), *Power, Money and Media*. Evanston, Ill.: Northwestern University Press.

Journalism Research Institute, Chinese Academy of Social Science (eds) (1983-1993) *Journalism Yearbook of China (Zhongguo xin wen nian jian)*. Beijing: Chinese Academy of Social Science Press.

Lane, K. (1990) *Sovereignty and the Status Quo: The Historical Roots of China's Hong Kong Policy,* Boulder, San Francisco: Westview Press.

Levins, R. (1962) 'Theory of fitness in a heterogeneous environment: the fitness set and adaptive function', *American Naturalist* 96 (November/December): 361–78.

Mosco, V. (1996) *The Political Economy of Communication*. Beverley Hills, Calif.: Sage.

Murdock, G. (1982) 'Large corporations and the control of communications industries', in Gurevitch, Curran and Woollacott (eds), *Culture, Society and the Media*. New York: Methuen.

Murdock, G. and Golding, P. (1977) 'Capitalism, communication and class relation', in Curran, Gurevitch and Woollacott (eds), *Mass Communication and Society*. London: Open University Press.

Pahl, R. and Winkler, J. (1974) 'The economic elite: theory and practice', in Stanworth and Giddens (eds), *Elites and Power in British Society*. Cambridge: Cambridge University Press.

Picard, R.G. (1989) *Media Economic: Concepts and Issues*. Newbury Park, Calif.: Sage.

Poulantzas, N. (1975) *Classes in Contemporary Capitalism*. London: New Left Books.

Shen, G. (1993) 'China's investment in Hong Kong', in Choi and Ho (eds), *The Other Hong Kong Report 1993*. Hong Kong: Chinese University Press.

Stinchcombe, A.L. (1965) 'Social structure and organization', in J.G. March (ed.), *Handbook of Organizations*. Chicago: Rand McNally.

Sung Yun-wing (1991) *The China–Hong Kong Connection: The Key to China's Open-Door Policy*. Cambridge: Cambridge University Press.

To Yiu-Ming (1995) 'Blowing in the wind: economic and political challenges to the press in political transition', in S. Cheung and S. Sze (eds), *The Other Hong Kong Report 1995*. Hong Kong: Chinese University Press.

Tsang Shu-ki (1994) 'The economy', in McMillen and Man (eds), *The Other Hong Kong Report 1994*. Hong Kong: Chinese University Press.

Yazhou Zhoukan (1995) 'Golden light under the shadow of political pressure' (in Chinese), 15 January: 15–19.

11 Directing Hong Kong

The political cinema of John Woo and Wong Kar-wai

Andrew M.J. Brown

Introduction

This chapter deals with political film making in Hong Kong during the run up to the handover of the colony from British to Chinese rule in 1997. This period is a particularly interesting one to study because of the general uncertainty about the immediate future and the competing ideologies behind the various parties' efforts to shape that future. On one side there was Britain, with its colonial history, promotion of free trade and a broad commitment to democracy. On the other side was the People's Republic of China (PRC), keen to reassert its territorial claim over Hong Kong and to use the process as a springboard for the eventual return of Taiwan but also concerned to preserve the territory's economic legacy.

Between these two was a third party – the people of Hong Kong. They had no say in the negotiations and were effectively sidelined by the political process, being allowed to participate only as members of the British team, never in their own right. In the face of the impotence of their politicians, the voice of Hong Kong's people was instead expressed through popular art forms such as cinema. It is the hypothesis of this chapter that in times of political restriction or inadequacy, popular films can be read as political statements, manifestos even, either reflecting or seeking to lead popular opinion. The wider argument is that the study of popular culture should be seen in the context of contemporary politics, and *vice versa*. This chapter will therefore also explore cultural issues and trace the parallels and transfer of ideas between the cultural and political spheres.

The specific focus of this chapter is on the films made by John Woo and Wong Kar-wai during the run up to the Hong Kong handover, in particular Woo's *The Killer* (1989) and Wong's *Chungking Express* (1994). To test the above hypothesis, I shall attempt a political/cultural reading of these film texts and consider their meaning within a historical context. I believe that many films of this period can be read as expressions of popular discontent, apprehension and confusion of identity during the negotiations.

This chapter was also written as part of a broader research project considering political cinema across China, Hong Kong and Taiwan. Despite the recent popularity of such films at film festivals and on the art-house circuit, the subject is still under-researched. Existing literature tends to fall into two categories: either describing broad cultural patterns or making close, biographical readings of individual directors' films. Examples of the former approach include Gold (1993) and Zha (1995), while Tam and Dissanayake (1998) is an example of the latter.

There is an equal lack of *political* film criticism dealing with the Hong Kong directors under consideration here. Existing work on the films of John Woo tends to deal with issues of masculinity and violence (e.g. Stringer 1997), while that on Wong Kar-wai emphasises visual style and characterisation (e.g. Tsui 1996).

However, there is an extensive literature on Chinese political history, and on the broader issues of globalisation, democratisation, modernisation and the spread of popular culture. This research aims to fill a gap in this literature by applying these general theories to specific film texts, viewing them both as political documents in their own right and as focal points for larger cultural and political debates, both in Southeast Asia and the West.

John Woo and *The Killer*

John Woo was born Wu Yu-sen in Guangzhou, southern China, in 1946. His family were devout Christians and fled persecution under communism, arriving in Hong Kong in 1951. They lived a hard life, being made homeless in a fire in 1953. Woo's father had tuberculosis and was unable to work, so his mother supported the family through construction work and manual labour. After his father died in 1964, Woo joined a local seminary and began training to be a priest, but he was ultimately turned down by the Church. In 1968, he started making amateur films with a local student theatre group and in 1973 joined Golden Harvest, a film company, directing his first film, *The Young Dragons*, in the same year. He made a number of somewhat formulaic films for the company before gaining mass popularity with *A Better Tomorrow* in 1986.

It is the phenomenal success of this film, and the others Woo made in the next few years, that gives him such significance in the popular culture of Hong Kong. In 1992, John Woo emigrated to the United States, but by this time he had become Hong Kong's most popular director, and his name had become synonymous with the genre of action films often known as 'heroic bloodshed'. Woo's popularity allows us to consider his films as expressions of the collective hopes and fears of mainstream Hong Kong society. This is one key way in which cinema can function politically: as a democratic/populist statement.

It is not my intention in the following analysis to consider Woo as an *auteur* (a director who intentionally constructs a unique world view throughout a body of films) but rather as a cultural mouthpiece, or representative of a certain social group, whose relevance is determined by the size of his audience. It is possible, then, to analyse his films historically and seek to understand the moments at which an audience could identify with the events shown.

The Killer is perhaps the clearest expression of this phenomenon. Its release in 1989 was against the background of China's publication of the first drafts of the Basic Law,[1] which effectively laid the foundations for mainland rule. China was also pressuring the British and Hong Kong governments to limit the pace and extent of democratic reform in the colony: official British policy at the time was to 'seek convergence' with the Chinese proposals. However, tensions in China itself had been rising for some time with the student-led campaign against government corruption, and this led to escalating confrontations with the government, culminating in the mass protests in Tiananmen Square in June 1989 and the building of the statue of the 'Goddess of Democracy'. Although the Chinese government reasserted its authority on the mainland, the management of the demonstration by the government kick-started massive anti-Beijing protests in Hong Kong. The strength of feeling in Hong Kong at this time, as well as the lack of British support for the protesters, is summarised by Bruce Herschensohn (1999: 8), as follows:

> Then came the massacre at Tiananmen Square. Any optimism was smothered .... [There were] massive demonstrations, unknown in Hong Kong, with somewhere between 500,000 and one million people .... A huge replica of the Goddess of Democracy was erected in Victoria Park. The British Government would not give it a permanent site (China, as expected, objected). Four months after Tiananmen Square, with protests against the People's Republic still on high, Governor David Wilson advised Hong Kong people to use their rights and freedoms 'with self-restraint'.

This was the background against which *The Killer* was released in Hong Kong cinemas, a critical juncture at which we should consider both the Hong Kong people's attitude towards Britain and China and the expression of such attitudes in this particular film.

The plot of *The Killer* revolves around the struggles of hit man Jeff (Chow Yun-fat) to make amends for his accidental blinding of night-club singer Jenny (Sally Yeh) during a job. It also involves his conflicts with the local crime syndicate under Johnny Weng and the efforts of Inspector Li (Danny Lee) to bring him to justice. During the course of the film, however, Jeff and Li become friends and eventually bury their differences and join forces to defeat the gangsters.

The first task of this analysis is to deconstruct the film's style, narrative structure and genre. Through this we can ascertain the film's thematic concerns and hence its political subtext and the cultural and ideological position taken in relation to China and the West and the attitude presented towards the Hong Kong handover itself.

Visual style, narrative structure and genre

The Killer is replete with visual imagery. The opening scene takes place in a lavishly decorated church, full of white candles and doves. Two shots emphasise a large wooden cross, backlit through a stained glass window, and a statue of the Virgin Mary. The first significance of this imagery is that it reveals the extent of the influence of Western culture on John Woo and Hong Kong. It is a reminder of the colonial history of Hong Kong and the zeal of British missionaries.

In the film's penultimate scene, the characters return to the same church for a violent showdown. During the crossfire, the Virgin Mary is blown to pieces. Woo immediately cuts to a shot of Jeff and Li, with a look of horror on both their faces. This suggests an abiding concern over the persecution of Christians in mainland China and their uncertain future in Hong Kong, an issue of personal importance to the deeply religious director as well as to many people in Hong Kong. The following is an example of these concerns, as discussed with Martin Lee, the leader of the Hong Kong United Democrats:

INTERVIEWER: In China, over the last several years, the persecution of Christians has been intensified .... Do you think [they] will be pressed down on here too?

MARTIN LEE: Any Christian who worries about the future of religious freedom has my sympathy. In China they have the Patriotic Church. Now everyone's supposed to be patriotic in Hong Kong too .... In China they want to control your thought.

(Herschensohn 1999: 80)

Or, as Woo himself said in an interview: 'those scenes show war can turn heaven into hell; anything that is pure and innocent is destroyed. The Virgin Mary symbolises purity, and she's shattered by bullets' (Wise 2000).

However, the story is not entirely one-sided. Woo's Christian characters are often paired with ones practising Chinese religion. In *The Killer*, Inspector Li is shown praying at a Buddhist shrine, and there is no real indication that he shares Jeff's Western beliefs. This uneasy coexistence between East and West underpins much of Woo's work and points to a key parallel with Hong Kong itself, where Western economics and culture sit uneasily beside Chinese traditions.

References to art and literature betray a similar contradiction: Woo's literary references are predominantly Western – the title of *Hard Boiled* (1992), for example, refers to the novels of Raymond Chandler and Dashiell Hammett. This film also contains the image of a murder weapon hidden in *The Complete Works of Shakespeare*. However, at a later point in this film we see a synthesis of East and West. Undercover detective Tony (Tony Leung) lives in a boathouse decorated with Western art prints, in front of which hang a multitude of distinctly Oriental origami birds.

We can see a further set of Western influences in Woo's wholesale appropriation of American classical narrative, a film-making formula first used in the Hollywood studio productions of the 1930s and 1940s. David Bordwell (1995: 157) defines classical narrative as follows: 'the classical Hollywood film presents psychologically defined individuals who struggle to solve a clear-cut problem or to attain specific goals. In the course of this struggle, the characters enter into conflict with others or with external circumstances'. Bordwell also highlights the use of the protagonist's character as 'the principle causal agent' and the dramatic structure of 'the deadline'.

If we apply this model to *The Killer*, we discover a remarkably close fit. The protagonist is Jeff, and his clear-cut problem is to raise enough money for Jenny's operation (the deadline being represented by her waning vision and the fear that the operation may come too late). Heroically, Jeff struggles to attain this goal, and in so doing he enters into conflict with both the syndicate and the police. The deadline in this instance has an additional metaphorical significance in the form of the July 1997 deadline. Woo (2001) revealed his own attachment to early Hollywood cinema in an interview on the DVD release of *Hard Boiled*: 'When I was very young my mother always took me to the movies ... I was especially fond of American classics like *Gone with the Wind* and *Waterloo Bridge*'.

Woo's wholesale appropriation of this American narrative formula can be seen as another example of Hong Kong embracing Western culture. Perhaps more significant, though, is the moral simplicity and sense of order inherent in classical narrative in that it constructs an idealised view of the world with an obvious divide between right and wrong and eventual narrative resolution. In the context of the tortuous and morally ambiguous negotiations for the handover of Hong Kong, a world with such rules and moral clarity must have seemed intensely appealing.

Somewhat more problematic is Woo's position within the action genre. Both Hollywood and Hong Kong action films rely upon visual spectacle (explosions), fast-paced filming (chases) and violence. However, John Woo has led Hong Kong film makers in creating a new breed of action film. He has taken Hollywood-style violence and modern weaponry and fused these elements with others drawn from traditional Chinese martial arts to create choreographed, highly stylised action films in which acrobatics are performed on motorcycles and characters wield two guns balletically as their predecessors used swords.

Film critics have typically sought to define genres through one of two approaches, namely iconography or thematic structures. In terms of iconography, Hong Kong action films barely deviate from their Western counterparts; guns, cops, cars, explosions – all these surface features remain the same. In thematic terms, however, we are entering new territory. The struggle between criminals and the law, culminating in the victory of the law-abiding hero, dominates modern Hollywood action films but is far less evident in Woo's work. Instead, we have an environment and heroes more akin to the Japanese samurai movies of Akira Kurosawa, with their portrayal of a lawless society and the man of violence with a code of honour. In interview, Woo has hinted at this interpretation himself: 'All of my movies are primarily about family, friendship, loyalty and honour' (Wise 2000).

This divergence can be seen most clearly in Woo's use of gangsters as sympathetic protagonists. For most Americans, 'good guys' and 'bad guys' can be defined in terms of cops and criminals, but for the Chinese, with an ideology based on Confucianism, it is more a case of those with honour against those without. These opposing ideologies can be seen in the following parallel sections of dialogue, in which an honourable character is set against a dishonourable counterpart. The first scene involves cops, the second gangsters.

POLICE CHIEF: Any progress in the Weng case?
LI: No, none at all. I nearly got the suspect, but he escaped.
CHIEF: Where's your razor-sharp intuition? Many people want me to fail, so this case means a lot to me. I don't need you letting me down.
LI: Sir, I don't do anything for anyone. I'll get the murderer; you'll get your promotion.

SIDNEY: You should let me handle Jeff. He's my responsibility.
WENG: What if he squeals on me?
SIDNEY: He's not that kind of guy.
WENG: I don't trust anyone … including you.
SIDNEY: I know the rules of the game; I'll keep my word.
WENG: Forget the rules. I want him dead because he exposed his identity. I'm the boss now and you'll do things my way.

It is interesting to note that the dishonourable characters are also the modernisers: Weng has killed his traditionalist uncle in order to take over the syndicate and run it his own way. The implication of this in terms of a political subtext is that it is the modern, communist China of Mao Zedong and Deng Xiaoping that is the enemy, not the traditional China represented by Confucius.

Ien Ang has identified the cultural processes at work behind the type of East/West anomalies discussed here – a form of globalisation by which local cultures appropriate foreign (usually American) cultural forms and fuse them with local, traditional elements to create something entirely new:

In the 1950s, Cantonese movies dominated the Hong Kong market …. Their popularity declined in the 1960s and early 1970s, when Hollywood films consistently out grossed locally produced Chinese films. By the 1980s, however, the most popular film genres in Hong Kong were once again locally produced, but evincing definite elements of 'indigenisation'.

The contemporary genre of Kung Fu movies, for example, appropriated and refracted James Bond-style film narratives by using fists and martial arts as weapons, as well as drawing on traditional Cantonese values such as vengeance for friends and kin, loyalty to close acquaintances and punishment of traitors.

(Ang 1996: 154)

This cultural globalisation can also be seen at work in the political and economic spheres, with the Chinese appropriation and adaptation of first Marxism and then capitalism. Consider, for example, the title and intent of Deng Xiaoping's crucial political text *Build Socialism with Chinese Characteristics* (1984). Here, as elsewhere, we can see changes in the political landscape paralleling those in the cultural.

Thematic concerns and political subtexts

Some thematic concerns have already been touched on, but the most important in *The Killer* is the sub-textual anxiety about the approaching handover of Hong Kong to China. Woo's attitude towards this event can best be demonstrated through an analysis of *The Killer*'s nihilistic ending.

Immediately prior to the final shoot-out Jeff says to Li, 'promise me one thing: if I don't make it, take me to a hospital, have them save my eyes for Jenny'. However, when Weng shoots Jeff in the face and blinds him, he simultaneously robs him of this last chance for redemption. Jeff and Jenny crawl towards each other across the blood-soaked turf, but due to their mutual blindness they miss each other and Jeff dies alone. Jenny is once again wounded in someone else's fight and now has no chance of recovering her sight. This emphasis on blindness and the act of blinding may be another reference to Shakespeare, specifically to *King Lear* with its parallel themes of fate, redemption and despair. It may also relate to the blindness of the people of Hong Kong towards their own future.

Meanwhile, Li pursues Weng, who has surrendered to the police. Li walks up to him and shoots him twice in the chest, an act that necessitates his own arrest. The bad guys have lost, but so too have all the good guys. The traditional happy ending is manifestly absent. An explanation for this can be found in the film's political context and the environment of widespread pessimism felt towards the approaching handover – the belief that regardless of whether Britain or China were to prevail in the negotiations, Hong Kong would lose out.

Even the climatic shoot-out can be read on an ideological level. The hundreds of anonymous assailants, identically dressed in black, can be identified with the communist Chinese masses. Jeff and Li, by contrast, can be taken to represent individualism and liberty. In their violent stand against the triad forces, Jeff and Li also embody the right to take up arms against an oppressive government (as enshrined in the American constitution). In this respect, Woo's films bear a striking resemblance to the American science fiction/horror films of the 1950s that warned against the Soviet 'red peril' by representing communists as hordes of zombies or hostile aliens (e.g. *Invasion of the Body Snatchers*, 1956). In this sense *The Killer* can be read as inciting the people of Hong Kong to stand up to China but also as a pessimistic warning about their low chance of success against such overwhelming odds.

The pessimistic climate surrounding the handover of Hong Kong to China is felt in virtually all of Woo's films. Although there are no explicit references to the handover, there are many signs that can be read on a metaphorical or allegorical level, all of which reveal an attitude that is verging on the apocalyptic. In the ironically titled *A Better Tomorrow* (1986), for example, we find the following dialogue, ostensibly about the triad lifestyle:

HO: Mark, we can't hang onto the past any more. So why stay?
MARK: You're right. We have very little now. If we don't watch out we'll
         have nothing.

And in a later scene:

MARK: I never realised that Hong Kong was so beautiful at night. It'll
         vanish one day – that's for sure.

In the second scene, we can also see an example of Woo's use of urban space. He contrasts the frenetic, violent activities within the city with the more serene or pensive moments when characters sit by the waterfront (as here) or in the hills overlooking the city of Hong Kong (in *The Killer*). The contrast of landscape and mood is therefore paralleled by that between tradition and modernity. The character of Mark is also highly important. As a cripple abused equally by police and gangsters, he can be viewed as a personification of the impotence and lack of self-determination felt by Hong Kong's citizens in their exclusion from the Anglo-Chinese negotiations. Li Cheuk-to (1996: 174–5) provides the following historical reading of *A Better Tomorrow*:

> The key to the film's popularity may lie in the Daya Bay Incident .... It was here that the Chinese authorities started to build a nuclear power plant. A pressure group in Hong Kong organised a petition, but the wishes of the million people who signed it were ignored by China. It was at this juncture that *A Better Tomorrow* was released. What better way for a frustrated public to give vent to pent-up feelings?

I would go one step further and claim that Woo's films in fact act as allegories of emotion (with narratives driven by the prevalent anxieties of the time) and that this is why their Hong Kong audiences identify so strongly with the characters and events.

In addition to the above discussion of *The Killer*, this claim can be substantiated through a reading of the emotional narrative of *A Better Tomorrow II* (1987). The plot of this film revolves around the character of Mr Lung (Dean Shek), who is set up by Ko, his trusted business partner. Ko subsequently kills Lung's daughter, driving him mad (perhaps another reference to *King Lear*) and then sends assassins after him when he flees to New York. This situation emphasises strong feelings of betrayal, paralleling those felt by many in Hong Kong towards the British. In the introduction to Mark Roberti's *The Fall of Hong Kong*, for example, leading Hong Kong Democrat Martin Lee says:

> We now know that British officials lied when they leaked word to the press that the constitutional provisions in the Joint Declaration (1984) were negotiated at the last minute and could not be fleshed out for lack of time. We now know that Britain knew all along – despite public assurances to the contrary – that China had no intention of allowing any meaningful measure of democracy in Hong Kong and that Beijing agreed to include provisions for an elected legislature in the agreement only at the eleventh hour to clinch a deal.
>
> (Roberti 1996: xix)

This is, admittedly, a somewhat loaded view, but it is one that is shared by the majority of Hong Kong's population, as demonstrated by the runaway success of Mr Lee's United Democrats in the 1991 and 1995 elections. In *A Better Tomorrow II*, it is therefore significant that the West fails to protect Lung, and it is only through returning to Hong Kong for a violent confrontation with Ko (China) that he regains his sanity.

Another emotion underpinning *A Better Tomorrow II* is nostalgia for a vanishing past and the values that it represented. In a key scene, Ho (Ti Lung) visits an artist who has been painting pictures of the events portrayed in the first film:

ARTIST: Many things are memorable. I've put down all the incidents in your lives into many stories .... The world nowadays no longer has people who are friends like you. Like Mark, how many are there like him?

However, this film also contains a potential break from the culture of nihilistic pessimism. In one of the film's last scenes, Kit (Leslie Cheung) is shot and fatally wounded while his pregnant wife is in hospital. Woo cuts from slow-motion shots of the fatal bullet to Kit's wife in labour, and then from the dying man to his newborn son. This appears to speak of the Daoist belief in the *yin* and the *yang*, the seed of good within evil, life within death and *vice versa*. The extension of this metaphor to the Hong Kong handover would mean that it cannot be entirely bad, and that within the rising darkness there must yet glow the light of hope.

Wong Kar-wai and *Chungking Express*

Wong Kar-wai was born in Shanghai in 1958, but his family emigrated to Hong Kong in 1963. Wong studied graphic design at Hong Kong Polytechnic, graduating in 1980, and went on to write scripts for television dramas. After a number of years as a scriptwriter, he joined an innovative new movie studio, Cinema City, directing his first film, *As Tears Go By*, in 1988. In 1992, when John Woo left Hong Kong to live and work in the United States, Wong remained behind and attempted to redefine his own cultural identity through his films.

In many ways, Wong's films form a counterpoint to those of John Woo. His reputation has been built primarily on the international art-house circuit, and his films speak to a narrower, more elitist audience. There is sufficient evidence in Wong's complex, multi-layered film texts, and in the interviews he has given to Western film critics, to view him as an *auteur* and to consider his films as part of a carefully constructed world view, with highly personal concerns and intentionally political subtexts. An example of this can be found in Wong's response to a question about the period setting of *In the Mood For Love* (2000):

> We ended [the film] in 1966. That was a critical moment in Hong Kong history. There was the Cultural Revolution in China, and in Hong Kong we had the anti-colonial riots. Those people who had moved from China to Hong Kong since 1949 had to realise that the place is easily influenced by the changes in China.
>
> (Romney 2000)

However, such differences exist against a background of shared cultural and political experiences, which create equally strong similarities: themes of violence and betrayal are at least as important to Wong's films as they are to Woo's. It is through a comparison of their films, using the same methodology, that we can ascertain how far these two directors represent a shared, collective agenda and to what extent they hold individual positions, with differing responses to their common experience of Hong Kong.

Chungking Express (1994) was Wong's third film and the one that brought him to the attention of Western critics and audiences. It was released at a time when Deng Xiaoping was withdrawing from active leadership, a move that heightened the uncertainty surrounding the future of both Hong Kong and China itself. Following the Tiananmen Square demonstrations in 1989, an atmosphere of mutual hostility and mistrust had developed between Britain and Hong Kong on the one hand and China on the other. Chris Patten had taken over the governorship of Hong Kong in 1992 and was attempting to secure a greater degree of self-rule, including, for the first time, democratic representation for the people of Hong Kong. He introduced bills to replace appointed officials with elected members, and to increase the elected proportion of the Legislative Council. This was to lead to the emergence of Martin Lee's United Democrats as the main party of Hong Kong, giving the people a legitimate political voice. However, Patten's failure to consult China on these reforms led to a further collapse in relations between the two, which ultimately led to China setting up rival institutions and announcing, in 1994, its intention to abolish the Patten-devised institutions immediately after the handover.

Meanwhile, the post-Tiananmen political atmosphere in the PRC had become one of zero tolerance towards dissidents and democrats. This did not bode well for the future of Hong Kong democrats, many of whom had already been branded by China as accomplices in the 1989 uprisings. On the intellectual front, Western academics and economists were developing the theory of Greater China (Shambaugh 1995) and were talking about the exchange of ideas, culture and trade between southeast China, Hong Kong and Taiwan, as well as the prospects for eventual political reunification.

Visual style, narrative structure and genre

Chungking Express is a film in two distinct parts, a blend of action and comedy. The plot is deceptively simple: the first story concerns Cop 223 (Takeshi Kaneshiro), who works in Hong Kong's notorious Chungking Mansions. Recently dumped by his girlfriend, he resolves to fall in love with the next woman to walk into his local bar – who turns out to be a heroin smuggler (Bridgette Lin). The second story centres on Cop 663 (Tony Leung) and the Midnight Express takeaway where he buys his dinner every night. Obsessed by the memory of his ex-girlfriend, he completely fails to notice the advances of waitress Faye (Faye Wong).

Perhaps the most immediately striking feature of *Chungking Express* is its visual style. Wong uses jerky handheld cameras and non-continuity editing through rapid jump cuts, often showing us the same action repeated from different viewpoints, while the action sequences are shot in blurred stop-motion. The antecedents of Wong's style are the experimental film makers of the French New Wave, such as Jean Luc Godard, but Wong moves beyond their 'style for style's sake' tendencies and uses these visual innovations, as well as the choice of location, as outward expressions of his characters' inner state.

While Wong's influences are very different to Woo's, they still betray a high level of Westernisation and stand in stark contrast to the slow-paced, static film style that is more typical in mainland China. Zhang Yimou, for example, in films like *Judou* (1990) and *Shanghai Triad* (1995), uses numerous long shots of rural landscape that are highly reminiscent of traditional Chinese painting and reflect an earthier philosophy of life. Both Wong and Woo, in their different ways, stand opposed to this style of cinema.

As with Woo, the issue of multiculturalism is also essential for an understanding of Wong's films. It can be seen, for example, in his use of language. Many of the characters in *Chungking Express* slip between Cantonese,

Mandarin and English, often within the same conversation. The smuggler also wears a blond wig, trench coat and dark glasses, which serve to mask her ethnic identity and make her appear Western. This reflects the cultural duality of Hong Kong itself and perhaps the idea that underneath its Westernised surface, the territory remains Chinese at heart.

The film's soundtrack also contains a number of cultural juxtapositions. It shifts from modern classical, through reggae and Western rock, to Cantonese pop. Different characters have their own theme tunes; thus scenes featuring Faye, who daydreams about moving to the United States, are accompanied by the Western pop track 'California Dreaming'. This particular choice of music can also be read as a comment upon the obsession with America exhibited by film makers like John Woo and their Hong Kong audiences.

There is also an important inter-textuality between *Chungking Express* and Wong's subsequent film *Fallen Angels* (1995). The first manifestation of this is in the use of locations, many of which are the same in the two films. The Midnight Express fast-food store crops up in the second film as one of the shops that He Qiwu breaks into and runs after hours. Second, Wong transposes dialogue between the two films. For example, in *Chungking Express* one character says, 'My name is He Qiwu. I'm a Cop PC 223', while in *Fallen Angels* another says, 'My name's He Qiwu. My prison number was 223'. To further complicate matters, the two characters are played by the same actor, although they have vastly different backgrounds and appearances – the first is smartly dressed and middle-class, while the second is an unkempt, unemployed mute with dyed blond hair. The third instance is one of body language. While serving in the Midnight Express, He Qiwu mimics Faye dancing to 'California Dreaming' with bottles of ketchup.

The significance of these scenes is that they show a confusion of personal identity within the cultural and political contradictions previously discussed. The characters are unable to define their own positions within a rapidly and traumatically changing society. This therefore relates to the problem of real people seeking to define their own cultural identity and understand what it means to be a citizen of Hong Kong at the close of the twentieth century. An example of this dilemma is provided by Wudy Heung of the Hong Kong Policy Research Institute:

> I'm sure that it's not difficult for you to appreciate my confusion of mind, because in a couple of days Hong Kong will be a Chinese territory. But what am I? I was born in Hong Kong, spent half of my life in the United States, and then in the last ten years I spent 70 percent of my time in China.
>
> (Herschensohn 1999: 65)

Wong's films ask these same questions through analogy. Will He Qiwu be the same person under Chinese rule as he was under British? Will the Midnight Express be the same place? The alternative realities Wong presents reveal a strong awareness of the radically different lives that the same people may be leading post-1997, depending on the choices made by their political masters. Wong is also asking his audience to consider these issues in relation to their own lives. Without presenting a solution, he is nonetheless encouraging people to be more aware and critical of the changes in the world around them.

In terms of genre, *Chungking Express* is a deliberate hybrid. Broadly speaking, the generic form of the first part is a crime/action thriller; it features cops, gangsters, gunfights, chases, double-crossing – all the central ingredients of a John Woo film. However, these elements are peripheral to the main narrative thrust, which is the tragicomic emotional plight of Cop 223.

In the first part we can therefore see a reinterpretation of a familiar genre, and this approach is continued into the second half, which plays out as a romantic comedy. Cop 663 is oblivious to Faye's advances, even when she breaks into his apartment and redecorates it. According to the conventions of the romantic comedy, the couple would inevitably end up together (just in time for a happy ending), but by the time Cop 663 finally catches on, Faye has quit her job, become an air hostess and boarded a flight to California. Wong revealed his idiosyncratic engagement with genre conventions in an interview with Tony Rayns:

RAYNS: Why are the men in both stories cops?
WONG: Partly because Hong Kong movies are supposed to be action orientated; they're full of cops and gangsters, and I chose cops. Partly because I like the idea of uniforms and service numbers.

(Rayns 1995: 14)

We can see here a clear contrast between Wong and Woo. Where Woo works strictly within the action format, respecting its conventions, Wong merely takes it as a starting point, manipulates its conventions and ends up with a film that defies narrative or generic classification. In *Fallen Angels*, Wong takes this process one step further, with a direct engagement in a number of scenes with the cinema of John Woo. Tony Rayns, in a preamble to the above interview, describes meeting the director on set: 'The hit man played by singer Leon Lai bursts in, causing the Indians to scatter in panic before one of them is gunned down. When I ask Wong Kar-wai about the scene he's shooting he grins and says, "Tonight, I'm doing John Woo"' (*ibid.*: 12).

On viewing the finished scene, the similarities are even stronger; Killer (Lai's character) dispatches his victims with two guns, shooting and reacting in an identical manner to Woo's heroes. The scenes are fast-paced and full of frenetic activity, with multiple armed assailants, all of whom are dispatched by the hyper-efficient killer. But this is not just a parody; the scene also contains an element of serious criticism. This can be seen in the aftermath of the shoot-out, when we see piles of dead bodies and cowering, terrified children, then notice that the camera lens is marked with small spots of blood, recalling documentary or news filming. The message here seems to be that Woo's lavishly stylised combat cannot be regarded outside the context of real violence, that you can never entirely glamourise murder. In the aftermath of the Tiananmen Square massacre, this message has a certain immediacy.

Thematic concerns and political subtexts

The key thematic concerns of *Chungking Express* are an exploration of personal isolation in urban society, the impossibility of love and the effects of time and memory. The first two themes form Wong's critique of the contemporary late capitalist society and culture of Hong Kong, while the third is directly related to the handover to China.

In the film, the theme of urban isolation can be seen in the characters' cramped single apartments, their lack of communication and under-standing, their constant betrayals, reliance upon technology and consumerism, and their lack of individual identity.

The issue of betrayal is obviously present in the romantic entanglements but can also be seen in other types of relationship. In the first part of the film, the smuggler is double-crossed by her contact, while in the second part the entire Midnight Express staff team open and read Cop 663's confidential mail. The key difference with Woo is that all Wong's characters are involved in betrayals of one type or another. He does not use this as a form of judge-ment but rather as a way of understanding the universal fallibility of human nature – a more complex approach than Woo's simplistic moral code of honour. This difference creates two different views of the Anglo-Chinese negotiations. Where Woo would be looking for the two sides to behave honourably, Wong would look for, indeed expect, a level of human fallibility and a betrayal of trust.

The reliance upon technology can be seen in Cop 223's relationship with May – their entire relationship is carried out via his pager. Other characters use TVs, stereos, guns and juke boxes as their emotional props. The film's clut-tered scenery is also filled with Western brand names such as Circle K, M&Ms and McDonald's. It is McDonald's that is the most prominent, with giant restaurant signs in a number of scenes, often dwarfing the characters them-selves. This throws up the issue of consumerism as the social product of late capitalism, a criticism particularly appropriate to Hong Kong, where the ideology of free-market economics has been elevated almost to the status of a national religion. It is also significant to note that it is Hong Kong's economy that makes it most attractive to China, and that in many ways it is busi-nessmen and corporations that have the most to gain from the handover. As Frank Martin, president of the American Chamber of Commerce, points out:

> Of course the reason why we believe that China is likely to take steps to ensure that Hong Kong remains stable and prosperous is because Hong Kong is the conduit for China's capital. Hong Kong companies have

over one billion dollars invested in China and employ over six million people. China's companies are listed on the Hong Kong stock market. That's where they're getting the capital for their future infrastructure development needs.

(Herschenshon 1999: 154)

Wong would seem to be unimpressed by such arguments. In his rejection of capitalism and materialism, he displays socialist values that are ideologically out of step with modern-day Hong Kong and are arguably more in tune with pre-Deng China. His references to McDonald's also appear critical of the process of economic globalisation, with its emphasis on institutions over individuals. In this respect, the West is just as guilty as China of oppressing the people of Hong Kong. We can therefore see in Wong's work a refusal to accept the black-and-white mentality of Woo, which supposes that everything Western is good and everything Chinese bad. For example, in *Days of Being Wild* (1991), which is set in the 1960s, the place of the McDonald's restaurant is taken by Queen's Cafe, a reminder of the imperial nature of colonialism and the feudal principle of ownership of people and places. This, at least, ended in 1997.

The lack of personal identity can be seen first in the naming of characters. Some have identical or similar names (May and Faye), while others remain almost entirely nameless (Cop 223 and Cop 663). This use of numbers as names is also an extreme example of commodification. There is an example of this in the script, which also contains a notably left-wing distinction between the attitudes of employers and those of employees.

MIDNIGHT EXPRESS BOSS: PC 633 is good with girls!
WORKER: That was 663, boss.
BOSS: Same thing.

The impossibility of love is a strong theme throughout all Wong's films, but whereas in *Days of Being Wild* this is the fault of the characters themselves, in *Chungking Express* it is due as much to the environment of urban overcrowding (with the resulting lack of community) and consumerism. This point is driven home when Cop 663 reveals why his girlfriend left him. Note the way in which people and relationships are treated as commodities:

COP 663: She said she wanted a change. She's right. If you can choose your food, why not your men?
MIDNIGHT EXPRESS BOSS: How does she know you're the best 'til she's shopped around? She'll be back.

Wong's treatment of the subjective nature of time and memory is initially through the use of clocks as a visual metaphor. There is a general emphasis on clocks in both *Days of Being Wild* and *Chungking Express*, but in *Fallen*

Angels Wong pushes their metaphorical use one step further with a scene in which Killer's partner is tidying an apartment dominated by a giant wall clock. She attempts, without success, to turn back the hands of the clock – to turn back time and prevent the inevitable, both in her relationship with Killer and in Hong Kong's with Britain. In addition to the metaphorical connections there is literal one: in 1994, the Chinese government set up a giant clock in Tiananmen Square that was set to count down the time remaining until Hong Kong returned to China.

Wong makes the same point more explicitly in *Chungking Express*, using the theme of sell-by dates. These can be found in many places, including Cop 223's collection of pineapple tins, all of which expire on 1 May. He sees this as a metaphor for the end of his relationship with May, but the viewer can see it as a further metaphor for the end of Hong Kong's relationship with Britain (on 1 July). Hence there is great deal of nostalgia and looking back in the film, as well as an intense awareness of impending change and an uncertainty about what the future will hold. There is also a key break here with Woo, who tends to prophesy disaster. Instead, Wong takes a more ambivalent, non-judgemental line, preferring to wait and see. Cop 223's narration indicates this metaphorical reading: 'somehow, somewhere, sometime everything expires. Swordfish expires, meat sauce expires, even cling-film expires. Is there anything on this earth that doesn't expire?'

By taking expiry dates as a metaphor for the end of colonial rule, even humorous dialogue takes on another meaning, as in Cop 223's argument with a shopkeeper who won't let him buy expired food: 'Why fresh? Think of the effort put into a tin of pineapple. It's grown, harvested, sliced. And you want to dump it? Think of the tin's feelings!'

More ominously, the smuggler's boss leaves her a sardine tin with an expiry date, again of 1 May, as a threat to kill her if she fails to turn up the missing drugs. This is a deadline in the literal sense and represents a bleaker view in terms of the handover parallel. However, the film's final conversation leaves us on a more positive if somewhat ambiguous note. It contains a clear reference to the uncertainty of the future as well as an awareness of diverging paths and possible destinations – potentially negative but also potentially positive:

COP 663:	Do you let people on with a boarding pass like this? It's today's date but I don't know where it's going.
FAYE:	Shall I give you another?
COP 663:	Please.
FAYE:	Where to?
COP 663:	I'm easy. Wherever you like.

This idea of a journey with potentially different destinations ties in with the prospect raised by some commentators that, despite China's impending political control of Hong Kong, it may ultimately be Hong Kong that changes China, through the more subtle spread of liberal economics, culture and politics. Wudy Heung hints at this cross fertilisation:

> [If] you look back to the late '70's and the early '80s, when we were talking about the transition of sovereignty back to China, people were thinking about how Hong Kong is going to be swallowed up by this big brother. Then ... people began to see that it might be the other way around, because as you come down from Beijing you see the influence of Hong Kong getting stronger and stronger.
>
> (Herschensohn 1999: 70)

This attitude is developed by Wong in his last pre-handover film, *Happy Together* (1997), which deals with a gay couple, Lai Yiu-fai (Tony Leung) and Ho Po-wing (Leslie Cheung), who move to Buenos Aires to restart their failing relationship. The allegorical nature of the storyline is indicated (as usual) through the dialogue. Lai says of Ho: 'For him "starting over" has many meanings'. For a politically inclined audience, it means Hong Kong 'starting over' with China and the West. The two characters, through their respective occupations, can be seen to represent the opposing political positions on this issue. Lai is a night-club host, welcoming Chinese tourists to a local venue, while Ho is a male prostitute for western clients:

HO: You think you're better? 'Welcome! This way!' Isn't that prostitution?
LAI: Not like you! You and your white trash!

Ultimately, the couple fail to reach an accommodation and Lai returns to Hong Kong – just in time to see the death of Deng Xiaoping on TV, with the resulting opportunity to 'start over' with the new leadership. Despite an air of negativity in much of his work, Wong is able to see beyond 1997 and point to the room for optimism that does exist. Significantly, Wong intended to name his first post-handover film 'Summer in Beijing', a reference to the potential for a thaw in Chinese relations with Hong Kong and an end to political oppression on the mainland. However, the film was never made.

Conclusion

From the above analysis, it can be seen that John Woo and Wong Kar-wai do indeed share a number of key concerns and are both responsive to the effects of globalisation. These shared concerns include, first, a sense of betrayal by Britain for ceding Hong Kong to China without obtaining sufficient democratic safeguards for the population. Second, there is a common anxiety over cultural and national identity, about what it means to be a citizen of Hong Kong in the run up to the handover. Finally, they share an attitude of uncertainty towards the future prospects for the territory beyond 1997.

Despite this common ground, the two directors construct very different responses to the issues raised. Woo sees no hope at all for Hong Kong beyond the handover; his anti-communism resulted in the restriction of options to one, namely emigration to an idealised United States. However, Wong is equally concerned about the West, in particular the American-isation and consumerism carried on the back of economic prosperity. His response is therefore to attempt to renegotiate a new identity for Hong Kong, based in part on the strengths of being Chinese while not ignoring the shortcomings of the PRC.

In terms of globalisation, both directors have produced films that owe at least as much to the West as they do to Chinese culture. Woo in particular can be seen to be operating largely within the parameters established by Hollywood film making. The key difference is that while Woo seems uncon-cerned by the erosion of Chinese culture by Western cultural and economic imperialism, Wong is clearly troubled by it, and his engagement with Western art forms is therefore more critical.

Woo's and Wong's common concerns indicate their shared social context, which according to cultural theorists like Barthes and Foucault is where the authorship of such texts is constructed. Foucault in particular has argued that an author is merely a distinctive patterning of pre-existing language, culture and ideology. He claims that 'the 'author-function' is ... not defined by the spontaneous attribution of a text to its creator, but through a series of precise and complex procedures; it does not refer, purely and simply, to an actual individual insofar as it simultaneously gives rise to a variety of egos and to a series of subjective positions that individuals of any class may come to occupy' (Caughie 1996: 289).

While the cultural background from which an author operates clearly *is* important, it seems to me untenable to extrapolate that the individual author does not in fact exist. A good artist, in whatever field, is usually aware of their cultural background and is more likely to challenge and engage with it than to be its unthinking minion. The opposing responses of John Woo and Wong Kar-wai to their shared environment clearly demon-strate the presence of very different ideologies, which are indicative of a wide range of viewpoints within Hong Kong as a whole. It could be argued, for example, that Woo is an 'author-function' for Hong Kong prior to the handover, but then Wong's films would be expected to follow the same pattern – and they clearly do not.

I feel that there is sufficient evidence of distinct political agendas in the two bodies of work examined to support the claim that at least some film directors are able to function as political *auteurs*, that is distinct individuals, representing different political viewpoints and putting across their manifestos in an attempt to either inform or convince audiences. Where the politicians have failed to impress their audiences, film directors may yet succeed.

On a historical note, it remains to be said that since the handover, both the greatest hopes and the worst fears of the various commentators have so far proved unfounded. China has so far attempted to meddle in minor legal and journalistic matters but has refrained from wholesale interference in politics and economics. The Beijing-appointed Hong Kong legislature, while remaining staunchly pro-Chinese, has also stood up for Hong Kong's business interests against mainland officials. However, Wong's plans for *Summer in Beijing* had to be shelved for political reasons:

> We wanted to make the film in Beijing, but we had problems with the censor's department in China .... For us, *Summer in Beijing* seems to be a very romantic title, but for them, obviously it's not. And we wanted to shoot some of the scenes in Tiananmen Square, and we had to stop that. And so I thought maybe we would have to stop this project, and start something else.
>
> (Morris 2000)

The film was replaced by *In the Mood for Love*, set in the 1960s, but Wong's next project, provisionally entitled *2046*, does promise a return to the complicated issue of Hong Kong's future relationship with China:

> It's more like a stage play. It happens in the future .... The idea came from a promise the Chinese Government gave in 1997[2]: They promised to leave Hong Kong fifty years unchanged. So 2046 is the last year of that promise, and I wanted to explore whether there will be anything unchanged. A lot of people in Hong Kong are afraid of change, but change is not a bad thing.
>
> (*ibid.*)

Notes

1   The full text of the Basic Law can be found in Buckley (1997), Appendix 5, pp. 195–224.
2   Actually, this promise was made in the 1984 Joint Declaration.

References

Ang Ien (1996) *Living Room Wars: Rethinking Media Audiences for a Postmodern World*. London: Routledge.

Benewick, R. and Wingrove, P. (eds) (1995) *China in the 1990s*. Basingstoke: Macmillan.

Berry, C. (ed.) (1991) *Perspectives on Chinese Cinema*. London: British Film Institute Publishing.

Bordwell, D. (1995) *Narration in the Fiction Film*. London: Routledge.

Browne, N. et al. (eds) (1996) *New Chinese Cinemas: Forms, Identities, Politics*. Cambridge: Cambridge University Press.

Buckley, R. (1997) *Hong Kong: The Road to 1997*. Cambridge: Cambridge University Press.

Cameron, I. (ed.) (1972) *Movie Reader*. New York: Praeger.

Caughie, J. (ed.) (1996) *Theories of Authorship*. London: Routledge.

Charity, T. (1995) 'Hong Kong Phewy', *Time Out*, August/September issue: 14–15.

Dannen, F. and Long, B. (1997) *Hong Kong Babylon*. London: Faber & Faber.

Denzin, N. (1992) *Images of Postmodern Society: Social Theory and Contemporary Cinema*. London: Sage.

Diamond, L. (ed.) (1994) *Political Culture and Democracy in Developing Countries*. London: Lynne Rienner.

Domes, J. and Shaw Yu-ming (eds) (1988) *Hong Kong: A Chinese and International Concern*. Boulder, Colo.: Westview Press.

Doyle, C. and Rayns, T. (1997) 'To the end of the world', *Sight and Sound* 7(5): 14–17.

Dwyer, D. (1994) *China: The Next Decades*. London: Longman.

French, K. (ed.) (1996) *Screen Violence*. London: Bloomsbury.

Gold, T.B. (1993) 'Go with your feelings: Hong Kong and Taiwan popular culture in Greater China', *China Quarterly* 136(4): 907–25.

Grant, B. (ed.) (1995) *Film Genre Reader II*. Austin: University of Texas Press.

Gross, L. (1996) 'Nonchalant grace', *Sight and Sound* 6(9): 6–10.

Herschensohn, B. (ed.) (1999) *Hong Kong at the Handover*. Oxford: Lexington Books.

Hicks, G. (ed.) (1990) *The Broken Mirror: China after Tiananmen*. Harlow: Longman.

Joseph, W. (ed.) (1997) *China Briefing: The Contradictions of Change*. New York: M.E. Sharpe.

Kane, A. (ed.) (1990) *China Briefing 1990*. Boulder, Colo.: Westview Press.

Kitses, J. (1969) *Horizons West*. London: Faber & Faber.

Lau Siu-kai (1984) *Society and Politics in Hong Kong*. Hong Kong: Chinese University Press.

Li Cheuk-to (1996) 'The Return of the father', in Browne *et al.* (eds), *New Chinese Cinemas: Forms, Identities, Politics*. Cambridge: Cambridge University Press.

Morris, M. (2000) 'Cool under pressure', *The Observer*, 1 October.

Morrison, S. (1995) 'La Haine, Fallen Angels, and some thoughts on Scorsese's children', *CineAction* (December): 44–50.

Patten, C. (1998) *East and West*. London: Macmillan.

Rayns, T. (1990) '*Diexue Shuang Xiong* (The Killer)', *Monthly Film Bulletin* (September): 260–1.

—— (1995) 'Poet of time', *Sight and Sound* 5(6): 12–16.

—— (1996) 'Fallen Angels (*Duoluo Tianshi*)', *Sight and Sound* 6(9): 42.

Roberti, M. (1996) *The Fall of Hong Kong: China's Triumph and Britain's Betrayal*. New York: John Wiley & Sons.

Romney, J. (2000) 'Mood music', *The Guardian*, 23 October.

Rosenbaum, J. (1997) *Movies as Politics*. Berkeley: University of California Press.

Shambaugh, D. (1995) *Greater China: The Next Superpower*. Oxford: Oxford University Press.

Stringer, J. (1997) 'Your tender smiles give me strength: paradigms of masculinity in John Woo's *A Better Tomorrow* and *The Killer*', *Screen* 38(1): 25–41.

Tam Kwok-kan and Dissanayake, Wimal (1998) *New Chinese Cinema*. Oxford: Oxford University Press.

Tasker, Y. (1993) *Spectacular Bodies: Gender, Genre and the Action Cinema*. London: Routledge.

Teo, S. (1997) *Hong Kong Cinema: The Extra Dimensions*. London: British Film Institute Publishing.

Tsui, C. (1996) 'Dissecting the visual artistry of Wong Kar-wai', *Hong Kong Film Connection* 3(5): 8–12, 25.

Wise, D. (2000) 'Wooed with violence', *The Observer*, 11 June.

Woo, J. (1993) 'John Woo in interview', *Sight and Sound* 3(5): 25.

—— (2001) *Hard Boiled*. DVD (widescreen version) released by Tartan Video, London.

Wright, W. (1975) *Sixguns and Society: A Structural Study of the Western*. Berkeley: University of California Press.

Yahuda, M. (1996) *Hong Kong: China's Challenge*. London: Routledge.

Zha Jianying (1995) 'China's Popular Culture in the 1990s', in R. Benewick and P. Wingrove (eds), *China in the 1990s*. Basingstoke: Macmillan.

Part IV

The overseas Chinese

12 Is there a British Chinese public sphere?

David Parker

Introduction

When I started researching this chapter, I hoped to explore the emergence of new media directed at, and in part produced by, Chinese people in Britain. My aim was to assess whether technologies such as satellite television and the Internet might become sites of communal elaboration and political mobilisation. At the close of my study in the spring of 2001, I found myself marching through the heart of London with several hundred Chinese protesting against the government; in part due to the efforts of a British Chinese website. Did this unprecedented public demonstration, cutting across class and generational differences, mark, as the organisers claimed, 'a turning point' in the history of the Chinese in Britain? Does the use of the Internet and the growth of other pan-European Chinese news media provide a new Chinese public sphere for the airing of debates, perspectives and sentiments? Do these emergent media forms help to constitute a British Chinese public – an audible, legible and visible community deliberating its past, present and future?

There are good reasons why a study of electronic media use by Chinese people in Britain might have something to offer the proliferating literature on cyberspace (Jones 1998; Dodge and Kitchin 2001) and diasporic identities (Naficy 1999). First, the Internet lends itself extremely well to drawing together a dispersed population such as Chinese people in Britain, the younger generations of whom are concentrated in educational institutions and professional employment, with ready access to computers. Second, the exploration of media practices within a particular migrant group can illuminate wider debates about transnationalism, diaspora and community. Some of the media being created and used by Chinese people in Britain are at the leading edge of emergent cultural formations, containing 'elements of the cultural process that are alternative or oppositional to the dominant elements' (Williams 1977: 124). The communication practices linked with globally emerging migrant communities may have a wider significance in constituting 'ethnicized translocal publics that, by restructuring ethnicity across space, have an unsettling effect on political schemes of ethnic difference' (Ong 1999: 158).

I explore these issues through a mixture of content analysis, interviews with some of the creators of electronic media, and dialogue with media users to ask the following questions:

- How do we conceptualise the impact of new communications media on the Chinese diaspora?
- Do they offer the perfect form of connection for scattered diasporic identities?
- Do they constitute 'subaltern counter-publics' comprising 'parallel discursive arenas where members of subordinated social groups invent and circulate counter-discourses, so as to formulate opposi- tional interpretations of their identities, interests and needs' (Fraser 1993: 14)?
- To what extent do these new cultural practices shape a virtual public sphere whose networks have the potential to mobilise the hitherto dispersed and politically disconnected British Chinese constituency?

The public sphere

The concept of the public sphere has been vigorously debated since the translation of Jürgen Habermas's key volume (Habermas 1989; Alejandro 1993; Calhoun 1992; Dahlgren 1995; Robbins 1993). The term initially referred to the realm of free discussion distinctive of eighteenth-century Europe's bourgeois salons, coffee houses and press. Here public affairs were debated openly on the basis of reasoned position taking, dialogue and nego- tiation through the force of argument, not arms. The public sphere's arena of critical discourse, distinct from the state, has, according to Habermas, been debased in the twentieth century by the growth of mass media and the incursion of bureaucratic state imperatives into the shaping of public opinion. Yet, as we shall see later, recent developments in communications technologies, most notably the Internet, and their appropriation by British Chinese audiences may revive features of the public sphere, albeit with new inflections.

The classical definition of the public sphere has been amended. It is no longer dependent on face-to-face interaction in agora-like locations. It is increasingly defined by long-distance networks rather than spatially contiguous assembly. In addition, perhaps in response to feminist critics such as Fraser (1997) and Young (1990, 2000), Habermas has begun to acknowledge a plurality of publics rather than one homogeneous public:

> The opinion-formation uncoupled from decisions is effected in an open and inclusive network of overlapping, subcultural publics having fluid temporal, social, and substantive boundaries .... Taken together they form a 'wild' complex that resists organization as a whole.
>
> (Habermas 1996: 307–8)

A contemporary definition of the public sphere is thus more open and contestable than the classical Hellenic model. First, it acknowledges the presence of many publics, not all of which may be immediately commensurate with an overarching consensus. Second, it does not rest within the terms of a narrowly defined communicative rationality or public reason. Emotion, passion and barely reflected-upon biographical experiences can be profoundly important forces animating discussion. Third, the forms and sites of communication comprising today's public sphere must draw energy from new sources: 'the vernacular practices of street talk and new musics, radio shows and church voices, entrepreneurship and circulation' (Black Public Sphere Collective 1995: 3).

Approaching the analysis of collective action and expression through a reconsideration of the public sphere is preferable to automatically positing the existence of a community such as 'the British Chinese'. The emphasis shifts to the proliferation of sites of discussion, where a sense of collectivity is elaborated and questioned, rather than assumed. The more open and pluralistic understanding of the public sphere as nesting a multiplicity of publics can perform two useful functions in exploring the development of a distinctly British Chinese political culture. First, no single physical or symbolic space should be privileged; no elite discourse should be given analytical priority. New indicators of 'publicness' may be necessary, particularly for a group without much social recognition. Second, the history of Chinese people in Britain is in no small measure a history of how they carved out 'safe spaces' for collective consolidation and edification, often in the midst of hostile conditions (*cf.* Black Public Sphere Collective 1995).

History of British Chinese publicity

Spontaneous and organised forums for Chinese life in Britain have always existed. The history of Chinese people in Britain can be told through changes in the nature and shape of these autonomous arenas. A simplistic portrait would trace a progression from close-knit, face-to-face daily contact in 'Chinatowns' via broadcast media obtained in, but consumed away from, Chinatowns, to the emergent virtual associations facilitated by satellite television and the Internet. However, a more complex analysis would highlight the residual traces of older formations in some of the new cultural practices.

Archival photographs of Chinese settlement in Liverpool and London indicate how laundries, cafes and boarding houses provided havens for a mainly male seafaring population in the first years of migration to Britain (Parker 2001; Wong 1989). The characteristic features of early twentieth-century Chinatown street life – the food stores and restaurants, language schools, Chinese churches and clan associations – have not disappeared but have re-emerged in different forms since the Second World War. In the postwar period, these informal spaces and activities developed more systematically. Mainstream cinemas, nightclubs and casinos have, from time to time, catered for a late-night Chinese audience, providing further encouragement for public gatherings.

Since the 1970s, the voluntary sector and local authority provision of services geared to the needs of Chinese people in specific cities and London boroughs have underpinned the development of Chinese community centres. Throughout Britain, these offer a mixture of advice, language classes and luncheon clubs for the elderly. All of these face-to-face, word-of-mouth congregations of Chinese people continue in different forms, but the deconcentration and dispersal of the Chinese population away from the 'original' Chinatowns has placed a premium on media forms as a means of distributing cultural commodities, information and opinions through the networks of temporary assembly.

Newspapers, radio and television

Any history of Chinese media in Britain should acknowledge the work of the Chinese Information Centre in Manchester. Responsible for *Siyu*, a bilingual community magazine, it played an important role in the late 1980s as a focus for information and mobilisation. Its publications were instrumental in energising the demonstrations throughout the country in response to the Tiananmen Square massacre of 4 June 1989.

The main Chinese-language newspaper published in Europe is *Sing Tao Daily News*, the parent company of which produces a daily with the same title in Hong Kong. It is based in London but is distributed throughout Europe, and it is published six days a week. Two-fifths of the 50,000 copies circulated daily are sold in Britain (information supplied by *Sing Tao*). The paper follows a regular format: world news on the cover; two pages devoted to Britain; two to Hong Kong and China; two to Taiwan; and one each to East Asia, Asian business news, Europe and France. *Sing Tao* acts as a notice board rather than a heavily editorialised opinion former. For example, the edition of 19 December 2000 contained the following stories: 'Birmingham Chinese Women's Association is to hold a children's Christmas party on 26 December'; 'The Man Clan has selected a new Chairman in Holland'; 'The Dutch Chinese Civil Engineers Association organised its third conference on 9th December 2000'; 'Paris has allocated land for the development of a Chinese school in district number 13'. Reading *Sing Tao*, one gleans a sense of some of the key Chinese community associations and their recognition by local and national government dignitaries. However, there are no columns, feature essays, editorials or readers' letters. The paper is a collection of news reports, not a forum for deliberative interchange between readers.

Compared with the Black and Asian British populations, radio stations have played only a minor role in British Chinese life. BBC local radio stations in Manchester, Liverpool and Newcastle have occasionally broadcast programmes dedicated to their local Chinese populations. The commercial station Spectrum Radio broadcasts a Cantonese strand for one hour each evening in London.

Terrestrial television has also offered little to the British Chinese population. Chinese programmes and appearances by Chinese actors still come around with the frequency of a lunar eclipse. The hunger for representation has only been appeased by occasional documentaries and even more occasional roles, often as gangsters, in police dramas and soap operas. Aside from three short serials of the documentary strand *Orientations* on Channel 4 in the 1980s, there has been no regular forum for the appearance of Chinese people before a national media audience or any formal mechanism for the exchange of views between Chinese people in Britain. The advent of new electronic media has begun to change this.

New Chinese transnational practices

Analysis of the global Chinese population has centred largely on the transnational business networks of overseas Chinese investors (Seagrave 1995). However, literature influenced by cultural studies has begun to explore the wider cultural practices and identities through which 'transnational publics are forming new Chinese subjectivities that are increasingly independent of place, self-consciously postmodern, and subversive of national regimes of truth' (Ong and Nonini 1997: 26).

New media forms circulate through, and thereby constitute, these publics. They have the potential to express a diasporic Chinese imaginary. Poised between past and future, the diasporic imaginary reflects on communal dispersal, familial migration and the resultant extraterritorial orientation towards China, Hong Kong and East Asia. It is defined by particular configurations of memory, ritual and travel and continually replenished by a flexible range of cultural cargoes; from food and newspapers, to clothes, satellite TV channels, videos, DVDs and CDs. These sustain the portable, transposable yet durable, manifestations of difference I have referred to elsewhere as the 'diasporic habitus' (Parker 2000).

The diasporic habitus refers to the embodied practices resulting from 'a confrontation between two distinct time/space constructions, a chronotope characterised by atemporality and seclusion, and one of dominant historical time and socio-political space. These are interpenetrating terms in a dialectic within which the diasporic subject is produced unevenly and in relation to a newly fashioned ethnic subjectivity' (Liu 1999: 344). The diasporic imaginary stages this 'confrontation' between nostalgia and engagement through the narratives and cultural practices that derive from transnational migration and its consequences. The use of the term 'imaginary' 'conveys the agency of diaspora subjects, who, while being made by state and capitalist regimes of truth, can play with different cultural fragments in a way that allows them to segue from one discourse to another, experiment with alternative forms of identification, shrug in and out of identities, or evade imposed forms of identifications' (Ong and Nonini 1997: 26).

A British Chinese public sphere would be a local 'scene' within a global network of flows through transnational space, offering possible counter-narratives to an exclusionary mainstream cultural formation. It would facilitate the exploration of the time/space of the 'here and now' in the light of the 'there and then'. Part of the diasporic habitus is the disposition to both remember and refashion the ideas of home and origins. Media forms such as satellite television are crucial for nurturing this disposition and punctuating the rhythms of everyday life. They generate 'a shared space of a common nexus of Chinese popular culture programming around the globe' (Yang 1997: 309) and a shared time of viewing the latest daily news from 'home', potentially extending the cultural reach of 'Greater China' (Sinclair *et al.* 1996). The Internet provides an additional resource for diasporic constituencies consonant with current reconfigurations of space and time (Shohat 1999).

Through examining the emerging discourses in British Chinese media, the consequences of migration, particularly for second-generation young people, become evident. The tension between diasporic identification, still oriented towards the homeland, and hyphenated ethnic affiliation (in my terms British Chinese) concerned with forging an existence in the land of migration, is recurrently negotiated (Liu 1999: 344). However, new media forms enable a mutual interplay between these subjectivities within the life practices of the same person. The consumption of Chinese television and the growth of Chinese-themed websites mark new forms of agency with a distinctly British Chinese inflection.

Recent developments in British Chinese media

Satellite television

There are two Chinese-language satellite television broadcasters in Europe, both based in London. Phoenix Chinese News and Entertainment is currently a free-to-air Mandarin-language service. It has grown out of Chinese News and Entertainment (CNE), initiated in 1992 and managed until 1998 by Betty Yao. It built up its programming and audience with a mix of Cantonese and Mandarin news and entertainment programmes. However, with the Asian economic crisis of the late 1990s, the station's backers required new capital. In August 1999, this was formally provided by the Chinese broadcaster Phoenix, whose Phoenix Chinese Channel has been broadcasting throughout Asia since 1996.

Phoenix CNE now broadcasts for eight hours a day, from 6pm to 2am UK time. Its programming and staff have become increasingly oriented towards the audience originating in Greater China rather than offering exclusively programmes derived from Hong Kong. Its daily schedule comprises five and a half hours in Mandarin and two and a half hours in Cantonese. The channel is in a developmental phase, keen to expand its broadcasting, drawing on Phoenix's links with many provincial television channels in China to match the interests of an increasingly diverse European Chinese audience. Phoenix CNE is part of a global Chinese-language media corporation that has just launched a North American channel. The parent company is 45 percent owned by an Asian subsidiary of Rupert Murdoch's News International, Star Television. It is thus bound up with the strategic ambitions of a media conglomerate eager to reach the worldwide Chinese-language market. The Phoenix annual report described the overall strategy of the company: 'Phoenix integrates the Chinese way of life with the modernity of the West to create a distinctive vision. Forging ahead with multi-media content and technology, the Phoenix vision reaches out to the Chinese community, globally' (Phoenix Satellite Television Annual Report 1999–2000: 2).

This sense of the British and European Chinese audience as part of a wider Chinese diaspora is also held by the second British-based Chinese television channel: the Chinese Channel. The Chinese Channel was established in March 1994 by Pacific Media plc and Shaw Media Corporation. Broadcast from the Astra satellite, it began by showing programmes in Europe only from midnight to 3am, but this was extended to 7am in 1995. In 1995, a majority stake in the channel was purchased by Hong Kong's major television station, TVB, and from March 1997 a day and night satellite television service was introduced, run by TVB International, an arm of the station specialising in the distribution of its output to the overseas Chinese.

Although based in Britain, the Chinese Channel has become increasingly pan-European in orientation. Its 'footprint' stretches over twenty-seven countries from Ireland to Scandinavia and Eastern Europe. It carries some advertising but is predominantly a subscription channel. In the UK, the current fee is £25 per month. The Chinese Channel's policies were explained in more detail during a discussion I had in September 2000 with assistant project coordinator Carmela Wong, programme producer Harry Cheung, presenter May Chau and researcher Gigi Wong.

The station has recently begun to expand beyond the safe programming schedule of repackaged Hong Kong television shows to address the everyday experiences of the British and European Chinese. Between July and November 2000, for example, the Chinese Channel produced three short series geared towards the European Chinese population and their experiences as migrants. Network Chinatown is the most recent local content programme, initiated in July 2000, with three series to date. The first run of programmes included features on the elderly, catering, Chinese medicine, discrimination and Chinese women.

MAY CHAU: These were quite innovative in a way because we created a platform for the Chinese people to speak on some issues openly, on air, and at the end there would be a thirty-second editorial trying to inspire them to go beyond and think deeper as to what they should do, for example as a Chinese woman in the UK.

The second series involved three programmes about the Chinese in Paris. The third included a discussion programme featuring young Chinese people. The station is keen to extend such connections with the audience.

MAY CHAU: When we were in Paris we talked a lot about the struggles of those people and what they went through and you had a lot of feelings in you. And it's good sometimes to have a forum for sharing and to generate more interests and discussions.

The formative role of satellite television in the Chinese diasporic habitus can be summarised very neatly:

INTERVIEWER: Is there something that unites the audience in the twenty-seven European countries to which you broadcast?
CARMELA WONG: That is being an overseas Chinese. If there is such a thing as homesickness, then our programmes would satisfy them in that way.

The small amount of published research on Chinese satellite television in Britain stresses its importance, particularly for the elderly: 'Thanks to a shared viewing experience, their sense of belonging to a larger imagined Hong Kong community is all the more heightened and intensified' (Peng 2001: 150). Since 1998, both Chinese television channels have shifted their output towards covering mainland China through programmes in Mandarin. This marks a recognition of the growing population who have arrived in Europe from several provinces in China, as opposed to the primary sources of early postwar migration to Europe – Guangdong and Hong Kong. The nesting of the British Chinese channels within rival media corporations, each disseminating similar packages to Chinese people across continents, lends weight to Yang's comment: 'There are increasing overlaps and commonalities in the programming that Chinese in these various places are viewing, making for the emergence of a transnational Chinese language imagined community in the next century' (Yang 1997: 309–10).

However, some of the younger audience are sceptical of the community-building capabilities of satellite television watched in homes late at night:

INTERVIEWER: Would you say those things formed part of a British Chinese public sphere or not?
ANGELA (BRITISH-BORN CHINESE, AGED 24): They don't set up any community feel to it. They're playing on the fact that Chinese people work long hours and relate more to the Hong Kong lifestyle and

certainly to the media. So it's 'let's buy TVB programmes and make money out of the fact that people watch them'. They're not looking to attract much of a community here.

Forms of self-generated solidarity may be more readily apparent on the Internet.

Digital diasporas

There has been an outpouring of literature on the Internet's potential for enhancing the public sphere (e.g. Dahlberg 2001; Rheingold 1994; Slevin 2000). Enthusiasts welcome its apparent ability to connect across space and time and enable new forms of association and identity to be shared. Virtual communities, no longer dependent on physical proximity, create 'incontrovertibly social spaces in which people still meet face to face, but under new definitions of both "meet" and "face" … passage points for collections of common beliefs and practices that united people who were previously separated' (Stone, cited in Benedikt 1991: 118).

Given the open architecture of the Internet, surprisingly little has been written about how diasporic social groups have made use of the medium (Mallapragada 2001; Mitra 1997) or how racialised identities and questions of racism are addressed through it. There is a possible tension between the 'identity play' that is held to be a feature of the Internet's anonymous and disembodied character and the formation of websites, chat rooms and discussion boards on the basis of clearly defined ethnic markers. Models of identity drawn from analysis of role playing (most famously Turkle 1995) may 'make it hard to envision how other subaltern publics might be formulating more fixed identities via the Web' (McPherson 2000: 129). It is important to appreciate that the Internet 'does not introduce totally new ethnic dynamics, but rather magnifies those that already exist' (Warschauer 2000: 167). Paradoxically, the medium often felt to be undermining fixed and categorical identities such as ethnicity may also be providing the means for their reanimation.

Analysts of the Indian diaspora's use of the Internet have stressed the depth of the reattachment to place of origin it can nurture: 'Negotiated here is the lost space of a nation, community, or tribe which is being re-created and reinvented on the other Internet space … the loss of geographic proximity is the raison d'être for the mobilisation of the Internet space' (Mitra 1997: 70–1). In postings to newsgroups and discussion forums stereotypes are consolidated, prejudices are ventilated, wounds of history are reopened, and intense affiliations are asserted rather than contested. However, these authors have addressed Internet sites most associated with the first generation of migrants, not the second or subsequent overseas-born generations. There has been little published specifically on Chinese-themed Internet sites geared to the emerging diasporic generations.

In assessing their content, it is important not to contribute to a narrative of degeneration that decries the Internet as another deformation of the public sphere (see Dreyfus 2001 for an occasionally intemperate discussion). Nor should we hail these new forms as a computopian realm of absolute freedom. The mere fact of regular communication via a network and a loose adherence to a flexibly defined set of discursive practices do not imply the existence of a community. Connection 'does not inherently make for community, nor does it lead to any necessary exchanges of information, meaning and sense-making at all (Jones 1998: 5).

Furthermore, social inequalities do not simply dissolve in the ether of cyberspace. All communities are formed through a variety of mediating structures: they 'are technologies of power that constitute subjects and their ethnic identities through material, symbolic practices' (Poster 1998: 196). On-line forums are not free of wider forces of power and inequality. With Internet sites devoted to a particular ethnic identity, especially one as specific as British-born Chinese, the cultural characteristics of those involved bring the site into being. The animating force often derives from passionate debates about the appropriate form of Chinese culture for the twenty-first century, what counts as authentic in the midst of globalisation, and who has the right to define an identity.

Chinese diaspora on the Internet

British Chinese Internet activity must be assessed against the background of the more general on-line Chinese presence. There are three main forms of Chinese-related website:

1   China-focused sites, which can be divided into those with a news or cultural emphasis. Among the more important news sites are the official government portals, such as www.chinadaily.com.cn, and business-driven information engines such as www.sina.com and www.chinaonline.com. The stated objective of the latter two to link Chinese communities around the world dovetails neatly with assembling a Chinese market for eager investors. Chinese entertainment and leisure sites such as www.muzi.com are driven by similar imperatives, connecting capital to the culturally different.

2   Chinese diaspora sites of varying degrees of commercialism and organisation exist worldwide. Those explicitly addressing the Chinese diaspora as a totality include the San Francisco-based site of the World Huaren Federation (www.huaren.org). The site's links make a point of foregrounding the memory of war, past antagonisms with Japan and the current plight of Chinese in Indonesia and thus makes an explicit stand in defence of what it regards as Chinese interests. It also disseminates a weekly electronic journal *Chinese Community Forum*.

3   The most high-profile of the sites with a diaspora inflection is rooted in a national context of the United States – asianavenue.com. As of December 2001, this site boasted over two million members. At all times when I have connected to the site, at least 5,000 members have been logged on. The site combines information and interaction, with a proliferation of forums, chat rooms and discussion sites.

There is a common theme to these sites: the vast geographical distances between where members and readers are currently located and the diversity of East Asian reference points they have. The much-noted dispersal of the Chinese population globally is mirrored in a nation like Britain. This makes the Internet potentially more significant as a form of connection, a forum for debate and a means of mobilisation. The next section will examine two of the main British Chinese Internet sites for their potential as counter-publics.

British Chinese websites

www.chinatown-online.co.uk

Chinatown-online was formed on 8 August 1998, and its original intention was to offer a website guide to Chinese restaurants in London. Since then, however, it has expanded from offering a history of Britain's Chinatowns to a series of community, business and information sites, funded in part by advertising and sponsorship, at one point by Amoy Foods, a French-owned maker of Chinese condiments. Chinatown-online has always hosted a discussion board, and in response to a thread one day enquiring why there was no site specifically for British-born Chinese people to share experiences and information, the site helped to establish one.

www.britishbornchinese.org.uk

This site was launched in autumn 1999 as a voluntary offshoot of Chinatown-online with a small number of articles and a discussion forum. The site's brochure describes its purpose as 'a forum for British born Chinese to exchange ideas, network and reaffirm their own distinctive identity'. Since its launch, the lightly moderated discussion board has spawned several themed segments: as of December 2001, these included 'the community centre', 'the town hall', 'the tea house', 'the restaurant', 'the comedy club' and 'the high street'. The eighteen discussion forums include 'Yin' for women and 'ID Parade' for issues related to identity.

Broadly speaking, five types of message are posted:

1   Of increasing importance as the site membership grows are invitations to social gatherings and comments on those that occur.

2   Dissemination of information about Chinese-related events: for example, 'alerts' about the rare appearances of Chinese actors on mainstream television, Chinese artistic performances.

3   Observations about China and its place in world politics. One of the longest threads asked 'Should the Chinese give back the spy plane without an apology from the U.S.?' The prevailing response was 'No!' There is a 'real-time' feed of news from China on the main page of the britishbornchinese.org.uk website. There are very few discussions about the political dynamics of Hong Kong, but it is Hong Kong's contemporary popular culture rather than China's that generates the most debates.

4   Postings about visiting, or working in, Hong Kong and other East Asian cities. Many of these draw attention to the particular position of being a British Chinese 'expatriate', in between both local East Asians and expatriate Western colleagues. See, for example, the thread from May 2001, 'Stereotyping in Shanghai'.

5   The most relevant messages for assessing the public sphere dimensions of the site are those concerned with British Chinese identity and experiences. A British Chinese style, ethos and repertoire of dilemmas and responses is expressed. Recurrent themes, common to most young people, include mixed-race relationships, sex and media stereotypes.

Yet the forum comes into its own when some uniquely formative experiences are addressed at length. For example, the 'rite of passage', helping out in the family catering business, is reflected in the fifty-six responses to the thread, 'What do all them nites in your parent's takeaway amount to?' One of the most telling responses was 'it's the realisation of ending up back there if you don't make it' and 'life in a takeaway is one of the toughest things you have to endure'. The sharpest interchanges about being British born Chinese extended through the 'CHinese rulez!!!!' (*sic*) thread within the forum 'Thinker's Corner', with 134 responses from January to May 2001. The initial message castigated British-born Chinese for forgetting their language and culture:

YOU WILL ALWAYS BE A CHINESE COS YOU ARE A CHINESE!!!!!!!! IF YOU CANNOT SPEAK CHINESE THEN YOU ARE A DISGRACE TO THE CHINESE COMMUNITY!!!!!!!!!!!
(27 January 2001)

This touched on perhaps the most sensitive issue spiralling through the discussion forum: what, if anything, is a necessary condition for being entitled to claim Chinese identity? Replies polarised between denouncing what many saw as a drive to purification and offering thoughtful accounts of why identity should not be reduced to language, race or culture. The words of one respondent eloquently summarise the predominant tone not just of this thread but of the site as a whole:

I hope we can agree on the principle that to aspire to recognise one's Chinese heritage is itself something to be encouraged, and whether we speak Chinese well or poorly, it is better to encourage that level of knowledge than to criticise it. Better to nurture than to alienate, better to embrace than reject.

(13 April 2001)

The number of segmented discussion boards has grown, with the notable addition of 'the World Service' for British-born Chinese expatriates, mainly in Hong Kong, China and Singapore, to exchange views and organise meetings. This is one example of how the site fosters a close link between on-line and off-line networking. Several months into the site, one of its users suggested holding a 'meet-up' in London specifically for British-born Chinese people and their friends. These are now a monthly fixture in London, attracting nearly one hundred participants. Smaller, more informal, social gatherings have taken place in other British cities, including Birmingham, Manchester, Leeds and Liverpool. A 'British-born Chinese in Hong Kong' group advertises its monthly meetings via this London-based site. Future plans will enhance the site's interactivity:

The new members' area will be free to access but require registration. It will have a large number of extra facilities, including the existing discussion forum plus the possibility of web-based e-mail, a calendar, the ability to post your own gallery of photographs, and a messaging service (a bit like mobile phone text messaging – if you are on line the message will appear in a little pop-up window on your screen).

(Steve Lau, site editor)

Throughout 2001, the site expanded rapidly; the number of members rose from about 100 to over 1,400 from January to December. The number of page impressions increased to around 120,000 per month, four times the rate of summer 2000. Success brought its own problems. As the number of postings grew to over 300 a day, their reflective quality diminished, as did the ability of the volunteer site moderators to scrutinise content. In November 2001, the site newsletter bemoaned 'the general slide of the discussion board area into trivia' and called for the website 'to move on, and grow up a little'. In practical terms, the site's moderation became more active, debarring user names with graphic sexual innuendo and reserving the right to delete messages 'likely to bring the British-born Chinese community into disrepute'. The next British Chinese website I will highlight also witnessed dramatic growth in the first few months of 2001, and in a different register also demonstrates how British Chinese forms of public expression are taking shape.

www.dimsum.co.uk

This site, launched in early 2000, grew out of its co-editors' shared frustration at the lack of a Chinese voice in Britain. I interviewed Jack Tan and Sarah Yeh, the site's London-based editors and founders, in August 2000. Jack is responsible for the editorial and business aspects of the site and Sarah for its creative elements. Together they own, run and manage the site, assisted by a core of four volunteers and a team of contributors.

JACK TAN: Initially when we talked about it, we were really excited and also frustrated that until now Chinese voices in this country had been really quiet .... We were sick of assimilation, of being quiet and being invisible, and Chinese people fading into the background and not making a fuss .... We want to make a fuss!

SARAH YEH: To voice our opinions, that kind of stuff.

JACK: The Internet seemed to be the best way – it's cheap and easy.

The site differs from britishbornchinese.org.uk in having a wider remit and a more inter-cultural feel. The site's title, 'Dimsum', gives the notion of a deliberative public sphere a Chinese ambience (*dimsum* are the light snacks characteristic of Chinese gatherings), and as the site introduction states, 'Often, the point of Dimsum is not so much the food as the discussion about politics and life' – the site tries to recreate 'some of the atmosphere of talk, discussion and sharing'. The majority of the site's content is editorialised, offering a forum of information and argument, updated periodically. Its initial intention was to stimulate debate rather than to offer the minute-by-minute interactivity of a discussion board.

JACK TAN: If there is any control over the site, it is that we don't want it to become a purely Chinese site. We've toyed around with the idea of having a message board or a chat line, but we thought no, *we* want to direct this.

Although dimsum.co.uk did in fact add a discussion forum several months after that interview, this has yet to achieve the traffic of the britishbornchinese.org.uk forums. Among the issues emphasised by Dimsum are 'mixed-race' relationships, the appreciation of Asian culture more generally, but martial arts and food in particular, and features about travel to East Asia. The site is interested in the wider cultural dynamics between East and West. Compared with the Britishbornchinese site, it is not so bound to the experiences of a particular collective. The cultural politics of the site is contested integration:

JACK TAN: I'd like to see a strong Chinese identity, but I'd like that to be a hyphenated identity, British in as much as we growing here, and I don't

want us to go the American way, we are not Chinese Americans, it's the
British part that sets us apart from the Chinese Americans, we're not
over the top, we're not cliquey. We just need a voice and I think the
British public appreciates a voice that is reasonable rather than one
which pushes down the throats of the white majority. We're here to live
with the white majority, their culture is our culture, it's important that
we fit in.

In the initial phase of the site's existence, there were very few specific
campaigns promoting Chinese people in Britain as a collective force.
However, this changed in early 2001. Two challenges to adverse media
representations highlighted the role that an electronic forum like Dimsum
can play in generating debate, bringing previously unrecognised perspectives to the attention of a wider public and encouraging political
mobilisation.

The first concerned a national newspaper columnist's provocative review
of the film *Crouching Tiger, Hidden Dragon* (2000). Journalist Charlotte
Raven had taken exception to the widespread acclaim heaped on Ang Lee's
martial arts epic: 'I have no doubt that if Crouching Tiger had been in
English, the script would have seemed unforgivably banal. In Chinese, delivered inscrutably, it seemed to contain multitudes' (*The Guardian*, 16 January
2001).

Several Chinese readers took exception to the use of the stereotypical
depiction of Chinese people as 'inscrutable'. Among them was the editor of
the Dimsum website, who helped to secure a response from the editor of *The
Guardian*'s review section, Ian Katz:

> I accept that the column caused real offence for which I offer sincere
> apologies .... This episode has at least served to heighten our sensitivity
> to the casual deployment of Chinese stereotypes. I will certainly look
> more carefully at stories touching on these subjects in future.
>
> (www.dimsum.co.uk/perspective/chen_katz_dimsum.html)

A few days later, *The Guardian*'s readers' editor reflected on the interchanges
of letters and e-mails:

> We should wean ourselves off it [the word 'inscrutable'] as quickly as
> possible. In the *Guardian* in the past 12 months we have asserted that
> Asia remains the world's most inscrutable continent, we have carried a
> headline 'Inscrutable East', and we have noticed a Japanese busi-
> nessman with an 'inscrutable smile'. I am not suggesting that this word
> only triggered the complaints about the column in the *Guardian* – clearly
> it did not – but it is taken by those it offends as symptomatic of an atti-
> tude that is lacking in respect.
>
> (*The Guardian*, 3 February 2001)

Since then both the Dimsum site and posters of messages on the Britishbornchinese site have drawn attention to media representations and sent e-mails and letters to the Press Complaints Commission and Advertising Standards Authority. These attempts to shift the boundaries of acceptable discourse regarding matters Chinese in Britain prefigured a more concerted challenge.

The second and most dramatic campaign was sparked by an allegation, first carried in *The Times* and *The Guardian* newspapers of 27 March 2001, that recycled waste food from Chinese restaurants in Newcastle fed to pigs in the northeast of England was the source of the outbreak of foot and mouth disease in spring 2001. The mass circulation *The Mirror* newspaper of 28 March 2001 had a front-page headline, 'Sheep and Sow source'. Its editorial alleged that with illegal meat being imported and sold in some takeaways and restaurants, 'Maybe the meal you last bought on an evening out was sub-standard or even diseased'. Thereafter, Chinese catering businesses reported a sharp loss in trade, up to 40 percent in London. Environmental health officers descended on Chinese supermarkets to remove imported meat products from the shelves.

In response to this, over the next few days the Dimsum website acted as one of the catalysts for an unprecedented mobilisation of Chinese people in Britain. Letters of protest about the coverage were sent to national newspapers. Together with business organisations associated with the older generation, such as the Chinese Takeaway Association, second-generation Chinese in London helped to organise a concerted campaign against mass media scapegoating of Chinese food. A public meeting in London Chinatown on 4 April 2001 inaugurated the Chinese Civil Rights Action Group (UK). This group called a demonstration for Sunday, 8 April in London.

Notable among the 500 or so who marched from Chinatown to Westminster was the mixture of families, community activists and Chinese business owners. Demonstrators chanted 'Mr Blair, be fair' in English and 'No justice, no takeaway' in Cantonese. A letter of protest was delivered to the Minister of Agriculture, Nick Brown, who met members of the group and issued a statement exonerating the Chinese catering trade and recognising the contribution of the Chinese community to a multicultural Britain:

> The delegates made a representation to me concerning the damaging effect on the Chinese community by this irresponsible reporting. I have been particularly concerned at the tone of some reporting, which seems close to carrying racist overtones. I deplore the scapegoating of the Chinese community. There is absolutely no justification for this. I, and the Government, stand shoulder to shoulder with the Chinese community against racism.
>
> (Ministry of Agriculture, Fisheries and Food, 8 April 2001)

Television news bulletins that evening and the following day's national

Plate 4 Protest by British Chinese communities against misrepresentation during the foot and mouth crisis, London, 8 April 2001

(photo courtesy of David Parker)

newspapers carried extensive coverage of perhaps the first widely reported recognition of Chinese people in Britain made by a government minister (see 'We don't blame Chinese', *Daily Telegraph*, 9 April 2001: 4). This, if nothing else, marks an important intervention by Chinese people in the public domain.

The longer-term consequences are unclear. The wider aims of the Chinese Civil Rights Action Group include building 'a national organisation capable of defending the interests of the Chinese community in Britain'. At the group's inaugural meeting, chairman Jabez Lam, a community activist of long standing, declared, 'We must put a stop to the portrayal of the Chinese as a foreign community ... stereotypes have to be broken and the image of the Chinese in Britain has to be positively promoted'.

As a result of the crisis and demonstrations, the hit rates for the Dimsum website rose dramatically: to over 110,000 page impressions in April 2001. The editors' conception of the site has also shifted:

SARAH YEH: The site was originally set up as a hobby, something small, and very much a part-time project. Since the foot and mouth campaign, we have decided that we feel most comfortable setting it up as a charity

Plate 5   Protest by British Chinese communities against misrepresentation during the foot and mouth crisis, London, 8 April 2001

(photo courtesy of David Parker)

so that we will be able to focus on more social and political issues that affect the Chinese community.

In the words of the Dimsum website, the mobilisation around the foot and mouth outbreak may mark 'a turning point in truly recognising the contribution of the Chinese community in Britain'.

Conclusion

There is a British Chinese public sphere of a new kind in the making. Several deliberative forums now exist to both encourage and organise traffic in meanings and opinions. Without them much would not have happened: no monthly meetings in London and elsewhere, no networking between several hundred British-born Chinese throughout the country and beyond, perhaps no demonstration in London and no Chinese Civil Rights Action Group. However, in the aftermath of the foot and mouth campaign, it is important to make a sober assessment of this activity, the role of the Internet in fostering it, and the possibilities that remain.

First, the alliances witnessed on the march through London in April 2001 are likely to be temporary. The conservative business-protective desires of the restauranteurs are likely to disengage from the radical impulses of those (mainly younger activists) concerned with issues such as stereotypical representations in the media, economic justice and political participation. Indeed, arguments within the Chinese Civil Rights Action Group over whether the first anniversary of the death of fifty-eight Chinese immigrants at Dover should be publicly commemorated on 18 June 2001 partly reflected these differences. Mapped onto this division are intergenerational differences in Chinese language fluency: aside from a few transliterations into romanised versions of Cantonese and Mandarin, the major British Chinese Internet sites are in English; the *Sing Tao* newspaper and the satellite Chinese channels are in Chinese. There is currently no British Chinese bilingual publication bridging the age and linguistic divisions. Due to these and other difficulties, the Chinese Civil Rights Action Group announced its dissolution on 27 March 2002. In leaving its legacy on the Internet, it correctly noted:

> A significant development has been the mobilisation of first and second generation British born Chinese bringing with them the ability to be articulate and through websites such as www.dimsum.co.uk and www.britishbornchinese.org.uk to communicate with peers at great speed and in great numbers.
>
> (www.ccrag.org/pages/en/legacy.html)

Second, the limitations of on-line communication as a proxy for collective action were already becoming apparent by summer 2001. The British-Born Chinese discussion forum was dominated by a small group of regular contributors. As of 2 June 2001, the thirteen individuals (2.6 percent of members) who had posted over 200 messages each accounted for nearly one-third of the total messages on the forum. One user asked 'has the BBC community peaked already? ... seems like there is lots of potential and expectation but not enough substance' (22 May 2001). The same could be said of British Chinese life as a whole. Its public sphere is decidedly embryonic. The transition from discussion to institutional influence has a long way to go:

> Theoretically, speech communities are democratic forums in which public opinion takes shape, opinion aimed at directing or influencing public policy, norms of behaviour, or political consensus. Although these are idealistic and perhaps unrealistic goals for counter-publics, which are by definition publics divorced from substantial control over how public power is deployed, they define the point of the analytic exercise nonetheless: not only speech but also action.
>
> (Holt 1995: 328)

It is sobering to consider that, once again, no Chinese candidates stood for parliament in the British general election campaign of June 2001. The presence of Chinese people in mainstream British life is still muted. Testament to this is the recent formation of the Chinese in Britain Forum (www. chinese-forum.co.uk). This national body, partly funded by central government, seeks to promote the involvement of Chinese organisations and individuals with voluntary institutions, local authorities and national policy making. Without such participation in wider civil society, the British Chinese public sphere will amount to a few thousand people talking to themselves.

Yet the wider recognition so long sought by Chinese people in Britain requires the foundation of a collective sense of purpose within such small-scale settings. Media forms such as satellite television and the Internet are a crucial element in nurturing an expressive culture of critical discourse among Chinese people worldwide. If the 'articulation of life stories is the activity through which meaning and purpose are inserted into life' (Bauman 2001: 13), then the most important role played by the sites discussed here could be the provision of narrative resources to enhance both personal and collective reflections. Every day, the recurrent dilemmas of family life, career aspirations and the trade-off between prosperity and fulfilment are posted and responded to. What makes these sites distinctive is their British Chinese inflection: for example, where else could you find exchanges such as '97 things Chinese people do', 'Adoption and Eurasians' or 'British born Chinese going to Singapore to work'? These sites and the discussions they generate provide an informal setting where 'new problem situations can be perceived more sensitively, discourses aimed at achieving self-understanding can be conducted more widely and expressively, collective identities and need interpretations can be articulated with fewer compulsions than is the case in procedurally regulated public spheres' (Habermas 1996: 307–8).

To read dimsum.co.uk and britishbornchinese.org.uk is to scroll through a collective subjectivity, a series of nuanced identity formations and evolving perspectives, a cast of intriguingly named characters, a variable sense of humour – in short, the beginnings of a cultural identity. These sites express experiences and perspectives unique to Chinese people raised in Britain. To have them aired in public, archived, capable of retrieval anywhere in the world, is a cultural innovation whose potential has yet to be explored. The demonstration in London on 8 April 2001 may be the first of many events generated by a British Chinese counter-public, connected by the Internet and satellite television, but increasingly willing to act well beyond those limited arenas.

References

Alejandro, R. (1993) *Hermeneutics, Citizenship and the Public Sphere*. Albany: State University of New York Press.

Bauman, Z. (2001) *The Individualized Society*. Cambridge: Polity Press.

Benedikt, M. (1991) *Cyberspace: First Steps*. Cambridge, Mass.: MIT Press.

Black Public Sphere Collective (eds) (1995) *The Black Public Sphere*. Chicago and London: University of Chicago Press.

Calhoun, C. (ed.) (1992) *Habermas and the Public Sphere*. Cambridge, Mass.: MIT Press.

Dahlberg, L. (2001) 'Extending the public sphere through cyberspace: the case of Minnesota e-democracy', *First Monday* 6(3), available at the website: http://www.firstmonday.dk/issues/issue6_3dahlberg/.

Dahlgren, P. (1995) *Television and the Public Sphere*. London: Sage.

Dodge, M. and Kitchin, R. (2001) *Mapping Cyberspace*. London: Routledge.

Dreyfus, H. (2001) *On the Internet*. London: Routledge.

Fraser, N. (1993) 'Rethinking the public sphere: a contribution to the critique of actually existing democracy', in B. Robbins (ed.), *The Phantom Public Sphere*. Minneapolis: University of Minnesota Press.

—— (1997) *Justice Interruptus: Critical Reflections on the Post-Socialist Condition*. New York and London: Routledge.

Habermas, J. (1989) *The Structural Transformation of the Public Sphere*. Cambridge: Polity Press.

—— (1996) *Between Facts and Norms*. Cambridge, Mass.: MIT Press.

Holt, T. (1995) 'Afterword', in Black Public Sphere Collective (eds), *The Black Public Sphere*. Chicago and London: University of Chicago Press.

Jones, S. (ed.) (1998) *Cybersociety 2.0: Revisiting Computer-Mediated Communication*, Thousand Oaks, Calif., and London: Sage.

Liu, P.D. (1999) *Asian/American*. Stanford, Calif.: Stanford University Press.

Mallapragada, M. (2001) 'The Indian diaspora in the USA and around the Web', in D. Gauntlett (ed.), *Web Studies: Rewiring Media Studies for the Digital Age*. London: Edward Arnold.

McPherson, T. (2000) 'I'll take my stand in Dixie-Net: white guys, the South and cyberspace', in B. Kolko, L. Nakamura and G. Rodman (eds), *Race in Cyberspace*. New York: Routledge.

Mitra, A. (1997) 'Virtual commonality: looking for India on the Internet', in S. Jones (ed.), *Virtual Culture: Identity and Communication in Cyberspace*. Thousand Oaks, Calif., and London: Sage.

Naficy, H. (1993) *The Making of Exile Cultures*. Minneapolis: University of Minnesota Press.

—— (ed.) (1999) *Home, Exile Homeland*. New York: Routledge.

Ong, A. (1999) *Flexible Citizenship: The Cultural Logics of Transnationality*. Durham, NC: Duke University Press.

Ong, A. and Nonini, D. (eds) (1997) *Ungrounded Empires*. London: Routledge.

Parker, D. (2000) 'The Chinese takeaway and the diasporic habitus', in B. Hesse (ed.), *Un/settled Multiculturalisms*. London: Zed Books.

—— (2001) '"We paved the way": exemplary spaces and mixed race in Britain', in T.K. Williams and C. Nakashima (eds), *The Sum of Our Parts*. Philadelphia: Temple University Press.

Peng, L.S. (2001) 'Satellite television and Chinese migrants in Britain', in R. King and N. Woods (eds), *Media and Migration*. London: Routledge.

Poster, M. (1998) 'Virtual ethnicity: tribal identity in an age of global communications', in S. Jones (ed.), *Cybersociety 2.0: Revisiting Computer-Mediated Communication*. Thousand Oaks, Calif., and London: Sage.

Rheingold, H. (1994) *The Virtual Community*. New York: Harper Perennial.

Robbins, B. (1993) *The Phantom Public Sphere*. Minneapolis: University of Minnesota Press.

Seagrave, S. (1995) *Lords of the Rim*. New York: Putnam.

Shohat, E. (1999) 'By the bitstream of Babylon: cyberfrontiers and diasporic vistas', in H. Naficy (ed.), *Home, Exile Homeland*. New York: Routledge.

Sinclair, J., Pookong, K., Fox, J. and Yue, A. (1996) 'Diasporic identities: Chinese communities and their media use in Australia', paper presented to the Culture and Citizenship Conference, Australian Key Centre for Cultural and Media Policy, 30 September – 2 October, available at the website: http://www.gu.edu.au/centre/cmp/Sinclair.html.

Slevin, J. (2000) *The Internet and Society*. Cambridge: Polity Press.

Thompson, J. (1995) *The Media and Modernity*. Cambridge: Polity Press.

Turkle, S. (1995) *Life on the Screen: Identity in the Age of the Internet*. New York: Simon & Schuster.

Warschauer, M. (2000) 'Language, identity and the Internet', in B. Kolko, L. Nakamura and G. Rodman (eds), *Race in Cyberspace*. New York: Routledge.

Williams, R. (1977) *Marxism and Literature*. Oxford: Oxford University Press.

Wong, M.L. (1989) *Chinese Liverpudlians*. Birkenhead: Liver Press.

Yang, M. (1997) 'Mass media and transnational subjectivity in Shanghai: notes on (re)cosmpolitanism in a Chinese metropolis', in A. Ong and D. Nonini (eds), *Ungrounded Empires*. London: Routledge.

Young, I. (1990) *Justice and the Politics of Difference*. Princeton, NJ: Princeton University Press.

—— (2000) *Inclusion and Democracy*. Oxford: Oxford University Press.

13 Children, media and the public sphere in Chinese Australia

Yingchi Chu, Stephanie Hemelryk
Donald and Andrea Witcomb[1]

Introduction

This chapter offers a perspective on the role of media in the formation and maintenance of citizenship in migrant communities. Focusing on Chinese Australian children, we argue that their media consumption and interpretative practices are highly important to the production of migrant identity in a settler nation. In the following case study of first-generation migrant children in Western Australia, we trace the agnostic relationship between residual parental memories, emergent parental and child settler identities, and children's attitudes to the parental homeland. The argument examines these sites of identity through media-related experience, but it also suggests that these sites are contingent and effective within the larger scope of political and social spheres of belonging. The premise of our suggestions is that the media are conditional to, although not guarantors of, a functioning modern public sphere.

The fieldwork on which this chapter is based took place between 1999 and 2001 in Perth, Western Australia, and Beijing, People's Republic of China (PRC). We conducted screenings, interviews and focus groups with parents, children and teachers in schools and local community organisations. The total sample of interviews and questionnaires was ninety in Australia and seventy-five in China. While this does not constitute a representative survey of either the country of settlement or the place of origin, the snapshot responses have given us scope for qualitative analysis of prevalent attitudes to children's media in both locations. The comparative data collected in Beijing allowed us to recognise issues that arose from the fact of migrancy rather than from common generational factors. The Beijing responses also clarified culturally founded issues, which helped to identify residual parental expectations in the migrant Australian sample.

Greater China in Chinese Australia

The history and constitution of the Chinese population in Australia is both typical of diasporic experience and peculiar to the Australian example.

Migration south has been occurring over (at least) 150 years, since the gold rush(es) of the 1850s. However, restrictions on entry for Chinese were in force both during the colonial period and after federation in 1901. In 1887, the reports of Chinese commissioners on the state of Chinese residents in Australia found that they suffered extensive and debilitating racism. The ensuing debate between Britain, China and Australia resulted in further restrictions on entry; the Chinese population fell from 38,000 in 1880 to fewer than 20,000 in 1920. The Naturalisation Act of 1903 made it impossible for anyone of non-European origin to become an Australian citizen. This legislation forced many long-term residents to leave Australia or to remain without the possibility of their immediate and extended families ever joining them. The White Australia policy, which continued in various guises until 1974, had also been enacted in 1901 (The Immigration Restriction Act) in the first wave of federal law making. 'White Australia' was specifically coined to exclude potential migration from the Asian region. In the 1980s and 1990s, the Chinese population grew, mainly due to business and skill-based migration. There were also one-off episodes of migration (and naturalisation) after the 1997 reunification of Hong Kong and the PRC, and following the 1989 Tiananmen Square massacre (Finnane 1998: 122–3). Most of the subjects in our interviews came into Australia in one or more of these recent categories (or as family members).

Currently, Chinese Australia includes old families, especially in Queensland and Victoria, but also first-, second- and third-generation Australians. Some are first-time migrants from the Chinese mainland; others are from Hong Kong, Taiwan or Southeast Asia. Of those from Southeast Asia, many have a personal or family history of multiple migration encompassing Southeast Asia, Europe and Africa. Our research focused on first-time migration from the mainland, but we also spoke with those who had experience of multiple migration. Unsurprisingly, perhaps, this group had markedly different attitudes to Chinese culture, at least in so far as it was available, or not, in media products.

Six popular terms are used to describe groups within the Chinese diasporic communities in Australia. These terms define differences between and across various communities. Some are borrowed from other regional centres of settlement (such as Malaysia). Their usage in Australia is suggestive of both Australia's place within the broader Chinese diaspora and the shared ways in which people think through their cultural and political identities. These groups are not fixed. They do not necessarily describe all Chinese Australians; nor should we expect any one Chinese Australian to identify exclusively with any one category. Migrant identities are by definition in flux (Wang 1991):

1   *luoye guigen* (fallen leaves return to the roots, the soil) – a nostalgic mentality held by an older generation of migrants. For example, in the first half of the twentieth century in Sydney, those who could afford it organised to send their ancestors' bodies back to their home towns.

2   *zancao chugen* (get rid of grass by pulling it out by the roots) – a mentality denying a home origin and striving for total assimilation by cutting off all prior connections.

3   *luodi shenggen* ('sink roots' in a foreign land and accommodate to the host society) – refers to those who make a new home in the host country through cultural accommodation; recent studies on the Chinese diaspora argue that there is a change in Chinese migrants from *luoye guigen* to *luodi shenggen* in the twentieth century (Chan 1997).

4   *xungen wenzu* (search for one's roots and ancestors) – a mentality of ethnic pride and consciousness based on the maintenance of cultural memory (Donald 2001).

5   *shigen lizu* (lose contact with ones roots and ancestors); in other words the uprooted, the alienated, the 'wandering intellectuals, away from their roots in historic China', in exile.

6   *taikong ren* (astronaut family) – those without assimilation, live in a plurality of terrains, transnational movement, Hong Kong and Southeast Asian Chinese (Beal and Sos 1999).

These categories of consciousness exist side by side within the context of the histories of migration and migration policy in Australia. They are useful for our analysis in so far as they separate out possible patterns of media consumption across and within migrant groups. Media consumption involves several variables, which are symptomatic of the particular matrix of migrancy. The key words in the definitions given above might be nostalgia, denial, assimilation, accommodation, alienation and transnationalism. None of these concepts is peculiar to the Chinese population and, taken together, could be said to be emblematic of Australian cultural identity. However, their salience in the mainstream is dependent on the contingent sharpness of their expression among recent migrants. In particular, we argue that they have especial poignancy in the expressive gap between adult migrant attitudes to media and those of their children.

Media as a condition of the public sphere

The long-running debate on the relation between media and the public sphere has tended to focus on models of liberal democracy and 'free speech'. Recently, however, scholars have recognised that a shift is needed to 'de-Westernise' media studies (Curran and Park 2000) and, furthermore, to acknowledge that publicness (Donald and Donald 2000) is a shifting paradigm of political expectation. Our study focused on two very different political cultures, neither of which fits the classic ideal of liberal democracy (arguably, nowhere does). Australia is a settler nation with an indigenous population and an ethnically diverse citizenry. The citizen body is far from homogeneous in terms of either political memory, immediate cultural parameters or family history. China is an authoritarian state organised through collective formations of social behaviour and socialist capitalism. The production of public opinion and discursive space is utterly unlike the ideal formation of the Habermasian public sphere. Nonetheless, there are sophisticated political competences at work in the performance of socio-political identity in the PRC. These performances take place in an imagined sphere of 'publicness'. This term may not fit (or not only) the model of an autonomous public sphere functioning between the state and the private but is a more general term for the *various* ways in which people in different political conditions share contemporary moments of political understanding. In order to participate in a moment of shared contemporary recognition, one must first possess local political competence and cultural literacy. We contend that such competence is articulated through all kinds of individual and collective behaviour and knowledge management, including media consumption and interpretation. We further suggest that the articulation of political competence is a necessary component in the performance of all types of political identity, including Australian citizenship. Therefore, the confidence of migrant communities in their competence within the new socio-political sphere is a qualitative measure of the successful functioning of publicness across all Australian citizens.

Media use among migrant communities in Australia has been documented in reference to the trans-border flows of media content in the Australasian region (Cunningham and Sinclair 2000). Media content is transnational, and even the moment of consumption is filtered through a time–space delay that underlines the border crossing of a daily act (Hawkins and Yue 2000). Migrants from Mainland china, Hong Kong and Taiwan are all active consumers of Chinese cultural products, as well as producers of and traders in Chinese cultural products. Melbourne and Sydney are centres for Chinese media, although there are distribution outlets all over the country. About ten major Chinese newspapers are published in cooperation with Hong Kong and Taiwan, and there are many small local Chinese newspapers published by mainland Chinese. In Perth, there are no Chinese newspapers directly associated with Hong Kong and Taiwan, but Chinese papers from Sydney and Melbourne are available in Chinese book stores in the city. There are also a couple of local Chinese weekly newspapers published by Australian mainland Chinese. Television product is available through pay TV, community TV (channel 31), and cable channels. Programming tends to be a mixture of local production and Taiwanese or Hong Kong imports. The Special Broadcasting Service (SBS) is a government-sponsored channel with a remit to broadcast multi-language news, documentary and entertainment programming to people from non-English-speaking backgrounds. It has also become a channel that carries cult movies and special interest shows. SBS carries news from Central Chinese Television (CCTV) but is otherwise underused by large numbers of Chinese viewers. Chinese films screened on SBS are described by the Chinese-speaking audience as too 'out of date' and too 'artistic'. They are perceived to be targeted at Australian film buffs rather than the mainstream interests of Chinese Australian audiences.

The turn from government and broadcast commercial channels to cable and satellite options is symptomatic of the failure of the national stations to cater for minority interests. There is also a strong tendency to provide alternative viewing both inside and outside the home, partly for adult pleasure and partly for the cultural education of children and teenagers. All Australian capital cities have Chinese cinemas where Hong Kong films are shown. Video shops associated with Hong Kong and mainland Chinese distributors distribute films and television series through cheap videotape and video CD copies. For first-generation migrants from mainland China, Hong Kong and Taiwan, especially retirees, domestic workers and overseas students, such videos are their main source of media entertainment. Children in these households are likely to be more comfortable with mainstream Australian products that tally with their peer group preferences. Nevertheless, the saturation of domestic media space with local and imported Chinese-language media products allows these young people to access several media cultures within the Australian environment. Parents may have different motivations in this respect. As our research has shown (Donald 2001), parents of young children are concerned about their cultural literacy in a Chinese context. Clearly, however, the parents' original decision to migrate does not suggest a serious desire for the children to 'go home'; the children know that they are already 'at home'. Rather, their access to competing and agnostic media spheres requires them to develop competence in Australian culture and political *praxis* while facilitating the translation of residual competences held by their parents. Their behaviour as media consumers shows that this generation has moved far beyond the simplistic notion of assimilation and into a transnational consciousness that is nonetheless resolutely Australian. A consequence of this multiple competence is to produce the children as the prime negotiators of family accession to Australian publicness.

Children as negotiators in the public sphere

INTERVIEWER (I): Why do you think your parents like watching Chinese films?

RESPONDENT (AUSTRALIAN CHINESE GIRL, 15 YEARS OLD) (R): Because that is something they are familiar with. They can say, 'look, when I was sixteen, I was like that blah, blah, blah'.

I: Do you participate with their nostalgia and memory?

R: No. I don't want to be rude. No, it is so far away from what I am. It is unimaginable.

I: Do you watch Hollywood films with your parents? Do you explain things to them while you are watching?

R: Yes. I explained what is going on, because they don't understand [the] cultural side of things. They are so confused. They don't know what is going on. Well, a little hard, but I want to do. I try my best to convince them to watch Hollywood films with me, as they did when they convinced me to watch Chinese films with them.

I: Why did you do that? I guess it must be very hard while you are enjoying your film and you have to explain?

R: I want to. I want them to see good sides of Hollywood films as they see good sides of Chinese films. Otherwise, they think Chinese films are so great, they are not! Hollywood films are better to watch, they make you feel good. The techniques are good, they are easy to watch, sometimes, the stories are good.

I: Do you like Australian television programmes?

R: Yes, there are some good ones, I love *Sea Change*. Sometimes I have to explain humour to my parents, you know, overseas migrants sometimes are not very good at seeing [the] funny side of the story. I don't think there are many good TV series in Australia, but there are some good Australian films: *Strictly Ballroom, Priscilla, Murial's Wedding*. I like them, sometimes I don't think my parents like them, because that is beyond their cultural understanding, something like *Priscilla*. I try to make them to see [the] funny side of it.

This interview is typical of conversations with young people in Perth. From an early age (either birth or the date of landing), migrant children live between two media worlds. At day-care centres and school and in social interactions with their friends, they access and interpret their lives through the music, television and merchandising of mainstream media products. At home, they watch Australian television and play with English-language multimedia, but they also participate in family viewing of Chinese soaps and Chinese news. Some young people take their responsibility as negotiators rather seriously (as does the young woman quoted above). Others may not but must always interpret themselves, their cultural preferences and the effects of media attitudes on their world outlook across at least two spheres of understanding. Their dexterity in, for one thing, acknowledging the existence of parallel media makes young migrant people extremely valuable social actors in the production of Australian citizenship. Their skills in negotiation allow them to embody and actively express the complexity of modern life in a settler society. Their contribution to parental access to the Australian media sphere, 'I try to make them see the funny side of it', is invaluable. However, this work of negotiation must be a two-way street if it is to create lasting and genuine cultural pluralism at the core of Australian political identity.

In our analysis of the interviews with parents and children, we therefore aimed to identify and describe both the ways in which children became active citizens and how parental memories of their own childhood media-viewing practices could be a useful tool in building a more inclusive media sphere. At the moment, in Australia, the childhood memories of migrants are not factored into the national responsibility for acknowledging multiplicity in society. Nor are they given much thought as an important factor in the process of settlement and in the difficult negotiations of the migrant with a host public culture. This is not surprising, given that the politics of difference require an identifiable, local context in order to function in the political sphere. However, we argue that more emphasis could usefully be placed on the trace of childhood media practices (whether it be revolutionary film, poster art, certain cartoon characters). This is because such traces sets the adult in a generation and articulate the parameters of acceptance or transgression by which they are likely to organise their own parental responsibility. The trace is both a fixer and a disturbance. It could well be understood as an extremely valuable constituent of the adult migrant. The trace of childhood difference could promote diverse and dynamic irruption into a host culture. Too often, such traces are described as nostalgic, or even encouraged to be so through glib multiculturalism (the anti-politics of folk dance and food festival). The anti-politics of the receiving culture inadvertently forces migrants to choose between a denial of the complexity and continuing relevance of their residual competences (to their identity and to the development of Australian political culture) and a self-protective alienation from the place of settlement.

When we talked with the children and got them to write down their reactions to the kind of media products familiar to their parents, a different picture emerged. Their comments evinced a comfortable familiarity with Australian media products, which they used as their measuring stick with which to assess the Chinese films we showed them. However, there was a quality of alienation from the parental culture embedded in their responses. After screening a clip from the film *Little Soldier Zhang Ga* (*xiaobing zhangga*, 1963), we found that the students responded in the first instance as modern filmgoers; they were unused to monochrome, and they did not understand poverty as a revolutionary context:

> I think that this sort of show wouldn't be acceptable in today's modern Australian television because, (a) black and white movies aren't very popular and usually detract people from it, (b) the theme is very oriental and thus might not suit the general target audience of the main broadcast in channels 7, 9 and 10. However, it would suit SBS very much. Myself, I don't mind *Little Soldier Zhang Ga* as it is interesting to see films of that genre and of that film era, but it's a show that is very retro and old-fashioned. A very unfamiliar sort of film.

(respondent 6, girl, 13–16 age group, Parkwood Chinese Language School)

This Chinese Australian teenager makes several observations in her response to a clip of the film. Her first point is a comment on its age – the film is not 'modern' (unlike modern Australia), and what is more off-putting, it is in black and white. Furthermore, the theme is 'oriental'. Now, whether this respondent is referring here to the storyline, the characters or to the mode of narration is not clear. However, what is apparent is that she recognises that its 'oriental' character is not part of the Australian 'modern' mainstream, although it would fit on SBS. She also allows the 'oriental' and the 'black and white' to slip simultaneously into the 'retro' and 'old-fashioned' categories. Not that this young Australian casts herself as part of that 'old-fashioned' culture. She does 'herself' find the film interesting – partly because she seems rather interested anyway in genre and film – but it is still unfamiliar and distant from her and from her media experience.

Other teenagers made less scholarly but similarly sceptical comments, which also emphasised the film's antiquity and cultural strangeness:

- 'It's black and white, sore losers, hard to see, loves to take revenge, they talk funny, they don't use their brain much only strength[en], they got funky haircuts, they are good tree climbers; very old-fashioned, look very farm-like, very tan, dress like sumo wrestler. I like funky hair' (respondent 16).
- 'The characters are different from the people we have today. They look weird. It might be better if it was coloured. They dress weird. Doesn't make sense, Don't understand'.
- 'The characters aren't recognisable. How the characters behave isn't like the kinds of people behave today …. Bare feet'.

Or, more wistfully:

- (in Chinese)'I think the film deeply shows the poverty and the mood of these children in China'.

It is not entirely surprising that the film looked strange and old-fashioned. It was made nearly forty years ago and is about the revolutionary wars thirty years prior to that. However, the film was selected for research after a survey in contemporary Beijing showed that most younger and older adults cited this as the most memorable film about children they knew. It was also recommended by Yu Lan, the erstwhile director of the Children's Film Studio in Beijing. Another respondent in China told us recently that it is also familiar to new audiences in China as it is screened regularly on CCTV movie channel 6.

However, we must compare those Australian responses with those of other Australian teenagers (aged 13–16), writing in Chinese and English, who did not distance themselves from the text either by period (although nobody praised the black and white photography) or through reference to place or ethnicity. They took it as another piece of film with some good qualities, and some surprising ones. Several responded positively and directly to the character portrayed. Others criticised it on the grounds of narration (black and white) and general picture quality (cinematography and reproduction), or commented on the level of violence in a movie made for a general (family) audience:

- (In Chinese) '[It] is very interesting. Zhang Ga is very bad but also very brave'.
- 'Little boys were very violent, which isn't commonly seen in family films'.
- 'There was a lot of fighting, which is not usually seen in a film for a family audience'.
- 'A bit boring ... family film ... the boys similar to boys in films nowa-days – maybe fight a bit more violent,.

What emerges from these discussions is that their confidence in naming this film as strange clearly showed that they were untroubled or even unaware of the cultural traditions that their parents have been concerned to retain and pass on. These children were completely naturalised into the Australian media sphere, but a sphere in which Chinese trace memories are hardly visible.

Residual memories

The parents targeted in this study were mainland migrants who had arrived in Australia within the last twenty years. Although they were generally very positive about their children's development, most also evinced anxieties about children's media in Australia. They felt that there was a deep lack of culture in Australian media products and therefore a lack of educational value (*jiaoyu*). As we have argued elsewhere, their opinion rested on a perception that historical consciousness was missing from media narratives, and that this was compensated for by undue attention to animal stories rather than human parables (Donald 2001).[2] This focus on the importance of history (*lishi*) to culture (*wenhua*) lies at the heart of the parents' notion of citizenship. Their children's ease with media products that did not have history at their centre therefore marked a cultural distance between the parents and their children. For the parents, history defined the educated person's cultural and civic experience. The transferral of civic competence from a Chinese context to an Australian one for the adults was therefore a very large task, as it involved the evisceration of a core value from the concept of culture. So what emerged from our discussions with the parents was that adult migrants bring a vocabulary of citizenship with them that proves hard to translate in the new context, especially the new cultural space of television for children. This accordingly limits their ability to direct their children's understanding and negotiations in local cultural space, and in the public sphere more broadly.

These fears are complicated by parents' belief that children need to see Australian products because they are becoming Australian, and that Chinese products are not assimilated without a great deal of historical explanation, to which the children refuse to listen! However, this brings up the second issue. As we describe below, much of the anxiety felt by parents is mirrored in the feelings of their peer groups in China itself. Problems that parents attribute to migration are also partly to do with generational patterns of consumption. The high level of foreign programming in Chinese children's television (varying between 25 and 48 percent in animation; see Goonasekera 2000) and in television generally destabilises the adult's sense of control. Their memories of what television has been and should be are constantly challenged by the 'glocalisation' of consumption. Children are dealing with a cultural field that some adults find perturbing:

> Cartoon films should be appropriate for children, for their age and their level of psychological development. But there are too many cartoons that do not do that. They are too commercial.
>
> (male teacher, grade 3, Beijing, 2000)

PRC adults also have to come to terms with a suite of alien national memories, at least as embedded in media product, although they do so from the stability of being at home. It is, if you will, a fair fight. Nevertheless, their concerns do resonate with diasporic or trans-cultural shocks. They sense a tension developing between the implied value systems of global products and the productions made in China for Chinese. Meanwhile, children assimilate sources of both entertainment and 'edu-tainment', confusing one with the other, and making global choices in a local–national environment. The interpenetration of global market products and local values, the glocalisation of twenty-first-century development, is impersonated in children's patterns of viewing and understanding. However, as these comments from children at Tsinghua Linked School, Beijing, make clear (and they are representative of several conversations), parents in the PRC have no compunction about *switching off*:

> I go home first, do my schoolwork, then I do the homework that my mother sets me. Then I wait for her to come home from work. When she gets back, we have a meal. Then we continue our study. I can only watch about ten minutes television every day.
>
> (girl, 8 years old)

> I am only allowed to watch television on Friday. But if I can't stay up till ten o'clock, then I won't go to bed at all!
>
> (boy, 9 years old)

A further issue arises from migrants' parents' self-perception and is encouraged in the prevalent formations of multiculturalism in Australia.

There is a tendency in many adults to move from the passion of a remembered incident or period of time to a general nostalgia for a whole other world, where everything is somehow better ordered and more congenial to one's ontological coherence. This nostalgia was echoed in China, for example by a teacher in his forties, who wanted his pupils to know and feel the extraordinary atmosphere in Beijing at the time of Zhou Enlai's funeral (1976). If they could only understand this, then they would, he implied, gain access to a greater world of revolutionary memory, morality and national sentiment. But as he discovered (and presumably will rediscover over and over again as new generations of schoolchildren pass through his classroom), the historical shift that has occurred in Chinese socio-political and economic life over the last twenty years has severed the children from this possibility of empathy.

The parental generation in China is experiencing a shift from memory to nostalgia, as the nature and context of cultural competence and national identity make it difficult for young people to understand the enduring value and social resonance of a revolutionary childhood. Given the extreme transformation of the Chinese economic and social environment in the past twenty years, the widening gap between generations is comparable to the chasm opened up through migration. However, although the comparative data remind us that media consumption is organised by generational contingencies, we also observe that migration poses particular added difficulties for the parental group.

The process of crossover from memory to nostalgia is perhaps beyond the scope of this paper to explore, but it is important to note (Wood 1999: 143–60). In migrant experience, the process of memory loss seems to speed up. In the preserve of media culture, particularly, parents are assuming that their memories are irrelevant to the host culture, and even to their own children. We would suggest that a deeper acceptance of difficulty and difference on the part of host cultures might impede the process by which adult political-cultural competence is re-articulated as nostalgic cultural performance on the margins of an inflexible public sphere. In terms of parent–child relations, cultural programming, which allowed for positive irruption of memory traces into public culture, would give a new balance of competence across the generations.

Conclusions

Our findings raise some serious questions around the possibility of achieving affective relationships to culture and history when living in a first-generation migrant household in Australia. This becomes most evident in the encounter with television directed at audiences of children. The children of recently arrived migrants are privileged and burdened by the necessity to negotiate this area of public culture on behalf of the family. They demonstrate competence in the mediated vocabularies of national reproduction and citizenship but are relatively ill at ease with mediated versions of their parents' remembered childhoods. By contrast, their parents are dispirited and unsure of their absolute ability to 'parent' in the new media environment. A dysfunction has emerged in the capacity of migrant parents' to direct (and monitor) their children's understanding and negotiations in local cultural space, and in the public sphere more broadly. This was poignantly expressed by parents who, on the one hand, do not want their children to watch television before school (the 6.30–8.30am slot) but on the other feel that they *cannot switch it off*. Similarly, parents articulated a desire for their children to share their memories of childhood, which, as visits to actual places and people were impossible, could best be done through mediated forms and through language learning. Yet they contended that while their children *should* see the films and shows they themselves remember, they also felt that their children probably would not understand their contextual impact (especially in the more violent moments of war films) and should therefore *not* see them after all.

How, then, could a media culture that embraced the traces of parental memories of their childhood viewing help? While we recognise the political and commercial challenges that would be raised through a commitment to active and even agnostic cultural pluralism, we still offer the following recommendations. First, we suggest that valuing the traces of memory in the public sphere would acknowledge individual and national relationships to other places in the contemporary moment. This echoes Ann Curthoys' recent call for a revision of the parameters of national history. She argues that it needs to be thought, written and represented in public institutions within a more inclusive framework of international influences and conditions (Curthoys 2001). In our case study, her paradigm would demand that a history of Australia would necessitate an understanding of Chinese history (and *vice versa*). Conversely, cultivating a mediated habit of description and acknowledgement might facilitate first-generation adult involvement in the Australian public sphere. In the Australian case, one of the strategies that might help would be the production of children's programming inflected with a notion of history. After all, despite these Chinese parents' comments, Australia does have history and culture(s).

However, it is not easy to incorporate Australian history into children's programming, given that it documents invasion, genocide and a racist immigration policy. Again, Ann Curthoys has demanded that these hard issues be honestly broached and made a dominant part of intercultural and international public debate if a useful revision of Australian nationhood is to be achieved. In the work here, we would accept her position and extend the conundrum. The debate needs to take place in the mediated public sphere, and in all areas of media product, including children's programming. In the process of such debate, traces of international and migrant competences must be valued as equivalent in order to destabilise the grounds of debate and admit diverse Australian political competences into the public arena.

Pragmatic strategies for acknowledging the traces of migrant childhood viewing might include co-productions with Chinese/Hong Kong and Singaporean companies; interactive youth programming, where children and adults tell stories to one another; international animation that is not revoiced for a local audience; and multilingual online feedback facilities. Such strategies would also recognise that children from migrant families operate between two worlds. The teenagers we interviewed were very focused on their Australian-ness, but they were also active in the local Chunghwa (Chinese) society in Western Australia. Media practices need to acknowledge and emulate young people's flexibility and multiple competences.

If strategies like these could be achieved, then migrant parents might feel more confident of their ability to participate in the mediated Australian public sphere. By the same token, the burden of negotiation carried by the children of migrants could be shifted to society. The phenomena of alienation, assimilation and denial could then be set aside in favour of dynamic and mutual processes of cross-cultural accommodation. The transnationalism of the 'astronauts' could become less a feature of business migrants and more a condition of Australian cosmopolitanism.

Notes

1   This research was funded through a small Australian Research Council grant to Donald and Witcomb (2000).
2   However, the researchers note that the co-production between ABC (Australia) and CCTV (China), *Magic Mountain*, effectively combines human values with animal characters.

References

Beal, T. and Sos, F. (1999) *Astronauts from Taiwan: Taiwanese immigration to Australia and New Zealand*. Wellington, New Zealand: Asia Pacific Research Institute.

Chan Kwok Bun (1997) 'A family affair: migration, dispersal, and the emergent identity of the Chinese cosmopolitan', *Diaspora* 6(2): 195–213.

Cunningham, S. and Sinclair, J. (eds) (2000) *Floating Lives: The Media and Asian Diaspora: Negotiating Cultural Identity through Media*. Brisbane: University of Queensland Press.

Curran, J. and Park Myung-jin (eds) (2000) *De-Westernising Media Studies*. London: Routledge.

Curthoys, A. (2001) 'History for the nation, or for the world?' *Australian Collections, Australian Cultures: Museums and Identities in 2001*, Museums Australia 6th annual national conference, 23–26 April, Canberra.

Donald, S.H. (2001) 'History, entertainment, education and jiaoyü: a Western Australian perspective on Australian children's media and some Chinese alternatives', *International Journal of Cultural Studies* 4(3): 279–99.

Donald, J. and Donald, S. (2000) 'The publicness of cinema', in C. Gledhill and L. Williams (eds), *Reinventing Film Studies*. London: Edward Arnold.

Finnane, A. (1998) 'Chinese in Australia', in G. Davison, J. Hirst and S. Macintyre (eds), *The Oxford Companion to Australian History*. Melbourne: Oxford University Press.

Goonasekera, A. (1999–2000) 'Multimedia for edu-tainment of children in Asia: the case of television in seven Asian countries', http://www.childresearch.net. CYBRARY/SYMPO/BOARD%5fE/ASIA2P.HTM#T2, accessed on 15 October 2000.

Hawkins, G. and Yue, A. (2000) 'Going south', *Culture/China: New Formations* 41: 49–63.

Lee, L.O.-F. (1991) 'On the margins of the Chinese discourse: some personal thoughts on the cultural meaning of the periphery', *Daedalus* 120: 207–26.

Lever-Tracy, C. and Ip, D. (1996) 'Diaspora capitalism and the homeland: Australian Chinese networks into China', *Diaspora* 5(2): 239–73.

Ong Aihwa and Nonini, D.M. (eds) (1997) *Undergrounded Empires: The Cultural Politics of Modern Chinese Transnationalism*. London: Routledge.

Wang Ling-chi (1991) 'Roots and changing identity of the Chinese in the United States', *Daedalus* 120: 181–206.

Wood, N. (1999) *Vectors of Memory: Legacies of Trauma in Post War Europe*. Oxford: Berg.

14 Talking about Jet Li

Transnational Chinese movie stardom and Asian American Internet reception

Julian Stringer

Introduction

> Some scholars of reception write as though 'experiencing' the text stops at the end of the show. Even if the audience has been perfectly bourgeois and quiet during the movie, talk happens afterwards, often in great quantity. To analyse the ideological, cultural and personal effects of film viewing, considering post-movie talk by spectators is exceptionally important. Here, the work of cultural studies and analysis of fandom contributes to writing the history of American film reception ....
>
> ... 'talk' continues to process the text, reworking it for the use of the spectator. Part of that spectatorial use seems clearly to be personal, but other use values are social – the creation of communities of people who use the text as the object through which to construct networks of attachment, discovery, and, sometimes, authority and power.
>
> (Staiger 2001: 26, 28–9)

As the above quotation indicates, a key dimension of political communication in the cultural sphere is the 'talk' generated around the rituals of film viewing. Individuals and groups engage in public discourse about movies as a means of working through the significance of issues felt to have both keen personal import and broad social relevance. Whether through face-to-face discussion at the multiplex or art cinema, the posting of computer messages or the publication of articles and letters in the pages of print magazines and fanzines, talk provides important – if often critically neglected – ways of imparting and sharing knowledge and opinion. By talking about issues important to them on a personal level, fans and other discussants help to constitute the group identities through which individuals strive to make sense of their movie-going experiences.

Within the diverse imagined communities that make up what is referred to as Greater China, the recent proliferation of media technologies such as the Internet has facilitated new and vital means of talking about cinema. As David Morley and Kevin Robbins (1995) and Arjun Appadurai (1996), among others, have pointed out, instant communications technologies have made deep inroads into popular culture and undercut previous boundaries of national identity. In a borderless world, the global 'mediascape' is characterised by the presence of bewilderingly large numbers of distinct communities who produce, circulate and consume rhetorical statements concerning aspects of cinema that matter most to them. Such groups are able to access and transmit information with the mere move of a mouse.

Some of these new forms of public dialogue would not be possible without the convergence of the Internet and popular cinema. Certainly, at the turn of the twenty-first century the bringing together of these two media appears to be a match made in heaven – it seems to make everybody happy. At the levels of production and distribution, the development of the information superhighway has added to the number of lucrative exhibition 'windows' currently available for the commodification of audio-visual products (complementing 'traditional' theatrical exhibition, video, television, cable, VCDs, DVDs, and so on). In Greater China today, more films than ever before are now being watched on an expanding number of different kinds of screen; these films are able to travel farther and wider than previously imagined; and with the possibilities opened by the technology of the World Wide Web, they have the potential to reach ever larger numbers of consumers and respondents. At the same time, the widespread proliferation of domestic forms of media spectatorship, together with the opportunities they create for interpersonal talk among diverse communities, has added a patina of intimacy to the relation between the corporate media and its publics. It is now possible for Internet users around the world to feel as though they have the ability to interact with, and hence participate in, the publicness of popular culture by exchanging responses to their personal film-viewing experiences.

Transnational Chinese movie stars have played a crucial role in focusing some of these new arrangements. As representative social 'types' (Dyer 1979), they embody private hopes and dreams in a relentlessly public manner. Stellar names such as Jackie Chan, Joan Chen, Chow Yun-Fat and Michelle Yeoh have projected compelling images of 'Chinese-ness' on the big and small screens of the global mediascape, generating in their wake a cacophony of chatter from fans and more distant observers alike. In the case of Asian fans, this talk is frequently concentrated around a range of key questions: to what extent do these icons speak to us? What do they say to us about our lives? How are we to decide what we think about them? These questions then shade into issues raised elsewhere by other commentators: why have *these* performers become international stars? Are they adequately up to the job of dramatising the life experiences of the social communities they ostensibly represent?

While recent work in film studies has usefully paid attention to the production and reception of transnational cinema in the Greater China context (Lu 1997; Yau 2001), it has to date concentrated far less upon the need to think through the relevance of these kinds of question. Of course, there has been work on internationally renowned Chinese movie stars (Fore 1997; Gallagher 1997; Stringer 2003), but the spread of the Internet and the concomitant volume (in both senses of the word) of its accompanying talk have opened up new research agendas, which have yet to be fully explored.

In pursuing these challenges, therefore, alternative approaches to both star studies and audience studies are called for. It is now a number of years since Richard Dyer's classic book, *Stars* (1979), pioneered the serious academic study of this subject. In one of that book's most influential formulations, the notion of the 'star image' was advanced as a way of theorising the broad social significance of movie personalities. For Dyer, a star image is a multidimensional sign comprising the accumulated inter-textual knowledge that circulates through the mass media about a public figure: it comprises promotion and publicity materials, commentaries of various kinds, and the meanings generated through film performances. Unfortunately, however, the widespread, not to say easy, acceptance over this period of Dyer's notion of the star image has inadvertently foreclosed the development of other, more audience-centred, critical perspectives.

Although this is not the place to go into great detail about what the limitations of this particular concept may be, one specific observation should be identified here, namely that a star image is, in part, constituted by audiences through the very act of talking about the personality in question. Consider the fact that the increased levels of dialogue on the Internet concerning performers such as Chan and Yeoh only serves to highlight these stars' *use value*. By focusing on specific reception contexts, it becomes possible to see how Chinese media icons function as forms of cultural currency exchangeable within and between distinct imagined communities. In this sense, the 'star image' may be thought of as more of a moving target than Dyer ever dreamed; indeed, it can at times come to resemble a mere effect of fans' desires, a 'text' to be 'used'. In short, a star image has no guaranteed ideological meaning, as some of Dyer's work tended to imply. Rather, within the Internet reception contexts explored in this chapter, whatever individual discussants proclaim or decide a star *should* mean in their discussion forums is what the star in question ultimately *does* mean – at least at that particular time and in that particular (electronic) space.

The choice of case study

As a way of illustrating this point, this chapter concentrates on one specific kind of reception of one contemporary Chinese film star, namely responses to martial arts icon Jet Li by certain Asian American Internet users.

Why Jet Li? And why Asian Americans? I have focused on Li, rather than any of the other bright lights of the 'Jade screen', for three reasons. First, he is a figure who spans some of the key cultural and geographical coordinates of Greater China. Li was born and first achieved fame in mainland China. He then moved to Hong Kong and became one of the most famous players in the domestic film industry. After attracting extraordinary transnational attention for his Hong Kong performances, he then reinvented himself yet again in the late 1990s by establishing a new career inside the US corporate media. Today, Jet Li is one of the most successful and best-known of the numerous Asian diasporic talents working at the heart of the Hollywood film industry.

Second, Li's international career is frequently viewed through the prism of a key term that circulates in discussions around him: authenticity. There are two aspects to this. To begin with, there is a longstanding – and by now rather tiresome – debate in some fan circles on the genuineness, or otherwise, of his martial arts abilities. Is he a true *kung fu* master, or someone in *need* of the wires and harnesses that so often hoist and pivot his body around during his most spectacular fight scenes? Is he a more 'real' fighter than, say, Jackie Chan, who has famously refused to use wires? More relevant to my immediate concerns is the perception of a different, albeit linked, notion of authenticity.

As a Chinese actor, Jet Li is frequently talked about in terms of cultural 'purity'. Perhaps because of the strong associations of Chinese nationalism projected in his celebrated roles as the folk icon Huang Feihong ('Wong Fei-hung' in Cantonese) in the *Once Upon a Time in China* series (Hong Kong, 1991–1993), his public persona has carried connotations of ethnic authenticity in a slightly different way to the images of the other stars listed above. As Hunt (1999: 95–6), quoting Sek Kei, puts it, 'If Bruce Lee seemed "westernised", Li's films make more of his "Chinese-ness". His Wong Fei-hung reinvents the Confucian patriarch as a new Chinese man who opposes China's traditional superstition as well as Western and Japanese imperialism ... thus representing the "perfect" Chinese man'. What interests me here are the very different connotations that such 'perfection' can be given by some Asian American audiences.

Finally, in recent years Li has proved beyond a reasonable doubt that he is more than up to the task of carrying major Hollywood star vehicles, even if these are all action films. Paradoxically, by working within this one limited (and limiting) genre, he has developed into a more straightforward leading man, a 'safer pair of hands' at the box office, than his Chinese contemporaries Jackie Chan and Chow Yun-Fat. Simply put, Chan is still perceived in the USA as producing ostensibly (often subtitled or dubbed) 'Hong Kong films', while Chow's ventures into romance (with *Anna and the King*, 2000) and 'art cinema' (*Crouching Tiger, Hidden Dragon*, 2000) have compromised his already less than smooth transition to Hollywood action star status (in *The Replacement Killers*, 1997, and other disappointing titles). By contrast, Jet Li has established himself as more of a sure-fire commercial bet. As an out-and-out action star, he has a built-in recognition factor. Every time you pay to watch one of Li's movies, you know he's going to kick and punch and spin and jab his way through it; and if you don't much care to see such things, why would you want to go to see a Jet Li movie in the first place? In other words, while Li is no A-list megastar, he is enough of a commercial package to be able to secure both regular work and habitual attention from the US 'infotainment' media. In the contemporary cultural climate, action films are popular enough for this to happen.

For all of these reasons, Jet Li has become to all intents and purposes an Asian American movie star. On the one hand, he now occupies a privileged position within the Hollywood firmament, having achieved a level of public recognition unusual among Chinese actors in the United States. On the other hand, in the process of moving from Hong Kong to America, he has subjected his Chinese heritage to a complete makeover. His star image now has the ability to speak in the most direct manner possible to the concerns of Asian American communities (predominantly, but not necessarily exclusively, Chinese American). As an icon able to represent them at some level, Jet Li is a figure about whom Asian Americans appear to talk a great deal.

Certainly, they have a special relationship with him. There is a lot at stake for Asian Americans in debating and intervening in the future shape of the effects of new media technologies and the publicness of commercial cinema on group identities in the United States. As a so-called 'model minority' and growing force in both the commercial marketplace and political sphere, Asian Americans are perceived as of particular significance by Hollywood. Asian Americans are now distinct target consumers for commercial US movies, and the Internet has become a key means for this particular social audience to access and transmit information and opinion regarding its products.

When thinking about how to approach the sheer amount of available resources on the Internet concerning the above subjects, one needs to tread carefully. In trying to identify what Jet Li has been made to mean by Asian Americans, I first conducted a mass trawl, sifting through pages and pages of data. Predictably enough, there are now any number of websites catering to Asian American communities from which information about fan talk around Jet Li may be extracted. However, it very quickly became apparent that a range of different kinds of source may broadly be identified.

For example, as one would expect, there are currently a number of sites devoted exclusively to Jet Li himself. Some of these are 'unofficial' sites, like jetlifanworks.tripod.com, which operate independently of the corporate media and have no links to the promotional machinery of the Hollywood studios. By contrast, 'official' sites, such as www.jetli.com, are more implicated in the business of commerce: they display clear connections to corporate bodies, acting for example as subsidiary commercial windows for the selling of videos and Jet Li paraphernalia, and the previewing of trailers for upcoming movies and television appearances.

Alongside these are the sites designed specifically to cater to and serve the Asian American community. None of the sites I visited in this category focuses exclusively on movies and popular culture, although many do so in passing. However, all address Asian Americans as a new kind of market and social and political force by focusing at every turn on the question of agency; that is, by foregrounding Asian American concerns as part of a counter-vision of US society that posits their voices as central at every turn. Examples of these sites include www.Asianworld.com, www.Asianvenue.com, www.Click2asia.com, www.Netasia.com, www.Asianamericanculture.com and www.Yolk.com.

Finally, there is a small but growing number of specialist Asian American film sites that provide discussion forums and opportunities to exchange information and opinion on all kinds of movie activity, including talk about stars such as Jet Li. Examples here are the pages at www.naaatanet.org (National Asian American Telecommunications Association) and www. ramen.itsc.org (APAnet Discussion Forum – Asian American Film and Video).

For convenience, I have by and large limited my focus in what follows to talk generated on just two specific websites. The first of these is perhaps the most active of the sites designed to facilitate discussion of all aspects of Asian American cinema, and as such it might be considered a particularly useful resource for my immediate purposes, namely Asian American Film (located at asianamericanfilm.com). This attractively produced venture is a combination official and unofficial site, and it is tied extremely closely to current activity in the independent production and distribution sectors. In addition, though, it includes reviews of contemporary Hollywood movies, regularly updated news stories and a community section comprising message boards and chat rooms, as well as a write-your-own-*haiku* page, 'Haiku Fu!', wherein readers are encouraged to submit specially composed poems 'about Asian American subjects so near and dear to our hearts!' (Asian American Film, posted on 16 February 2002).[1] The *haiku* page of most relevance to this chapter shows an 'inspirational' photo of Jet Li jumping in the air, ready to kick a foe, and an encouragement that readers compose and send in their own poems on the subject of Li and his films.

The second site I have looked at in some detail is *Giant Robot* (at www.giantrobot.com). Again, this is an electronic resource that claims to speak to and from the heart of Asian American community concerns. The print version of *Giant Robot*, published every quarter in Los Angeles, has established itself as one of the most successful of the 'hip', young Asian American publishing ventures of the 1990s. As a relatively glossy 'lifestyle' magazine, *Giant Robot* is concerned with all aspects of the Asian American experience. However, it appears disproportionately preoccupied with the importance and attractions of popular culture, including movies. Such concerns also animate discussion in the pages of the electronic version of the magazine.

In summary, both Asian American Film (hereafter abbreviated to AAF) and *Giant Robot* (hereafter abbreviated to GR) are highly self-conscious about the positions they occupy in the broader community; each projects a compelling vision of Asian American subjectivity and agency. Inevitably, such perspectives help to determine the specific ways in which Jet Li is made sense of in each of the sites.

Jet Li and minority representation

A popular *kung fu* actor, Jet Li was known as Li Lianjie when he won the national championship at the age of 8 in mainland China, a title he held for five consecutive years. His screen debut was *The Shaolin Temple* (directed by Zhang Xinyan, 1982). He moved to Hong Kong and starred in numerous martial arts films, including *Once Upon a Time in China* (directed by Tsui Hark, 1991), *Fong Sai Yuk* (directed by Yuan Kui, 1993) and *The Tai-chi Master* (directed by Yuan Heping, 1993). Li's best screen roles are those of legendary heroes of masculinity and moral integrity who rescue suffering victims and defeat evil victimisers (foreign as well as domestic). By contrast, his contemporary roles, as in *The Bodyguard from Beijing* (directed by Yuan Kui, 1994), are not generally successful. In the mid-1990s, Li started playing in Hollywood films, one of them being *Black Mask* (1997) (Zhang 1998: 217–18).

To update this encyclopaedia entry, one would be obliged to mention the fact that since 1998 Jet Li has starred in four Hollywood feature films (while continuing to work in Asia): *Lethal Weapon 4* (1998), *Romeo Must Die* (2000), *Kiss of the Dragon* (2001) and *The One* (2001). In addition, he created much interest among Asian American communities for his earlier role in *Once Upon a Time in China and America* (1997) – a Hong Kong title that nevertheless provides a clear 'bridge' to Li's work in the USA (it was shot in Texas) – not to mention his numerous promotional appearances on US network television and in other media. Gossip and rumour circulating around the star provides another focus of attention. For example, the knowledge that Li turned down the lead male role in the smash hit *Crouching Tiger, Hidden Dragon* extends the range of 'what if' speculation and fantasy narratives that so often circulate around public icons, especially 'minority' ones burdened with the weight of a particular community's hopes and dreams.

The Asian American Internet sites I have chosen to concentrate on in this chapter tend to talk about Li's four showcase Hollywood roles in two distinct ways. First, there is what may be termed the 'advocacy position', wherein Li's appropriateness as an authentic pan-Asian cultural icon is debated in terms of the twin issues of masculinity and sexuality.[2] Second, there is what I want to call the 'pragmatic position'. Here, discussion is oriented towards awareness of the very real material constraints that have greeted this Chinese actor's aspirations to Hollywood leading man status. Linking these two positions is sensitivity to the performative nature of Jet Li's public life as a Chinese movie star.

As a way of exploring the advocacy position, it is helpful to start by quoting an observation made by a contributor to yet another relevant website:

The success of these martial arts movies is evident in both the Asian American community and American society as a whole. However, it also demonstrates the fine line that the Asian American community must walk. On the one hand, most of us are proud of the success of these martial arts movies and their Asian and Asian American stars. However, we must be wary of the possibility that these movies will only reinforce and perpetuate the cultural stereotype that all Asians know martial arts.

(anonymous article, 'Martial arts movies and hip hop', at Asian-Nation: The Landscape of Asian America, www.asian-nation.org, accessed on 2 April 2002)

The central structuring argument of this and so many other quotations is that when it comes down to the politics of 'ethnic' representation, Jet Li's US movies are in some sense not sufficiently 'adequate'. Now, there can never be such a thing as 'adequate' minority representation; if there were, there would be no need to push for any improvements. Minority stars like Jet Li therefore become a forum through which Asian American fans talk about the limits of existing images and the need for new ones – or, put differently, the 'fine line' that spectators must walk between gratitude for and resentment of some of those images already on offer.

Different fans have different perceptions of the positions occupied by Jet Li between these two poles. For some, his Hollywood titles are simply awful. 'Uncle Benny' is not alone in articulating this point of view:

I mean, Jet Li for instance, the films that he has made here in the U.S. have been horrible, all of them. The ones he did in HK, with probably much less production value were so much better. Anyway he is not a viable asian leading man, he is a martial arts action hero without much screen presence.

(Yolk.com, 18 February 2002)

As an extension of this kind of complaint, the question inevitably arises as to how far Jet Li should be considered a representative Asian American in the first place:

It should be asian-AMERICANS who are venerated for achievements in this country and abroad. I mean Chow Yun-Fat and Jet Li are cool but the last time I heard, they're not U.S. citizens, an obvious requirement to be considered asian-AMERICAN.

('Logan Canyon', APAnet Discussion Forum – Asian American Film and Video, 20 May 2001)

The working assumption behind comments such as these may be summed up in the terms Martin Wong chooses to advance in an article on the breakthrough release of *Lethal Weapon 4* published in the print version of *Giant*

Robot: 'this is his [Li's] first big-budget American studio-backed movie. This is also the first time he's played a bad guy' (Wong 1998: 31). Or, as one of Asian American Film's Haiku Fu! poems put it, 'Once upon a time/Before Lethal Weapon 4/Jet Li was The One!' (Jennifer Li, AAF, posted on 16 February 2002).

In making a distinction between Li's Asian and Hollywood roles, then, the former are often presented as 'good' and the latter as 'bad', even though it is the US movies that arguably more explicitly connect Li's performances to the life experiences of Asian Americans. And across the websites, it is Li's maleness that frequently allows such distinctions to be presented and talked about. Masculinity is the lens through which many fans negotiate the meaning of Li's Hollywood performances, as well as the perceived (in)authenticity and (in)adequacy of his star image. In this sense, the attractions and shortcomings of Jet Li's US roles are used as a means of making advocacy claims on behalf of the wider community.

More specifically, the theme of masculinity tends to be approached from three different angles: first, the validation of Jet Li as a powerful martial artist and so a compelling bodily presence; second, the more common perception of weakness and emasculation as key elements of his Hollywood film roles; and, third, through a discourse on romantic and erotic behaviour. In each of these cases, Jet Li is revealed as no 'perfect' Chinese man or 'legendary hero of masculinity'.

First, then, there is the claim that Jet Li represents a strong masculinity, an argument made on fewer occasions than one might initially expect. This point of view represents clear sympathy for a Chinese actor fighting symbolically against the odds:

> Despite lacking a sexual presence and a mastery of acting, Jet Li takes the Asian martial artist away from the image of the Kungfu Buster Keaton, thus re-creating a powerful masculinity that is not necessarily detrimental to the Asian male image in American media.
>
> (Kamemoto Mamatsu, AAF, 7 July 2001)[3]

The flip side to this discussion of Asian masculine strength is consideration of Jet Li as a weak male image. Here, the Chinese folk hero is revealed as an emasculated Asian American man, and indications of gender and sexuality are presented in terms of their corollary, namely appeals to political pride and political power. As 'J' puts it in a message posted at AAF on 6 July 2001:

> It's a Catch22 ... do we want success for our community in Hollywood, visual representation, etc. bad enough that we settle for the typical chopsocky fare or do we protest and demand more realistic portrayals but at the same time risk underrepresenation because of the lack of such opportunities? When we're NOT doing chopsocky characters, we're

getting beat up like little girls – see Rick Yune get his head pummeled in *Fast and the Furious* along with his Asian sidekick getting beat down by none other than a girl! So, either we're ultra-powerful (and mysterious /exotic) or we're ultra-weak, in both cases – asexual. It's a bittersweet success story. Romeo Must Kiss ....

Emerging out of this last quotation is a greater sense of just how these discussion networks of attachment, discovery, authority and power are constructed through the appropriation of Jet Li as a form of Asian American cultural currency. Clearly, the community being imagined in the above example is a very male-oriented one ('none other than a girl!'), suggesting that the focus on Jet Li's gender weaknesses characterises anxieties projected within a homosocial reception environment. Indeed, further proof of this is demonstrated through a message posted on AAF by a female Jet Li fan highly self-conscious of her devalued 'girlie' identity: 'Even for a girly girl like me, the final action sequence [of *Kiss of the Dragon*] is pretty cool' (Emily Ting, AAF, film review, 16 February 2002). And consider too the example below, wherein 'ThatGirlJing' (AAF, 29 June 2001) talks about the same film:

> There were awkward moments of comical relief at the expense of emasculating Jet Li, for example: a horribly-acted emotional breakdown by Bridget Fonda as Jet comforts her, where, to my dismay, the camera pulls away for a shot showing Bridget in her hooker boots towering over Jet, losing any sense of emotional strength Jet's character could have developed. And surprise, surprise: Jet does not get any play!

Push the sort of comment made above one step further, and the logical outcome of this preoccupation with male weakness is the perception, not just of Li's emasculation, but of his complete asexuality. Jet Li may be an action star with a longstanding record of 'moral integrity' on screen; however, for many Asian Americans, he appears to be a sexless leading man. One of the main points of interest here is that such a position represents both a reversal and a reinvention of one of the key continuing stereotypes of Asians in the US media: the (mysterious, exotic) sexual deviant (Lee 1999: 83–105). Rather than being seen as sexually sick and perverse, Asian sexuality is now repositioned as that which is healthy and good. The only problem, though, is that while being in a unique position to possess and project healthy and good Asian sexuality, Jet Li is perceived as not actually having any.

This masculine 'lack' is both exposed and compensated for through intense discussion of subjects such as movie romance and kissing on the big screen. Indeed, it is the latter subject that takes up by far the most discussion space, by both male and female contributors, on the sites I visited. There are numerous examples through which this point could be made, one of the most detailed of which is as follows:

I agree with the fact that Asian male are still being portrayed as being a-sexual through the media and society. I never realised this stereotype existed until I read about it .... The fact that moviemakers only allow asian actors to act a-sexual only enforced this stereotype. In *Kiss of the Dragon*, Jet Li plays an a-sexual cop .... In his first western movie *The Master*, about ten years ago, he acted like a normal guy. He kissed both the white girl and asian girl and behaved like a normal young man with healthy romantic and sexual feelings .... In the upcoming movie *The One*, Jet also only hugs his wife and doesn't kiss her. It's rediculous. Bruce Lee always had sex with women in his films. He acted sexualy normal, which is realistic. Although Jet is one of the coolest heroes on earth, he can still learn those social things from the big man Bruce and his son Brandon. Jet should also get laid in a movie sooner or later, because right now he's not doing very well on shaping the western-asian image ('JL fan', AAF, 9 November 2001).

'Normal' and 'healthy' sexuality are here equated with sexual drive and its representation, something perceived to have been lost since the time of *The Master* (a Hong Kong movie shot on location in Los Angeles) in 1992. As Jet Li has become more visible in the United States, then, he is also assumed to have become more sexually 'safe' (unthreatening?) ('Kamenriderv3', AAF, 4 November 2001, writes: 'More like an old fashioned conservative Chinese custom. Jet Li married twice so I think he spread his Chi Kung a bit already. None of that chastity to increase the kung fu power.').

This is a perception that also lies behind the following contributions to *Giant Robot*: 'Ugh! I hate it when cinematic interacial couples don't consu-mate. It's one of my biggest peeves. You can tell there is a producer somewhere saying, "Whoa! Hold on, that won't play in Iowa". It's worse now than in the 80's' ('Willie D', GR, 3 November 2001); 'Actually Jet NEVER kissed anyone in any of his movies. I don't even think I've ever heard him go out with any women at all either! That my friends is dedication to the martial arts' ('Citruskid', GR, 3 November 2001); 'They never hook up asian men with non-asian women ... but asian women are hooked up with non-asian men often. And i mean HOOK up *wink wink*' ('Nancyk', GR, 4 November 2001). Other contributors to Asian American Film make remarkably similar observations: 'This movie was pretty good but one thing strikes me about it. THE ASIAN GUY CAN NEVER HOOKUP WITH THE GIRL. Especially if it's a white girl. This is perpetuating the stereotype that Asian men in the media are a-sexual' ('Tai', AAF, 7 September 2001); 'as for jet li and asian men ... there's a girl at the theatre where i work that's from bosnia and thinks he's cute, which is funny, because out of all asian men ... jet li? hm' ('phism', AAF, 11 July 2001).

Across the range of subjects raised so far (about which consensus has clearly not been reached) – for example, the relation between the US and Hong Kong films, the nature of Li's masculinity and sexuality, the comparison of this particular Chinese icon with the images of white and African American performers – one issue remains of paramount importance. Whatever Jet Li may mean *over there*, in Asia, is not the same as what he means *over here*, in the United States. For Asian America, Jet Li does not speak in quite the same language as he does elsewhere. On the one hand, he is a transnational Chinese icon deserving of support; on the other hand, his 'adequacy' as precisely this kind of cultural and political icon is questioned at every turn.

Against this foregrounding of advocacy issues exists what I have termed the pragmatic response to Jet Li and his work. This position constitutes what may be characterised as a different kind of 'defence' of Jet Li and his Hollywood films. While the advocacy position is largely concerned with issues of textual representation, the pragmatic position is more interested in extra-textual considerations. This latter position therefore affords Asian Americans the opportunity to engage in slightly different varieties of talk about this particular movie star. More specifically, discussion threads of this kind pick up on the perceived 'moral integrity' of Li's transnational star image but place it within the context of the day-to-day dilemmas and choices faced by the displaced Chinese performer in a largely hostile environment, namely Hollywood itself. The theme of moral integrity, then, is now displaced on to the actor himself and takes the form of the broadly based rhetorical question once asked by Lenin: what is to be done?

As a key indication of this point of view, the advocacy position's concern with performativity (i.e. whether or not the Chinese actor 'adequately' represents community concerns) is refocused around a more prosaic question: what are the material conditions, the limits of his profession, that allow Jet Li to perform at the US box office? Responses suggest a keen awareness that these are *career choices* that Jet Li is making, and hence demonstrate a sensitivity to the behind-the-scenes politics of Hollywood representation.

Again, there are numerous examples to choose from here. For example: 'Sure', writes 'Roxanne' at AAF on 15 December 2001: 'It would be great if Jet Li actually kissed someone in his movies but if he doesn't want to then leave him alone, even though I've always hoped he'd kiss the girl in his movies I've come to expect that he doesn't so I don't get dissapionted'; 'Yes, I would love to have asian american men be portrayed in a multifaceted way and not be relegated to waiter/nerd/nucelar scientist/gansters, etc. But movies like this does move the image of the AA men away from one of weakness. And this obsession some people have with "an Asian guy must get some on the big screen" is ludicrous .... I say take it one step at a time' ('Bing', AAF, 7 July 2001).

The above comments represent an affirmative pragmatic position, but others are much more hostile. For example, there is among many voices a tendency to blame the actor personally for bad career moves in the United States: 'What do you expect from Jet Li. His acting sucks major ass and he can't say any more than 3 engrish words in a row without some serious post production editing. He can kick and grunt but god bless him when he speaks engrish' ('old school yukio mishima', AAF, 18 October 2001); 'Depends on which film industry, Asian men get poontang in Asian movies. They don't get much action in American movies. Either way, sex is a bigger taboo than violence in Asian cinema .... I think some Asians are partly to blame because they want to be the chaste hero all the time. Jet Li doesn't skin in any of his movies. He doesn't see Aunt 13's pink even though Wong Fei Hung eventually married her in real life .... So I think both it's cultural and The Man keeping the Asian brother down' ('Kamenriderv3', AAF, 4 November 2001); 'Well, it's a little unfair ... to compare it to his work in HK. He is not a star here like he is in HK. He isn't exactly getting flooded with scripts I'm sure, or at least by scripts which don't suck ass (like KOD). It's like blaming a b-movie actor for not starring in blockbuster movies. I'm sure he'd love to but ya gotta play the hand you're dealt' ('Mikio4', AAF, 18 October 2001).

As this last quotation suggests, such debate over to what extent Li should be 'left alone' or chastised for 'choosing' to be the 'chaste hero all the time' extends to repeated comments on the importance of his agent. Clearly, this figure is deemed to be a crucial mediator in the transformation of Jet Li's star image to the US context. Indeed, the activities of the professional agent preoccupy many minds in both the affirmative and hostile strands of the pragmatic position, as these examples testify: 'Jet Li has the worst agent in the business' '('Red Elephant', GR, 17 October 2001); 'that scence where he picks up that motorcycle and tries to smash himself over the head did it for me, he should get a new agent though' ('SHATTERSTARNYC', GR, 17 October 2001); 'jet li definitely needs a new agent. i bet you 2 features from now, his movies will be straight to video. I think a major impedence on his american acting career is his limited english skills. It's not like they can cast him as a lead (or support) for projects like "shakespeare in love"' ('tim just tim', GR, 18 October 2001).

The issue of 'limited English skills' is, finally, another key term of the pragmatic position. To what extent is it desirable for an actor such as Jet Li to represent English-speaking Asian Americans? As 'sifuhotga' puts it (GR, 18 October 2001): 'did u see Jet on Leno the other night? ... it was painful watching him struggle through the interview. Leno was actually being very nice about the questions he wasn't getting answered, but the whole scene just reminded me of Long Duk Dong being questioned by his host family in Sixteen Candles. 'sigh''. To which 'd@m@n' responds (GR, 18 October 2001): 'ah come on! give him a break! he did alright I think. much better than the first time when he promoted lethal weapon 4'.

Awareness of other possibilities inherent in the performative nature of Jet Li's star image are only very rarely glimpsed. 'digininja' (AAF, 11 November 2001) writes of *The One* that 'the best part though was seeing mug shots of all the jet li's in other universes that got killed ... pimp jet li, womanly jet li, businessman jet li, funny stuff. muahaha'. This occasional focus on fantasy is sometimes collapsed with the preoccupation with the figure of the agent to create a synthesis, within an overall pragmatic position, of the hostile and affirmative tendencies: 'it is was jet li I would have requested, no, I would have DEMANDED a bootylicious scene with the ebony princess alliyah' ('shatterstarnyc', GR, 11 June 2001); 'I would have had that put in my contract if I was jet: 'MUST have bootylicious scene with aaliyah''' ('iron-monkey', GR, 11 June 2001).

Conclusion

These are only a few examples of a much wider and much more intricate electronic conversation. As Staiger (2001) argues, 'talk' does indeed happen after (and before and during) a movie show, and often in great quantity. Linguistic statements such as those presented in this chapter continue to process 'the text' around use values both personal and social. However, the point needs to be made that within such discursive networks, the star image functions in specific rhetorical ways – as a 'text' to be consumed, to be sure, but also as a form of cultural currency, or as the language through which community members talk to one another about matters of importance to them.

In the case of Asian American responses to Jet Li, a double consciousness is at work. While many discussants of his Hollywood roles exhibit a desire to debate the adequacy of his 'perfect' Chinese-ness, others foreground the limits and constraints of the performer's own working environment. 'Masculinity and moral integrity' are retained as key terms, but they undergo a transformation of meaning within this specific reception context. Furthermore, in many discussion threads, the conclusion reached is that the more successful Jet Li becomes in the USA, the more he needs to be interrogated by Asian American audiences. The implicit question behind all of the comments quoted in this chapter is this: do 'we' want to decide that Jet Li is an 'adequate' representation, or do 'we' want to insist that he is somehow 'not enough'?

Asian American Internet reception of other transnational Chinese movie stars will no doubt present slightly different variations on the significance of such questions and answers. After all, Jet Li, Jackie Chan, Joan Chen. Chow Yun-Fat and Michelle Yeoh do not all represent exactly the same social 'type'. As female Chinese star images, for example, Chen and Yeoh (or Maggie Cheung and Brigitte Lin) project very different life histories, personality traits and social values. As a result of these differences, diverse communities within Asian America itself will invest in a range of conflicting positions regarding the interest of their on- and off-screen lives.

Finally, it is important to remember that the kinds of response I have explored in this chapter are specific to Asian America and would doubtless not appear in quite the same form in other areas of Greater China, such as the mainland, Taiwan and Hong Kong. Li, Chen, Yeoh and all the rest will be made to mean something else in these different reception circumstances; they will circulate as another kind of cultural currency. One of the most exciting prospects for work on the production and reception of transnational cinema in the Greater China context, then, is the need to pluralise transnational stars such as these through focused and localised audience research. Star studies and cultural studies, as well as Asian studies and the study of political communication, can only benefit from further consideration of the fan talk generated around the rituals of film viewing in these diverse cultural spheres.

Notes

1   All quotations from websites in this chapter preserve original punctuation and spelling.
2   My choice of terminology here owes a lot to the work of Jun Xing, who talks about the 'advocacy network' that nurtures Asian American film activity. This network includes 'community-based organizations and non-profit media arts centers, such as Visual Communications in Los Angeles, Asian CineVision in New York, and the National Asian American Telecommunications Association (NAATA)' (Xing 1998: 177).
3   Significantly, this sense of pride in Asian masculinity is occasionally aligned with a comparison with African American masculinity – the two are widely perceived to be compensatory mechanisms to stand in lieu of the achievement of wider social power. For example, consider this comment on *Kiss of the Dragon* by 'Kiss of the Dragon DJ': 'With Jet Li being the albeit reluctant hero, he got a little bit further than Denzel [Washington] with Julia [Roberts] in *The Pelican Brief*' (AAF, 31 March 2002).

References

Appadurai, A. (1996) *Modernity at Large: Cultural Dimensions of Globalization*. Minneapolis: University of Minnesota Press.

Dyer, R. (1979) *Stars*. London: British Film Institute.

Fore, S. (1997) 'Jackie Chan and the cultural dynamics of global entertainment', in Sheldon Lu Hsiao-peng (ed.), *Transnational Chinese Cinemas: Identity, Nationhood, Gender*. Honolulu: University of Hawaii Press.

Gallagher, M. (1997) 'Masculinity in translation: Jackie Chan's transcultural star text', *Velvet Light Trap* 39: 23–41.

Hunt, L. (1999) 'Once upon a time in china: kung fu From Bruce Lee to Jet Li', *Framework: The Journal of Cinema and Media* 40 (April): 85–97.

Lee, R.G. (1999) *Orientals: Asian Americans in Popular Culture*. Philadelphia: Temple University Press.

Lu, S.H.-P. (ed.) (1997) *Transnational Chinese Cinemas: Identity, Nationhood, Gender*. Honolulu: University of Hawaii Press.

Morley, D. and Robins, K. (1995) *Spaces of Identity: Global Media, Electronic Landscapes and Cultural Boundaries*. London: Routledge.

Staiger, J. (2001) 'Writing the history of American film reception', in M. Stokes and R. Maltby (eds), *Hollywood Spectatorship: Changing Perceptions of Cinema Audiences*. London: British Film Institute.

Stringer, J. (2003) 'Scrambling Hollywood: Asian stars/Asian American star cultures', in T. Austin and M. Barker (eds), *Contemporary Hollywood Stardom*. London: Edward Arnold, forthcoming.

Wong, M. (1998) 'King Kong vs. Jet Li', *Giant Robot* 11 (summer): 30–1.

Xing Jun (1998) *Asian America Through the Lens: History, Representations and Identity*. Walnut Creek, Calif.: Alta Mira Press.

Yau, E.C.M. (ed.) (2001) *At Full Speed: Hong Kong Cinema in a Borderless World*. Minneapolis: University of Minnesota Press.

Zhang Yingjin (1998) 'Jet Li', in Yingjin Zhang and Zhiwei Xiao, *Encyclopedia of Chinese Film*. London: Routledge.

Conclusion

15 Greater China, globalisation and emancipation

Neil Renwick

Introduction

The object of this chapter is to explore the performative and discursive claims to legitimacy and authority underpinning the late modern state in Greater China in relation to the complex forces of societal rationalisation and globalisation. In particular, by drawing upon and developing further a largely Habermasian methodology, this conceptually focused study seeks to tease out the potential implications of these forces for fundamental individual and collective existential issues of identity, meaningfulness, self-transcendence and emancipation central to continued motivational support for the late modern state. The continuing centrality of the developmental state to Greater China and the sheer extent of change experienced by these societies over the past twenty years makes it a particularly interesting case study to explore these questions. Although the chapter addresses Greater China as a whole, the analysis focuses particularly upon China as the fulcrum of contemporary transition.[1]

Greater China

The following discussion is not primarily concerned with the continuing debate over the validity or otherwise of the concept of 'Greater China', as the genealogy and highly contested merits of the term are well elaborated elsewhere (Harding 1995: 8–34). Rather, the conceptual label is accepted here as a shorthand descriptor for a core entity comprising the People's Republic of China (China), the Republic of China (Taiwan), the Hong Kong Special Administrative Region (SAR) and Macau, and also Singapore, in economic and cultural terms. Greater China is a simultaneously experienced mass of centrifugal and centripetal dynamic processes, endogenously and exogenously derived perspectives, and normatively driven analytical ambitions reflecting variegated ambitions for political reunification.

Greater China is to be understood as a multidimensional experience that cannot be equated unconditionally with a geographical, economic, cultural or institutional singularity. Certainly, it is constituted by *spatial* and *temporal* associations. Here the notion of 'trans-border space' (Scholte 1997,

1999) – dissociation between territoriality and social relatedness – becomes interesting for the conceptualisation of Greater China. The distinguishing analytical referent is a discernible progressive supplementation and incremental eclipsing of 'cross-border' and 'open-border' relations through more extensive and intensive flows of money, goods and information, increasingly conducted through cybernetically ordered transmission belts. As Ngai-Ling Sum (1999: 129) has illustrated, these processes within 'trans-border space' compress 'spatial scales' and 'temporal horizons'. Such compression disturbs 'time–space governance', defined as 'the strategic networks of trans-border actors (both public and private) involved in coordinating and stabilising divergent trans-border modes of growth and their capacities to manage self-reflexively the material, social, discursive, and time–space dimensions of these modes of growth' (*ibid.*: 130).

To these spatial and temporal considerations of Greater China should be added an additional and *necessary* criterion of identity formation: that is, Greater China as a symbolic or semiologically charged, supraterritorial 'imagined community'. After Anderson (1991: 6), the point is that 'all communities ... are imagined. Communities are to be distinguished, not by their falsity/genuineness, but by the style in which they are imagined'. Geographical distance, ideologically imposed barriers, hyphenated national citizenship affiliation or generational outlook can intervene to restrict the closeness of such communal imagining, 'yet in the minds of each lives the image of their communion' (*ibid.*), and indeed absence may make the heart grow fonder. In this imagined sense, the wider Chinese diaspora of Southeast Asia and beyond also forms a constitutive part of Greater China, understood as 'a global Chinese culture' that involves 'increasing cultural interaction of people of Chinese descent, again across international boundaries' (Harding 1995: 20).

Globalisation

The established processes of identity formation or collective imagining associated with the territorially bounded and nationally defined state are clearly called into question by globalisation. For Scholte, the global relations of this 'fourth dimension of social space' (after longitudes, latitudes and altitudes) are 'place-less, distance-less, borderless interactions and interdependencies between persons' (1996: 44).

Critically, globalisation represents a series of significant challenges to established organisational and value systems. Held *et al.* usefully summarise the areas subject to challenge. These include spatio-temporal, organisational, conjunctional, diversity of modalities, reflexivity, contestation, regionalisation, Westernisation, territoriality, state forms and democratic governance (Held *et al.* 1999: 429–31). Globalisation is considered in this chapter as economic, socio-cultural and political, with these various cross-currents of challenge introduced at appropriate points in the discussion.

The first dimension examined here is economic globalisation. 'Globality' in this context can be seen in transactional flows; viscosity, velocity, and unevenness; and procedural normativity. Three factors contribute to an exponential growth in transactional flows: the interconnectedness of cross-border production, trade and capital networks; communications technologies, representing a qualitative and quantitative shift in the transmission belts of cross-border transactionalism; and transnational corporations as trans-border prime movers of the interconnectedness and principal beneficiaries of the new technologies. These corporations spur transnational flows through their intra-firm capital transfers; intra-firm vertical and horizontal production systems; and intra-firm trade, distribution and marketing networks. Global fluidity, speed and spread centre upon post-Fordist processes of flexible accumulation, greater mobility and accelerated speed of capital and production related to major centres of gravitational pull. The societal implications of these changes are focused upon the creation of 'anti-economies' grounded in 'social exclusion'. Procedural normativity builds through the development of open-border institutions and value-driven neo-liberal regimes.

Clearly, economic structures and agencies are inextricably intertwined with socio-cultural value systems, and the second major aspect of globality is that of cultural globalisation. For Stuart Hall, the economic and political forces of globalisation are weakening the nation-state construction of identity producing simultaneous moves towards the global and local. At the global level, identification is located within 'a new form of global mass culture ... dominated by the modern means of cultural production, dominated by the image which crosses and re-crosses linguistic frontiers much more rapidly and more easily, and which speaks across languages in a much more immediate way' (Hall 1991: 27). This mass culture is centred in the West (particularly the USA) and is characterised by 'a homogenising form of representation, enormously absorptive of things'. But this homogenisation is self-consciously neither absolute nor complete as it seeks to:

> recognise and absorb those differences within the larger, overarching framework of what is essentially an American conception of the world .... it is very powerfully located in the increasing and ongoing concentration of culture and other forms of capital. But it is now a form of capital that recognises that it can only ... rule through other local capitals, rule alongside and in partnership with other economic and political elites. It does not attempt to obliterate them; it operates through them. It has to hold the whole framework of globalisation in place and simultaneously police that system: it stage-manages independence within it, so to speak.
>
> (*ibid.*: 28)

Understood in this latter sense, then, cultural globalisation is about a simultaneously experienced constitutive homogenisation and heterogeneity, *dis*location and flux that corrodes the rigidities of modernity's identities and sources of existential meaning (Renwick 1996: 154–71). Jürgen Habermas (1994: 119) describes this experience as:

> the fantastic unbinding of cultures, forms of life, styles, and world perspectives that today no longer simply encounter each other, but mutually open up to one another, penetrate each other in the medium of mutual interpretation, mix with one another, enter into hybrid and creative relationships, and produce an overwhelming pluralism, a decentred, hence obscure multiplicity, indeed a chaos of linked but contingent, nearly indecipherable sounds and texts.

Just to confuse matters, then, globalisation is *also* about the 'disorganisation of capitalism' and its uneven or 'unbalanced development – the reach, penetration, intensity and implications of each of its economic, cultural or political forms – across the globe (Lash and Urry 1994). It is also about forces of globality coexisting, coalescing, diverging and confronting those of internationalism (Nicholson 1999: 23–34; Hirst and Thompson 1999).

This decentred, unevenly experienced, unstable condition generates impulses towards the local as well as the global – towards 'face-to-face communities that are knowable, that are locatable, one can give them a place' (Hall 1991: 35). The search for reconstituted places within which to relocate identity is inextricably tied to individual and collective disorientation within ever more complex societal conditions of late (or for some post-) modernity. Central to this condition is the steady emasculation of humanity through societal rationalisation, evident in the pervasive grip of 'techno-scientific consciousness' and everyday technocratic specialisation.

Such rationalisation detaches people from familiar individual and social ethical-moral parameters. Following Giddens (1992: 21), these complex forces of change 'sequester' experience whereby 'for many people, direct contact with events and situations which link the individual lifespan to broad issues of morality and finitude are rare and fleeting'. The degree to which life is felt to be meaningless should be comprehended in terms of 'a repression of moral questions which day-to-day life poses, but which are denied answers'. Giddens defines this experience of meaninglessness as 'existential isolation', by which he means 'a separation from the moral resources necessary to live a full and satisfying existence' rather than a separation of individuals from each other (*ibid.*: 22).

Globalisation raises critical questions regarding the status and role of the individual in relation to the key collectivised intersubjective realisations of society and state. This brings us to political globalisation. The greater societal complexity influenced by economic and cultural globalisation provokes a deeper questioning of the emancipatory trajectory of human progress in the discursive characterisations and self-avowed practices of the modern society and state. In particular, the foregoing issues of identity, societal complexity and rationalisation, 'sequestered experience' and 'existential isolation' within increased globality are central to contemporary challenges not only to the established *performative* bases upon which states in Greater China (as elsewhere) have claimed legitimacy and authority but also to their *discursive* claims.

The political issue here is the political management of socio-economic change and the dynamics of opportunities opened up for some and the costs experienced by others by processes of change. The unevenness of the economic and cultural impact of globalisation may adversely influence patterns of social exclusion. On the one hand, in circumstances of extreme transitional tension, globalisation may also contribute to challenges to the motivational and consequent political legitimacy to the state, leading to pathologies of violence, repression and 'defensive' national identities exhibiting nationalism, xenophobia or racism.

On the other hand, opportunities for renewed individual and collective identity and self-worth or meaningfulness may also be generated by globalisation. Thus, as Lash and Urry (1994: 3) argue, while there is 'increasing meaninglessness, homogenisation, abstraction, anomie and destruction of the subject', there is evidence of simultaneous processes at work that 'may open up possibilities for the recasting of meaning in work and in leisure, for the reconstitution of community and the particular, for the reconstruction of a transmogrified subjectivity, and for heterogenisation and complexity of space and of everyday life'.

Together, these three dimensions of globalisation are important for our comprehension of Greater China insofar as they raise useful analytical connections with issues that are at the heart of the following analysis. These issues include socially rationalised complexity; the 'transformative character of globalisation' (Scholte 1999: 14–15); processes of identity formation, social meaningfulness and emancipation; and critical performative and discursive legitimation/trans-border governance challenges facing Greater China's late modern states.

Issues of theory and method

The theoretical approach developed to explore these issues in this study begins with the writings of Jürgen Habermas and, following Axel Honneth, a reconstitution of Habermas's ideas of 'discursive democracy' and discursive ethics through Levinas's informed ideas of asymmetrical intersubjective relationships, and Charles Taylor's perspectives on recognition and 'misrecognition' (Honneth 1996: 289–323).

Habermas's long-term project has been heavily influenced by his personal identificatory location. He was socialised in the generational after-shadow of the Holocaust, so his work reflects a deep concern with the loss of freedom and the search for progressive legitimate bases for self- and collective realisation, equality within a renewed 'public sphere' free from repression, and the reconstitution of ethical-moral emancipatory concerns through discursive democracy. His upbringing within the context of a divided German condition of 'two states, one nation' finds expression in a recurrent thematic return to questions of individual and societal identity and meaningfulness. The problems of East Germany's 'bureaucratic socialism' crystallised Habermas's reconstruction of Weberian notions of societal rationalisation, state delegitimation, lost freedom and emptied meaning. Relatedly, Habermas's concerns regarding German reunification find resonance in his insights into the processes of societal transition – particularly the 'entry costs into a market economy' for a bureaucratic socialist state – and of democratisation.

Habermas's engagements with the complex societal processes of rationalisation and transition, state legitimacy crises, emancipatory aspirations, enhanced meaningfulness through expanded opportunities for the attainment of human potentials, and the possibilities for such transformative experiences to be realised through deliberative action in a public sphere free from duress together offer powerful conceptual insights for the explanation of change in contemporary Greater China.

What makes Habermas's contribution particularly interesting as an analytical starting point for the study of contemporary Greater China is that the PRC, and until relatively recently Taiwan, Hong Kong and Macau, have exhibited discursive and actual constructions of society and state understood as constitutive of a 'collective subject'. This collective subject, in turn, is understood as the agency for transcending individual limitations. Science and technology, encased in a positivistic discourse of 'instrumental' or 'purposive' rationality in which 'knowledge' is self-affirming, have formed the principal emancipatory mechanisms of collective and thus individual liberation from multiple and mutually reinforcing historical restraints. As the recent history of Greater China has demonstrated, the continued legitimacy of society and state grounded in this instrumental 'rationalisation of society' rests upon a capacity to meet collective needs. The 'complexification' of society restricts the ability of social institutions to perform their transcending function, undermining their legitimacy and opening new problematics regarding the relationship between collective and individual. This is particularly apposite given the post-1978 economic reform process ('market socialism') in mainland China, the political reforms in Taiwan since the mid-1980s, and the new governmental culture instituted in Hong Kong and Macau following their reversion to mainland China. When conjoined with the transformative potentialities of globalisation suggested above, additional complexities arise for the capacity of society and state to deliver collective and thus individual needs and reinforces questions of continued legitimacy.

Following from Habermas's critique of the crises in capitalist economy during the 1970s, however, the capitalist state itself has been subject to the challenge of legitimacy (Lechte 1994: 187). The capitalist state's capacity to determine and meet the needs of its citizenry effectively is subjected to the complexities derived from globalisation – not least its ability to raise revenues from globally footloose corporations in order to fund its social support programmes. The transmission of values via globalisation promotes and perhaps necessitates a greater emphasis upon the individual as the primary agency for the realisation of human potentials within a conception of the capitalist state that is itself flawed. This realisation propels to the forefront of debate the questions at the heart of Habermas's own vocational quest of how to avoid an intensification of social pathological forms and what can act as the basis for a better, and thus more rational, society directed towards, as Michael Pusey (1987: 14) puts it, 'collective needs rather than to arbitrary power'.

Habermas's 'strategy of critique' allows us to raise particular questions regarding Greater China. Is complexification making it more difficult for the established idea of the 'collective subject' and the state to retain legitimacy? Is 'society', including that of the PRC, moving under the twin (and related) pressures of domestic changes and globalisation towards an atomistic reality – one more consistent with the Anglo-American philosophical tradition of 'freedom from' than 'freedom to'? What does this mean for tendencies towards pathological forms on the one hand and Habermasian aspirations towards social betterment through a revivified social rationality on the other?

These questions take us to the core of Habermas's political theorising and to his conception of a more ethically sound and politically progressive basis for intersubjective understanding. His notion of discursive democracy is of a public sphere wherein discussion takes place at a multiplicity of discursive sites free from undue constraint and pathological distortion. The intersubjective basis for these lies in a communicative competence characterised by intersubjective equality. Yet Habermas's emphasis on equality leaves his approach exposed at this point. Given the continuing structural pathologies of financial and political concentrations contextually distorting intersubjective relationships in the late modern state, equality *per se* is likely to be insufficient for a restored belief in the capacity for self-transformation, revived existential meaningfulness, motivational renewal and a resuscitation of the emancipatory project.

Here Levinas's concern with knowledge, ethics and morality, intersubjectivity, 'the order of sameness' and 'alterity' offer a theoretical way forward. Levinas's writings concentrate upon the need for greater reflexivity regarding the social and, in his view, consequently more moral conditions governing the constitution and utility of knowledge in pursuit of 'the good' rather than primarily 'the true'. Particularly, Levinas argued that the collapse of faith in positivist versions of universal truth necessitated a reconstitution of 'the good' as a source of human meaningfulness. But how to define 'the good' without falling into the trap of merely repeating the folly of instrumentalised positivist truth claims? Levinas's answer was to stress the idea of 'alterity'. This is 'the alterity of the face, which is not a difference, not a series, but strangeness – strangeness which cannot be suppressed, which means that it is my obligation that cannot be effaced (Wright *et al.* 1988: 179). He argued that 'In ethics, the other's right to exist has primacy over my own' (Levinas and Kearney 1986: 24). This he justified on the grounds that 'the self cannot survive by itself alone, cannot find meaning within its own being-in-the-world, within the ontology of sameness' (*ibid.*). Such alterity is necessarily one in which 'man's relationship with the other is better as difference than as unity: society is better than fusion' (*ibid.*: 22). This, then, is intersubjectivity understood as a prior asymmetrical obligation towards, and transcendent reaching out to, the face of the other beyond one's own selfhood.

This asymmetrical (or 'dissymmetrical' as Levinas terms it) obligation would seem to be at odds with the ideas of equal treatment central to modernity's codified notions of justice and law (Honneth 1996: 289–323). For Levinas, justice is founded upon ethics. Justice is tethered to the political and institutional realm and the compromises necessarily required in the moral choices between competing and conflicting duties of care within a framework of law and equal treatment and responsibility. Ethics, understood as asymmetrical obligation and responsibility grounded in 'alterity' and 'the good', provides an unbounded 'violence in justice'. Here 'justice is always a justice which desires a better justice' (Wright *et al.* 1988: 177), and without this ethical relationship to the other, justice in the former sense of equal treatment or in the sense of 'solidarity', 'the moral principle of reciprocal concern' (Honneth 1996: 318), is unsustainable. But, as Levinas acknowledges, the two forms of justice conflict (although these constitute a productive tension in Derrida's reformulation; see Honneth 1995: 314–15). Habermas's conceptualisation of law in his later writings dissects it into two dimensions in tension with each other. Law can be understood as 'administrative power' and an instrument of social control. But, significantly for the issue of justice, Habermas also sees law in a liberal state as embodying a normative moral quality of 'communicative power' in promoting basic political rights, 'solidarity' and a new basis for societal legitimation (White 1996: 11).

But this still leaves us with the question of justice embedded in a discursive democracy predicated upon the primacy of equal treatment. Georgia Warnke points out that this is also a 'top down' and 'neutral' conceptualisation (1995: 133), and she poses the critical question of what if 'one's conception of the good requires more from the society than neutrality? Suppose the survival of one's culture requires a conception of a collective right to cultural survival as opposed to the individual rights secured by liberal principles?' (*ibid.*) Warnke's incisive study of Habermasian principles, liberal principles and cultural values appropriately draws upon the insights into recognition to be found in the writings of Quebecois philosopher Charles Taylor. Importantly for the study below, Taylor's studies demonstrate a convincing argument whereby asymmetrical/'dissymmetrical' moral orientations and a normatively conceived sense of justice can be evoked legitimately in relation to universalised precepts of equal treatment in a liberal or liberalising state.

The central focus is the condition of the late modern state. Although Habermas's project has been directed primarily towards a better understanding of the critical challenges being faced by modernity's liberal capitalist state, he has also offered insights into 'bureaucratic socialist states' and the challenges incurred in transition from command economies to market economies. Both liberal capitalist and bureaucratic socialist states are twin versions of modernist-driven notions of the state and are subject to late modernist challenges to the performative and discursive claims to legitimacy and authority. In the context of Greater China, what is of interest here are the implications for the 'truth claims' of the state arising from the PRC's move towards 'market socialism'; Taiwan's socio-economic and political liberalisation; and the reversion of Hong Kong and Macau to PRC governance. These transitional societies are raising major challenges to the 'central organising principles' underpinning relationships between state and society.

The legitimating 'truth claims' of the late modern state are intimately bound to societal 'rationalisation'. This is experienced in two mutually reinforcing experiences:

1   The extensification and intensification of the complexity of late modern societies and the late modern state evidenced by the distorting media of a suffocating centralised state; excessive financial and productive concentrations; and a pervasive techno-scientific specialisation, i.e. rationalisation in everyday living. This carries consequences for (1) modernity's pathologies – 'an unbalanced development of its potential' (White 1995: 8); (2) individual and collective meaningfulness and self-transformations; and (3) 'sequestered experience' and 'existential isolation'.

2   (Truth claims) 'techno-scientific consciousness' or 'scientism' – knowledge formations and discursive power. Characteristic of 'scientism' in its positivistic or 'instrumental' form of reason is a consequential reduction of 'ends' to 'means'; of ethical-moral concerns to technical problems open to technocratic resolution.

For the societies of Greater China, techno-scientific progress has become a central discursive mantra of state development binding self-transformations to the technocratic resolution of problems, discourse and performance being inextricably entwined with the destiny of state and society, deemed synonymous. Yet pathological distortions in these societies – oppressive state-centrism, high concentrations of wealth and power, and deliberative repression – have formed corrosive challenges to performative and discursive 'truth claims'; subjective and intersubjective loss of identificatory meaning, worth and ethical-moral value; and a loss of motivational support and challenges to the legitimacy of the state.

Such issues of meaningfulness and motivation require an understanding of subjectivity, intersubjectivity, and symmetrical and asymmetrical recognition. Habermas is engaged with the German philosophical tradition, with its interest in society wherein the individual is an integral part of the pre-eminent collective whole and is 'a transcendental history-making subject'. The collective psychology of the people is understood 'as a collective subject, and in the stronger Hegelian version, as a spiritual and cultural entity that transcends the individual' (Pusey 1987: 16). This is clearly so different from philosophical traditions identifying the individual as the primary locus of agency and society merely 'an aggregation of individuals each pursuing his or her own 'private' benefit' and which reject 'all ontologically grounded concepts of Society that transcend the individual' (*ibid.*). For the German tradition, then, 'Society is more naturally conceived as a collective embodiment of knowledge, of reason, and of the identity of a people. Social institutions are more readily understood as the achievements of a collective "will and consciousness"'. Society and state each offer 'positive and rational potentialities'. As Pusey describes it, 'In different ways each is seen as a medium through which individuals may rationally transcend the arbitrary limitations of individual and private life and together realise their larger purposes' (*ibid.*: 17).

Habermas's writings, with their normative emphasis upon the progressive and emancipatory thrust of reason, understood in what Habermas regards as the original hermeneutic, interpretative sense of the European Enlightenment; their concern with the relationship between the social or collective world – the 'self-regulating system whose imperatives override the consciousness of the members integrated into them' – and the 'lifeworld' (*Lebenswelt*) – the world of consciousness, identity formation and communicative action; their problematisation of 'society' and of 'state' legitimation; and their interest in establishing an ethical basis for communicative interaction stand as a return to the German tradition and as a further development of it (Lechte 1994: 186–91). For Habermas, the notion of discursive democracy conveys a normative character grounded in empowerment, emancipation, transition and deliberative freedom free from repression in a genuine 'public sphere' facilitating a capacity for personal and societal learning and self-realisation through communicative action.

Globalisation and Greater China

Economic globalisation

Central to our understanding of Greater China and economic globalisation are processes of greater 'openness and integration' (Ruggiero 1997: 1) within

Greater China and between Greater China and the wider globalising economy. The core of the economic relationships of Greater China lies in a pattern of synergistic interdependencies in production networks, investment flows and trade exchanges.

Taiwan has recorded significant and sustained levels of growth in gross domestic product (GDP), GDP *per capita*, merchandise exports, and outward foreign direct investment (OFDI). Much of its merchandise exports and OFDI go to Asia, especially China through Hong Kong. Hong Kong's growth has been sustained on the basis of both merchandise exports and imports and provision of commercial services. Hong Kong has significantly benefited from acting as a 'third country' re-export corridor for Taiwanese capital, goods and firms entering China and for repatriated earnings to Taiwan. Hong Kong also acts as an entrepôt for manufactured goods from China (mainly the Pearl River delta, and Guangdong and Fujian provinces) to global markets. China's spectacular post-1978 economic growth is by now exhaustively documented. Without any doubt, China represents the linchpin of economic growth and deepening interconnectedness in Greater China. It has built its economic renaissance through substantial inward foreign direct investment (IFDI, much of this from Hong Kong and Taiwan), the relocation of labour-intensive factories (again many from Hong Kong and Taiwan) largely for preferential tariff 'processing trade' production,[2] and export-led growth.

These dynamic synergistic forces of growth have established a Greater China economic centre of gravity within wider networks and flows of global interconnectedness. To demonstrate this, the following brief review adopts the three categories of economic and business globalisation detailed above, namely *transactional flows*; *viscosity, velocity, and unevenness*; and *procedural normativity*.

Transactional flows

Beginning with *transactional flows*, we need to consider three factors: (1) the interconnectedness of cross-border production, trade and capital networks; (2) the revolution in communications; and (3) transnationalised business.

The interconnectedness of cross-border production networks in Greater China can be evidenced by three factors: the relocation of labour-intensive manufacturing firms from Hong Kong and Taiwan to the PRC, the associated industrial structural adjustment in Hong Kong and Taiwan to high-technology, high added-value knowledge-intensive industry; and a significant shift in all three economies towards service sector pre-eminence. Evidence of Taiwan's industrial redeployment to China indicates that by 1998, Taiwanese investors had committed US$40 billion to over 40,000 business enterprises employing over 10 million people and forming a critical contributing factor to China's tax base (Tucker 2000: 260; Chiu 2000: 139; *Far East Economic Review*, 5 July 2001: 60–1). Further evidence for this is provided by the composition of trade. A significant portion of imports into China from Hong Kong and Taiwan is accounted for by machinery, transport equipment and industrial materials, supplemented in the case of Taiwan by investments in electronic and electrical appliances, base metals and plastic products (MOEA 2001). Much of this Taiwanese activity was located in Jiangsu and Guangdong. Structural adjustment towards service-oriented economies in all three countries can be seen in the 85 percent share of GDP accounted for by services in Hong Kong, 64 percent in Taiwan and 50 percent in China (CIA 2000).

Greater China's economic interconnectedness represents a significant centre of gravity within the wider globalising economy. For Hong Kong, China is its largest import and second largest (after the USA) export partner, accounting for 30 percent of domestic exports and 43 percent of imports in 2000. Re-exports are now the lifeblood of its trading position, accounting for 89 percent of all its exports. Asia-Pacific Economic Cooperation (APEC) countries receive 78 percent of these exports; China accounts for 35 percent, the USA for 22.3 percent and Japan for another 6 percent (GOHK 2001). Asia accounts for 52 percent of Taiwan's exports, with 21 percent to Hong Kong (with over half being re-export goods for China) and 11 percent to Japan; 56 percent of Taiwan's imports originate in Asia, with Japan supplying 28 percent). China's merchandise trade position reflects a significant relocation of Hong Kong and Taiwanese manufacturing and as a prominent 'processing trade' country. China's total export growth from 1990 to 1999 was 135 percent, with processing trade accounting for 56.9 percent or US$104.6 billion (WTO 2000).

Global trading blocs form significant building blocks in the globalising economy, and flows of Greater China's trade represent important markers to its global reach. For example, the North America Free Trade Association attracts 31 percent of Macau's exports and provides 11 percent of imports, and 26 percent of Taiwan's exports and 18 percent of imports. Obviously critical here is the role of the USA. The USA is a vital market for Greater China's goods, accounting for over 22 percent of Hong Kong re-exports, 22 percent of Chinese exports, 48 percent of exports from Macau, and 25 percent of Taiwanese exports. The EU receives 15 percent of Hong Kong's re-exports (again largely from China), 11 percent of Taiwanese exports and 11 per cent of Macau's exports.

Vital to the growth in global merchandise trade is the lubricating role of an increasingly globalised trade in commercial services. In Greater China, it is Hong Kong that is the principal player. Hong Kong recorded over 20 percent annual growth in commercial service trade in the early to mid-1990s (WTO 1995: 11–12), with exports of US$35 billion and imports of $22 billion in 1999. But China is catching up, recording exports of US$27 billion and imports of $32 billion in 1999. Taiwan, with a more restrictive regulatory regime, still recorded significant commercial services trading in 1999, with exports of US$15 billion and imports of $23 billion.

Clearly, foreign direct investment (FDI) represents the other vital lubricant of economic interconnectedness within Greater China and between Greater China and the globalising economy. In terms of the total stock of FDI held by the Greater China economies, China is far and away the strongest performer, attracting a major inflow of foreign investment from the 1980s, amounting to almost 19 percent of IFDI in developing countries by the mid-1990s. Singapore accounts for another 8 percent and Hong Kong for over 3 percent.

The top four developing countries for OFDI are Hong Kong, Taiwan, China and Singapore. In terms of OFDI, 33 percent of Hong Kong's investments go to the USA, but 66 percent go to East, Southeast and South Asia. Of this Asian investment, a substantial portion is directed towards the neighbouring Chinese provinces, particularly Guangdong. A major share of this latter investment in China originates from Taiwanese sources and is rerouted via Hong Kong.

The overall significance of IFDI is magnified for developing countries, and this is particularly accurate for Greater China economies, with IFDI accounting for 73 percent of GDP for Singapore, 21 percent for Hong Kong and 18 percent for China. Taiwan, with its concern for possible security implications, is the exception, with IFDI accounting for only 6.6 percent of GDP. Estimates of 2001 IFDI levels anticipate a 13 percent rise to US$44 billion in inward flows to China and US$4.4 billion for Taiwan (*Far East Economic Review*, 1 February 2001: 48–50).

The communications revolution has spurred a qualitative and quantitative shift in the character of the transmission belts of cross-border transactionalism. The emergence of the Internet and the mobile phone are of particular significance. In 2000, there were 6.4 million Internet users in Taiwan (31 percent of the population), 1.85 million in Hong Kong (26 percent of the population), 40,000 in Macau (9 percent of the population) and 12.3 million in China (0.97 percent of the population). Of these, 5 million users in China, 610,000 in Hong Kong and 2.6 million in Taiwan access the Internet from work (iamasia, June 2000 and July 2000).

While the present level of Internet use is relatively low in international terms, a rapid rate of increase and the potential for growth excites great expectations (Nua Internet Surveys 2000; China Internet Information Centre 2000a, 2000b). In 1992, there were only 250 Internet users in China, so the increase to over 15 million by 2001 represents a phenomenal rate of growth (*Far East Economic Review*, 1 February 2001: 46–7). The PRC government is facilitating internal inter-city interconnectedness with a series of investments in information technology infrastructural projects and in Chinese e-commerce enterprises by external investors. Access potential may also increase rapidly with the advent of Internet-accessible PCs, new Internet set-top boxes available to China's 300 million televisions, and especially the potential development of Internet-connected mobile phones. With 60 million mobile phone subscribers currently in China, expected by some observers to rise to 200 million by 2010, a rapid and substantial expansion of Internet access is likely (Hiscock 2000: 4). However, as is well reported, the extent to which the Internet business potential is realised in China, particularly with respect to trans-border transactionalism, will depend upon a relaxation of government restrictions, which currently appears unlikely in the short term given recent police raids on and prosecutions of cybercafes (*The Times*, 28 January 2000: 21; *Wall Street Journal*, 3 October 2000).

Transnational businesses are the prime movers of trans-border transactional flows and the principal beneficiaries of the communications revolution. These features are particularly evident in the degree of intra-firm capital flows, vertical and horizontal production systems, trade, distribution and marketing. Large transnational corporations (TNCs) are well represented in Greater China, including Microsoft, McDonald's, IBM and General Motors (GM) (*Far East Economic Review*, 28 December 2000&–4 January 2001: 46–89). These corporations, global in reach, have started to move into less obvious parts of Greater China to establish operations: for example, GM's recent decision to establish a manufacturing base in China's impoverished Guangxi province (*Far East Economic Review*, 1 February 2001: 42).

However, the character of transnationalised business in Greater China is distinct from that of TNCs from North America, Western Europe or Japan. Transnational businesses in Greater China tend to be small or medium in size, to be single-sector oriented and to possess familial decision-making structures and processes, ownership patterns and institutional organisation. While acknowledging the potential for caricature here, the essence of the enterprise culture within Greater China is to be found in networks of personal and family connections and obligations (*guanxi*) embedded in the historically and culturally grounded worldwide Chinese diaspora. Given the intra-regional character of trade and investment and trans-border transactions noted above, the circulation of capital, production, distribution and marketing is sited deep within these distinctive Chinese 'networks of relationships' (Dicken 1999: 201). Globalisation is also influencing the corporate behaviour of these enterprises, with mergers and acquisitions becoming ever more evident in Greater China (*Far East Economic Review*, 7 June 2001: 46–7).

Viscosity, velocity and unevenness

Greater China clearly experienced a dramatically increased intensity in the circulation of goods and capital during the 1990s. Here the focus is on post-Fordist flexible accumulation (Harvey 1990), with circulation creating both splintering (a *dis*location of the 'inter-national' by a 'global' division of labour) and agglomeration (centres of gravitational pull). The transnationalisation of production and subcontracting networks across Greater China noted above is restructuring labour according to global market imperatives.

The emergence of megacities, the network 'hubs' of the global economy located within urban industrial/financial 'corridors' such as Taipei–Hong Kong–Guangzhou–Shanghai or Fujian–Okinawa–Taipei representing high-density gravitational centres, consolidates patterns of uneven globalisation within Greater China. The rapid growth of Internet use in Greater China facilitates the speed and intensity of transactions through these corridors (*Far East Economic Review* 4 March 1999: 11). In the fastest-growing Internet system in Greater China, that of China, 67 percent of use in 1999 was for technology-related information and 45 percent for business information (*Far East Economic Review*, 4 March 1999: 10–14).

However, our concern here is directed towards the unevenness of the globalisation experience, in particular the emergence of 'anti-economies' grounded in 'social exclusion': poverty distribution and the widening gap between rich and poor such as that experienced by China, with 11.5 percent or 106 million of the rural population still in absolute poverty and the majority of these living in the western provinces (World Bank Group 2000f). Uneven economic growth and social development is also increasingly associated with Internet access in an economy shifting towards 'knowledge' industries. The 'digital divide' is evident in the geographical distribution of Internet use. In 1999, Only 6 percent of China's Internet users were located in the western provinces, and 45 percent of eastern provincial users were located in Beijing (25 percent), Guangdong (12 percent) and Shanghai (6 percent) (*Far East Economic Review*, 4 March 1999: 12). Part of the problem is clearly infrastructural (being tackled by high levels of state investment in IT) and part linguistic. The Internet's global universalism has rested upon English 'domains', thereby excluding many people in Greater China not conversant with English. Although this is being challenged by East Asian consortia working towards a multilingual web, there is still some way to go before this is realised (*Far East Economic Review*, 22 February 2001: 38–40).

Procedural normativity

If we turn to what I term *procedural normativity* – open-border economic institutional and the development of value-driven neo-liberal regimes – then conventional wisdom holds that East Asia is in the process of being integrated into a global neo-liberal economic regime. There is much to this argument. Globalisation in this sense is cloaked in the guise of the World Trade Organisation (WTO), the International Monetary Fund, the APEC forum and associated organisations such as the Pacific Economic Cooperation Council. Overlapping memberships simply serve to reinforce a continuing process of opening up economies to freer market forces. APEC's agreement to work towards establishment of an APEC free trade area is illustrative of such momentum. With respect to our concern with Greater China, the admission of China into the WTO represents a most potent symbol of the apparent universalisation of economic globalisation and of the neo-liberal values that lie at its heart. In particular, as a rule-oriented organisation dedicated to non-discriminatory multilateral trade cooperation, membership carries with it the obligation for governments to adapt or change national trade regulations to the rules of the WTO. Such adaptation is necessarily not exclusive in nature, as trade policies and regulations cannot be isolated from those relating to fiscal policy, investment, employment and industry. Indeed, adaptation may carry (as it clearly does in the case of China) significant implications for the very character of the national political culture itself. As Higgott has pointed out, the experience of the Asian financial crisis illustrates resistance to such spill-over. From this perspective, this was indicative of a deeper contestation over the pervasiveness of the neo-liberal economic order and a useful corrective to universalising assumptions about neo-liberal economics and the passing of the East Asian developmental state (Higgott 2000: 254–63; Higgott and Rhodes 2000: 1–19). However, with Habermas's warning that the late modern state can turn to repression rather than democracy when faced with a challenge to its legitimacy in mind, governmental attempts to return the genie to the bottle by quarantining the political culture from the repercussions of WTO membership may elicit authoritarian suppression of the socio-political discursive space.

Socio-cultural globalisation

The foregoing analysis has illustrated the extent of regional economic interconnectedness. This economic activity has established significant rates of growth and rising levels of *per capita* income (UNDP 2000). This has obvious significance for the indices of poverty and particularly basic needs. Available evidence indicates that Greater China has made significant progress on all of the basic, health and education needs on demographic indices and, to some extent, on environmental indices (UNDP 2000). However, the implications of fundamental economic change for socio-cultural conditions are clearly profound, with potential consequences for motivation/legitimation crises in Greater China. The concern here is with the emergence of 'anti-economies' or sites/spaces of social resistance grounded in social exclusion.

Again, China is the principal focus of attention. Double-digit growth rates, rising GDP *per capita*, expanding exports and rising capital imports, massive urban regeneration and improved health and education provision stand testament to 'open door' economic development (UNDP 2000). However, looking beyond these indices, there are deeper socio-cultural issues and implications. The penetration of China by TNCs (as in Taiwan and Hong Kong) has been accompanied by the entry of transnational subcontractors. These latter enterprises then establish supply links to local subcontractors. These small and medium-sized enterprises may be 'green field' operations, but many in China involve mergers and particularly acquisitions of uncompetitive state-owned enterprises suffering from the loss of state subsidies. These transnational networks can pass on the costs of global economic competition or downturn to local subcontractors, with adverse consequences for employment, wages, health and safety, rights of association and gender abuse (Greenfield 1997). Moreover, the mediated gap between the large transnational and the local supply network underlines the 'footloose' capability of these transnational businesses.

The facilitation of these 'glocalisation' links through the alignment of China's industrial restructuring policies with those of the international neoliberal order is increasing disparities in economic growth and spatial poverty traps between the coastal/southern provinces and those of central and western China (Jalan and Ravallion 1997). These are spurring mass migration, with consequent rural depopulation, an ageing demographic profile and land degradation, and urban employment, housing, health and environmental pressures, creating a young, educated, urbanised technocratic *nouveau riche*.

Additional signs of social differentiation can be seen in a generational 'digital divide' evident in Internet use, with 52 percent of China's Internet users in 1999 under 25 years of age (*Far East Economic Review*, 4 March 1999: 12). The rural/urban, north/south and east/west, rich/poor, employed/unemployed, male/female, old/young divisions are creating identity gaps that are unsustainable in the absence of a legitimating 'central organising principle' or authoritative discourse and carry the seeds of motivational crisis. While the government has made periodic use of anti-'spiritual' or 'cultural' pollution campaigns against debased Western materialism and consumerism over the years, it is a campaign that cannot be won. The increasing numbers of Chinese travelling overseas for tourism or study, increasing contact with foreign visitors to China, and the arrival of English soccer stores, McDonald's, Western films, *Nike* fashion, German cars, and music such 'hip-hop' from New York's Bronx are contributing to a irreversible cultural transformation grounded in a shared assertion of freedom of expression among the affluent sections of China's youth in cities such as Shanghai (*Far East Economic Review*, 22 February 2001: 64–6).

The point here is that public aspirations are rising in China, and periodic surveys reinforce this with respect to the urbanites of Beijing, Shanghai and Guangzhou. There is caution regarding China's economic development but a perception of an improvement in the overall quality of life. While nonmaterial hopes for happy relationships and health predominate, material aspirations focus upon housing, education and prestige cars (*Far East Economic Review*, 4 March 1999: 72–6). To fulfil these aspirations requires political management, and for many in China, transition has lessened rather than increased the prospect of realising their potential and aspirations.

Political/ideational globalisation

Is globalisation merely Westernisation and this, in turn, merely Americanisation? Does Greater China's engagement with globalisation carry ideational consequences for the respective political cultures? Certainly, globalisation carries with it a range of core values embedded in Western notions of civil society: freedoms of expression and association, equality of treatment under the law, equality of opportunity, full political participation of citizens, and a minimal state role in society. These values are central to the political cultures of Western Europe and North America and underpin membership of the world's major multilateral political and economic institutional order. Economic, cultural and political globalisations provide powerful transmission belts that are simultaneously formal and informal, conscious and unconscious, direct and indirect.

While seeking to avoid caricature, the essence of authoritarian rule may be said to rest with the perceived need to maintain ultimate control over society and its development. Authoritarian leaders may see economic globalisation as a potential means of shoring up their diminishing legitimacy through economic and social rewards to the people, but it also evident that ideational globalisation ultimately threatens both the rationale and practice of control by opening up new identificatory spaces beyond the established control of the state. The Falun Gong, cybercafes, Christian adherents and Uigur nationalist separatists all in their own distinctive ways represent different faces of this ideational challenge of political polycentrism (*Far East Economic Review*, 22 February 2001: 32; *The Sunday Times*, 10 December 2000: 23).

Knowledge and the free flow of information are the lifeblood of the late modern society and discursive democracy. One must distinguish between form and substance. In Hong Kong, the provisions of the Basic Law enshrine freedoms of speech and association and access to government. Yet informal and by now well-honed instincts for self-censorship belie the muted formal application of government regulation. But in China, new Internet laws, police raids on Internet cafes and the imposition of severe prison sentences on transgressors, continued censorship of the media/press (both formal and self-censorship), restricted access to foreign satellite television and radio broadcasts, the closed penal system and large-scale state executions, a sizeable army of informants and secret police, and an opaque legal system reflect a continuing state ambition to retain control over the flow of information and knowledge, deploying the loosely defined catch-all term 'state secrets' to rationalise the policing of knowledge flows and access to them, and ultimately controlling public discourse.

In China, the government has sought to fill the void of legitimacy with nationalism ('patriotism') as the basis for a new inclusive discourse. The trumpeting of the reversion of Hong Kong and Macau, the failure to win the 2000 Olympic Games, the protracted delays in China's accession to the WTO, continued international criticism of human rights practices, and the state-sanctioned public protests over NATO's bombing of the Chinese embassy in Belgrade in 1999 all stand testament to raised nationalist discourse in China. The decision 13 July 2001 by the International Olympic Committee to award the 2008 Olympic Games to Beijing may give rise to the so-called 'Olympics effect'. Critically, the decision offers the recognition and acknowledgement that China's leaders have craved as validation for the reform path they have pursued. External scrutiny and popular engagement with the wider world may accelerate the process of political emancipation and may inject a significant level of global capital into the host economy from TNCs. However, a major test of change may be whether there is a pre-Games roundup of 'hooligans' and tolerance of peaceful demonstrations before, during and after the Olympians have departed.

Towards discursive democracies in Greater China?

For Higgott and Rhodes (2000: 16), 'there is still no substitute for the state as the repository of sovereignty and rule-making and as provider of national security. It is also the socialiser of risk in the last resort and the orchestrator of coordinated policy responses to the challenges thrown up by the processes of globalisation'. But, what if the orchestrator has lost the ability to offer practical leadership when faced with greater societal complexity and a relocation of decisive decision-making power beyond its sovereign realm? Or, perhaps more crucially, what if the state is perceived by its citizenry to have lost the necessary credibility, legitimacy and authority to act as the socialiser of risk and orchestrator of policy? Faced with a degree of socio-economic and political complexity derived from globalisation, the practical exercise of political sovereignty is fundamentally undermined and a legitimation crisis is either created or an existing crisis intensified.

Taiwan has sought successfully to address this potentiality through processes of economic and socio-political liberalisation. China has yet to confront this issue, and the jury is still out on the capacity of the Chinese state, albeit one in transition, to follow the path of discursive democracy. This choice of this path depends upon recognition by the ruling elite that there are opportunities as well as costs in the process of change. This, in turn, depends on tackling issues of social justice or poverty arising from indigenous change and from the spaces of engagement between indigenous change and the complex forces of globalisation. Central to discursive democracy is communicative action. Communicative action is, in Habermas's theory, action that 'relies on a cooperative process of interpretation in which participants relate simultaneously to something in the objective, the social, and the subjective worlds, even when they thematically stress only one of the three components of their utterances (Habermas 1981/1989: 333). Such utterances, when made free from constraint, offer the potential for recognition rather than misrecognition, a reconstitution of identity and meaning, and for self-realisation of the potential by individual and collectivity alike.

Peter Harris's penetrating short portrait of the 'aimless' Chinese state takes us closer to an understanding of the Chinese state in a context of fundamental societal transformation:

> It is a society struggling to restore half-forgotten loyalties and try new forms of association as it emerges from the rubble of the Mao era, and from the corporatist straitjacket of the Deng transition – a cluster of communities with common interests coming to terms with the loss of moral authority of the state, corrupt in both theory and practice. All these trends are depriving the state of its *telos*, its purposes, and moving it inch by inch in the direction of a state as *societas*. Like the other shore of a wide river, the aimless state in China is still out of reach; but its contours can be made out in the distance.
>
> (Harris 2001: 109)

But the present is still dominated by a Chinese state with specific 'aims', the interests of which are synonymous with those of the Communist Party. The maintenance of power is to be attained through the rejuvenation of the economy through internationalisation, a consequential easing of the popular mood through greater provision of social goods and a redefined national consciousness grounded in popular nationalism. The danger is that the state finds itself adrift, unable to control the forces it has unleashed, and unable to command the confidence of a distanced citizenry. This scenario of legitimation and motivational/existential crisis presents a sharp choice for government with consequences for Greater China as a whole. On the one hand, there could be a genuine governmental shift towards discursive democracy and communicative action and, on the other, desperate and ultimately destructive authoritarian attempts to retain control. The key to what may happen lies with the changeover to the next generation of leaders, due in 2002. Much attention has been directed towards Hu Jintao. Hu, a Politburo member since 1992, state vice-president and vice-chairman of the Central Military Commission, has long been regarded as Jiang Zemin's heir apparent (*Far East Economic Review*, 22 February 2001: 17–20). Hu is likely to tolerate a steady expansion in the freedom of expression within China, but only within a continued tight party/state framework of control while overseeing the structural adjustments required under WTO membership conditions. This amounts to a steady-as-she-goes gradualist approach. However, the dynamics of transformation may not offer the Chinese state the time and capability to sustain this precarious balancing act between rapid and fundamental economic reform and socio-political control. As this chapter has argued, the ultimate challenge facing the next party chairman and state president is to take China towards a genuine discursive democracy. On this may turn the future of Greater China in the twenty-first century.

Notes

1 The argument in this chapter is also to be found in the author's study 'Critical security and civil society in Northeast Asia: problems and prospects', an unpublished paper presented at the ISA Annual Convention, Los Angeles, March 2000, and in Renwick (2002).

2 Defined by the WTO (2000) as countries that have 'modified their import regime by granting, under certain conditions, duty-free access to those imports which are bound for the processing and assembling of goods destined for exports. This preferential tariff treatment was initially limited to trade that went through specific areas (e.g. the Special Economic Zones of China ...) but often extended thereafter to companies located outside these specifically designated areas'.

References

Anderson, B. (1991) *Imagined Communities: Reflections on the Origin and Spread of Nationalism*. London: Verso.

Ash, R.F. and Kueh, Y.Y. (1995) 'Economic integration within Greater China: trade and investment flows between China, Hong Kong and Taiwan', in D. Shambaugh (ed.), *Greater China: The Next Superpower?* Oxford: Clarendon Press.

Central Intelligence Agency (CIA) (2000) *The World Factbook 2000* (http:// www. odci.gov/cia/publications/factbook/geos/ch.html).

China Internet Information Centre (2000a) 'Investigation on Internet development in China' (http://www.cnnic.net.cn/develst/e-about.shtml).

—— (2000b) 'Semiannual survey report On Internet development in China' (http:// www.cnnic.net.cn/develst/e-cnnic2000.shtml).

Chiu, L.-I.C. (2000) 'Taiwan's economic influence: implications for resolving political tensions', in G.W. Gong (ed.), *Taiwan Strait Dilemmas: China–Taiwan–U.S. Policies in the New Century*. Washington: Center for Strategic and International Studies.

Cohen, R.A. (ed.) (1986) *Face to Face with Levinas*. Albany: State University of New York Press.

Davis, C. (1996) *Levinas: An Introduction.*Cambridge: Polity Press.

Dicken, P. (1999) *Global Shift: [Transforming the World Economy]*, 3rd edition. London: Paul Chapman.

Giddens, A. (1992) 'Modernity and self-identity: self and society in the late modern age', in Frascina and Harris (eds), *Art in Modern Culture: An Anthology of Critical Texts*. London: Phaidon/Open University.

Government of Hong Kong (2001) 'External trade statistics' (http://www. info.gov.hk /censtatd/eng/hkinf/ext_trade/trade1.htm).

—— (2001) 'Trade by main country/territory' (http://www.info.gov.hk/censtatd/ eng/hkinf/ext_trade/trade4.htm).

Greenfield, G. (1997) 'Transnational capital and workers in China' (http://www. amrc.org.hk).

Habermas, J. (1972) *Knowledge and Human Interests*. London: Heinemann.

—— (1981/1986) *The Theory of Communicative Action*, Volume I. Cambridge: Polity Press.

—— (1981/1989) *The Theory of Communicative Action*, Volume II. Cambridge: Polity Press.

—— (1994) *The Past as Future*. Cambridge: Polity Press.

—— (1997) *Between Facts and Norms: Contributions to a Discourse Theory of Law and Democracy*. Cambridge: Polity Press.

Hall, S. (1991) 'The local and the global: globalization and ethnicity', in A.D. King (ed.), *Culture, Globalization and the World System*. Basingstoke: Macmillan.

Harding, H. (1995) 'The concept of "Greater China": themes, variations and reservations', in D. Shambaugh (ed.), *Greater China: The Next Superpower?* Oxford: Clarendon Press.

Harris, P. (2001) 'China's aimless state', in Huang Xiaoming (ed.), *The Political and Economic Transition in East Asia: Strong Market, Weakened State*. London: Curzon.

Harvey, D. (1990) *The Condition of Postmodernity*. Oxford: Basil Blackwell.

Held, D., McGrew, A., Goldblatt, D. and Perraton, J. (1999) *Global Transformations*. Cambridge: Polity Press.

Higgott, R. (2000) 'Regionalism in the Asia-Pacific: two steps forward, one step back?' in Stubbs and Underhill (eds), *Political Economy and the Changing World Order*. Oxford: Oxford University Press.

Higgott, R. and Rhodes, M. (2000) 'Asian crises and the myth of capitalist "convergence"', *The Pacific Review* 13(1): 1–19.

Hirst, P. and Thompson, G. (1999) *Globalization in Question*. Cambridge: Polity Press.

Hiscock, G. (2000) *Asia's New Wealth Club*. London: Nicholas Brealey.

Honneth, A. (1996), 'The other of justice: Habermas and the ethical challenge of postmodernism', in S.K. White (ed.), *The Cambridge Companion to Habermas*. Cambridge: Cambridge University Press.

Interactive Audience Measurement Asia (iamasia) (June 2000) 'NetKnowledge China report' (http://www.iamasia.com).

—— (July 2000) 'NetKnowledge Taiwan report' (http://www.iamasia.com).

Jalan, J. and Ranallion, M. (1997) *Spatial Poverty Traps – Rural China*. Washington: World Bank Group research working paper.

Lash, S. and Urry, J. (1994) *Economies of Signs and Space*. London: Sage.

Lechte, J. (1994) *Fifty Key Contemporary Thinkers: From Structuralism to Postmodernity*. London: Routledge.

Lee Yeon-ho (1997) 'The limits of economic globalization in East Asian developmental states', *The Pacific Review* 10(3): 366–90.

Levinas, E. (1969) *Totality and Infinity: An Essay on Exteriority*. Pittsburgh: Duquesne University Press.

—— (1985) *Ethics and Infinity: Conversations with Philippe Nemo*. Pittsburgh: Duquesne University Press.

—— (1987) *Time and the Other*. Pittsburgh: Duquesne University Press.

—— (1996) *Basic Philosophical Writings*. Bloomington: Indiana University Press.

Levinas, E. and Kearney, R. (1986) 'Dialogue with Emmanuel Levinas', in R.A. Cohen (ed.), *Face to Face with Levinas*. State University of New York Press.

Liu Guoguang, Wang Luolin, Li Jingwen, Liu Shucheng and Wang Tongsan (eds) (2000) *Economics Blue Book of the People's Republic of China, 1999*. Armonk, NY: M.E. Sharpe.

Lyotard, J.-F. (1985) 'Letter to Jessamyn Blau, Milwaukee, May 1, 1985', in J.-F. Lyotard (1992), *The Postmodern Condition Explained to Children – Correspondence 1982–1985*. Sydney: Power Institute of Fine Art.

Mainland Affairs Council, Cross-Straits Exchanges, The Executive Yuan, Republic of China (http://www.mac.gov.tw).

Marris, R. (1999) *Ending Poverty*. London: Thames & Hudson.

Ministry of Economic Affairs (MOEA), Republic of China (2001) 'Economic Statistics' (http://www.moea/stat/four/english/d6–1t.htm).

Nicholson, M. (1999) 'How novel is globalization?' in M. Shaw (ed.), *Politics and Globalization: Knowledge, Ethics and agency*. London: Routledge.

Nua Internet Surveys (2000) 'Wireless Web grows slowly in China' (http://www.nua.ie/Surveys/index.cgi?f=VS&art_id=905356061&rel=true).

Pusey, M. (1987) *Jürgen Habermas*. London: Tavistock Press.

Renwick, N. (1996) 'Re-reading Europe's identities', in Krause and Renwick (eds), *Identities in International Relations*. Basingstoke: Macmillan.

—— (2002) *Northeast Asian Critical Security*. London: Palgrave.

Ruggiero, R. (1997) 'China and the world trading system', *WTO News 1995–1999 Speeches*, Former WTO DG, Beijing University 21 April 1997, available at the website http://www.wto.org/english/news_e/sprr_e/china_e.htm.

Scholte, J.-A. (1996) 'Globalization and collective identities', in Krause and Renwick (eds), *Identities in International Relations*. Basingstoke: Macmillan/St Antony's.

—— (1997) 'Global capitalism and the state', *International Affairs* 73(3): 427–52.

—— (1999) 'Globalization: prospects for a paradigm shift', in M. Shaw (ed.), *Politics and Globalization: Knowledge, Ethics and Agency*. London: Routledge.

Sen, A. (1997) *On Economic Inequality*. Oxford: Oxford University Press.

—— (1999) *Development as Freedom*. Oxford: Oxford University Press.

Shaw, M. (ed.) (1999) *Politics and Globalization: Knowledge, Ethics and Agency*. London: Routledge.

Sum Ngai-Ling (1999) 'Rethinking globalization: re-articulating spatial scale and temporal horizons of trans-border spaces', in Olds, Dicken, Kelly, Kong and Yeung (eds), *Globalization and the Asia–Pacific: Contested Territories*. London: Routledge.

Tucker, N.B. (2000) 'Dangerous liaisons: China, Taiwan, Hong Kong, and the United States at the turn of the century', in T. White (ed.), *China Briefing 2000: The Continuing Transformation*, Armonk, NY: M.E. Sharpe/Asia Society.

United Nations Development Programme (UNDP) (2000) *Human Development Report 2000*. New York: Oxford University Press.

Warnke, G. (1995) 'Communicative rationality and cultural values', in S.K. White (ed.), *The Cambridge Companion to Habermas*. Cambridge: Cambridge University Press.

White, S.K. (1996), *The Cambridge Companion to Habermas*. Cambridge: Cambridge University Press.

White, T. (2000) *China Briefing 2000: The Continuing Transformation*. Armonk, NY: M.E. Sharpe/Asia Society.

World Bank Group (2000a) 'The World Bank and the East Asia and Pacific Region' (http://wbln0018.worldbank.org/eap/eap.nsf/General/8BACD5416E7C795385256 96700852520?OpenDocument).

—— (2000b) 'Regional overview: East Asia's recovery: maintaining momentum', Washington, 30 November (http://www.worldbank.org).

—— (2000c) 'Japan at a glance' (http://www.wto.org).

—— (2000d) 'Global poverty monitoring' (http://www. worldbank. org/research / povmonitor/index.htm).

—— (2000e) 'Social policy and governance in the East Asia and Pacific region: social indicators' (http://www.worldbank.org/eapsocial/indicat/index.htm).

—— (2000f) 'Poverty assessment summary: China – overcoming rural poverty', Washington (http://wbln0018.worldbank.org/dg/povertys.nsf).

World Trade Organisation (WTO) (1995) *Annual Report*. Geneva: WTO.

—— (1998) 'Hong Kong, China: December 1998, trade policy reviews' (http://www.wto.org/english/tratop_e/tpr_e/tp97_e.htm).

—— (2000) 'Developing countries merchandise exports in 1999 expanded by 8.5% – about twice as fast as the global average', *WTO News: 2000 Press Releases* 175, 6 April.

Wright, T., Hughes, P. and Ainley, A. (1988) 'The paradox of morality: an interview with Emmanuel Levinas', in Bernasconi and Wood (eds), *The Provocation of Levinas – Rethinking the Other*. London: Routledge.

Index

Page references in *italics* refer to tables